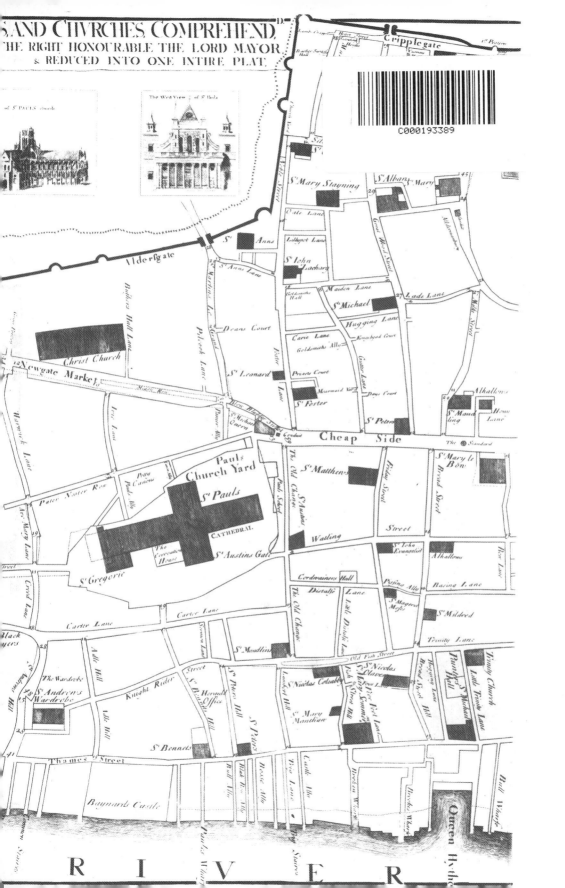

'A More Beautiful City'

Robert Hooke and the Rebuilding of London after the Great Fire

M<small>ICHAEL</small> C<small>OOPER</small>

SUTTON PUBLISHING

For Jennifer

First published in the United Kingdom in 2003 by
Sutton Publishing Limited · Phoenix Mill
Thrupp · Stroud · Gloucestershire · GL5 2BU

British Library Cataloguing in Publication Data
A catalogue record for this book is available from the British Library.

ISBN 0-7509-2959-6

Endpapers: George Vertue's 1723 engraving of London streets immediately after the Great Fire. Based on John Leake's 1666 manuscript map (Figure 44) it shows the new street widths in feet. (*Guildhall Library, Corporation of London*)

Typeset in 10/14.5pt Photina.
Typesetting and origination by
Sutton Publishing Limited.
Printed and bound in England by
J.H. Haynes & Co. Ltd, Sparkford.

CONTENTS

LIST OF ILLUSTRATIONS

Where possible I have used images of original sources for the illustrations and tried to reproduce many of them as they were originally presented, not merely as ornaments to a text, but integrated with it to tell the reader more than text alone could do.

I would like to express my appreciation to the following individuals and organisations who have given permission to reproduce material in their possession. The American Physical Society. Ashmolean Museum, University of Oxford. Beinecke Rare Book and Manuscript Library, Yale University. The British Library. The Company of Clockmakers. Corporation of London Records Office. Guildhall Art Gallery, Corporation of London. Guildhall Library, Corporation of London. Derek Hull. Lisa Jardine. The Joint Grand Gresham Committee. Micro-g Solutions Inc. Museum of the History of Science, University of Oxford. C.L. Ogleby. The Royal Institution of Chartered Surveyors. The Royal Society. The Master and Fellows of Trinity College, Cambridge. University College London Library Services. Willen Church Council. Specific illustrations are acknowledged in the captions to the Figures.

ACKNOWLEDGEMENTS

My interest in Robert Hooke began in 1986 when the late E.C. Hambly gave a lecture on him at City University, London, in which he challenged his audience to do something to uncover Hooke, the hidden City Surveyor. Feeling under some obligation to meet the challenge, I was grateful when Gresham College Council awarded a grant to my university that enabled me to take sabbatical leave and begin my research. Aware of the shallows and deeps awaiting anyone venturing for the first time into historiography, I sought advice from various historians, all of whom gave generously of their time over a period of several years. I would like to thank in particular Jim Bennett, Michael Hunter and Lisa Jardine for convivial conversations in which I gained more from their knowledge of Hooke and his times than I feel I gave in return. I would also like to thank Ann Saunders for her support and advice on London's places and people. I have received assistance for my work in various archives and libraries. I am grateful to the President and Council of the Royal Society for a grant to support my transcription of all Hooke's City Papers. Jim Sewell (Corporation of London Records Office), Rupert Baker and Christine Woollett (Royal Society Library), John Fisher and Jeremy Smith (Guildhall Library), Peter Williams and Sheila Munton (City University Library) and Ursula Carlyle (Mercers' Company Archivist) and their colleagues have all met my requests with cheerful efficiency. Vanessa Harding, Michael Hunter and Michael Nauenberg have read drafts of this book and made valuable and constructive comments, which I acknowledge with gratitude. Suggestions from Jaqueline Mitchell, my editor at Sutton Publishing, have resulted in improvements to my original text. Having spent much of my academic career analysing errors in measurements, I know it is impossible to eliminate them completely, despite the best of intentions. Whether the errors which remain here, after all the assistance I have had, are random, systematic or gross, they are certainly my own; I can only hope they are not significant.

St Albans
June 2003

INTRODUCTION

Gusts of wind swirled around the streets of London on the morning of Tuesday 7 June 1664. Broken low cloud drifted south-eastwards, but above, high in the sky, clouds were moving rapidly towards the north. Around 3 o'clock in the afternoon claps of thunder were heard and soon heavy rain began to fall. In Piccadilly people were going about their daily activities. A woman sitting on a cart of peas drawn by a pair of horses was travelling towards the city. On the other side of the road several brickmakers and carpenters were working on a house. When the rain came, two of them went to stand beneath a lean-to shelter where another was seated at the end of a wooden bench. Another man sitting at an open window of his lodgings in a house in Pall Mall was startled as a lightning flash lit up the paper on which he was writing and a hideous clap of thunder rent the air, seeming to come from somewhere close by. At that instant a gatekeeper standing at the entrance to a house near the Poet's Head, not far from St James's Palace, saw a bolt of lightning glowing like a piece of red-hot iron come with a great noise and force of wind from the direction of the Palace to strike the roof on the west side of a corner house in Piccadilly, throwing off tiles and bricks into the street, exposing broken laths and leaving the smell of brimstone hanging in the air. The horses pulling the cart of peas reared up at the noise, upsetting the cart on to the woman who was riding in it. She was badly bruised, but the horses were unharmed. The two workmen standing in the shelter were thrown to the ground by the blast. At the same time their colleague seated at the end of the wooden bench was lifted up and thrown down again in the middle of it. They were unharmed, but two other men standing together outside the shelter were struck down. One fell to his knees but the other (an old bird-catcher) fell down as if dead. Later he was found to be alive though badly bruised and bleeding profusely from what seemed to be a wound to his mouth, rather than from some internal cause. He was incapable of coherent speech, although by the following day he had recovered. The house where the lightning had struck was badly damaged. Glass in some of the east-facing windows was broken, their timbers torn and scorched, but lower down some panes of glass remained whole, held together by the melted leads. In a room at the top of the house, just below the place where the lightning had struck, pieces of the ceiling lay scattered across the floor. The walls of the room were scarred as if they had been raked by gunfire. Outside, a door at the west end of the house was splintered and the surrounding brickwork greatly damaged.

We know all these details (and many more) of this incident in Piccadilly because the lodger writing at the open window of a house in Pall Mall was the Royal Society's Curator of Experiments, 29-year-old Robert Hooke, the greatest experimental scientist of his time. When someone came to tell him that the lightning which had so recently startled him had also damaged a building and injured a man in Piccadilly he hastened to the scene. His curiosity was aroused, not in the hope of finding an exciting, or newsworthy, sight of horror or tragedy, but because he had an opportunity to see at first-hand some of the effects of a lightning strike and perhaps understand more about thunderstorms. He intended to discover as many facts as he could and report them the following day to the Royal Society at its weekly meeting in Gresham College in the City of London.

The report of the thunderstorm illustrates many facets of Hooke's complex character and intellect. His concentrated and detailed interest in natural phenomena, even when they took place in public places and were witnessed only by people with no scientific training or interest in natural philosophy,[1] is apparent in his report. The incident in Piccadilly was not an experiment in a laboratory, but a fairly common natural event in a public place. Although he himself was not present at the place where the lightning struck, others were, so he sought them out and asked them questions about what they had felt, seen, heard or smelled at the time. Throughout his life Hooke sought greater understanding of the natural world by careful and accurate observation and recording, whether as part of a laboratory experiment designed to give answers to specific questions or when going about his work or leisure in the streets of London. This book attempts to rectify some of the neglect and misunderstandings about Hooke by examining his work in London as City Surveyor after the Great Fire and relating this to his work in science.

In his report to the Royal Society Hooke described not only what he was told, but who told him, where they were standing and what they were doing at the time. Such additional information could be used in deciding which of two conflicting pieces of evidence was the more reliable. The report also shows that Hooke was able to mix easily with workmen and other citizens whose social lives were far removed from those of the aristocrats, courtiers, physicians and clerics who dominated the Royal Society at the time. Three years later, when he was called upon as City Surveyor to supervise the work of bricklayers, masons and carpenters as they rebuilt London out of the ruins of the fire, his knowledge of their methods and the tools of their trades was vital. He could work with trained craftsmen in their workshops, but he could also discuss Euclidean geometry, the philosophy of Descartes and why planets moved in elliptical orbits with men such as Robert Boyle and Christopher Wren in their private houses – the house in Pall Mall where he was lodging belonged to Lady Ranelagh, Robert Boyle's sister. His genius lay in his ability to bridge the worlds of the mechanic's workshop and the learned man's philosophical speculations.

His report of the thunderstorm also illustrates two particular subjects which were of great interest and importance to him, and which would be fundamental to his rebuilding of the city: his technical interest in building construction and his scientific interest in light and air. He had, as a matter of course that morning, observed how the winds were blowing and the way the clouds passed overhead in sufficient detail to be able to describe what he had seen to the Royal Society, even though while he was observing the state of the atmosphere he had no idea that he would later have to write a report on it. He thought it was important to take pains to understand more about air and light because both were essential to mankind. His observations for the Royal Society to discover the physical properties of light and the atmosphere were not undertaken out of mere curiosity: he believed that such discoveries would lead to improvements in the health and well-being of the citizens of an overcrowded and noisome city. His science had a purpose beyond the gaining of knowledge for its own sake.

Hooke's pursuit of knowledge and his efforts to create a beautiful and healthy new city were partly fuelled by a desire for fame and fortune. His life was not one of intense contemplation, remote from the lives of others in the way that his contemporary, the great, vindictive genius Newton's was for much of his life. Hooke was a gregarious and generous man who worked amid the tumult of London's lanes and streets and met daily with friends and colleagues. In London's coffee houses and inns he was just as likely to be found arguing about whether light was a pulse or a wave motion as writing a certificate to compensate a citizen for ground taken away to widen a street, or giving instructions to a ship's captain who was about to leave for remote lands on what to bring back for the Royal Society to discuss, or simply having a convivial evening eating and drinking with his friends, gossiping and comparing the effectiveness or otherwise of various purgative drugs they had taken. Returning at night to his lodgings in Gresham College he would work in his rooms designing and making new scientific instruments, preparing his experiments for the Royal Society's weekly meetings and writing his lectures.

A condition of Hooke's appointment as Professor at Gresham College in 1665 was to remain celibate. He died, childless, thirty-eight years later. Hooke had no students who would follow where he had led and develop his ideas and practice, nor any children to defend his reputation after his death. His character and achievements were either forgotten through misfortune or denigrated. The gregarious, generous and inventive genius who did more than anyone to rebuild London after the fire disappeared from memory, while evidence of his surveying lay hidden in scattered documentary records. For 300 years he has been generally thought of as misanthropic, reclusive and bitter, envious of the achievements of greater men. However, even in his account of the incident in Piccadilly a more sympathetic side to his character can be seen. He reported that on the day following the incident the old bird-catcher had recovered from his injured mouth and was able to speak again. This means that Hooke, by the time he had finished writing his report, had taken the trouble to find and speak to the old man to see how he was. Pepys wrote that Hooke 'is the most, and promises the least, of any man in the world that I ever saw'.[2] Pepys was with Hooke after his unanimous election to the Royal Society at its meeting in Gresham College on 15 February 1665, where he saw Hooke perform experiments on burning charcoal, with and without air, and with the addition of nitre, that is, potassium nitrate.[3] After the meeting Pepys went to the Crown Tavern, according to the normal custom of the leading members of the Society, including Hooke, where the company had 'excellent discourses till 10 at night'.[4] Pepys easily saw through Hooke's unprepossessing appearance to the nature of the man behind – many others have not been as acute.

Hooke's work as scientist and surveyor was almost entirely carried out within London. Gresham College was in the north-east corner of the city between Bishopsgate Street and Broad Street, on the site now occupied by the building known as 'Tower 42'.[5] Gresham College was not only the place where Hooke lived; it was here, too, that he had his workshop, performed his experiments in front of the Royal Society and gave his public lectures. It was also the place occupied by London's rulers and administrators in the years after the fire when Guildhall was uninhabitable. London's streets were Hooke's workplace and its buildings his laboratory. The world in which he operated was that of Restoration London, a vigorous and highly competitive milieu where he made friends and enemies among such great and diverse men as Wren, Pepys, Newton and Boyle.

I have had to take account of the changes in meanings of technical words since Hooke was writing. After Newton, 'force' and 'power', for example, have separate and distinct scientific meanings or definitions. A scientist now would never use them in a professional context to refer to the same thing. However, Hooke and his contemporaries often used them indiscriminately as a name for the same phenomenon. 'Force' and 'power' are used now in everyday speech much as Hooke and his contemporaries used them, as synonyms. When writing about Hooke's science, I have endeavoured to use such terms in their modern scientific sense, but when quoting from seventeenth-century sources I offer explanatory notes from time to time, which I hope will avoid confusion.

Another area of difficulty arises from the widespread use now of mathematical concepts and notation by scientists in their work. The custom became routine for scientists and engineers in the eighteenth century as the contents of Newton's *Principia* were more widely read, understood and applied using calculus. But Hooke and his contemporaries usually expressed mathematical relationships verbally. When writing about Hooke's science I have therefore not used equations, except occasionally in the notes so that a reader who is familiar with elementary algebraic expressions can find there further explanation of what Hooke was doing, while others need not feel inhibited about avoiding such details.

I have discussed Hooke's science because it was related to the way he carried out his surveying duties, but this is not a book about his science. Other writers on Hooke have treated that aspect of his life and thought, some in great detail, and continue to do so. His complexity encourages scholars from different disciplines to write about him from their various standpoints: many of the results are cited in the Select Bibliography. Nor is this book a general biography. The tercentenary of Hooke's death this year has brought a wider interest in him, shown by conferences and other commemorative events, television and radio programmes and books. Inwood (2002) and Jardine (2003b) have added greatly to Margaret 'Espinasse's excellent short biography, which is now almost fifty years old.[6] Bennett *et al.* (2003) looks at four of the many aspects of Hooke's life and work.

In writing this book I wanted to do something different – to show what Hooke did, as a scientist and a man of his time and place, in the rebuilding of London after the disastrous fire of 1666. Part One is a general introductory account of his extraordinarily busy social and professional life, including his important contributions to the new experimental science. In Part Two I have made use of previously hidden archival evidence to describe in detail how he served the needs of citizens desperate to rebuild their houses and their lives, and laid out the foundations of much of the London we see today. By showing how his motives and work in science and in surveying had much in common, I hope he will come further out of the shadows cast by two great men, his friend Christopher Wren (Figure 1), and his enemy Isaac Newton (Figure 2).

1. Portrait of Sir Christopher Wren by Johann B. Closterman. (© *The Royal Society*)

2. Portrait of Sir Isaac Newton by Charles Jervas. (© *The Royal Society*)

PART ONE
ASPECTS OF A LIFE

1

❧❧❧

FINDING BY MY OWN TRIALS

Born at noon on 18 July 1635, Robert Hooke was not expected to survive beyond childhood. He was the youngest of four children of the Revd John Hooke, curate of the parish church of All Saints at Freshwater in the Isle of Wight, and his second wife Cecelie (née Gyles).[1] The young Robert Hooke's weak constitution could cope only with a diet of milky foods and fruit. When he reached the age of seven years, his father, seeing that his youngest child was, after all, likely to live to maturity and would have to earn a living, decided that he should follow him into the Church. Hooke was not strong enough to be sent away to school so his father began to teach him at home. After learning some English grammar Hooke's frequent headaches interrupted his education. As his father's health slowly declined, his education at home came to an end and he was left alone to follow his own inclinations.

His great interest in the workings of mechanical devices was evident early on. He tried to imitate everything he saw done by local craftsmen, sometimes even making improvements of his own. After watching somebody take an old brass clock to pieces in order to repair it, he made similar parts out of wood, put them together and produced a clock which worked well enough. He also made a 3ft-long fully-rigged model ship fitted with a device which fired the ship's guns as it sailed across the small harbour at Freshwater. He showed a similar talent for drawing and painting, making his own materials from ruddle and chalk to make copies of the prints hanging on the walls at home. The painter John Hoskins when visiting the Isle of Wight was surprised that an untutored boy could draw so well. For these reasons Hooke's father thought his youngest son should be apprenticed to a trade such as watchmaking or limning, now that his scholarly education at home had been abandoned.

These well-known details of Hooke's childhood come from a short *Life* by Richard Waller, Secretary of the Royal Society from 1687–1700, which he incorporated in his edition of Hooke's posthumous works published in 1705, only two years after Hooke's death.[2] Waller did not get to know Hooke until about 1680, so his account of Hooke's childhood is not first-hand. However, Waller claimed that the details he published came from the beginnings of an autobiography, now lost, that he found in Hooke's papers. Hooke had begun to write an autobiography in 1697, but did not take it beyond the death of his father in October 1648, at which time Hooke was thirteen years old. John Aubrey, who also knew Hooke well and often borrowed money from him (which he rarely repaid),[3] also records John Hoskin's surprise that the young Hooke was able to make his own drawing materials from coal, chalk and ruddle and produce creditable sketches.[4]

We might be suspicious of these accounts because they give glimpses in the younger Hooke of exactly those attributes which strongly characterised his maturity – concentrated powers of observation, mechanical genius, curiosity about things around him, exceptional draughtsmanship and general ill-health. I do not, however, propose that this is a clear case of the man having become father to the imagined child. Other circumstances of Hooke's childhood can be linked with varying levels of confidence to events in his adult life. The social milieu in which Hooke grew up was strongly royalist and Anglican, centred around a few individuals and places in the Isle of Wight. John Hoskins, who was so impressed by Hooke's draughtsmanship, was painter of miniatures to Charles I. The teacher at the school in Newport where Hooke's elder brother John was educated was William Hopkins.[5] Sir John Oglander, a prominent royalist living in the Isle of Wight, was a friend of Hopkins. Hooke's father had been curate at Brading Church, near Oglander's home at Nunwell, prior to his appointment at Freshwater. Cardell Goodman, rector of the church at Freshwater when Hooke's father was curate there, had attended the royalist Westminster School and Christ Church Oxford. Soon after King Charles I arrived at Carisbrooke Castle in the Isle of Wight after escaping from Hampton Court in November 1647, Oglander led a group of royalist supporters living in the island to pay their respects to the king. It is very probable that Hooke's father, Cardell Goodman and William Hopkins were among them.[6] These men, and others who shared their political and religious views, had a strong influence on Hooke's formative years. At around the time Hooke left for London in 1648, they were beginning to suffer punitive fines exacted by the parliamentarians from known royalists. It is possible that the death of Hooke's father, whose health had been poor for some time, was hastened by fears of losing his appointment and ruining the future of his bright younger son Robert. But the Isle of Wight royalist connections would later work to Hooke's advantage.

Hooke's two sisters were more than seven years older than he. His elder brother was away at Newport, so we can imagine that the young man was often alone, following his natural inclinations by making and trying out mechanical models. Untutored except for what he learned from local craftsmen, he discovered the importance of using the right materials and how to shape them into different forms. John Aubrey wrote that Hooke made things for himself 'never having had any instruction. His father was not Mathematicall at all.'[7] But Hooke's father might have provided him with simple tools such as the village blacksmith was capable of making. By concentrating his hand, eye and mind on these activities, alone in an out-house or unused stable, the boy probably quickly forgot his sickness. Despite Hooke's ailments, Waller says he was 'sprightly and active in Running, Leaping, &c. tho' very weak as to any robust Exercise'.[8] In fine weather he was able to walk over the downs above the chalk cliffs and along the sandy beaches at their foot. Natural phenomena began to engage the young boy's attention. He would have noticed periodic changes in the natural world around Freshwater, such as the slow monthly rhythms of tide and moon, the annual cycling southward and northward of the setting sun on the western horizon, and the regular turning of constellations of stars around Polaris, high in the sky to the north. It is not too fanciful to think that his many experimental investigations and speculations for the Royal Society into natural motion and change had their source in such childhood observations and his own artificial rhythmic recording device – the little working wooden clock.

Not all nature's changes were rhythmic and predictable. Freshwater is on the island's western peninsula, almost surrounded by water and air. Hooke saw storms, gales and gentle breezes, clear skies, clouds and mists, all constantly changing for no apparent reason, sometimes threatening the lives of seafarers. The wanderings of the moon and planets were seen in marked contrast to the regular motions of the stars. Perhaps his childhood fascination with restless and unpredictable natural phenomena and their consequences led him, in maturity, to make barometers, thermometers and devices for measuring the direction and speed of the wind in order to understand the causes of changes in the weather. Such knowledge could be used to predict storms and improve living conditions in London's dark and airless alleys and courts. We have surer grounds for seeing in his childhood the beginnings of another of his many important scientific speculations and his practical interest in building materials if we look at the geology of the land around his home.

The most spectacular of many interesting features of the geology of the western part of the Isle of Wight are the Needles. Originally formed by the accumulation of layers of calcareous life-forms on the bottom of the sea, they were solidified by pressure, turned on edge and thrust upwards by tectonic movement. The chalk, of which the Needles are the most obvious part, runs like a spine east–west across the island. Fossils contained in the chalk lie all around the cliffs and can be seen embedded in the layers of rock where it has been exposed. As Ellen Tan Drake has shown,[9] Hooke's boyhood explorations of the coastal cliffs around his home were more than a child's idle wanderings. He looked carefully at what he saw and wondered how it was possible for the shells of sea creatures to be found at the tops of hills, far above sea level. Such childhood musings led much later to a series of lectures he gave at Gresham College (the last in 1699) which were published posthumously as *A Discourse on Earthquakes*.[10] In these lectures Hooke speculated with a prescience which astonishes many geologists today that the daily interactions between land, sea and air over a long period of time produced the landforms and deposits we see today. Underlying all his observations and speculations was a strong urge to use the knowledge he had gained for practical purposes. One illustration of how his interest in rocks and their constituents led to practical use can be found in his microscopical observations with Christopher Wren of the structure of a limestone they

3.   The surface of Kettering-stone, or 'Ketton stone', as seen by Hooke through his microscope and published in *Micrographia*. The diameter of his published engraving is about 160mm. (*Hooke 1665, Schem. IX, Fig 1:* © *The Royal Society*)

were using for building (Figure 3). Called 'Kettering-stone' by Hooke, it is now known as 'Ketton stone' named after the quarry at Ketton, near Kettering, in Northamptonshire. On seeing the details of the stone's structure Hooke performed a simple experiment to test its porosity. He sealed both sides of the sample with cement, except for two small areas opposite one another on each face. Then, having moistened with spittle one of the unsealed areas, he placed his mouth against it and blew into the stone. He found that bubbles came out of the unsealed area on the opposite side. He deduced that the stone was very porous – an important property which influenced its use in building.[11] The accuracy of Hooke's microscopical observation of limestone can be seen by comparing his illustration in *Micrographia* with images of the same material obtained recently using an optical microscope with reflected illumination (Figure 4) and with a scanning electron microscope (Figure 5).[12]

Hooke's father died in October 1648, bringing the boy's childhood at Freshwater to an end. He left his younger son 'forty pounds of lawful English money, the great and best joined chest, and all my books . . . [and] Legacies due to my children, which their Grandmother Ann Gyles gave unto them as will appear by her Will, viz . . . To my son Robert Hooke 10 pounds.'[13]

With a fortune of £50 the thirteen-year-old orphan was far from being poor, but he had no other source of income and needed to earn a living. His childhood had been

4.   The surface of a fracture plane of Kettering-stone photographed through a modern optical microscope with reflected illumination and reproduced here at roughly the same scale as Figure 3. It illustrates the difficulties in illumination and depth of focus which Hooke had to overcome. The grains are about ½mm in diameter. (*Derek Hull*)

5.   The surface of a fracture plane of Kettering-stone photographed using a scanning electron microscope and reproduced at roughly the same scale as Figure 3. By comparing the detail shown here with that in Figure 3 it can be seen how well Hooke was able to overcome problems of illumination and depth of focus. (*Derek Hull*)

dominated by his interest in the natural and artificial worlds around him, but in the seventeenth century there were no careers in science. Knowing that his father favoured an apprenticeship for the young Hooke (and that his brother had been apprenticed to a grocer in Newport), his father's friends thought he should make use of his intuitive yet practical talents through apprenticeship to a tradesman such as a clockmaker or painter. Accordingly, Hooke left the Isle of Wight for an apprenticeship in London – the city where he would spend almost all the rest of his life.

The friends and colleagues of Hooke's late father who could give Hooke advice and support were out of favour with the parliamentarians, but the royalists' connections were still in place and could be used to take care of the education and employment of one of their orphans. We do not know how Hooke began his apprenticeship to the portrait painter Peter Lely, and can only guess at the reasons that led the thirteen-year-old Hooke to Lely's studio in particular. Perhaps John Hoskins arranged for him to go there. In any case, Lely's studio was a good place to serve an apprenticeship. Born in Westphalia to a Flanders family, Peter Lely came to England around 1643. Four years later he was made a freeman of the Painter-Stainers' Company of the City of London and was able to take in apprentices.[14] Known at first as a landscape artist, he turned to portraiture and was soon in demand by wealthy patrons, including the king (he painted the younger children of Charles I), but by the time Hooke arrived at his studio in late 1648 Lely had turned his attention to painting the mythological subjects more in favour during the Commonwealth period. By 1650 he had the largest practice of any portrait painter in the Kingdom. He easily found favour in the restored court after 1660, painting a succession of 'Windsor Beauties' and showing with particular skill the voluptuousness of the sitters and the texture of their silk and satin garments.

Although Lely's studio in Covent Garden was a sort of academy for young and ambitious apprentice painters who learned their craft filling in the backgrounds to the portraits, or delineating the stylised positions of the sitters' hands and the objects they held, Hooke did not stay there long. We know only a little more about why he left than we do about why he went there in the first place. Waller tells us that Hooke left after 'I suppose but a short time; for I have heard that the smell of the Oil Colours did not agree with his Constitution, increasing his Head-ach, to which he was ever too much subject'.[15] On the other hand, John Aubrey says that Lely 'liked [Hooke] very well; but Mr Hooke quickly perceived what was to be donne; so thought he, why cannot I doe this by myselfe and keepe my hundred pounds?'.[16] There is probably some truth in both these accounts, but it is likely that the royalist Anglican network, especially Dr Richard Busby, headmaster of Westminster School, and Cardell Goodman also had much to do with Hooke's early departure from Lely's academy and his entry into Westminster School.

Richard Busby (Figure 6) was a very important early influence on Hooke. He was appointed Head Master in 1638 and only relinquished the position when he died in 1695, aged eighty-nine years, the most renowned schoolmaster in England in the seventeenth century. Despite being a well-known royalist and Anglican churchman, his sound judgement and familiarity with power and with those who wielded it enabled him to find a way through the political and religious upheavals of the Interregnum and the Restoration. He seems to have forfeited no favours, either by his refusal to sign the National Covenant of 1644 or by the appearance of his name in the list of those in Cromwell's funeral procession. After the Restoration he and his school became more prosperous than before. It was not only the longevity of his reign at the school but also the manner of it that has brought him fame. He combined rigorous physical and academic disciplines in teaching which earned him the lasting affection of some famous men who had been his pupils and the dislike of others. In the 1620s a scholar was required to read, write and orate Latin and Greek verse and prose. Cicero, Livy, Virgil, Isocrates, Euripides, Homer and Xenophon were among the writers whose works were studied. The boys were roused at 5.15 a.m.

They then said Latin prayers, washed and walked two-by-two to College Hall, where the first classes started at 6 a.m. and ended at 8 a.m., when the boys took refreshment known as 'Beaver'.[17] Busby's syllabus was liberal, including music, mathematics, Hebrew and even Arabic alongside the traditional Latin and Greek, but his flogging was rigorous. John Aubrey, who expressed very liberal views on education, said he had heard from some of Busby's former pupils that '[Busby] hath made a number of good Scholars, but I have heard several of his Scholars affirme, that he hath marred by his severity more than he hath made'.[18] John Locke, Christopher Wren and John Dryden were pupils at Westminster around the time Hooke was there, but Wren did not stay long. He started in 1641 when he was nine years old but in 1646 his father, who had been Dean of Windsor, removed his son from the threatening proximity of Parliament.

6. Dr Richard Busby, Head Master at Westminster School, in whose house Hooke stayed as a pupil. An engraving by Robert White based on a posthumous picture of Busby by Henry Tilson. (*Author's collection*)

Busby took into his own house a succession of young and able boys. He admitted rather more than he should have done according to the school's statutes. A disgruntled master at the school complained to the school governors that instead of the statutory four boarders, Busby 'all his time has had between thirty and forty at a time, and they Boarded at excessive rates in his own House'. The complaint was one among many against Busby made to the school governors by Edward Bagshawe, appointed temporarily Second Master in 1656 and confirmed in that post the following year. He and Busby were mutually antagonistic, but despite the likelihood that at least some of his complaints were justified, he, not Busby, was suspended, and he left the school in 1658. Such was Busby's influence.[19] It is hard now to say what 'excessive rates' were. Busby probably charged a scholar for lodgings as much or as little as he thought possible or necessary in the particular circumstances. Hooke's legacy of £50, assuming it was still intact after only a short time with Lely, was probably sufficient to pay for tuition, clothes, lodgings and food throughout his time there,[20] but if not then his early performance at Westminster would have convinced Busby of his special talent and merit for scholarship.

Busby's admiration of Hooke continued throughout his life. The two men became friends, often dining together at Westminster at a time when an application of the geometrical principles Hooke had studied – architecture – was of interest to both men.

7.   The interior of the church of St Mary Magdalene at Willen in Buckinghamshire. A colour wash by Louisa Benthall (1820–59). The church was designed and built by Hooke for Richard Busby. An apse was added to the west end later in the nineteenth century. (*Willen Church Council*)

In the 1670s Busby decided to build at his own expense a parish church at Willen (Figure 7) in Buckinghamshire, and chose Hooke as his architect. Ten years later, when Busby decided to pay for the repair of a chapel at his birthplace, Lutton in Lincolnshire, he again chose Hooke to undertake the work. Busby died before the work could be completed, but he made provision in his will for it to be finished:

And whereas I have long intended to have repaired and beautified the Chapel at Lutton in the County of Lincoln the place of my nativity and have already by the assistance of Dr. Hooke begun the said work now my Will is that if it should please God that I happen to die before the same be finished that then my Executors with the advice and assistance of the said Dr. Hooke do finish and complete the same in such manner as I have acquainted the said Dr. Hooke I intended to have performed.[21]

Although Hooke applied himself diligently to learning Latin and Greek at Westminster, he was no more than competent in those subjects. However, according to John Aubrey he earned Busby's admiration by mastering the first six books of Euclid in a week and learned to play the organ after only twenty lessons.[22] Busby's liberal syllabus allowed him to develop his exceptional gifts. He gained a knowledge of Hebrew and of some other Eastern languages (possibly Arabic and Sanscrit) but:

he fell seriously upon the study of the Mathematicks, the Dr. encouraging him therein, and allowing him particular times for that purpose. In this he took the most regular

Method, and first made himself Master of Euclide's Elements, and thence proceeded orderly from that sure Basis to the other parts of the Mathematicks, and thereafter to the application thereof to Mechanicks, his first and last Mistress.[23]

This passage by Hooke's first biographer, Richard Waller, reveals the importance in Hooke's education of Busby's idiosyncratically liberal view of what should be taught. Competence in Latin and Greek was essential, even for those whose interests were more in the nature of things than in the nature of man; but for certain boys (Hooke was one, Wren probably another) mathematics and its application in mechanics were not only proper subjects for study, but time was made available for suitable students to pursue such unusual scholarly activities. The child whose intuitive understanding of mechanical devices enabled him to make working models of a clock and a sailing-ship was now discovering the abstract geometrical forms and relationships that his mechanisms made real. Euclid's circles, intersecting planes and scalene triangles became Hooke's cog-wheels, vanes and sails. His excitement and zeal at the realisation of how abstract concepts could lead to useful objects and actions never left him.

Hooke told John Aubrey that 'At Schoole here [Westminster] he was very mechanicall, and (among other things) he invented thirty severall wayes of Flying', and Aubrey goes on to say 'I have heard Sir Richard Knight (who was his School-fellow) say that he seldome sawe him in the schoole'.[24] What can we make of these two statements except to say that Busby allowed Hooke to spend a lot of time away from school pursuing his interest in practical mechanics in craftsmen's workshops, attempting to make flying-machines? Busby's encouragement of these extra-curricular activities is at first very surprising. At the time boys preparing for admission to university studied a corpus of traditional subjects and mainly classical texts. Practical mechanics was certainly not generally thought of as a fit subject for study by young gentlemen, even in Busby's liberal curriculum. It was more a topic for a seven-year apprenticeship to a master craftsman.

An explanation of Busby's unusual management of Hooke's education lies in the publication of a modest instructional book written in the vernacular by John Wilkins (Figure 8) entitled *Mathematicall Magick, or the wonders that can be performed by mechanical geometry*. Dr John Wilkins (1614–72), generally favourable towards the parliamentarian cause, was appointed Warden of Wadham College, Oxford, in 1648 to replace the royalist incumbent. In 1659 Richard Cromwell appointed him Master of Trinity College Cambridge.[25] Wilkins had been a leading figure among a number of physicians, clerics and aristocrats who began in the 1640s to meet informally in London and then in Oxford, to put into practice Francis Bacon's idea that cooperative observation and open debate was the best way of gaining knowledge of the natural world. Following the Restoration they moved to London and were joined there by some men from the exiled Stuart court. At this time they held their meetings in Gresham College, Bishopsgate. On 28 November 1660 Wilkins and about twenty other men, including Robert Boyle and

8. Portrait of John Wilkins by Mary Beale. (© *The Royal Society*)

Christopher Wren, regularised their activities by forming what was to become the Royal Society, meeting weekly in London at Gresham College. Although Wilkins lost his appointment at Cambridge as a consequence of the Restoration, he was soon back in favour and was appointed Vicar of St Lawrence Jewry in the heart of the City of London next to Guildhall and close to Gresham College. He completed his transformation from favoured parliamentarian to favoured royalist when he was appointed Dean of Ripon in 1663 and Bishop of Chester in 1668,[26] but it was in London that he played a key role in linking Hooke to the Royal Society and to the City of London, a connection which became extraordinarily important for both institutions and for Hooke himself.

It is likely that Wilkins first heard from Busby about Hooke's attempts at Westminster School to make flying-machines, a task to which he often returned. Late in his life he recalled that in Oxford in 1658–9:

> I contriv'd and made many trials about the Art of flying in the Air, and moving very swift on the Land and Water, of which I shew'd several Designs to Dr. Wilkins then Warden of Wadham College, and at the same time made a Module, which, by the help of Springs and Wings, raised and sustain'd itself in the Air; but finding by my own trials, and afterwards by Calculation, that the Muscles of a Mans body were not sufficient to do any thing considerable of that kind, I apply'd my Mind to contrive a way to make artificial muscles; divers designs I shewe'd also at the same time to Dr Wilkins, but was in many of my Trials frustrated of my expectations.[27]

Richard Waller found some sketches of flying-machines among Hooke's papers after his death, but chose not to publish them because they were 'so imperfect, that I do not judge them fit for the Publick'. One of the machines seems to have had blades like those on a modern autogiro which, turned by the wind, assisted the motion of hinged bat-like wings fixed to a man's arms and legs.[28] John Aubrey says that Hooke's earliest attempts at making flying-machines at Westminster School were known to 'Dr Wilkins at Wadham College at that time, who gave [Hooke] his *Mathematicall Magick* which did him a great kindness'.[29] Wilkins's *Mathematicall Magick* was published in 1648.[30] In two parts, the first dealing with manual machines and their operation, the second with mechanical automata, it was the combination of theory and practice in the book which appealed to the young Hooke's imagination and ambition, and would drive him to extraordinary achievements. A copy of *Mathematicall Magick*, probably the one given to him by Wilkins, was in Hooke's possession at the time of his death.[31] Wilkins intended the book to lead to practical ends, quite different from the usual objectives of studying didactic texts. In the address 'To the Reader' Wilkins wrote 'a divine power and wisdom might be discerned, even in those common arts which are so much despised'.[32] *Mathematicall Magick*, particularly that introductory comment, was further inspiration to the young Hooke. Here was an authoritative and esteemed cleric and academic making public his view that it was morally and intellectually proper to engage with hand and mind in the mechanical arts. Hooke came to understand that by following his natural aptitude for mechanics he could exercise his powers of reasoning and at the same time serve a divine purpose. This conviction stayed with him throughout his life. In developing experimental science and in rebuilding the City of London, he had a common aim – to bring benefits to his fellow man. In 1665 in his Preface to *Micrographia*, his first important publication, he paid fulsome tribute to his mentor Wilkins. He said that if the contents of his book:

shall be any wayes useful to inquiring men, I must attribute the incouragement and promotion of them to a very Reverend and Learned Person, of whom this ought in justice to be said, That there is scarce any one Invention, which this Nation has produc'd in our Age, but it has some way or other been set forward by his assistance. My Reader, I believe, will quickly ghess, that it is Dr. Wilkins that I mean. He is indeed a man born for the good of mankind, and for the honour of his country.[33]

Elsewhere in *Micrographia* Hooke wrote 'the Arts of life have been too long imprison'd in the dark shops of Mechanicks themselves & there hindered from growth, either by ignorance, or self-interest'.[34] Through the inspiration of Wilkins and the liberality of Busby's ideas on education, the schoolboy Robert Hooke received a singular education which included practical experience in London's 'dark shops of mechanics' and in music, as well as the more bookish studies of the traditional classical texts.

Elections to Christ Church Oxford, or to Trinity College Cambridge, were made each year from among the scholars at Westminster.[35] Hooke was not elected by examination to Christ Church, but was awarded a choral scholarship, 'a pretty good allowance' according to John Aubrey,[36] and a sinecure in the Interregnum, when church music was banned. Waller tells us that:

[Hooke] went to the University of Oxford, in 1653. but as 'tis often the Fate of Persons great in Learning to be small in other Circumstances, his were but mean. I find that he was a student of Christ-Church, tho' not of the Foundation, but was, as I have heard, a Servitor to one Mr. Goodman, and took his Degree of Master of Arts several Yeares after, about 1662, or 1663.[37]

A servitor was usually paid by a wealthier student, or by one of the clergy, to carry out menial tasks, but there is no record of anyone at the time named Goodman at Christ Church. The Goodman mentioned by Waller who provided Hooke with financial support at Oxford was probably Cardell Goodman, rector at Freshwater at the time of Hooke's father's death and one of the witnesses to the will in which he was referred to by Hooke's father as one of his 'worthy and well beloved friends'.[38]

Hooke soon gained a reputation in Oxford circles as a clever and exceptionally practical young man. By making changes to its pendulum, he improved the accuracy of the clock used for timing astronomical observations by his teacher Seth Ward, Savilian Professor of Astronomy, later Bishop of Salisbury. A year or two after beginning his studies at Christ Church Hooke was employed by Dr Thomas Willis, the physician and chemist, who identified the part of the brain now known as the 'circle of Willis' and was also the first to discover the form of diabetes known as diabetes mellitus.[39] Willis was an iatrochemist, that is to say he was interested in understanding how the chemical compositions of various substances were related to their medicinal properties. Hooke worked in Willis's laboratory, preparing and dispensing medicines for his patients according to prescription, and performing chemical experiments. He lodged in Willis's accommodation in Beam Hall, opposite Merton College Chapel. Although Willis employed Hooke because of his exceptional abilities, once again a royalist/Isle of Wight connection can be seen, which was to Hooke's advantage: Willis's brother-in-law John Fell (who later became Vice-Chancellor and Dean of Oxford) was the son of Dr Samuel Fell, rector at Freshwater when Hooke's father was appointed curate there in the 1620s.[40]

Wilkins's presence at Wadham College was a continuing benefit to Hooke: it was probably Wilkins who recommended Hooke to Willis and soon afterwards to a man who would also have an important influence on Hooke's intellectual development – the Right Honourable Robert Boyle, seventh son of the Earl of Cork, chemist and Christian gentleman of private means (Figure 9). Boyle had been living on his estate at Stalbridge in Dorset, where he had his own chemistry laboratory. He was invited by John Wilkins to move to Oxford to join the group of natural philosophers then meeting at Wadham College, where Wilkins was Warden. In the winter of 1655/6 Boyle moved to Oxford and set up a laboratory in a building in High Street belonging to the apothecary John Cross. Wilkins, Willis and Boyle were quite different from one another in temperament, politics and social backgrounds, but such differences were of little consequence when it came to their common interest in science. They all saw Hooke as a young man with exceptional talents and ambition who could make a considerable contribution to their scientific objectives: before long Hooke was working for Boyle, who was then facing a formidable technical problem.

During the 1650s Boyle had made experiments on respiration and the properties of air. He gave the matter his attention because air was known to be essential for life and therefore it was important to know something of its properties. Boyle knew about the work of Otto von Guericke in Magdeburg, who had demonstrated that air had weight by showing that a vessel emptied of air weighed less than when it was full. Von Guericke had also demonstrated the existence of atmospheric pressure and the great effort needed to overcome it by showing that two teams, each of four men, could not pull apart two copper hemispheres, 200mm in diameter, from which the air had been removed. Only after the vacuum had been released by opening a valve was it possible to separate the 'Magdeburg hemispheres'.[41]

Boyle intended to go beyond what von Guericke had done and perform experiments inside a chamber containing air at higher or lower pressures than normal. He needed to use a glass vessel for the chamber so that the experiments inside could be seen. He also needed an air-pump for drawing air out of the vessel and for pumping air in, with a seal for

9.   Portrait of the Honourable Robert Boyle by Johann Kerseboom. (© *The Royal Society*)

maintaining the reduced or increased pressure during the experiments that could be controlled from outside the vessel. Boyle had commissioned Ralph Greatorex (1625–1712), one of England's most highly skilled makers of mathematical instruments, to make the air-pump for him, but unfortunately it did not prevent air leaking back into the evacuation chamber.[42] Boyle now asked Hooke to design and make a new pump.

Hooke eagerly accepted the invitation and set out for the London workshops where he knew from his time at Westminster he could obtain suitable materials and machines such as lathes for doing what was required. He later described Greatorex's air-pump as 'too gross to perform any great matter'.[43] Greatorex had served a seven-year apprenticeship with the doyen of English scientific instrument makers, Elias Allen, and had made instruments for John Wilkins and Christopher Wren among others. We should not be too hard on Ralph Greatorex. His apprenticeship was in making finely engraved, accurate opto-mechanical mathematical instruments using materials and techniques quite different from those necessary for the heavy-duty performance of an air-pump. Nevertheless, his failure to extend his skills and knowledge to meet Boyle's requirements makes Hooke's achievement all the more spectacular.[44] We do not know to what extent Hooke himself machined the cylinder barrel and made the numerous other components, but we can be sure the apparatus was made to his design and under his supervision in the 'dark shops of mechanics' (Figure 10). Back in Oxford he assembled the pump and chamber, which he and Boyle then used successfully for several experiments in the late 1650s and early 1660s, some of which gave rise to a further series of experiments which led to Boyle's Law, one of the best-known laws of physics: in brief, 'the volume of air at constant temperature is inversely proportional to its pressure'.

The 'spring' of the air could be felt with each stroke of the pump, whether it was being used to compress or rarify the air. Boyle and Hooke wanted to discover the relationship between the pressure on a volume of air and the space it occupied. They guessed from the work of others and from their own experience that if you doubled the pressure, the volume would be halved, but did this relationship always hold? If you increased the pressure ten-fold, did the volume decrease to a tenth of its original value, and so on? They devised an experiment to test the hypothesis that what they guessed at was true. They used a glass tube shaped like the letter J with air trapped in the shorter, closed arm (Figure 11). They poured mercury into the top of the open longer arm until it reached different levels, each time measuring the lengths of the columns of mercury in both arms. These measurements indicated the pressure and volume of the air trapped in the shorter, closed arm shown as Fig. 4 in Figure 11. The experiment was probably performed many times before they were satisfied that they had found the best procedures for making and using the apparatus and for taking the measurements.

There were many aspects of their experiment that were new then but have since become commonplace in science. In the first place, they published in great detail how they performed the experiment and the precautions they took. They described the difficulties they found (the longer arm of the glass J-tube was at least 8 feet long, so they had to position it in the stairwell of Boyle's house) and how they tried to overcome them. Even the way they published their measurements was new. They showed them all in the form of a table (Figure 12), but presented not only the measured values of volume and pressure, but also the pressure values which would be expected if the hypothesis were true. By simply comparing the measured pressures with the hypothesised, or calculated, values, anyone could see that they were not exactly the same. Small measurement errors are inevitable, but the pairs of measured and hypothesised values are close enough to one another to say that this experiment shows the hypothesis to be true. The excitement that Boyle and Hooke felt as they calculated, one by one, the expected values and found them coming out to lie very close to the measured values can be seen in the middle of the technical account where they said they experienced 'delight and satisfaction' at what they observed.[45] In accord with Francis Bacon's promotion of independent cooperative observations as a way of understanding nature, others could now do more experiments in different places and with different apparatus to see whether or not the hypothesis was generally observed. Neither Boyle nor Hooke claimed to have discovered a law of nature. They demonstrated that the hypothesised relationship between the volume and pressure of air was valid, within the limits of accuracy of their measurements. That is quite different from claiming to have discovered a law of nature. Boyle's Law was a later name given to the outcome of their demonstration. In an extended and generalised

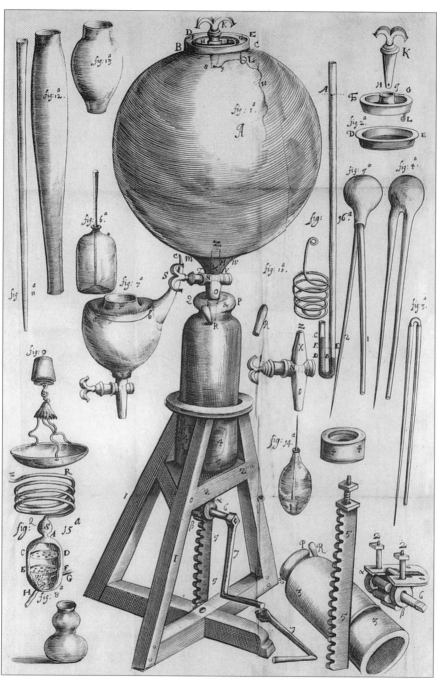

10. Boyle's air-pump and associated apparatus, designed and made by Hooke and used for the experiments published in *New Experiments Physico-Mechanicall, Touching the Spring of the Air, and its Effects*. The radius of the roughly spherical glass chamber was about 5 inches (130mm). The hole in the top of the chamber was wide enough 'to put in a man's arm cloathed'. (*Boyle 1660, frontispiece: © The Royal Society*)

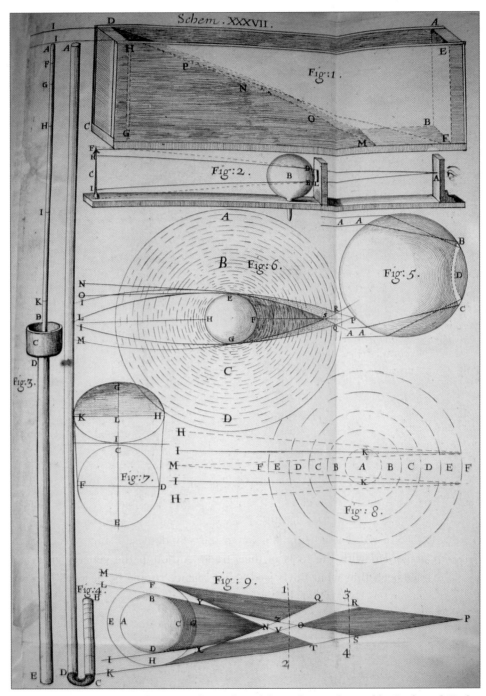

11. Diagrams in *Micrographia*. Fig 4 shows the 8 ft-long glass J-tube used by Boyle and Hooke to demonstrate Boyle's Law and Fig 3 shows the glass tubes they used in experiments for the rarefaction of air. Figs 1 and 2 illustrate apparatus for investigating the effects of refraction, whereas Figs 5–9 show Hooke's speculations on how rays of light are refracted when they pass through the earth's atmosphere. (*Hooke 1665, Schem. XXXVIII: © The Royal Society*)

(60)

divisions in the shorter Tube, the several Observations that were thus successively made, and as they were made set down, afforded us the ensuing Table.

A Table of the Condensation of the Air.

A	A	B	C	D	E
48	12	00		29 2/16	29 2/16
46	11 1/2	01 7/16		30 9/16	30 6/16
44	11	02 13/16		31 9/16	31 12/16
42	10 1/2	04 6/16		33 8/16	33 7
40	10	06 3/16		35 5/16	35 ..
38	9 1/2	07 14/16		37 --	36 15/19
36	9	10 2/16		39 1/16	38 7/8
34	8 1/2	12 8/16		41 9/16	41 2/17
32	8	15 1/16		44 3/16	43 11/16
30	7 1/2	17 2/16		47 1/16	46 3/5
28	7	21 2/16		50 5/16	50 --
26	6 1/2	25 3/16		54 5/16	53 10/13
24	6	29 11/16		58 2/16	58 8/8
23	5 3/4	32 3/16		61 5/16	60 18/23
22	5 1/2	34 7/16		64 1/16	63 6/11
21	5 1/4	37 2/16		67 1/16	66 4/7
20	5	41 9/16		70 11/16	70 --
19	4 3/4	45 --		74 2/16	73 11/19
18	4 1/2	48 12/16		77 14/16	77 2/3
17	4 1/4	53 11/16		82 12/16	82 4/17
16	4	58 2/16		87 14/16	87 7/8
15	3 3/4	63 15/16		93 1/16	93 3/5
14	3 1/2	71 5/16		100 7/16	99 6/7
13	3 1/4	78 11/16		107 13/16	107 1/13
12	3	88 7/16		117 9/16	116 4/8

(Column C, vertical:) Added 29 1/8 makes

A A. The number of equal spaces in the shorter leg, that contained the same parcel of Air diversly extended.
B. The height of the Mercurial Cylinder in the longer leg, that compress'd the Air into those dimensions.
C. The height of a Mercurial Cylinder that counterbalanc'd the pressure of the Atmosphere.
D. The Aggregate of the two last Columns B and C, exhibiting the pressure of the included Air.
E. What that pressure should be according to the *Hypothesis*, that supposes the pressures and expansions to be in reciprocal proportion.

For the better understanding of this Experiment it may not be amiss to take notice of the following particulars:
1. That the Tube being so tall that we could not conveniently make use of it in a Chamber, we were fain to use it on a pair of Stairs, which yet were very lightsom, the Tube being for preservations

12. Data published in 1662 by Boyle and Hooke in *A Defence* to show that they had confirmed by measurements the hypothesis that the pressure and volume of a given mass of air at constant temperature are in inverse proportion. Volume measurements (in different units) are in columns A; pressure measurements are in column D. The values of the pressure which would be expected if the hypothesis were true are in column E. (*Boyle 1662, 60: © The Royal Society*)

form it has been used in a wide range of applications in science and technology, just as Boyle and Hooke expected it would be.

The successful scientific cooperation between Boyle and Hooke was a very unusual, probably unprecedented, relationship. Boyle's aristocratic origins, independent income and refined social manners marked him as an honourable gentleman. Hooke would have been seen by people outside Wilkins's circle as another of Boyle's technicians, paid to work with tools and lathe at a bench similar to the way domestic employees worked in the kitchen or garden with the tools of their trade. Although the general view at the time might have been that what Boyle said about science should be believed because of who he was, and what Hooke said should carry less weight, this was not a view held by Boyle or by the formative members of the Royal Society who were capable of practising experimental science. Social differences, although respected by Hooke in his public modes of addressing Boyle, were of no consequence in their private debates and actions. Edward B. Davis has shown how, over many years, Boyle and Hooke in private thought and acted as equals in mathematics and natural philosophy where they each contributed to the other's understanding. Their relationship was mutually beneficial in personal matters too, with Boyle's other-worldliness and Hooke's busy engagement in everyday affairs enabling them to find ways of resolving difficulties arising from conflict between conscience and expediency.[46] Through Busby and Wilkins Hooke had come to see that mechanics had intellectual and moral value. By working with Boyle he found that measurements of natural phenomena using mechanical devices could reveal important and useful knowledge of the natural world made by God: measurement could be a moral act.

In working for Boyle, Hooke came to understand that by setting aside personal and social differences and by cooperating in pursuit of a common objective, great things could be achieved in science. It took craftsmen's skills, Boyle's wealth, Hooke's ingenuity and earlier scientific investigations by others (such as Evangelista Torricelli, Blaise Pascal, Richard Towneley and Henry Power) to demonstrate the validity of Boyle's Law. Hooke's firm belief in the importance of cooperative effort in human affairs was apparent again in his rebuilding of London after the Great Fire, when he worked closely with uneducated labourers, skilled craftsmen, wealthy merchants and members of the court for the common good.

From his childhood in the Isle of Wight as a self-taught but intuitively gifted mechanic, Hooke had honed his practical skills and widened his knowledge of materials and methods in the workshops of London and the laboratories of Oxford. By the time he reached his early twenties he had an exceptionally deep mechanical insight, shown by the successful making of the pump that Boyle required, but he was also showing a capacity for scientific investigation that was just as exceptional at that time. He had impressed many men with his lively mind and eager enthusiasm and had received their sponsorship, employment or other support. The most important of these men for his future career were Boyle and Wilkins. In Boyle he had the trust and support of a man of propriety, integrity and inherited wealth, dependent on nobody for his livelihood; in Wilkins he had the support of a clever man, hospitable, at ease in the affairs of university, Church and State, who had the respect of important men in many different walks of life, including the City of London. Hooke's astronomy teacher Seth Ward, Boyle and Wilkins had between them provided a sort of intellectual, moral and technical apprenticeship in Oxford to prepare Hooke for a career that would be crucial to the objectives of the Royal Society and to the rebuilding of London after the Great Fire.

2

THESE MY FIRST LABOURS

When Robert Boyle visited London from Oxford he stayed with his sister Lady Ranelagh in Pall Mall, where he set up another laboratory. In the early 1660s Hooke was working for Boyle in London as well as in Oxford. He was a young, ambitious man already making a name for himself as an experimental philosopher, but he had no private income. As so often happened in Hooke's early maturity, one or two influential men recognised that he had talents which could be useful to them, so they set about obtaining his services. He was soon appointed Curator of Experiments for the Royal Society, an institution in which he found first exhilaration, then frustration and finally, in the last year or so of his life, anxious despair. There were times when it seemed that without Hooke's vigorous physical and intellectual presence at its weekly meetings the Royal Society would have foundered.

In the first year or so of the Society's existence, progress in natural philosophy was disappointingly slow. Experiments of the quality that Boyle and Hooke were performing in Oxford could not be carried out at the Society's meetings in Gresham College: something as important as Boyle's Law could not be discovered each week. Debates on written reports and discussions about curious objects that had been brought in or sent to the Society were the main activities at the early meetings; a way of managing their experiments effectively had not yet been found. Individual members were nominated as curators of specific experiments, each of them being responsible for preparing and performing his experiment in front of the assembled members at one of their weekly meetings, but too many of them were ill-equipped by experience, upbringing or inclination to make mechanical devices. The Society's operator (or technician) employed at an annual salary of £4[1] was a craftsman of average ability, quite incapable of making the new instruments that were needed, or of understanding why and how they were to be used. The Society's amanuensis (or shorthand clerk, whose annual salary was also £4)[2] was sometimes ordered to make the equipment, but unsurprisingly he too usually failed to do what was necessary. [3]

Hooke's name is mentioned for the first time in Royal Society records[4] on 10 April 1661, when the Society decided to debate at its next meeting his publication *Attempt for the Explication of the Phænomena*.[5] The work described how water rose inside a number of thin glass tubes of differing diameters under a variety of conditions. Hooke speculated upon the cause of what he observed in terms of active properties of matter he called 'congruity' and incongruity'. The hydrostatical phenomenon is now referred to as capillary attraction, explained by surface tension. Debate in science was not enough; it was also necessary in the new learning to test the validity of any conclusions arising from debate and experiment by making further, independent, experiments and observations, but this was something the members were failing to do. On the day they intended to debate and repeat Hooke's experiments to test the findings he wrote about in *Attempt for the Explication . . .* it seems they were prevented from doing so because the apparatus was not ready. There is no record of any experiments or debate on Hooke's observations that day, but they ordered the amanuensis to make a list of all the orders for experiments that had not yet been executed.[6] Many experiments by nominated members of the Society were planned and some were performed during the rest of 1661 and most of the next year, but too many were not completed.

Sir Robert Moray (1608–73) was a formative member of the Royal Society. Through his position at court and his friendship with King Charles II he had gained the latter's approval of the formation of the Society in 1660 and its Charter of Incorporation as 'The Royal Society of London' in 1662. Moray now decided that the Society should act to change its custom of performing only simple experiments of little consequence. On 5 November 1662 at a meeting of the Royal Society in Gresham College he proposed:

> a person willing to be employed as a curator by the society, and offering to furnish them every day, on which they met, with three or four considerable experiments, and expecting no recompense till the society should get a stock enabling them to give it. The proposition was received unanimously, Mr. Robert Hooke being named to be the person.[7]

It is not surprising that Hooke was named: many of the members present had heard about his ingenuity from Wilkins, or knew about his work with Boyle at Oxford, or had read and debated his speculations in *Attempt for the Explication . . .* Following Moray's proposal Boyle was asked if he would release Hooke from his employment in Oxford.[8] At the meeting the following week Sir Robert Moray formally proposed Hooke as Curator of Experiments to the Society, Boyle having agreed. The proposal was accepted unanimously and the Society:

> ordered that Mr Boyle should have the thanks of the society for dispensing with him for their use; and that Mr. Hooke should come and sit amongst them, and both bring in every day of the meeting three or four experiments of his own, and take care of such others, as should be mentioned to him by the society.[9]

There was no doubt in the minds of the members that Hooke was the ideal man to get them through their difficulties in performing experiments, nor that he would readily accept the appointment and the opportunity it offered, even though there was little prospect that the Society would have funds to pay the curator's salary. Despite his talents he did not yet have any income, except from Boyle.

Not all responsibility for performing experimental demonstrations was passed to the new curator. On the day Hooke was appointed, the Society's President, Lord Brouncker, decided that he (Brouncker) would be curator of the experiment to find what 'force' is required to raise one pound through one foot in one second.[10] Although Hooke was clearly expected to perform experiments proposed by members of the Society, he was also expected to 'sit amongst them'. From the start his position was ambiguous: sitting with the Fellows as their intellectual equal, taking instructions from the Society's Council, but with little prospect of any remuneration in the near future. His name is recorded in the list of Registered Fellows approved by the Council of the Royal Society at its meeting on 20 May 1663,[11] but he was specifically exempt from all charges such as the quarterly subscription of 13*s* 0*d* and other fees.[12]

Hooke lost no time in showing the Society what he could do. Only a week after being appointed he was in front of the members demonstrating the different sounds that glass bubbles containing a partial vacuum made when they were broken – another use for his air-pump, but the demonstration would have been more entertaining for the Fellows than instructive. Hooke put down in writing some questions arising from what had been observed during the experiments, and made suggestions about the design of further tests and experiments to provide answers. He was ordered to bring to the Society's meeting the following week a written report on weighing glass bubbles, some filled with air and some partially evacuated. He told the Society that he would show an experiment on the 'tenacity' (compressibility) of air and also spoke of an engine for experiments on condensation. He was ordered to make it as soon as possible.[13]

Thus began Hooke's activities for the Royal Society which were to continue for many years. When he was ordered to make what he thought were more in the nature of entertaining demonstrations than experimental investigations he did not argue against performing them. Instead, he usually ignored them and put forward his own ideas for demonstrations and experiments, but was reprimanded from time to time and reminded that he had not yet performed what had been ordered and had failed to do what he had himself proposed. He found it hard to resist the urge suddenly to throw all his energies into a new line of enquiry that had engaged his attention, or to design and make a new instrument that he had conceived before finishing the matter in hand. He did not have a group of technicians and a workshop stocked with the materials and tools needed for making the new instruments from his design drawings, nor a laboratory with a few skilled operators who could test the instruments and perform and record experiments. He was expected somehow to do all these things himself, aided by one operator in his workshop in Gresham College, where he now had accommodation as Gresham Professor of Geometry, and to perform several experiments each week. His enthusiasm for science and ideas for instruments to provide measurements to aid his investigations enabled him to do far more than anyone else in the Society. His ideas seemed boundless.

Added complications were the great diversity and lack of discrimination in the Society's experiments in their early years. As a consequence of the members' enthusiastic optimism for science Hooke was expected to make microscopical and astronomical instruments and observations, experiment with skin grafts and blood transfusions, test the explosive power of different kinds of gunpowder, measure the earth's gravitational attraction, make instruments for recording the weather, investigate the refraction of light, find a way of taking soundings at sea without using a lead-line and find out and record the effect on himself and others in the Society of continually breathing the same quantity of air.[14] Some of the anatomical experiments he was called upon to perform caused him distress. In November 1664 he investigated by canine vivisection the way in which air mixed with blood in the lungs. His report of the operation, presented to the Royal Society on 9 November, described how the dog was kept alive for more than an hour by a pair of bellows pumping air into its lungs through a tube inserted into its wind-pipe. The heart continued to beat long after the thorax and belly had been opened. Hooke's detailed, but factual, account makes gruesome reading.[15] Writing of the experiment to Boyle on 10 November Hooke said 'I shall hardly, I confess, make [it] againe, because it was cruel'. He went on to say that although he examined and handled the working lungs, heart and other organs and discovered something of 'the necessity of fresh air and the motion of the lungs for the continuance of the animal life' he was unable to discover what he 'most looked for' which was a passage for air to pass from the lungs into either the heart or the blood vessels. He continued:

> I shall hardly be induc'd to make any further trials of this kind because of the torture of the creature but certainly the enquiry would be very noble if we could any way find a way soe to stupify the creature as that it might not be sensible which I fear there is hardly any opiate will performe . . . There are several that are much awakened by this experiment and, I find, intend to prosecute it much further of which I hope I shall have a certain account.[16]

Hooke's compassion for a suffering animal was sufficiently deep to place a limit on what he personally would do in the quest for natural knowledge, but he wanted to know what happened when others less sensitive than he was went ahead with new investigations by vivisection. Not all members of the Royal Society had such compassion. On 7 June 1665 Wilkins performed another experiment, similar to the one Hooke had done, but with the added interest of drawing off five or six ounces of blood from the dog's heart and transferring most of it into the vein of a bitch, 'but without any sensible alteration of the bitch'. After further investigation into the effect on its breathing of holes cut into its thorax, the dog died.[17] Hooke was listed as among those present. He probably watched his mentor's experiment with a keen eye, but, one imagines, with a troubled conscience.

During the first two years of his appointment Hooke continued to work part-time for Boyle in Oxford. When in London he lodged at the Pall Mall house of Boyle's sister, Lady Ranelagh, where Boyle had a laboratory. Under the influence of Wren, Hooke made a series of microscopical examinations, which he showed from time to time at the Society's meetings. Although most members were fascinated by what the microscope revealed, they were apprehensive when Hooke prepared to publish *Micrographia*, a book about his observations that he described as 'these my first Labours'.[18] He intended to publish not only his drawings but also to make public his conjectures about why the objects he had looked at appeared the way they did. Members of the Royal Society were uneasy about public reaction to the book, suspecting that Hooke's conjectures might be taken as their collective and dogmatic opinions – something completely against their Baconian principles. Publication of the book was delayed for several months while it passed between the members for their scrutiny. Hooke and the Society were faced with recognising and acknowledging the important role of speculation in science. *Micrographia* was eventually published in early 1665. The author is described as 'R. Hooke, Fellow of the Royal Society'. The book opens with Hooke's dedication to the king, then his disclaimer to the Royal Society in which he asserts his adherence to the Society's rules 'of avoiding Dogmatizing, and the espousal of any Hypothesis not sufficiently grounded and confirm'd by Experiments'. He then goes on to say that in his treatise:

> there may perhaps be some Expressions, which may seem more positive then Your Prescriptions will permit; and though I desire to have them understood only as Conjectures and Quæries (which Your Method does not altogether disallow) yet even if in those I have exceeded 'tis fit that I should declare, that it was not done by Your directions.[19]

Micrographia was a great public success: it can even be said to be the first best-selling book on popular science. It revealed details seen by Hooke through his microscope that nobody had seen before, such as the cellular structure of plants and the complex beauty of the scale of a fish (Figure 13) and the delicacy of mould (Figure 14). Pepys saw early copies of *Micrographia* at his binders and immediately ordered one, which he collected a fortnight later. The following day he sat up until 2 a.m. reading 'the most ingenious book that I ever read in my life'.[20]

Despite Hooke's enthusiastic optimism for the new learning, shared by some members, he and the Society began to suffer from lack of resources brought about by the failure of too many members to play their part, either by paying their dues (which were intended to cover costs, such as employees' salaries) or by active and informed

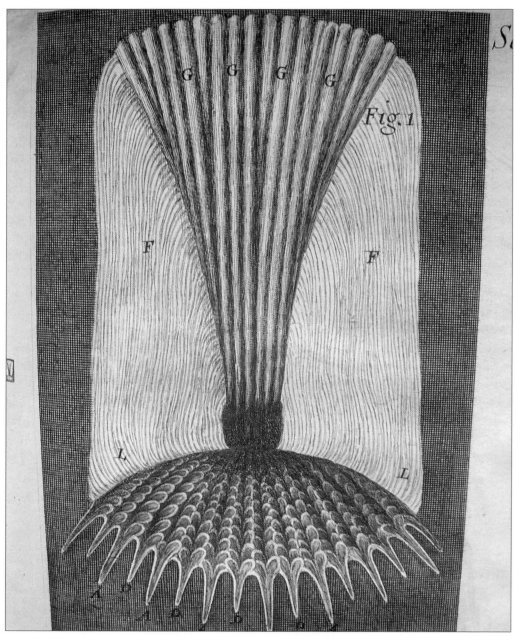

13. The scale of a sole, one of many illustrations in *Micrographia* of hitherto unregarded objects in nature. The small rectangle at the left-hand edge of the illustration represents the true size of the object; the dimensions of the published view of the sole's scale magnified are about 120mm × 190mm. (*Hooke 1665, Schem. XXI: © The Royal Society*)

14. Even commonplace white mould – a species of Mucor (Ainsworth 1976) – growing on the red sheepskin covers of a small book was revealed by the microscope as beautiful and delicate. Hooke wrote 'The whole substance of these pretty bodies was of a very tender constitution, much like the substance of the softer kind of common white Mushroms.' (*Hooke 1665, Schem. XII Fig 1:* © *The Royal Society*)

participation in an orderly and feasible programme of experiments. The Society had to find ways of managing and directing its unique activities. In particular, its finances were a continuous source of anxiety. During the first two years of employment at a notional annual salary of £30, Hooke was in fact paid nothing by the Society. He received £50 during the following two years, but it was not until 1675, after he had been working for the Royal Society for thirteen years, that all arrears of his salary as Curator of

Experiments had been paid.[21] Members who had been elected because of their wealth or influence failed to bring to the Society the benefits of patronage that were expected of them. Some grandees in the Society were more interested in being entertained than enlightened by experiments and demonstrations performed by Hooke. Having little understanding of, or interest in, the difficulties Hooke faced in making and testing new apparatus almost each week they became impatient when an experiment ‘failed’, seeing it simply as a fault of their philosophical servant.

Some historians take the view that Hooke’s independence as a natural philosopher was compromised by his inferior social position as an employee, dependent on others for his livelihood.[22] Most of the active formative members of the Royal Society who had themselves made and used instruments in furthering their knowledge of the natural world (Boyle, Wilkins and Wren in particular) did not take that view. Nor did those members who later chose to attend his Cutlerian Lectures regularly.[23] If Isaac Newton had thought Hooke’s authority was compromised by his social position he would not have taken the trouble to denigrate his work in the manner or to the extent that he did.

Hooke’s indefatigable powers of observation, experiment and rational speculation in natural philosophy continued until the late 1670s, from which point, for a multitude of reasons, both institutional and personal, the intensity of his experimental activities began to decline. He was now more than forty years old. The physical energy he had expended in surveying and scientific research during the decade after the fire was beginning to take its toll on his body. His insomnia during this time was a frequent cause of anxiety, as his many diary entries show. His physician colleagues in the Royal Society were keen to offer suggestions for new therapeutic regimes to cure his growing list of ailments; he frequently suffered from giddiness, headaches and vomiting, as he had as a child, and he experimented with drugs, out of scientific curiosity, recording in his diary what he had taken and how it affected him. The long-term effect of such self-dosing was more sickness and discomfort, which he then tried to cure by taking more and different medicinal drugs. He had, as Lisa Jardine has pointed out, succumbed to self-experiment.[24]

Three of the Royal Society’s most active formative members, Sir Robert Moray, John Wilkins and the physician Dr Jonathan Goddard (ever willing to prescribe medicines for Hooke), had died by the mid-1670s, and former active members such as Robert Boyle and Seth Ward stopped attending the weekly meetings, some of which were cancelled through lack of numbers.[25] No longer beset by incessant demands for new experiments, and becoming less physically active as his health deteriorated in the late 1670s, Hooke turned his mind to publishing some of his Cutlerian Lectures. Between 1674 and 1680 he published the only major works which appeared in his lifetime, apart from *Micrographia*, which was by now in its second edition. His mental energy had not abated.

Hooke was elected to the Society’s Council from time to time, and spent a few years as the Society’s secretary, but without relinquishing his role as curator. It was an impossible combination of roles. At the Society's meetings he was expected, as their secretary, to sit with other Council officers at the cloth-covered table bearing the mace, making notes for the Society's record of the experiments being performed in front of him. At the same time, as the Society's Curator of Experiments, he was expected to be at the wooden bench facing the officers and the Society, performing the experiments. His time as secretary was not a success. In the 1680s a new generation of members with ideas for reforming the Royal Society appointed curators for different subjects. Hooke was becoming increasingly ill and at odds with his fellow scientists.

His final act on behalf of the Royal Society was to lobby Parliament in 1699 to delay the passage of a bill which would allow the Gresham Trustees to demolish Gresham College in order to rebuild it, but with accommodation for rent as well as for the Gresham Professors. Rent income from a rebuilt college would help clear the Mercers' debt which they had accumulated largely as a result of their extravagant rebuilding of the Royal Exchange after the fire, against Hooke's advice. Hooke's reason for lobbying to delay the bill, until it was eventually lost when Parliament was dissolved, could have been to save the Royal Society from eviction. It was also to save losing, through the extravagance he had warned against, the rooms where he had lived and worked for almost forty years.

Hooke's 'first labours' had shown that observational techniques could reveal natural wonders to everyone. His experimental performances in front of the Royal Society resembled dramatic presentations, a wooden bench and scientific instruments serving as stage and set. It seemed as if natural philosophy was not only exciting and fruitful, but could also be regularly entertaining for onlookers. During the first two years of Hooke's curatorship it gradually became clear to many members of the Royal Society that their high expectations were not going to be realised quickly. Many members blamed Hooke for the slow progress, but others understood that it was necessary to plan experiments carefully and carry them out patiently. The Royal Society was a learned society, which, in accordance with Baconian principles, undertook experiments in order to learn more of the natural world. In doing so, it was also learning that financing and managing a learned society for natural philosophy are quite different from financing and managing research. Hooke was at the centre of these early difficulties in science, but his enthusiasm for experimental philosophy never left him, and his active presence sustained the Royal Society throughout its precarious first decade.

3

❧

A PERSON LEARNED IN GEOMETRY

Soon after he started to work for the Royal Society, Hooke's association with two of the leading figures in the City of London began. One was Sir John Lawrence, who was to become his true friend, the other Sir John Cutler, who brought Hooke continuous and debilitating anxiety for the next thirty years. In 1664, after he had worked for the Royal Society for two years, the members were still seeking ways of paying him his annual salary of £80. The influence of Sir John Cutler, a wealthy grocer, can be felt not only in the institution of the Cutlerian Lectures on the History of Trades, for which Cutler offered to pay Hooke £50 annually, but in Hooke's initial defeat for the post of Gresham Professor of Geometry.

In the mid-1660s the Royal Society was keen for Hooke to live in Gresham College, where he would be readily available to carry out his tasks, living and working in the building where the Society held its meetings. Gresham College (Figure 15) had been the London residence of Sir Thomas Gresham (1519–79), the Tudor merchant who made his fortune through banking and finance, particularly in the Low Countries where the Antwerp Bourse inspired him to set up the Royal Exchange in London. In his will he stipulated that his mansion should be used to house seven professors (of Divinity, Astronomy, Geometry, Music, Law, Physic and Rhetoric) whose annual salaries of £50 would be paid from income received from rents and leases of merchants and traders at the Royal Exchange. Gresham College was intended to be quite different from the universities at Oxford and Cambridge, but over the years various men moved both ways between an appointment at a university and one at Gresham College. Each Gresham Professor was required during term-time to give one lecture a week in English, as well as in Latin, to anybody who was interested enough to attend the public Reading Hall at Gresham College. Gresham's intention was to bring the new learning into such practices as navigation, building, mechanics, trading and manufacturing to the benefit of England as a whole and to the citizens and institutions of the City of London in particular.

Thomas Gresham's will was administered by Trustees (officially 'The Joint Grand Gresham Committee' but hereafter referred to as 'the Gresham Trustees') made up of representatives from the Mercers' Company and from the City.[1] The 'Mercers' Side' was responsible for appointing professors of Law, Physic and Rhetoric, the 'City Side' for appointments in Astronomy, Divinity, Geometry and Music.[2] When, in December 1663, Isaac Barrow decided he would vacate his position as Gresham Professor of Geometry in order to take up an appointment in Cambridge,[3] the Royal Society tried to arrange for Hooke to take lodgings four days a week in Gresham College so that he would be conveniently placed to prepare experiments the Society was planning to show to the king in the hope of gaining royal financial support for their objectives. It is highly likely that John Wilkins spoke to the City Side about Hooke's suitability to succeed Barrow.[4] When the City Side met on 20 May 1664 to elect Barrow's successor, there were two candidates, Hooke and Arthur Dacres, a physician.[5] The report of the election seems clear enough:

> . . . two learned persons viz. Dr Arthur Dacres and Mr Robert Hooke being suited for the same, their petitions being Read theire ample Certificates considered and the matter debated The Court proceeded to election and made theyreof the said Dr Dacres to supply the said place of Geomitry Reader in the College.[6]

A little over two weeks later, on 8 June 1664, the Royal Society Council questioned the validity of Dacres's appointment 'upon information given, that the lord mayor of London was not of the committee, and yet by his presence had carried the election by a casting vote'.[7] John Wilkins was influential on the Society's behalf in getting the City Side under the chairmanship of the new Lord Mayor, Sir John Lawrence, to look into the matter on 20 March 1665. Lawrence found that the appointment of Dacres had been illegal because the previous Lord Mayor, Sir Anthony Bateman, was not a member of the City Side but had taken the chair at the meeting and misreported the voting. The City Side, now under Lawrence, declared there had been a 'mistake' and 'that Robert Hooke was the person legally elected and accordingly ought to enjoy the same with the Lodgings proffits and all accomodations to the place of Geomitry Reader appertaining'.[8] The Royal Society had got what it wanted and shown that it had influence in the City.

In seeking an explanation for the 'mistake', it is noteworthy that it was made at the time when Cutler had Hooke in mind as his Lecturer on the History of Trades, and would therefore have had an interest in preventing Hooke's appointment as Gresham Professor of Geometry. Cutler could do little directly to ensure Dacres would be elected. He was not a member of the City Side, but he had friends and family who were. In May 1664, soon after Dacres had been 'elected', Hooke met Cutler by chance in a public house and told him of his disappointment by the City Side, which included a relative of Cutler.[9] He told Hooke not be too upset because he intended to pay him an equally good salary to enable him to continue the good work he had heard so much about. This chance meeting between Cutler and Hooke took place just before the Royal Society first heard of Cutler's intention to found a Lectureship.[10] A conspiracy between Cutler, Foote, Sir Anthony Bateman and his two brothers to save Hooke for Cutler's personal sponsorship is a possible explanation of the 'mistake'.[11]

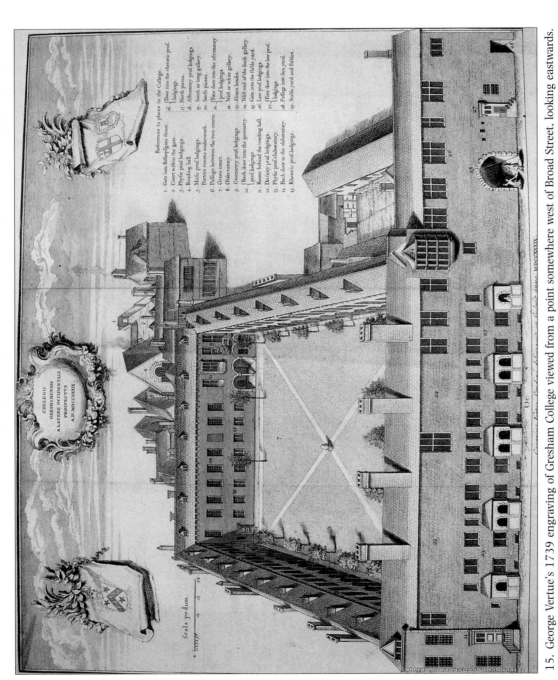

References to places in the College

1. Gate into Bishopsgate street.
2. Court within the gate.
3. Physic prof lodgings.
4. Reading hall.
5. Music prof lodgings.
6. Passage between the two courts. Porters rooms underneath.
7. Green court.
8. Observatory.
9. Geometry prof lodgings.
10. [Back door into the geometry prof lodgings.]
11. Room behind the reading hall.
12. Divinity prof lodgings.
13. Physic prof elaboratory.
14. Back door to the elaboratory.
15. Rhetoric prof lodgings.
16. [Door into the rhetoric prof lodgings.]
17. North piazza.
18. Astronomy prof lodgings.
19. South or long gallery.
20. South piazza.
21. [Stair door into the astronomy prof lodgings.]
22. West or white gallery.
23. Alms houses.
24. West end of the south gallery.
25. Gate into the stable yard.
26. Law prof lodgings.
27. [Fore door into the law prof lodging.]
28. Passage into Sun yard.
29. Stable yard and stables.

COLLEGII
GRESHAMENSIS
A LATERE OCCIDENTALI
PROSPECTVS
A.D. MDCCXXII.

Scala pedum.

15. George Vertue's 1739 engraving of Gresham College viewed from a point somewhere west of Broad Street, looking eastwards. The Dutch church Austin Friars and the church of St Peter-le-Poer, which escaped the fire, could have been used as standpoints for the drawing. (*Guildhall Library, Corporation of London*)

Before Dacres's illegal election had been rectified, Sir John Cutler offered to pay Hooke £50 a year to give a public lecture each week during vacations in Gresham College on the History of Trades. The Royal Society saw a way out of its difficulties. If Hooke were paid £50 annually by Cutler, then the Society could reduce his salary as curator by the same amount, leaving only £30 to find annually. Moreover, it seemed to the Society that Cutler was proposing to sponsor a new Gresham Professorship, with free lodgings in Gresham College for Hooke, so Hooke's failure to be elected Gresham Professor would not inconvenience the Society's work. Cutler's offer was just the sort of sponsorship the Society was seeking. There were, however, three difficulties: Cutler had made the offer to Hooke, not to the Royal Society; the offer was to sponsor public lectures, in Cutler's name, on the History of Trades, but public lectures and the subject chosen by Cutler were not among the main activities of the Royal Society; and the offer did not include the provision of free accommodation in Gresham College as a Gresham Professor. Such difficulties were important, but the Royal Society set them aside: knowing that Hooke's experimental gifts and expertise were crucial to their objectives, members were so desperate to retain his services and find him a salary that they negotiated a deal and signed a bond of agreement with Cutler in 1665 without informing Hooke.

Once Hooke had taken up the appointment as Gresham Professor of Geometry he continued to give his Cutlerian Lectures on the subject of the History of Trades, but soon used them instead to announce some of his scientific work. Although he began to pay Hooke his annual salary of £50 from the time of the first Cutlerian Lecture and throughout most of the late 1660s, Cutler's dissatisfaction increased as he saw the Royal Society continuing to ignore the arrangements set out in its signed bond of agreement with him – so he stopped paying. Hooke continued to read his lectures in the public Reading Hall at Gresham College, but they became associated more with the Royal Society than with the public, taking place in the hour before the Society's weekly meetings. The subjects of the lectures soon became very different from what Cutler had intended. It is not surprising that the relations between Hooke, his employers and his sponsor became strained, especially as Hooke had at the time received no salary from the Royal Society.

In the 1670s Hooke began to realise that he might have to resort to litigation to get Cutler to pay him his arrears of salary, in which case he would need evidence that he had fulfilled his obligations. He therefore began to publish his Cutlerian Lectures separately and in a collected edition.[12] He suspected that Cutler was spying on his lecturing with the intention of gathering evidence of his own to show that Hooke should forfeit his salary because he had failed to meet his obligations. A case in point occurred in July 1677, when Hooke noted 'Attend lecture of Sir J. Cutler in the Hall with Mr. Haak. Drew scheme of comet in the hall. Capn. Panton came for lecture but noe more, he gave me his designe for Academy. Axe here to spy.'[13] Hooke decided he should continue to record evidence that he was giving his lectures by writing on his lecture

16. The end of the manuscript (detail) of Hooke's Cutlerian lecture to the Royal Society on 18 December 1689 where he recorded the names of some of those present. (*Classified Papers xx, 80, f. 179r: © The Royal Society*)

notes the names of people who were present and who witnessed his performances, such as in this example (Figure 16): 'This Lecture was Read before the Royall Society Dec: 18. 1689. Present Sr. Joseph Williamson Mr. Pepys. Mr. Bemde. Mr. Hill Aubery. Lodowick. Dr. Mapletofte Dr. Tison Dr Slare Slare [sic] Mr. Evelyn Mr. Pitfeild. and severall others.'[14] Despite the problems, Hooke's Cutlerian Lectures display the wide range of his scientific interests and the originality of his ideas at that time, including his attempt to prove by observations that the earth moves around the sun (a motive in the design of the Monument as a telescope), methods for improving scientific instruments, studies of combustion, the law of elasticity (which now bears his name) and the nature and orbits of comets. The great confusion underlying Hooke's Cutlerian Lectureship caused him much anguish. Eventually he received all the salary owed to him by Cutler, paid from Cutler's estate, after lengthy litigation which ended with a Court of Chancery ruling in Hooke's favour on his 61st birthday.[15]

4

THE PLAINNESS AND
SOUNDNESS OF OBSERVATIONS

Before the Great Fire of 1666 Hooke's London, with its cramped and confused layout and dark, airless living quarters amid workshops and furnaces, was a medieval city in need of major reform. Attempts to make improvements had been generally ineffective, and although fire made reform necessary, designs for an ideal new city had to be set aside so that the inhabitants could resume their domestic and business lives without undue delay. When Wren and Hooke worked with craftsmen to replace the old medieval city and improve the lives of its inhabitants, they were also striving with their colleagues in the Royal Society to replace the medieval understanding of the natural world by a new learning which would bring other practical benefits. Wren and Hooke let light and air into the streets and buildings of London and rid them of the dirt of centuries that had accumulated in the decaying alleys and enclosed courtyards. They also investigated the nature of light and air, two phenomena necessary for life, in order to understand them better and make use of that understanding. Through countless acts of designing, listening, observing, measuring, reporting and directing the work of others, Hooke brought improved health and well-being to London's citizens. At the same time he was also the leading experimental scientist in England, where his designs for instruments and procedures, measurements, observations and reports revealed new and useful knowledge about the natural world.

In science, Hooke contributed to the sweeping aside of complex and sterile scholastic arguments about the natural world. The use of authoritative texts since the time of Aristotle as a basis of arguing from first principles in order to explain the natural world was leading nowhere. Experiment, observation, measurement and rational argument held out more promise of success. The Royal Society's motto *Nullius in Verba* (on no man's word) was a statement of principle. By working with men such as Seth Ward, Robert Boyle and John Wilkins, Hooke had come to see that experimental science could bring great benefits to mankind and that it was morally and intellectually an acceptable activity, an uncommon viewpoint at the time.

Boyle, Wilkins, Wren and other formative members of the Royal Society were individually and collectively influenced in their actions and thoughts in science by the

17. Portrait of the Lord Chancellor, Francis Bacon, Baron Verulam and Viscount St Albans. From the studio of Paulus von Sumer. (© *The Royal Society*)

writings of the lawyer and natural philosopher Francis Bacon (Figure 17).[1] Bacon's hugely ambitious scheme to transform the way knowledge about the natural world was acquired brought about an intellectual change in seventeenth-century England based on his writings on natural philosophy in 1620 under the general heading *Instauratio Magna* (the *Great Instauration*, or *Renewal*). Rejecting the principle held by many natural philosophers since Aristotle that new knowledge of the natural world should be obtained through logical deductions based on authoritative texts, Bacon proposed instead that we should start by making observations of natural phenomena and then apply reason to them in order to come to conclusions about their likely causes. The old procedure is known as deduction, or arguing logically from given, or

defined, causes to explain their effects. The new procedure, arguing from observed phenomena and drawing conclusions about their causes, is known as induction. Deduction is sometimes referred to as a priori reasoning and induction as a posteriori reasoning. In place of fossilised Aristotelianism, material empirical evidence, obtained cooperatively, would be the basis for revealing natural causes through reason. Bacon introduced a natural philosophy in which action as well as thought was essential. Bacon's philosophy of action appealed to the formative members who founded the Royal Society in 1660 in accord with another Baconian idea published posthumously in 1627 in *The New Atlantis*. Bacon foresaw an institution which he referred to as 'Saloman's House', where natural philosophers could collectively make experimental observations and engage in rational debate about the natural world. In following Baconian principles of thought and action, Hooke became the greatest experimental scientist of his time.

Members of the Royal Society had to be careful not to overstate their case and give offence to the monarchy or the Church. Already some of their experiments, such as those involving the weighing of air, were causing amusement at court, where they were seen as nothing more than the futile pursuits of eccentric virtuosi. Pepys recorded that at a meeting in the Duke of York's chamber the king mocked Sir William Petty, a leading member of the Royal Society and 'mightily laughed at [the Royal Society] for spending time only in weighing of aire and doing nothing els since they sat'.[2] The truth is, wrote Hooke, 'the Science of Nature has been already too long made only a work of the Brain and the Fancy; It is now high time that it should return to the plainness and soundness of Observations on material and obvious things.'[3] In the Preface to *Micrographia* he outlined the principle which underpinned his experimental investigations. He said that mankind's senses, memory and reason are all imperfect (brought about by the Fall in the Garden of Eden) and they must all be improved by artifice if they are to lead to more useful empirical evidence, fewer erroneous conclusions and the improvement of life. To remedy defects in our senses Hooke proposed using instruments for observations:

> By the means of Telescopes, there is nothing so far distant but may be represented to our view; and by the help of Microscopes, there is nothing so small, as to escape our inquiry; hence there is a new visible World discovered to the understanding. By this means the heavens are open'd, and a vast number of new Stars, and new Motions, and new Productions appear in them, to which all the antient Astronomers were utterly Strangers. By this the Earth it self, which lyes so neer us, under our feet, shews quite a new thing to us, and in every little particle of its matter, we now behold almost as great a variety of Creatures, as we were able before to reckon up in the whole Universe it self.[4]

Hooke's enthusiastic optimism breaks free here and elsewhere in *Micrographia* from the factual contents of the book – one reason why the Royal Society was anxious about its publication. Although his descriptions of what he saw are carefully and objectively written, they nevertheless reveal the excitement at what must have seemed to him and his colleagues in the Royal Society a prospect of infinite benefits to come from the new learning. His excitement was shared by an astonished book-buying public. *Micrographia* did much more to enhance the Society's standing than prosaic experiments on the properties of air.

By publishing pictures and written accounts of what he had seen through his microscope and telescope, Hooke was assisting his and our memories. But he went much further. In accordance with the Baconian principle of cooperative observations, he published in *Micrographia* diagrams and detailed instructions (Figure 18) for making the sort of microscope he had used so that anyone else could see for themselves whether or not his drawings and verbal descriptions of the objects under examination were accurate. He even foresaw the time when artificial aids – biological, chemical or mechanical – would be devised to increase our other senses, of smell, hearing, taste and touch. Hooke used *Micrographia* to show very large and distant objects as well as the very small and nearby. When he showed a diagram of the positions and brightness of stars in the constellation Pleiades, he filled up 'a pretty large corner' of the printing plate with a telescopic observation of a small part of the moon's surface (Figure 19).

Hooke wrote in *Micrographia* that he intended to set out and publish a scheme for natural philosophy. It was not published in his lifetime, but a draft entitled *A General Scheme, or Idea Of the Present State of Natural Philosophy, and How its Defects may be*

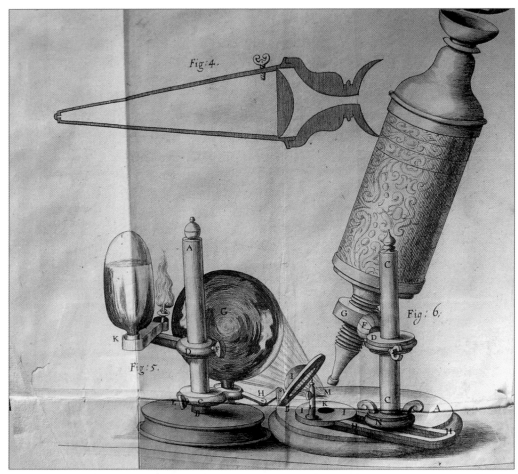

18. Hooke's microscope in *Micrographia*. Fig 4 shows a scheme of an eye lens and an objective lens with a very small aperture. Fig 5 shows the device for concentrating light from an oil lamp (K) on to the specimen under examination by means of a globe containing a clear solution of brine (G) and a plano-convex lens (I). (*Hooke 1665, Schem. I: © The Royal Society*)

Remedied by a Methodical Proceeding in the Making Experiments and Collecting Observations . . . was published in *Posthumous Works*.[5] Hooke did not see nature as a machine, whose complete workings could be fully understood by human observations and rational thought, but he commended the use of mechanical analogies as a way of concentrating the mind and raising and testing hypotheses in order to get closer to a full understanding of nature. His genius lay in his ability to combine thought and action in experiments designed to give useful evidence about the natural world. In his quest for accurate and reliable numerical data from experiments with instruments specially designed for measurement he was following Galileo (1564–1642), to whom he paid tribute in *Micrographia*, saying that if:

this method were followed with diligence and attention, there is nothing that lyes within the power of human Wit (or which is far more effectual) of human Industry, which we might not compass; we might not only hope for Inventions to equalize those of Copernicus, Galileo, Gilbert Harvy, and of others, whose Names are almost lost, that were the Inventors of Gun-powder, the Seamans Compas, Printing, Etching, Graving, Microscopes, &c.[6]

This comment illustrates Hooke's belief that 'inventions', both as discoveries and as artifacts, are equally worthy and that 'human Wit' and more importantly 'human Industry' are necessary if useful inventions are to be achieved. His innate understanding of mechanical operations enabled him to conceive new scientific instruments for specific purposes that were unprecedented in their variety and originality.

Hooke and his colleagues in the Royal Society suspected that the earth's gravitational attraction changed as one went higher above the earth's surface or deeper below it. Henry Power (1623–68), a physician member of the Royal Society, had carried out some experiments in the

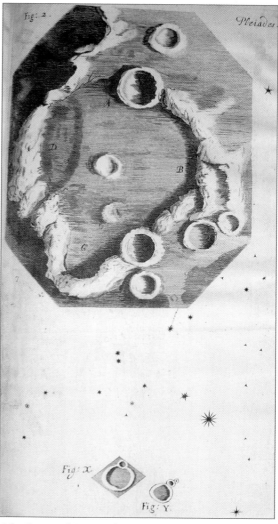

19. Crater of Hipparchus as seen by Hooke through a telescope with a 30ft objective in October 1664, just before the moon was half full. His illustration shows much more detail of the area than had been seen before. To demonstrate the point he reprinted views of the same area of the moon published by the astronomers Hevelius (Fig X) and Riccioli (Fig Y). *(Hooke 1665, Schem XXXVIII: © The Royal Society)*

vertical shaft of a coal mine 68 feet deep near his home at Halifax in Yorkshire to discover how the weight of a body changed as it was lowered from the top to the base of the mineshaft. He found the body 'to weigh lighter, by an ounce at least, than it did at the top', but members of the Royal Society were unconvinced by his short and vague account of what he had done.[7] Following Hooke's appointment as Curator of Experiments on 12

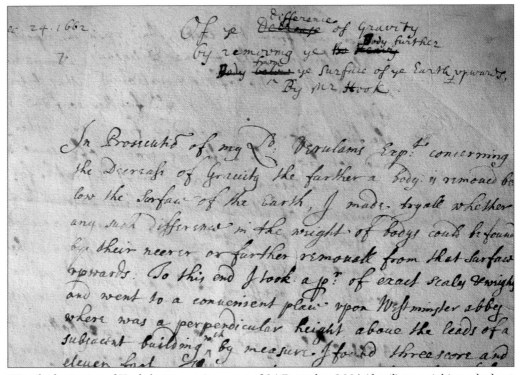

20. The beginning of Hooke's manuscript report of 24 December 1664 (detail) on weighing a body at different distances from the roof of Westminster Abbey; 'my L^d. Verulam's Exp:^ts' were Bacon's 'crucial experiments' (Bacon 2000, 163–4) of observations at the tops of high buildings and in deep mines to discover the variation of terrestrial gravity. (*Classified Papers xx, 7, f. 11r: © The Royal Society*)

November 1662, one of the first experiments the Royal Society required him to perform was to repeat Power's experiment, but from the roof of Westminster Abbey instead of from the top of a mineshaft at Halifax. On Christmas Eve 1662 Hooke delivered to the Royal Society verbally and in writing (Figure 20) an account of his experiment. A full transcription is given below because it is the earliest official experimental report in Hooke's hand that we have, and can be regarded as the first report by a professional scientist, showing that at the outset of his career he had already found a way of reporting clearly on all the relevant details of what he did and thought:

In Prosecution of my L^d. Verulam's Exp^ts concerning the Decrease of Gravity, the farther a body is removed below the Surface of the Earth,[8] I made tryall whether any such difference in the weight of bodys could be found by their neerer or further removall from that surface upwards. To this end I took a p^r: of exact scales & weights, and went to a convenient place upon Westminster abby, where was a perpendicular height above the leads of a subjacent building, w^ch[9] by measure I found three score and eleven foot.

There, counterpoising a peice of iron (which weighed about sixteen ounces troy) and packthread enough to Reach from the top to ye bottom, I found the counterpoise to be[10] of troy weight seventeen ounces & 30 graines. Then letting down the iron by the thread 'till it almost touched the subjacent leads, I tried w^t alteration there had happend as to its weight, and found, that the iron preponderated the former counterpoise somew^t more than 10 graines, Then drawing up the iron and thread wth all the Diligence possibly I could, that it might neither gett nor loose any thing by touching the perpendicular wall, I found, by putting the iron and packthread againe into its scale, that it kept its last equilibrium, And therefore concluded, that it had not received any sensible Difference of weight from its neerness to[11] or Distance from the[12] earth. I repeated the[13] tryall in the same place, but found, that it had not alter'd its equilibrium (as in the first tryall) neither at the bottom nor after I had drawn it up againe, which made me ghess that the first preponderating of ye scale, was from the moisture of the air, or the like, that had stuck to ye string, and soe made it heavier. In pursuance of this Exp^t, I remov'd to another place of ye abby, that was just the same Distance from the ground that the former was from the leads. And upon the repeating ye tryall there wth the former Diligence, I found not any sensible alteration of the equilibrium; either before or after I had drawn it up. wch further confirm'd me that the first alteration proceeded from some other accident and not from the Differing gravity of ye same body.

I think therefore it were very Desirable for the Determination of Dr. Powre's tryalls wherein he found such difference of weight, that it were examind by such as have opportunity, first w^t Difference there is in ye Density and pressure of the air, And w^t of that condensation or gravity may be ascribed to the differing degrees of heat and cold at ye top & bottom, which may be very easily try'd wth a common weatherglass[14] and a seald-up Thermometer;[15] for the Thermometer will show w^t of the change is to be ascribed to heat & cold, and the weather-glass will show the Differing condensation. Next for the knowing whether this alteration of gravity proceed from the Density & gravity of ye ambient air, it would be requisite to make use of some very light body, extended into large Dimensions, such as a large globe of glass carefully stopt that noe air may get in or out; for if the alteration proceeded from the magneticall attraction of ye parts of ye earth, that ball will loose but a 16th parts of its weight (supposing a lump of glass hold the same proportion that Dr Powre has found in brass) But if it proceed from the Density of the air it may loose half, or perhaps more. further it were very Desirable that the current of the air in that place were observ'd, As Sir R. Moray intimated the last Day. Fowrthly I think it were worth tryall to counterpoise a light & heavy body one against another above, and to carry down the scales & them to the bottom, and observe w^t happens. fiftly It were Desirable that tryalls by the letting down of other both heavier and lighter bodys as Lead, Quicksilver, Gold, Stones, Woods, liquors, animall substances, & the like. Sixtly it were to be wisht that tryall were made how that gravitation does Decrease wth the Descent of the body that is by making tryall how much the body growes lighter at every ten or twenty foot Difference. these tryall if accurately made would afford a great help to ghess at ye cause of this Strange phenomenon.[16]

Hooke's experiment on gravity bears a close resemblance to earlier experiments at Westminster Abbey by Boyle and Hooke using a weather-glass to measure the variation in atmospheric pressure with changes in height.[17] Hooke's later account of his gravitational experiment at Westminster Abbey shows that he adopted the experimental procedure already worked out by Boyle and himself for the air pressure experiment. Two different phenomena were under investigation, and two completely different instruments were used, but the same place and the same procedure served each purpose. Hooke continued to use London's tall buildings as sites for scientific experiments until after the construction of the Monument to the Great Fire, a building which he and Wren contrived to serve also as a zenith telescope.[18]

In Hooke's account of the gravity experiment at Westminster Abbey we can see characteristics of scientific investigations which are now commonplace, but were far from being so at the time. He describes how he went to a place on the roof of the Abbey where he found by measurement that there was a vertical drop of 71 feet (21.6m) to the roof of an adjacent building. He weighed a piece of iron and a ball of string in the balance. Then he unwound the string, attached the iron to one end of it, lowered the iron through 71 feet and attached the upper end of the string to one arm of the balance, re-weighed the iron and string and found that their weight had increased by more than 10 grains (about 650mg). But Hooke was not satisfied with what he had observed. He wanted to be more confident that the change in weight he had observed was not caused by anything other than a change in gravity. So he raised the iron with great care, to ensure that it did not touch the Abbey wall, and re-weighed it. He found its weight had not returned to the original value, but remained 10 grains heavier than at the first weighing. He was puzzled. If it had gained 10 grains in weight through a change in gravity when it was first lowered, it should have lost 10 grains when it was raised and so returned to its original weight. This had not happened. Hooke then repeated the experiment a few times and found, whether or not the iron was raised or lowered, that it weighed 10 grains heavier than it had at the first weighing. He did not ignore the awkward and anomalous observation that the weight had increased by 10 grains when the iron was first lowered, or explain it away by saying the experiment 'had failed' at the first attempt, or fail to report it. What appeared to be an anomaly might be highly significant. He sought a rational explanation.

Why had the first trial shown an increase of 10 grains in weight on lowering that was not repeated in later trials? Why did the weight not decrease by 10 grains when it was first raised? Can a rational explanation be found? Hooke thought that the most likely explanation of the observed increase in weight was not an increase in gravity as the weight was lowered, but an increase in the weight of the string through absorbing moisture from the air as it was unwound during the first lowering of the weight. The experiment was carried out in December, with the River Thames nearby. Under those conditions we can imagine a thick mist in the air. But Hooke was still not satisfied that he had found the right explanation. He saw little point in further repetition under exactly the same conditions, so he decided to move to a different place on the roof which was the same height above the ground as the former place was above the roof of an adjoining building. Once again, he found no observable change in weight. He thereupon concluded that there was no measurable change in gravitational attraction when a body was moved vertically through 71 feet. This is not the same as saying that there was no change.

In the last paragraph of his report, Hooke's fertile imagination is shown in full flow when he suggests six further experiments or observations that should be carried out at the mineshaft in Halifax in order to clarify the inconsistency between the outcomes of Power's experiments and his own. He did not expect that his proposed experiments would reveal a law of nature. At best they would 'afford a great help to ghess at the cause' of the decrease in weight which Power had observed. His use of 'ghess' (guess) indicates that he did not think he was close to discovering a truth, although that was an aim. Many more experiments in different places and with different procedures would be necessary to get closer to the 'Discovery of the more internal Texture and Constitution' of nature. Although that ambition was enough of an incentive for Hooke to make further investigations, the experiments on gravity had a practical purpose. They had been started by the Royal Society with the objective of rating the accuracy of timekeepers for finding longitude at sea. If this could be done, more accurate navigational charts would make the seas safer for mariners and bring increased power to the nation and wealth to its citizens through greater overseas trade.

Hooke was very wary of publishing his discoveries and inventions in case somebody took them up and profited from them before he had an opportunity to do so. In particular he suspected the Royal Society's secretary, Henry Oldenburg, of trafficking in scientific information by telling Christiaan Huygens about his design for a spring-balance watch. On the other hand, the prestige arising from being the first to reveal a property of nature is a very strong incentive for most scientists. A way of announcing one's priority in discovery without revealing exactly what has been found is to publish a brief description of the topic with the key part written in the form of an anagram. When the author is ready, the anagram can be unravelled and a full account made public. Hooke chose to do this in relation to what is now known as Hooke's Law of Elasticity, his most well-known achievement. In 1676 he published ten of his 'Inventions' in this way at the end of one of his Cutlerian Lectures:

To fill the vacancy of the ensuing page, I have here added a decimate of the centesme of the Inventions I intend to publish, though possibly not in the same order, but as I can get opportunity and leasure; most of which, I hope, will be as useful to Mankind, as they are yet unknown and new.

The third of the ten is

The true Theory of Elasticity or Springiness, and a particular Explication thereof in several subjects in which it is to be found: And the way of computing the velocity of Bodies moved by them. ceiiinosssttuu.[19]

Two years later Hooke unscrambled his anagram in *De Potentia Restitutiva, or of Spring Explaining the Power of Springing Bodies*, the sixth and last of his published Cutlerian Lectures. It begins:

The Theory of Springs, though attempted by divers eminent Mathematicians of this Age has hitherto not been published by any. It is now about eighteen years since I first found it out, but designing to some particular use, I omitted the publishing thereof.

About three years since his Majesty was pleased to see the Experiment that made out this Theory tried at White-Hall, as also my Spring Watch.

About two years since I printed this Theory in an Anagram at the end of my Book of the Descriptions of Helioscopes, viz. ceiiinosssttuu, id est, Ut tensio sic vis; That is, The Power of any Spring is in the same proportion with the Tension thereof:[20] That is, if one power stretch or bend it one space, two will bend it two, and three will bend it three, and so forward. Now as the Theory is very short, so the way of trying it is very easie.[21]

To make it easy for others to carry out their own experiments, Hooke, as usual, accompanied his description of what he did with drawings. He gives instructions for making three different kinds of spring from steel, or iron, or brass wire: a helix, a spiral (or watch spring) and a straight wire (Fig 1, Fig 2 and Fig 3 respectively in Figure 21). He shows eight different weights and illustrates how they stretched the helical spring by amounts proportional to their values when they were placed in the scale pan. He then goes on to say he followed the same procedure by placing the weights in the scale pan of the spiral spring in Fig 2 and found the measured extensions were in the same proportion as before.[22] A similar procedure was followed and the same outcome observed for the straight wire in Fig 3, but it was tens of feet long, suspended from a nail in a rafter and needed much greater weights than those used for the first two springs. Hooke adds that similar results can be found:

if trial be made, with a piece of dry wood that will bend and return, if one end thereof be fixt in a horizontal posture, and to the other end be hanged weights to make it bend downwards.

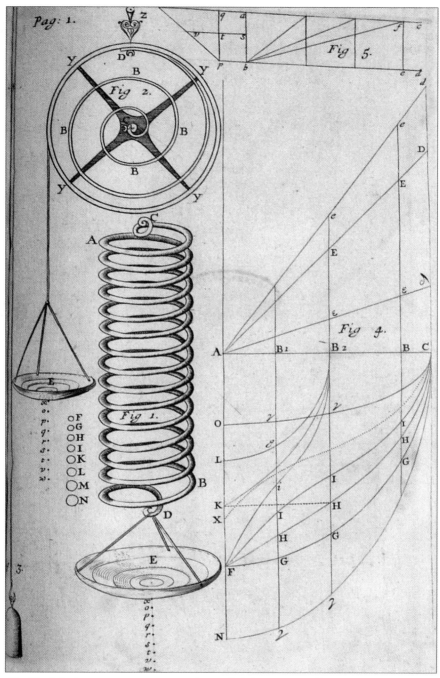

21. Hooke's diagram accompanying his verbal description of how to verify or refute what is now known as 'Hooke's Law of Elasticity' – the extension of a spring is proportional to the force applied, or as he first put it *Ut tensio sic vis* (As stretching, so power). Published in the Cutlerian Lecture *De Potentia Restitutiva, or Of Spring* and later in Hooke 1679. (*Hooke 1678a, 1: The Company of Clockmakers*)

The manner of trying the same thing upon a body of Air, whether it be for the rarefaction or for the compression thereof I did about fourteen years since publish in my *Micrographia*, and therefore I shall not need to add any further description thereof.[23]

Here again, Hooke is giving some importance to the generality of the relationship he is proposing. It applies not only to different-shaped bodies (straight, coiled and helical) but to different materials: metals, wood and even air. He clearly sees Boyle's Law and Hooke's Law as equivalent.[24]

Although the experiments which led to Hooke's Law involved static bodies, his main interest was in motion and in finding answers to questions such as, 'how does a weight move at the end of a spring when it is pulled down and released?' and 'what is the nature of the vibration?' Hooke showed it must be isochronous (that is, the times between successive lowest or highest positions are the same) when the restoring force is proportional to the extension. Answers to these questions were of great practical importance if springs were to be used to regulate watches. But his interest in the motion of bodies in general is clear when he speculated in *Of Spring* that all particles in the universe were in continuous motion and came close to proposing an early kinetic theory.[25] When he went on to write, 'Two or more of these particles joyned immediately together, and coalescing into one become of another nature, and receptive of another degree of motion and Vibration, and make a compounded particle differing in nature from each of the other particles',[26] he is close to describing a relationship between atoms and molecules. He had much more to tell the world in *Of Spring* than was useful for making a spring-balance watch.

His Westminster Abbey experiment on gravity and his work on springs are examples of the purpose and method of making experiments he set out in his undated statement published posthumously by William Derham in 1726 under the heading 'Dr. Hooke's Method of making Experiments':

The Reason of making Experiments is, for the Discovery of the Method of Nature, in its Progress and Operations.

Whosoever therefore doth rightly make Experiments, doth design to enquire into some of these Operations; and, in order thereunto, doth consider what Circumstances and Effects, in that Experiment, will be material and instructive in that Enquiry, whether for the confirming or destroying of any preconceived Notion, or for the Limitation and Bounding thereof, either to this or that Part of the Hypothesis, by allowing a greater Latitude and Extent to one part, and by diminishing or restraining another Part within narrower Bounds than were at first imagin'd, or hypothetically supposed.

The method therefore of making experiments by the Royal Society, I conceive, should be this.

First, To propound the Design and Aim of the Curator in his present Enquiry.

Secondly, To make the Experiment, or Experiments, leisurely, and with Care and Exactness. Thirdly, to be diligent, accurate, and curious, in taking Notice of, and shewing to the Assembly of Spectators, such Circumstances and Effects therein occurring, as are material, or at least, as he conceives such, in order to his Theory.

Fourthly, After finishing the experiment, to discourse, argue, defend, and further explain, such Circumstances and Effects in the preceding Experiments, as may seem dubious or difficult: And to propound what new Difficulties and Queries do occur, that require other Trials and Experiments to be made, in order to their clearing and answering: And farther, to raise such Axioms and Propositions, as are thereby plainly demonstrated and proved.

Fifthly, To register the whole Process of the Proposal, Design, Experiment, Success, or Failure; the Objections and Objectors, the Explanation and Explainers, the Proposals and Propounders of new and farther Trials; the Theories and Axioms, and their Authors; and, in a Word, the History of every Thing and Person, that is material and circumstantial in the whole Entertainment of the said Society; which shall be prepared and made ready, fairly written in a bound Book, to be read at the Beginning of the Sitting of the said Society: the next Day of their Meeting, then to be read over, and further discoursed, augmented or diminished, as the Matter shall require, and then to be sign'd by a certain Number of the Persons present, who have been present, and Witnesses of all the said Proceedings, who, by Subscribing their Names, will prove undoubted testimony to Posterity of the whole History.[27]

The statement outlines many of the procedures Hooke followed in his experiment at Westminster Abbey on Christmas Eve 1662 so we can be confident that by that time he had already decided on its contents.[28] He later wrote about them in more detail and incorporated them into a broader view of his ideas for natural philosophy.[29] Unfortunately, the early Royal Society was unable to organise and carry out a systematic programme of experiments. Hooke himself, despite his call to perform experiments 'leisurely', was far too often carried away in the middle of a series of experiments by his genius for conceiving new instruments for other purposes, and starting off enthusiastically in a new direction. Despite these frequent diversions he was able over the years to perform a series of coherent experiments and report on them in his published Cutlerian Lectures.

5

AT THE TOP OF PAUL'S STEEPLE

London's tallest buildings were a feature of Hooke's twenty-year obsession with experiments to measure the earth's gravitational attraction and the way it changes with height above the earth's surface. They provided him with convenient standpoints from which he could drop weights, swing pendulums and weigh bodies hanging at different heights above the floor beneath. The greater the vertical distance from a standpoint to the ground, the better the chances of measuring the change in gravity. The tallest building in London in the early 1660s was old St Paul's, so it was inevitable that he would make use of it for his gravity experiments.

Hooke had become interested in the earth's gravitational attraction when he was at Oxford in the late 1650s trying to make a spring-driven timekeeper for finding longitude at sea. He needed to find a way of testing the accuracy of his instrument in different places. The most accurate timekeepers were regulated by pendulums, which were affected by changes in the earth's gravitational attraction: a given pendulum swings faster if it is taken to a place where gravity is greater, and slower where gravity is less. Hooke's experiments at Westminster Abbey in 1662 to find a variation in the earth's gravitational attraction had failed to detect any change in the weight of a body when it was moved vertically through 71 feet (21.6m). He thought that his experimental procedure had not been at fault, but the circumstances under which it had been carried out were. One way of proceeding was to weigh a body over greater distances than the 71 feet he had access to at Westminster Abbey. He had suggested some new experiments for Henry Power to perform using a 68-yd (62m) deep mineshaft to discover if a measurable change in weight could be detected, but he was not prepared to wait for news from Halifax. In any case, he did not expect that Power would be much more meticulous in performing and reporting his new experiments than he had been in the past.

Hooke decided to find other ways of measuring the earth's gravity and its variation that did not involve weighing at different heights. He thought that if gravitational attraction varied with height, the free-fall of a body would be different at different heights. On 7 January 1663, two weeks after Hooke presented the Royal Society with his ideas for further experiments by Power at the coal mine in Halifax, he proposed two experiments for the following week's meeting. One of these was an investigation 'Of the force of descending bodies from different heights'.[1] This was not a success, as the record of the meeting on 14 January 1663 shows: '[Hooke] made an experiment of the force of falling bodies to raise a weight; but was ordered to try it by himself, and then to shew it again in public.'[2] Hooke was, as usual around this time, doing too many difficult experiments too quickly. The Royal Society did not attempt to restrain him. On the contrary, they added to his work with ideas of their own for further experiments.

A week later he 'shewed the scheme[3] of an instrument for making the experiment of the force of falling bodies; which was ordered to be made against the next meeting'.[4] Two weeks passed before he again performed the experiment in front of the Society, but, 'the instrument used for that purpose being defective', Hooke was 'ordered to make it better fitted against the next meeting and then to repeat the experiment'.[5] His 'Wit' and 'Labour' were fully engaged. He had made some progress by the following week when the instrument was used in an experiment that was partially completed. The Royal Society members had seen enough to approve the experiment in principle, and Hooke was ordered to 'try this by himself at home, as exactly as might be, and to bring in a written account of it at the next meeting'. But another idea had come to fruition in his mind. In addition to measuring the 'force' of a falling body, he could measure its 'celerity', or speed, so he proposed, as soon as he could do so, to attempt that too.[6] On 18 February Hooke presented to the Royal Society a diagram (Figure 22) of his instrument for measuring the 'force' of a freely-falling body in a full report of how he had used it in an experiment, what the results had been and the conclusions he had come to.[7] His idea was to allow a body F to fall vertically on to the plate at the right-hand end of the balance arm (G in Figure 22) and to record the lowest height from which it was able to move the weight H at the left-hand end which was kept in place by a light spring L. He expected to find that when the speed of a body falling from rest is doubled (by quadrupling the distance it falls) the weight it can move is doubled, but he reported the:

> tryalls though they Doe not answer our[8] Expectation as to the accurate exhibiting the strength of a moved body, yet[9] the tryalls[10] seeme to prove that a body moved wth twice the celerity acquires twice the strength, and is able to move a body as big againe.[11]

In his written report to the Royal Society Hooke shows that he had given much critical thought to shortcomings in the apparatus and his procedures. He goes on to describe and explain the difficulties, identifying correctly mechanical reasons why his results were inconclusive.[12]

Despite the difficulties he faced, Hooke was optimistic:

> Now As exact tryalls of this kinde may be very use full in Mechanics, soe could they be made wth bodys perfectly solid would they be for the Establishment of one of the cheifest Philosophicall principle[s] namely to shew the strength a Corpuscle moved,

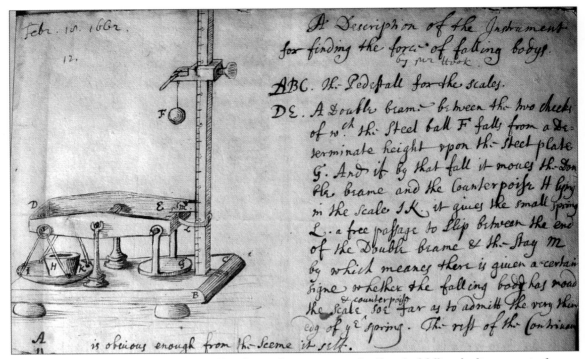

22. A sketch by Hooke (detail) of his device for measuring the 'force' of falling bodies as part of his experimental investigations into the earth's gravitational attraction. (*Classified Papers xx, 12, f. 20r: © The Royal Society*)

has to move another. And though Des Cartes put it as a principle That [if a body C is at rest and is larger than B, then B will never move C, no matter how great the speed with which B hits C] Yet these Experiments doe seem to hint that the least body by an acquired celerity may be able to move the greatest, though how much of its motion is imparted to the bigger body, and how much of it is recoyled into the smaller be not Determined by these Experiments.[13]

Hooke is arguing here that his experiments, although not yet satisfactory, have already hinted that one of the principles proposed by Descartes as the basis of natural philosophy by deduction has been shown to be erroneous. Despite the setback with his device for measuring the force of falling bodies, Hooke was as determined as ever to find a way of measuring the earth's gravitational attraction and how it changed with height. He now turned his attention to timing the rate of fall of bodies, rather than weighing them or measuring the force of their impact. If gravitational attraction varies from place to place, then the rate at which the speed of a freely-falling body increases will vary accordingly – its acceleration will be greater if the gravitational attraction is greater, and vice versa. So if a difference in acceleration could be measured, it would show how gravitational attraction varied. A very accurate timing device, itself unaffected by gravity, would be needed to do this, but none was available. Moreover, Hooke knew from his experiments with different-shaped bodies falling through various fluids that the earth's atmosphere would slow down the rate of descent of a falling body, so it would be necessary to know the magnitude of atmospheric 'drag' and make an allowance for its effect. Such difficulties, far from dissuading Hooke from pursuing his objective, made him even more determined to press ahead.

On 22 June 1664 the Society decided at a meeting the following week that 'The celerity of falling bodies with Mr. Hooke's new instrument, . . . be tried from Mr. Wilson's room.'[14] Hooke was still working on the design and construction of his accurate timing device and was not yet ready to demonstrate it in front of the Royal Society. His first demonstration took place on 13 July, but the measurements were affected by the wind.[15] His next demonstration was on 3 August when three lead balls of different diameters – the smallest a little less than 1 inch (25mm), the largest a little less than 1¾ inches (44mm) – were allowed to fall through 61 feet (18.6m). The measured times of fall were

three vibrations of half seconds and 15''' or 16'''. So that the difference between them was but 1'''.[16] Mr. Hooke was desired to find some convenient place in Westminster or Paul's for the prosecution of these experiments in a place free from wind; and to request such persons of the society for his assistance, as he could get.[17]

The report implies that Hooke had made a timing device, beating every half second, which could record a time interval of less than 2 seconds to an accuracy of ⅒th of a second. For a simple pendulum to beat half-seconds, it would have to be about 9¾ inches (250mm) long.[18] He made further trials with his timing device to test its consistency and reported to the Royal Society on 17 August that he had found by repeated trials that a lead ball let fall from rest fell 15½ feet in the first second.[19] Enthused by the success of the new device, the Royal Society quickly proposed other uses for it than the one for which Hooke had designed it and diverted Hooke away from his immediate objective. Members thought that after a little modification it could be used for finding the speed of a bullet, so they promptly ordered it to be done. The following week an experiment in ballistics took place. Unfortunately we do not have a drawing by Hooke of his timing device, but Henry Oldenburg in a letter to Boyle dated 1 September described the experiment in detail.[20]

Hooke was now making plans to continue his investigations into gravity and atmospheric pressure by experiments inside old St Paul's (Figure 23). It was far from an ideal experimental location, but its great height was essential for Hooke's purpose. Lightning had struck the spire in June 1561. Within four hours all the roofs and the steeple had been destroyed by fire, but by the end of the year the great east and west roofs had been rebuilt and re-leaded.[21] Rebuilding of the north and south transept roofs

23. Wenceslaus Hollar's engraving of old St Paul's, undated, but before 1658. It shows Inigo Jones's classical portico of 1633 at the west end and St Gregory's Church adjoining at the south with the cloisters behind. Hooke's experiments took place from underneath the shallow roof of the tower. (*Guildhall Library, Corporation of London*)

was not finished until April 1566. The spire was not rebuilt; the steeple was truncated and capped by a low-pitched pyramidal roof.[22] It was just below the steeple roof that Hooke intended to work. At some time in the week following the Royal Society's meeting on 17 August 1664 he went to investigate what experiments he might be able to perform there. During the visit he used his half-second timing device for rating a very long pendulum and discovered by a simple surveying measurement that the tower was about 30 per cent higher than it was generally thought to be. He wrote to Boyle on 25 August 1664:

. . . I have since your departure been on the top of Paul's steeple, in order to make several experiments, which will be prosecuted this week; but it being the first time I had been there, I could not be so well provided with an apparatus as I found was requisite; and therefore I was fain to return with only making some observations. One was, that a pendulum of the length of one hundred and eighty foot did perform each single vibration in no less time than six whole seconds; so that in a turn and return of the pendulum, the half second pendulum was several times observed to give twenty four strokes or vibrations.[23] . . . In another place of the Tower, where I had very clear perpendicular descent, I with a plum-line found the perpendicular height of it two hundred and four foot very near, [62m] which is about sixty foot [18m] higher than it was usually reported to be. In which place I shall, with some other company, this week try the velocity of the descent of the falling bodies, the Torricellian experiment,[24] and several experiments about pendulums, and weighing.[25]

On Monday 29 August 1664 Hooke and five other members of the Royal Society met at St Paul's, eager to make a number of experiments. Oldenburg wrote to Boyle on 1 September:

. . . There were Sir R. Moray, Dr. Wilkins, Dr. Goddard, Mr Palmer, Mr Hill, Mr Hook, and some of them went to the top of the steeple, and let downe a pendul of 200 foot long, with an appendant weight of [four] pound, and found 2 vibrations thereof made in 15". Time would then not give leave to proceed to the other Experiments, that were designed, among which will also be the Torricellian: but they will be set upon within 2 or 3 dayes.[26]

It is not surprising that time ran out before such an array of the Royal Society's grandees could do more than perform a very short simple experiment of little consequence. They had at their meetings made suggestions for experiments which needed careful planning and execution, but it is likely that each man probably had his own ideas on how the experiments should be performed, and in what order. Hooke, their greatest experimenter, and Richard Shortgrave, the Royal Society's operator, or technician, were capable of doing all that was necessary. They had achieved more on their first visit when they were not accompanied by such a forbidding array of the Royal Society's leading members.

The scene inside St Paul's during the experiment can only be imagined, but there can be little doubt that Hooke was one of the men who climbed to the top of the tower, taking his timing device in readiness for the free-fall experiments. Good communication between the grandees standing on the floor and Hooke and Shortgrave 204 feet above them in the gloom at the top of the tower was necessary when timing the long pendulum. Shouting out detailed instructions would have been ineffective in the cavernous Gothic interior, so simple pre-arranged signals to synchronise actions were probably used. The weight at the end of the 200ft-long pendulum was pulled aside from its rest position and held there. When the timing device had been made ready, a signal from aloft to release the weight at the end of the pendulum was made at the same time as the timing device was set in motion. The oscillations of the long pendulum and the short half-second pendulum of the timing device were counted. After an agreed number of oscillations of the large pendulum, the timing device would be halted and the number of complete oscillations, and the fractional part, of its half-second pendulum recorded.

Hooke visited St Paul's again the following week, eager to make progress, but this time his problems were more technical than organisational. He wrote to Boyle on the night of Thursday 8 September 1664, telling him in some detail how he had modified his mercury barometer in order to keep it airtight and intact while it was being hauled up and down through more than 200 feet between the floor and the top of the interior of the tower. He told Boyle that he had found the mercury to be half an inch lower at the top of the tower than at the floor beneath. Such a simple result was not easily arrived at, as Hooke explained:

The steeple being without any kind of lofts, but having only here and there some rotten pieces of timber lying across it; I caused a rope to be stretched quite cross the top, and fastned, in the midst of which I fixed a pully, through which I let down the string and weight to the bottom (for only in the very middle of the steeple was there a broad clear passage from top to bottom) and to this I could not at the top approach within eighteen foot:) having thus let down the rope, those that were at the bottom hung on this mercurial tube (which I had exactly marked, and stopped, and set ready before I went up) a large weather-glass (which moved by the rarefaction and condensation of the air only, which I had likewise marked and stopped) and a sealed thermometer, which I had likewise marked. After these were drawn up, and, by a contrivance of another pully, I had drawn them to me, I found the thermometer, the glass being but thin, broken. The quick-silver, upon opening the cock, I found to fall very considerably, which since, upon measuring, I find $2\frac{5}{8}$ of an inch: the weather-glass I found to be risen somewhat more than two inches: then closing them again, I caused them to be let down, and giving them charge not to let it quite down till I called to them from below, I went down myself, and found, upon opening the mercurial tube, that it rose exactly to its first station; as did also the weather-glass. I had designed to have tried many others then; but the night came so fast, that I could hardly see to get up again, and give order for the clearing of the lines. But I design, within a day or two, to make several other experiments.[27]

Hooke was now in charge, directing operations from the floor and from the top of the tower, hurrying up and down the narrow stairs, taking readings from his mercury barometer and weather glass. The agile boy who explored the cliffs and downland in the fresh air of the Isle of Wight had become an energetic thirty-year-old man, eagerly clambering around the gloomy walls and stairways inside old St Paul's, seeking measurable evidence of the earth's atmospheric pressure and gravitational attraction. He did not let physical danger hinder him in his work. His bravery can be seen in many small and incidental duties, whether experimenting on himself in reduced air pressure, or under water, or with pharmaceuticals in pursuit of biological knowledge, or descending into a space beneath the foundations of a collapsed party wall after the fire to seek evidence of a citizen's encroachment under a neighbour's cellar, or ascending to the top of the damaged and crumbling steeple of a parish church to decide whether it was dangerous and should be taken down, or safe enough to be repaired. In such cases he reported only what was necessary for the purpose. He was now trying to perform very sensitive measurements high in the tower of old St Paul's, standing on a cantilevered platform of timber boards surrounding a gap at least 18 feet wide – his only safeguard against falling 200 feet to the stone floor beneath. The boards had been placed there as part of the makeshift repairs to the steeple following the fire of 1561 and by now they were rotten. He was working in a dark enclosed space at the top of a tower high above the rest of London, buffeted by winds. No place could be found stable enough for securing a 200ft-long pendulum and his half-second timing device for accurate measurements. Delicate instruments had to be hauled up and down by two sets of ropes and pulleys. Despite all these difficulties, his enthusiasm was unabated as he climbed up and down the tower, giving instructions to the Royal Society's operator Richard Shortgrave and his assistants, setting up his apparatus, taking readings from his instruments and recording the results. His insatiable curiosity led him that same week to make a new discovery in the night sky where he 'found the stars in Orions-belt, which Mons. Huygens made but three to be five'.[28] Hooke was expected to make such discoveries; the casual brevity of his record of it hides the time he spent at night on his careful telescopic examination of stars and the moon.

Work at St Paul's continued during September. Lord Brouncker and Sir Robert Moray went with Hooke to repeat some of the earlier experiments and reported on what they had done.[29] Hooke wrote in what was at this time his regular Thursday letter to Boyle a longer account of their latest experiments.[30] They made further measurements of the time of swing of the 200ft pendulum. A lump of lead weighing 28 pounds avoirdupois was first attached to the end of a line made of 'a treble hard twist, one about the bigness of a very small goose-quill; the weight of it somewhat more than half a pound'. They found that when the amplitude of swing (to either side of the vertical position) was between 12 and 14 feet, the pendulum made '13 vibrations in 100 seconds pretty exactly; this we repeated several times and found the same'. They then repeated the experiment, but with an amplitude of swing reduced to 'not above a foot' and found the vibrations 'somewhat quicker; that is, 13 vibrations in 98 seconds'. They then repeated the measurements, but in place of the treble twist line they used 'a small wire about a 32 part of an inch in diameter, to which we hung the same weight'. They found very little difference from the previous measurements. The consistency of their measurements, given the length of the pendulum and its unstable point of suspension, are surprisingly good.

Hooke and his colleagues hastened to complete the St Paul's experiments in 1664, but the hours of daylight were diminishing as the autumnal equinox approached. They started a second experiment on weighing at different heights. They used a 'very curious beam' to counterpoise a 15 pound lump of brass with 'a company of smaller brass-weights tied in a small canvass bag together with the former small line' at the top of the tower. They then 'hung the beam over the very middle of the steeple', let down the bag of weights by means of the line and 'with long adjustening . . . found that the counterpoising bag and string was grown lighter by a drachm'.[31] This significant decrease in weight was not easy to explain. Although part of the balance was missing, it was so sensitive 'that a very small weight, as some very few grains, would very sensibly turn it'. The only explanation that seemed reasonable was that the loss of weight had been brought about by the increased density of the air at floor level compared with air 200 feet higher inside the steeple and the consequent increase in buoyancy. But the Torricellian experiments had shown a difference of only half an inch of mercury between the top and the bottom of the tower which seemed far too little to explain the observed loss in weight of the bag of brass weights. Hooke had used his weather-glass and device for timing falling bodies for making some measurements, but they were 'so imperfect, that I shall not, till we make them more accurate, trouble you with an account of them; nor of some other attempts till I have farther perfected them'.

The Royal Society, on hearing Brouncker's report of the unsatisfactory results, decided the experiments on weighing and falling bodies should be tried again,[32] but windy conditions prevented accurate measurement and they were inconclusive. The Society decided that the President and Moray should seek permission to use the king's 'statera' or balance, for further experiments which would be performed together with the experiment on falling bodies. The same small group of men who were present at the recent experiments were ordered to meet again at St Paul's on the following Monday, 26 September, at 11 o'clock in the morning to try again.[33] Meanwhile, having received Hooke's letter of 15 September giving details of the difficulties he was having with his St Paul's experiments, Boyle wrote to Henry Oldenburg, the Royal Society's secretary, putting forward some ideas for further experiments very similar to those Hooke had proposed to Henry Power almost two years earlier, in December 1662.[34]

Too many powerful men in the Royal Society were becoming personally involved in the experiments. They were enthused by the idea that the great height of the tower of old St Paul's would allow them to make useful measurements of all kinds, and they were proposing far too many. The problems already encountered had not yet been resolved. The unstable platform, vibration from winds and fading light made accurate measurements inside the tower not only difficult but dangerous. The effects of greater buoyancy in the denser air at the bottom of the steeple had not been satisfactorily examined. The balances used for weighing were still suspect. Hooke's timing mechanism was giving trouble, while the effect on the apparatus of magnetic attraction of the iron cramps in the stonework was unknown. Too many doubts had to be resolved and winter was approaching. Hooke's obligations to Sir John Cutler were beginning to cause him some anxiety. The Royal Society's Council was seeking the best way to get some much-needed funds from the king, the Duke of York and Prince Rupert.

Boyle's letter to Henry Oldenburg was read at the meeting of the Royal Society on 28 September, but no new experiments at St Paul's were ordered.[35] In a letter to Boyle dated 6 October 1664 Hooke explains why the experiments had ceased:

> Most honoured Sir,
>
> I have forborn all this time to give you the trouble of one of my scribbles, that I might have been able to have made it somewhat less troublesom, by giving you an account of some further trials made on Paul's. But such have been the disappointments, from winds, and rains, and divers other accidents, that we have not as yet made any further proceeding in that business. The magnetical experiments also which you were pleased to propound should long ere this have been tried, had not the multitude of iron bars, wherewith all the top stone, and indeed all the stones of the steeple are tied together, wholly spoiled that design: and indeed I fear (the winter weather coming on so fast) we shall hardly make any more trials there before the next spring . . .
>
> Most honoured Sir, your most faithful and most humble servant, Ro: Hooke.[36]

Hooke would make no more trials at old St Paul's the following spring, or at any other time. News of people dying from plague in Holland had first reached London in the spring of 1664. Ships from Dutch ports entering the Thames were quarantined. The City ordered that any persons or goods from Holland found in London without a quarantine certificate were to be shut up in their houses or store-rooms as if they were infected.[37] Such trade ceased in February 1665 when war with Holland was declared. The very cold winter of 1664/5 probably slowed the spread of the plague in England (twenty-one deaths in Portsmouth were reported in July 1664), but an epidemic broke out soon after the freezing winter came to an end in March 1665. The Lord Mayor at the time, Sir John Lawrence, whose friendship with Hooke during the years after the Great Fire was so important to the rebuilding of London, had the courage and sense of duty to stay in London, but those who could left for safer places. Henry Oldenburg, the Royal Society's secretary, also remained in London throughout the plague where he organised the publication of the new *Philosophical Transactions*. He was probably motivated as much by his eagerness to safeguard his position at the centre of communication of scientific intelligence as by a sense of duty. He kept up his correspondence with members of the Royal Society and other scientists at home and overseas, particularly with Huygens in Holland, Hevelius in Danzig and Auzout in Paris. Evidence of their disagreements with one another and with Hooke came regularly to his notice.

The Royal Society resolved to discontinue its Wednesday meetings after 28 June 1665, but the President exhorted members to bear in mind the various tasks that had been given them to carry out during the recess.[38] Hooke was charged with working on three devices: a machine for grinding lenses, chariot wheels and watches.[39] He was not told to continue his experiments which related directly or indirectly to the earth's gravitational attraction, but he fully intended to do so. Boyle and several other leading members of the Royal Society had already left London for Oxford, the town to which the king had transferred his court and administrators. On 8 July 1665, before leaving Gresham College, Hooke wrote to Boyle saying that he (Hooke), Sir William Petty and John Wilkins were planning to go with their implements and Richard Shortgrave to Nonsuch, a royal palace near Ewell in Surrey, owned at the time by the Queen Mother, Henrietta Maria.

Soon after Hooke had written to Boyle he found that Nonsuch had been taken over by the Exchequer of Receipt, temporarily removed from the Palace of Westminster, so Hooke and the small party from the Royal Society went instead to Durdans, near Epsom in Surrey, the seat of George, the 9th Baron (later 1st Earl of) Berkeley and a member of the Royal Society. Durdans turned out to be so convenient for experiments 'such as one cannot every where meet with an opportunity of doing' that we might suspect Hooke intended all along to go there.

It soon becomes clear from his letters to Boyle that 'the large catalogue of experiments' he had in mind was the same programme that in December 1662 he had presented to the Royal Society with a recommendation that Henry Power should perform it at a mineshaft near Halifax, and some of which he had performed at Westminster in the winter of 1662 and in old St Paul's in the autumn of 1664. He needed better conditions than he had found at Westminster and St Paul's and more time for a prolonged period of repeated and careful observations. Instead of making use of a great height above the earth's surface for observations, using a great depth below it might be more fruitful. In any case, there were many other experiments he wanted to carry out below the surface of the earth. Deep wells in the chalk at Banstead Downs, not far from Durdans, provided an opportunity at last for him to make the investigations he had planned almost three years previously. He began his new experimental programme by repeating Henry Power's 1662 experiment of weighing a body at the surface of the earth and below it. He reported his results in a letter to Boyle dated 15 August 1665:

I have made trial since I came hither, by weighing in the manner, as Dr. Power pretends to have done, a brass weight both at the top, and let down to the bottom of a well about eighty foot deep, but contrary to what the doctor affirms. I find not the least part of a grain difference in a weight of half a pound between the top and bottom. And I desire to try that and several other experiments in a well of threescore fathom deep, without any water in it, which is very hard by us.[40]

Hooke's mail during the plague was forwarded to him at Durdans from Gresham College. He continued his correspondence with Boyle and Oldenburg, but some letters failed to arrive. Their loss is regrettable because Hooke seems to have used them as the main record of the details of his experimental measurements and observations. On hearing that one letter he had sent to Boyle had failed to arrive, he wrote in the next:

> I was a little troubled at the miscarriage of my last letter, and so much the more, because I could not till now find an opportunity of repeating my request I therein made. I did therein, as I remember, send an account of some trials I had then newly made in a well not far from us, which, upon measuring, I found to be no less than three hundred and fifteen foot in its perpendicular depth . . .[41]

After re-stating, as best as his memory would allow, the experimental results and his 'catalogue' of further experiments that were in the lost letter, Hooke goes on to repeat his earlier request to Boyle to send his own suggestions for a 'catalogue of such experiments as you shall think fit to be tried to it, which was indeed the chief business of my last scribble'.

There were comings and goings at Epsom during the period of the Royal Society's recess, which diverted Hooke's attention away from his programme of experiments on gravity. Boyle arrived there from Oxford at about the same time that Hooke arrived from London, in early July 1665. They worked together on some of the experiments which Boyle published the following year in *Hydrostatical Paradoxes, Made out by New Experiments (For the most part Physical and Easie)*. He stayed for about a month before returning to Oxford.[42] On 7 August 1665 John Evelyn passed through Durdans on his way from his family estate at Wootton in Surrey to London. He saw Wilkins, Petty and Hooke busy contriving chariots, ships' rigging, a racing wheel and other mechanical inventions. Evelyn noted 'perhaps three such persons together were not to be found else where in Europe, for parts and ingenuity'.[43] Later that month Petty left Epsom for Salisbury.[44]

Hooke had personal reasons for leaving Durdans. In late September or early October 1665 he paid a visit to the Isle of Wight: since his mother's death there in June 1665 restrictions on travel to the island because of the plague had prevented him seeing his family. During his visit he dealt with various family matters and re-traced some of his childhood climbs and walks around the chalk cliffs and downland of the island, taking careful notes and sketches of fossilised remains of sea creatures found high in the cliffs, and speculating on how they might have got there – notes later to be published posthumously by Richard Waller.[45] Hooke returned to Epsom at some time during the winter of 1665/6 and continued with his experiments at the wells on Banstead Downs. He went back to London as soon as it was safe to do so in February 1666 and presented an account *On Gravity* to the Royal Society, in which he summarised his experimental work and made some speculations about the universal nature of gravitational attraction which would later be part of one of the most acrimonious disputes in science when Isaac Newton published *Principia* in 1686.

6

❧❧❧

A SORT OF DOMESTICITY

Gresham College was not only the place where Hooke had his workshop, demonstrated his experiments before the Royal Society and gave his Cutlerian and Gresham Lectures; it was also his home, where he lived for nearly forty years until his death in 1703. His set of rooms (Figure 24) included a garret in the roof, a library, a parlour and two other rooms on the first floor, a workshop on the ground floor and cellars below, all located in the south-east corner of the college quadrangle. Hooke lived out his domestic life in the company of his servants, relatives and the Royal Society's operators, Richard Shortgrave and, later, Harry Hunt. Although in the last decade of his life he let out his parlour to the Royal Society for their meetings, only a few of his many friends and colleagues called to see him in his rooms, and even fewer dined with him there. He was visited on matters of surveying business by some of the more important building contractors after the fire, such as Thomas Fitch, and by craftsmen in building and mechanical trades. Among the relatively few of his close personal friends who visited him in his rooms were John Aubrey and Theodore Haak, a frequent visitor with whom Hooke played chess in the evenings. Thirty years older than Hooke, Haak was a scholar from Germany and one of the earlier members of the Royal Society. Another friend, Richard Blackburne, nearly twenty years younger than Hooke, lodged with him for a short while before going to Leiden where he qualified as a physician. His friendship with Hooke continued after his return to London, at which time he became 'Dr Blackburne' in Hooke's diary instead of simply 'Blackburne' – Hooke was meticulous in the way he wrote names in his diary, Wren becoming 'Sir Chr. Wren' after receiving his knighthood instead of 'Dr Wren'. Robert Boyle was always 'Mr Boyle' and John Oliver, 'Oliver'. Hooke was sensitive to such social distinctions.

Most of his hectic social life took place away from Gresham College, in the taverns and coffee houses of London and in the private houses of his friends and colleagues from the city and the Royal Society. He was interested in almost everything that came up for discussion in that milieu, but his diary entries record far more about national and city politics and news from home and overseas than about art, literature and music. Despite a talent for playing keyboard music when a schoolboy, and the discovery after his death of two harpsichords among his belongings, his diary gives no indication that he performed music, although he often sang to block out noises in his head when working

24. Detail from Vertue's print of Gresham College (Figure 15). Hooke's rooms (9) and back door (10) are in the south-east corner of the quadrangle. The gateway (1) at the top of the Figure leads into Bishopsgate Street. The building with the steeply pitched roof (4) is the reading hall where Hooke gave his lectures. The remains of the timber framework for Hooke's zenith telescope can be seen (8) on the roof above Hooke's lodgings. (*Guildhall Library, Corporation of London*)

in his workshop late at night, and he was very interested in the mathematical and acoustic properties of music and its notation.

He occasionally went with friends to the theatre, not always with pleasure. In June 1676 he went to see Thomas Shadwell's play *The Virtuoso*, a mocking portrayal of the Royal Society's members and their activities. The main character, Sir Nicholas Gimcrack, was shown as a figure of fun, engaged in fruitless but expensive activities with his microscope and other gadgets. Gimcrack bore some resemblance to specific members of the Royal Society, including Hooke, who was offended by what he saw as trivialisation of the worthy intentions of the Royal Society. His annoyance when people in the audience recognised his having been personally picked out for ridicule can be seen in his diary entry: 'With Godfrey and Tompion at Play. Met Oliver there. Damned Doggs. *Vindica me Deus*. People almost pointed.'[1]

Hardly a day passed when he was not out and about in the city, measuring and inspecting, gossiping and arguing, eating and drinking, mixing his social life with his professional duties as scientist and surveyor, moving easily from settling disputes at construction sites about rising costs of building, or encroachment by a neighbour on to another's land, to a discussion with seafarers about the tides and currents they had found on their travels and what flora and fauna he wanted them to bring back from their next trip. He would return late to Gresham College where he would prepare an experiment in his workshop, write his diary, dose himself with a variety of medicinal and other drugs and spend too little time asleep.

Hooke's health was seldom good. From childhood he suffered from headaches and dizziness, which bothered him increasingly as he got older. From adolescence he suffered from a stoop, recently attributed to Scheuermann's kyphosis, which untreated can lead to deterioration with age;[2] Pepys had commented on his unprepossessing appearance.[3] Richard Waller, who knew Hooke only in his latter years, described Hooke's body as 'very crooked' which:

> made him but low of stature, though by his Limbs he shou'd have been moderately tall. He was always very pale and lean, and laterly nothing but Skin and Bone with a meagre Aspect, his Eyes grey and full, with a sharp ingenious Look whilst younger; his Nose but thin of a moderate height and length; his Mouth meanly wide and upper Lip thin; his Chin sharp, and forehead large; his Head of a middle size. He wore his own Hair of a dark brown colour, very long and hanging neglected over his Face uncut and lank, which about three Year before his Death, he cut off and wore a periwig. He went stooping and very fast (till his weakness a few Years before his death hindred him) having but a light Body to carry, and a great deal of Spirits and Activity, especially in his youth.[4]

John Aubrey, who knew Hooke before his years of decline, described him as 'of midling stature, something crooked, pale faced, and his face but little belowe, but his head is lardge; his eie full and popping, and not quick. A grey eie. He has a delicate head of Haire, browne, and of an excellent moiste curle.'[5]

By the time he began to keep a diary in 1672 he was regularly taking medicinal drugs. Noises in his head, sleeplessness and nausea were chronic conditions which he tried to alleviate by a variety of drugs enthusiastically prescribed for him by his physician friends in the Royal Society, particularly Jonathan Goddard. Metallic compounds including iron, mercury and antimony, tincture of wormwood (unfermented absinthe), laudanum, sal ammoniac, flowers of sulphur and Dulwich water (a proprietary mineral water which he used as a purgative, sometimes apparently with spectacularly satisfying results) were regularly taken, often with boiled milk, eggs and ale. Hooke also self-prescribed drugs in attempts to cure his illnesses, but they only brought on new discomforts which he then attempted to alleviate by more pharmaceutical experiments, which generally led to further deterioration in his health. He treated his body as an experimental device and used his diary as a laboratory record of his intake of drugs for purging and vomiting and of their effects on his mind and body.[6]

As a Gresham Professor he was required to remain celibate. He had serial sexual relations with a few women who at the time were employed by him as his domestic servants. In the early 1670s he was having infrequent sexual relations with his housekeeper Nell, noting them in his diary using the zodiacal symbol Pisces to mark his orgasms, and typically laconic statements such as 'Played with Nell – [orgasm] – hurt small of Back', 'with Nell [orgasm] *supra*' (on top) and 'Slept pretty well. *mane* [in the morning] [orgasm] Nell'.[7] He seems to have become fond of Nell, recording his disappointment when he suspected her of going with other men. But Nell did not intend to spend her life serving Hooke. In 1673 she married a barber named Young and left Gresham College to set up as a needlewoman near the Fleet Channel, where she made and repaired Hooke's clothes. They remained friends, visiting one another from time to time throughout the next twenty years. Sometimes Hooke entertained Nell to dinner in his rooms at Gresham College and bought presents for her children.[8] As late as 1693 Hooke recorded 'N Young D[ined] here, chick[en]'.[9] There are no indications that during Nell Young's visits to Hooke after her marriage they engaged in anything more than friendly gossip, discussing the latest news from the Isle of Wight (where Nell had some connections with the Hooke family) and dealing with cutting and sewing new clothes for Hooke. Nell's replacements as housekeeper were less congenial. Bridget Taylor was dismissed after three months, possibly for a liaison with Hooke's lodger, Richard Blackburne. She was followed by Doll Lord who was 'intollerable' and lasted only a few weeks after her first sexual encounter with Hooke. Her successor in Hooke's household and bed, Bette Orchard, was not only intolerable, but careless and clumsy as well. On 30 September 1674 Hooke recorded 'Paid Bette 15sh for her quarters wages. Discharged her. Mary first came to serve me for 20sh per quarter.'[10] Mary Robinson became his domestic servant, but nothing more, for the next ten years.

By 1672 Hooke's niece Grace, the daughter of his elder brother John, was growing up in Hooke's household. Her father sent money for her lodgings, but Hooke bought her gifts of clothes and jewellery and treated her to visits to Bartholomew Fair and other entertainments. Grace attended a school in the city and was apparently under an obligation to marry the son of Sir Thomas Bloodworth, Lord Mayor at the time of the fire, an obligation from which Hooke eventually obtained her release in 1673 when he wrote 'writ to brother and sent a second coppy of T. Bloodworth's Release'.[11] Hooke's affection for his niece developed into a sexual affair in June 1676, a few weeks after her sixteenth birthday. On Hooke's part at least it is not too fanciful to say that the relationship developed into one of love. Under parliamentarian law Hooke would have been liable to prosecution for incest, a capital offence. However, after 1660 and the repeal of such legislation, if the affair had become public Hooke could have faced prosecution by an ecclesiastical court. Hooke and Grace were often together in public, taking evening walks in Moorfields. The difference in their ages of twenty-three years was not a matter of much social importance at the time.

Grace Hooke attracted the attention of many men besides Hooke, who was upset by her liaisons with younger men. There is some evidence that during a visit to the Isle of Wight Grace was made pregnant by Sir Robert Holmes (Governor of the island and former admiral) and subsequently gave birth to a baby girl there in 1678, who could have been Holmes's illegitimate daughter Mary. John Hooke's mounting debts and his knowledge of his daughter's sexual relationship with his brother Robert and others, and possibly of her pregnancy, might have contributed to his suicide in March 1678.[12] When Grace fell ill after eating fruit on 24 July 1679, Hooke could see that her life was in danger. He wasted no time. The next day he called in his Royal Society physician colleagues and an apothecary, Whitchurch, who was a fellow habitué of Garraway's coffee house. They diagnosed smallpox, the disease from which Hooke's nephew Tom Gyles had died two years previously when he was lodging with Hooke as a recalcitrant pupil. The medical and pharmaceutical treatments given to Grace were unlikely to have had any beneficial effect, but in any event by the time her mother Elizabeth arrived at Gresham College from the Isle of Wight on 31 July the crisis had passed and Grace slowly recovered her good health. She died from undiscovered causes nearly eight years later in February 1687, aged twenty-nine.

The loss of his beloved Grace hastened Hooke's declining health. He had been ridiculed in the theatre and his contribution to Newton's work which came to fruition in *Principia* was denied by its author. He was fighting hard to recover his rightful dues from Sir John Cutler by litigation. For thirty years he had drawn heavily on his mental and physical resources to the benefit of science and the City. Decades of inquisitive pharmaceutical experiments and self-medication were by the 1690s having a serious and increasing toll on his body. Most of the friends and colleagues he had known in the early days of the Society, when his vibrant presence at their formal and informal gatherings was so important to them, were now infirm or had died. In their place were younger men, who saw Hooke only as an increasingly ill and rancorous old man, claiming achievements which were not substantiated by recorded evidence. Hooke suffered for his acute perceptions. He believed that the earth was slowing down, that its poles moved, that chalk now high up in cliffs was once under the sea and that once there were species of life that are extinct – but he could prove none of those things. The days when Wren had told Hooke in a letter 'I know you are full of employment for the Society wch you almost wholly preserve together by your own constant paines' had long gone, and were largely forgotten.[13]

He found solace in the company of old friends who came to see him in Gresham College, or met him in the city places he had frequented for more than thirty years. John

Godfrey, Clerk of the Mercers' Company, and Francis Lodwick, merchant (elected to the Royal Society when he was more than sixty years old), figure frequently in his later diary as 'Gof' and 'Lod'. He was particularly close to his protégé Henry Hunt ('Harry'), now the Royal Society's official operator and factotum. Hooke went for walks outside the city with friends, as he had with Grace, taking the air in Moorfields with other citizens who were probably admiring the grandeur of his Bedlam[14] Hospital. He visited booksellers' shops and auctions almost daily and had reading glasses made or repaired as his eyesight deteriorated. He resumed his diary in 1688,[15] its contents showing that he continued, well into the 1690s, to make perceptive speculations on natural phenomena, to design buildings for private clients, to supervise building work at Westminster Abbey and to take an interest in the latest gossip, national politics and news from overseas. He continued, too, to give his lectures and come up with new ideas for scientific instruments and, for a while, maintained his fastidious dress, noting purchases of new cloth and buttons. But in the last years of his life the deterioration in his physical condition was severe. Richard Waller described how Hooke led:

> a dying Life for a considerable time, being more than a Year very infirm, and such as might be call'd Bed-rid for the greatest part, tho he seldom all the time went to Bed but kept in his Cloaths, and when over tir'd lay down upon his Bed in them, so that at last his Distempers of shortness of Breath, Swelling, partly of his Body, but mostly of his Legs, increasing, and at last Mortifying, as was observ'd after his Death by their looking very black, being emaciated to the utmost, his Strength wholly worn out.[16]

Waller's 'active, restless, indefatigable Genius' died on 3 March 1703 in his sixty-eighth year. Stephen Inwood has recently brought to light another account of Hooke's death written by his old friend the seafarer Captain Robert Knox. As Hooke lay dying, he ordered a maidservant who was with him to fetch Knox to his bedside. Knox and Henry Hunt laid out Hooke's body in his clothes, gown and shoes as he had died, sealed up all the doors of Hooke's apartment with Knox's seal and left to arrange the burial.[17]

Three days later Hooke was buried in his parish church of St Helen Bishopsgate,[18] where the mortal remains of his 'good and sure freind' Sir John Lawrence and of his niece Grace already lay. He was buried 'decently and handsomely . . . all the members of the Royal Society then in Town attending his Body to the Grave, paying the respect due to his extraordinary merit'.[19] Hooke had drafted a will a few days before he died, but it was unsigned and he died intestate.[20] He had amassed a fortune of at least £10,000, most of it in cash, which by his draft will he intended should be shared equally (after specific dispositions) by four friends he did not name. Instead his estate passed to his nearest relative, his second cousin Elizabeth Dillon (formerly Stephens), and from her into oblivion. His papers and other possessions were dispersed by his relations and his books were auctioned in the Strand on 29 April 1703.[21] Some of his papers were rescued and published posthumously by Waller, and by William Derham after Waller's death, but his survey books were probably discarded as worthless. His earlier and more detailed diary disappeared, or was thought to have been written by someone else, until it was acquired by the Corporation of London and eventually edited and published at the tercentenary of Hooke's birth in 1935.

In late 1891, almost two centuries after his death, a start was made on lifting the floor of the church of St Helen, Bishopsgate, prior to repairing the nave pavement, but a Home Office order was quickly issued on 7 November directing certain measures to be taken to prevent the church 'becoming or continuing dangerous or injurious to the public health'. According to a journal kept by the Rector, J.A.L. Airey,[22] on lifting the floor a 'horrible view' was revealed of 'loose, confused and intermingled bones with which the ground was filled to several feet in depth . . . effluvia from the decaying remains below was free to rise from the floor of the church, and pollute the air'. Out of the intermingled remains of '700–1,000 persons' only about ten individuals could be identified. The coffins had been crushed under the weight of successive burials and re-burials over the centuries.

The remains were removed 'with utmost reverence and decency and care . . . no vulgar or mere wanton curiosity at any time', placed in seventy cases and taken to a cemetery at Wanstead where they were re-buried in a vault alongside the remains of parishioners of the amalgamated parish of St Martin Outwich. The mortal remains of Hooke, Sir John and Lady Lawrence and Grace Hooke were not among those that could be identified, so it must be assumed that they now lie at the City of London Cemetery and Crematorium, Wanstead, in a mass grave (square 222, Grave 3833) paid for from the Parish Poor Fund. An inscription on the memorial (Figure 25) at the site reads:

25. The burial site and memorial in 2003 at the City of London Cemetery Wanstead where, in 1892, the remains of hundreds of parishioners of the church of St Helen Bishopsgate, probably including Hooke and his niece Grace, were re-interred in a mass grave (number 53833, square 222). (*Author's collection*)

> Sacred to the memory of many generations of the parishioners of St Helen Bishopsgate in the City of London who died in the Lord and were buried within the walls of the parish church and whose remains were removed to this cemetery and decently and reverently re-interred in a vault hereunder by Order of the Queen in Council A. D. 1892 . . . 'The Lord Knoweth them that are His.'

There is at present (June 2003) no memorial to Hooke in London.

7

SYSTEMS AND CONTRIVANCES

Hooke's character was distorted into caricature soon after his death and as recently as 1983 reputable scholars were describing him as a 'melancholy, deformed, even sordid person'.[1] He made many powerful enemies in the scientific field by over-reacting to real and imagined slights and refusals to recognise what he believed to be his prior claims in discovery. He never lacked confidence in himself, a trait which too often induced exaggerated and boastful reaction to criticism. He managed to aggravate Huygens, Flamsteed, Hevelius and Leibniz, but he made an enemy of one of the greatest scientists of all time, Isaac Newton. It was this enmity that fuelled the denigration of Hooke as a man and as a scientist after his death, but his achievements in two aspects of science deserve to be recognised: intuitive speculation and ingenious experiment.

SYSTEMS

Hooke's attempt to dispute Newton's priority in explaining planetary motion was crushed by the latter's towering mathematical genius and arrogance. Although Newtonian mechanics is one of the greatest creations of the human imagination, Hooke's claim to have contributed something to that achievement should be recognised. From the time an essay on Newton was published by Rouse Ball in 1893[2] drawing attention to Hooke's contribution to Newton's celestial dynamics, the topic has received a great deal of attention from scholars, much of which is highly technical. Although recent work, particularly by Michael Nauenberg, has cleared away some misconceptions about Hooke's thoughts on dynamics, the dispute will probably continue to be written about and argued over because it can be approached from so many directions. It shows up the differences both in the characters of the two men and in their approaches to scientific enquiry. Newton's isolation from the world prior to the publication in 1687 of *Principia*[3] and his intense concentration on the mathematical abstractions of planetary motion were quite different from Hooke's busy engagement in the lives of his fellow citizens in the heart of mercantile London and his ingenious efforts to understand natural phenomena by performing experiments. The only characteristic (except for a capacity for intense inquiry) the two men had in common, it seems, was pride, and Newton's was much more aggressive.

The animosity between the two began in 1672, when Hooke wrote a hasty but sharp criticism of Newton's discoveries in optics, claiming that he (Hooke) had already written about such matters.⁴ Newton, the younger man, was deeply offended by the tone of Hooke's criticism, which might explain why he published nothing more on optics until after Hooke's death. Newton's resentment did not ease as the dispute rumbled on, with Hooke making assertions which, quite properly, Newton thought he (Hooke) should justify. The two men were persuaded to make conciliatory moves, which they did, but without much sincerity. When Newton wrote to Hooke 'If I have seen farther, it is by standing on the shoulders of giants' it is probable that the stooping Hooke thought it more offensive than complimentary, and that Newton fully intended it to be taken that way.⁵

The German astronomer Johannes Kepler (1571–1630) showed that harmony and simplicity lay behind the apparently wayward motions of the planets through the sky as seen from earth.⁶ The natural philosophers of the second half of the seventeenth century, excited by simplicity and harmony in nature, sought an equally simple and harmonious explanation of planetary motion. What kept the planets in their orbits? Why were the orbits elliptical? What stopped a planet from crashing into the sun, or from flying further and further away from it? Were the motions of the moon and comets part of the same system? What use could be made of the relationships revealed by Kepler? Questions like these concerned Hooke and Wren and other clubbable members of the Royal Society when they met and debated at Gresham College and in the coffee houses and inns of London. The questions also engaged the minds of Huygens in Holland and Newton at Trinity College Cambridge.

We know that Hooke grappled in London for three decades, until the end of the 1680s, with the problem of explaining planetary motion by sequences of experiments, demonstrations and speculations. Only a few weeks after returning to the city from Banstead Downs in the wake of the plague, Hooke followed up his paper 'On Gravity', in which he described his experimental work, with another paper of speculations 'concerning the inflection of a direct motion into a curve by a supervening attractive principle'. After considering and rejecting the idea that a planet in its orbit is continually deflected from a straight line by the resistance of the medium through which it travels, he suggested that:

> the second cause of inflecting a direct motion into a curve⁷ may be from an attractive property of the body placed in the center; whereby it continually endeavours to attract or draw it to itself. For if such a principle be supposed, all the phænomena of the planets seem possible to be explained by the common principle of mechanic motions; and possibly the prosecuting this speculation may give us a true hypothesis of their motion, and from some few observations, their motions may be so far brought to a certainty, that we may be able to calculate them to the greatest exactness and certainty, that can be desired . . .⁸

The use of 'we' shows Hooke knew that true Baconian cooperative effort should yield the answers. Nevertheless, for the first time, the key to an explanation of planetary motion was explicitly and clearly stated: planetary motion is a combination of motion along the tangent of an elliptical orbit with motion towards a centre – the sun at a focus of the ellipse. Hooke says very little more here about what might be the cause of the inflected motion towards the centre, or how it might vary with distance from the centre. After reading his paper to the Royal Society, he made some demonstrations with conical pendulums[9] to the assembled members to illustrate what he meant by a combination of tangential and central motions.[10]

  Shortly after these demonstrations he started his onerous work as City Surveyor, which took much of his time. When he returned to the topic of gravity in his first published Cutlerian Lecture, *An Attempt to Prove the Motion*[11] *of the Earth from Observations Made by Robert Hooke Fellow of the Royal Society*, published in 1674, but which he had read in Gresham College in 1670, he added some more elements to his scheme of planetary motion.[12] *An Attempt . . .* is mainly about Hooke's use of a zenith telescope (one which points vertically upwards, towards the zenith) to detect the changes in direction to a given star as a result of the Earth moving along its orbit around the sun. The changes in direction are known as the star's 'annual parallax' which varies from one star to another depending on their distances from the Earth. Hooke built a zenith telescope in his rooms in Gresham College (Figure 26) and he and Wren ensured that when the Monument was built it could also be used to measure annual parallax (Figure 27).[13] At the end of *An Attempt . . .* he says at some time in the future he will:

explain a System of the World differing in many particulars from any yet known, answering in all things to the Rules of Mechanical Motions: This depends upon three Suppositions. First, that all Cœlestial Bodies whatsoever, have an attraction or gravitating power towards their own Centers, whereby they attract not only their own parts, and keep them from flying from them, as we may observe the Earth to do, but that they do also attract all the other Cœlestial Bodies that are within the sphere of their activity; and consequently that not only the Sun and Moon have an influence upon the body and motion of the Earth, and the Earth upon them, but that Mercury also Venus, Mars, Jupiter and Saturn[14] by their attractive powers, have a considerable influence upon its motion as in the same manner the corresponding attractive power of the Earth hath a considerable influence upon every one of their motions also. The second supposition is this, That all bodies whatsoever that are put into a direct and simple motion, will so continue to move forward in a streight line, till they are by some other effectual powers deflected and bent into a Motion, describing a Circle, Ellipsis, or some other more compounded Curve Line. The third supposition is, That these attractive powers are so much the more powerful in operating, by how much the

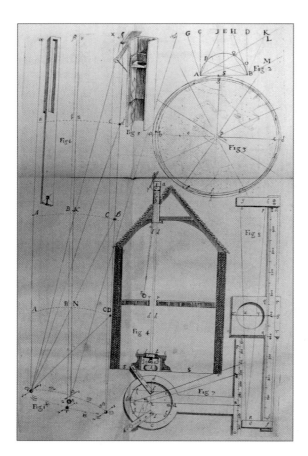

26. Hooke's design drawings in *An Attempt* for the components of a zenith telescope with a 36ft objective lens set into the roof of his rooms in Gresham College used for measuring the small changes in a star's position as the earth moves around the sun. Fig 1 (bottom left to centre top) shows how the positions of stars appear to change as the earth moves around the sun. (*Hooke 1674a: The Joint Grand Gresham Committee*)

nearer the body wrought upon is to their own Centers. Now what these several degrees are I have not yet experimentally verified; but it is a notion, which if fully prosecuted as it ought to be, will mightily assist the Astronomer to reduce all the Cœlestial Motions to a certain rule, which I doubt will never be done true without it. He that understands the nature of the Circular Pendulum and Circular Motion, will easily understand the whole ground of this Principle, and will know where to find direction in Nature for the true stating thereof. This I only hint at present to such as have ability and opportunity of prosecuting this Inquiry, and are not wanting of industry for observing and calculating, wishing heartily such may be found, having my self many other things in hand which I would first compleat and therefore cannot so well attend it. But this I durst promise the Undertaker, that he will find all the great Motions of the World to be influenced by this Principle, and that the true understanding thereof will be the true perfection of Astronomy.[15]

These speculations show how much further Hooke has gone since 1666, setting out his 'System of the World' with deep intuition and literary economy and in a form which

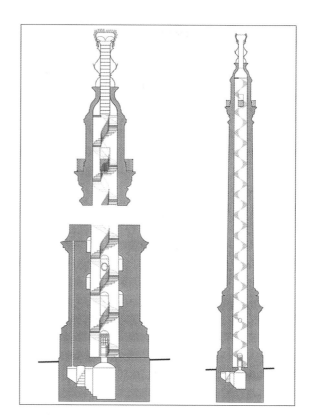

27. Vertical sections through the Monument revealing its intended use as a zenith telescope. When the two hinged semi-circular iron doors at the top were opened, an observer in the underground observation chamber at the base of the column could measure with a micrometer eyepiece the changes in position of an overhead star throughout the year. (*Lisa Jardine*)

resembles very closely Newton's world-view as it eventually appeared seventeen years later in *Principia*. Here at least Hooke has justification for claiming priority. He suggests that an attractive power exists between bodies in the solar system (but he does not say the property is universal) and that it increases as the bodies come closer to one another (no mention of an inverse square law). Once again, however, he seems to expect that someone else will use his hypothesis and find the law of attraction that will explain planetary motion. His excuse that he could not do it himself because of his civic duties can be accepted to some extent, but one is left with a strong suspicion that he was beginning to understand that a law of gravitational attraction was impossible for anyone at that time to detect by experiment, and that his mathematical ability was inadequate to do it by analysis – a point which Newton homed in on later.

Despite the difficulties Hooke did not give up. His diary entries between late 1675 and early 1680 show him thinking about ways of using Kepler's laws of planetary motion and Huygens's representation of centrifugal force[16] to deduce what 'the several degrees are' of the 'attraction or gravitating power towards their own Centers' of celestial bodies. In company with his Royal Society colleagues he performed and discussed experiments where balls were sent rolling around the inside surfaces of upturned cones of different shapes. As Lohne has shown, it is likely that by about 1676, through such cooperative efforts, Hooke, Wren and Edmond Halley[17] had used centrifugal force and Kepler's third law to deduce that the law of attraction for uniform motion of a body in a circular orbit is an inverse square law.[18] Showing that an inverse square law of gravitational attraction could produce an elliptical orbit is more complicated because the speed of the body in its orbit and its distance from the centre (a focus of the ellipse) are not constant.

It was at this stage that Newton came into the picture. As far as anyone knew he had done no work on planetary orbits, although as a member of the Royal Society he would have been aware of the subject through the publication of the work of others, including Hooke. Following the death of Henry Oldenburg, Hooke was elected secretary of the Royal Society. On 24 November 1679 he wrote a polite letter to Newton in an attempt to make a new start in their personal relations and, as secretary, to bring Newton closer to the Royal Society, in particular with their speculations on planetary motion.[19] Unaware of the strife he was about to release, he wrote that he hoped Newton would continue:

> your former favours to the Society by communicating what shall occur to you what is philosophicall, and for returne, I shall be sure to acquaint you with what we shall receive considerable from other parts or find out new here . . . For my part I shall take it as a great favour if you please to communicate by Letter your objections against any hypothesis or opinion of mine, And particularly if you will let me know your thoughts of that of compounding the celestiall motions of the planetts of a direct motion by the tangent & an attractive motion towards the centrall body, or what objections you have against my hypothesis of the lawes or causes of springiness.[20]

It is possible that in asking Newton to comment on his (Hooke's) idea of combining inertial rectilinear motion along the tangent to the path with an attractive motion towards the centre, he was hoping Newton would use the idea and contribute to the search for 'the several degrees' of attraction to the centre and so 'reduce all the Cœlestial Motions to a certain rule', something Hooke and his colleagues in the Royal Society had so far failed to do. Newton's reply held out little hope of cooperative research with Hooke or anyone else. In a letter to Hooke dated 28 November 1679, he first brushed aside with disdain Hooke's invitation to exchange letters on 'what is philosophicall' by saying;

> I have had no time to entertain philosophical meditations . . . for some years last [I have] been endeavouring to bend myself from philosophy to other studies . . . unless it be perhaps at idle hours sometimes for a diversion' [and so I am] almost wholly unacquainted with what philosophers at London or abroad have of late been imployed about.[21]

As to Hooke's request for Newton's opinion on his (Hooke's) hypothesis that planetary motion is the result of compounding a direct tangential motion with an attractive central motion, Newton replied that because he was unaware of what philosophers in London were doing:

> you will incline the more to believe me when I tell you that I did not, before the receipt of your last letter so much as heare (that I remember) of your hypothesis . . . and of the lawes and causes of springyness, though these no doubt are well known to the philosophical world.[22]

The superior tone of this reply would have rankled with Hooke, particularly as Newton's letter contained evidence that he had in fact already come across Hooke's hypothesis.[23] Hooke simply did not believe what Newton had written, a viewpoint which was fully justified nearly seven years later when in a letter to Halley Newton admitted that he had earlier read of Hooke's hypothesis in *An*

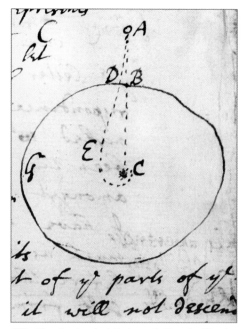

28. Newton's sketch in a letter to Hooke dated 28 November 1679 (detail) showing the trajectory of a body let fall freely from the top A of a tower AB on a rotating earth and allowed to pass unhindered through the earth. Newton speculated that it would come to rest at C, the centre of the earth. (*MS R.4.48, p. 2: The Master and Fellows of Trinity College Cambridge*)

Attempt . . . .[24] Newton continued his letter to Hooke by proposing a test to demonstrate that the Earth rotates from west to east about its axis by dropping a heavy object from the top of a tower and noting where it landed.[25] He speculated that if the heavy object could continue falling and pass through the interior of the Earth unhindered, it would follow a spiral path and end at the Earth's centre. To illustrate his point he included a diagram, the first of four that were to become important in the dispute between Hooke and Newton (Figure 28).

Hooke seized on a careless error in Newton's speculation and wrote a reply on 9 December 1679,[26] in which he pointed it out and announced that a few days earlier he had read Newton's letter of 28 November 1679 to the Royal Society.[27] Newton's pride was severely damaged at being corrected by Hooke, particularly so because he saw that Hooke's explanation of why he (Newton) had got the path wrong, although ingenious, itself contained an error. Hooke had written 'my theory of circular motion makes me suppose [the path] would be very differing [from yours] and not at all akin to a Spirall but rather a kind Ellipteuid' (Figure 29).[28]

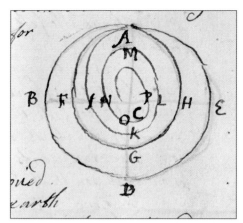

29. Sketch from a copy of Hooke's 9 December 1679 letter to Newton (detail) showing the trajectory of a body if it were allowed to fall freely through the earth. (*Misc. MS 2582, F-1: Beinecke Rare Book and Manuscript Library, Yale University*)

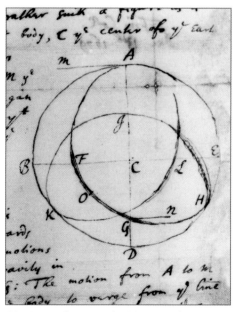

30. Part of Newton's 13 December 1679 letter (detail) to Hooke showing the trajectory of the imagined freely falling body to be quite different from Hooke's. In contrast to Hooke's hasty sketch (see Figure 29) Newton's careful drawing gives every appearance of having been based on calculation. (*Add. MS 37021: British Library*)

It is easy to see why Newton was annoyed by his own carelessness in putting forward such an idea, but Hooke's references to 'my manner of circular motion' and his offhand statement later in the same letter would have turned Newton's annoyance to cold rage:

I could adde many other conciderations which are consonant to my Theory of Circular motions compounded by a Direct motion and an attractive one to a Center. But I feare I have already trespassed to much upon your more Usefull thoughts with these my Impertinants yet I would desire you not to look upon them as any provocations to alter your more mature and serious Resolutions. Go on and Prosper and if you succeed and by any Freind let me understand what you think fit to impart anything from you will be Extremely Valued . . .[29]

Here was the nuisance, Hooke, expounding his 'theory' but not bothering to use it to construct or calculate the orbit. All Hooke had done, it seemed to Newton, was to invent an ingenious way of looking at the problem[30] and produce only a rough sketch of what he alleged the orbit would be in consequence. He then had the effrontery to ask Newton to let him know through a friend if he made any progress in calculating the path. Newton decided that he would show Hooke the sort of thing that someone who was claiming to have a 'Theory of Circular motions' should do in order to justify the claim.

In his reply of 13 December 1679 Newton included a diagram of the path of a body falling freely through the Earth to show how far he had gone towards reducing 'all the Cœlestial Motions to a certain rule' (Figure 30). On seeing the illustration Hooke would have known immediately that Newton had been able to calculate the path, but not *how* he had done it. Newton kept that to himself, except to say that he had based it on a constant force towards the centre of the earth. Exactly how Newton calculated the path shown in his diagram (and why he made a small error in his construction) has been revealed by Michael Nauenberg by ingenious mathematical detection work.[31] It is now clear that Newton made use of Hooke's idea of combining tangential and central motions, which he had denied being acquainted with, but later admitted to having known. Newton ended his letter in ironic imitation of Hooke:

> Your Acute Letter having put me upon considering thus for ye species of this curve, I might add something about its description by points quam proxime. But the thing being of no great moment I rather be[g] yor pardon for having troubled you thus far wth this second scribble wherein if you meet wth anything inept or erroneous I hope you will pardon ye former & ye latter I submit & leave to yor correction remaining Sr Yo^r very humble Servant
>
> Is. Newton.[32]

Hooke knew that Newton had got the path more or less right because it agreed with his own observations of the path of a ball rolling inside an inverted concave cone, where the force towards the centre is almost constant. But this path was still not planetary motion. Hooke took an opportunity to push Newton even further. When he replied from Gresham College on 6 January 1680 he told Newton 'your Calculation of the Curve by a body attracted by an equall power at all Distances from the center Such as that of a ball Rouling in an inverted Concave Cone is right'.[33] He went on to say 'But my supposition is that the Attraction always is in a duplicate proportion to the Distance from the Center Reciprocall'.[34]

This is Hooke's first known statement of his belief that planetary motion is based on an inverse square law of attraction. He has now moved the debate away from finding the path of a body imagined falling freely under a constant central force through the Earth, and directed it towards planetary motion where the orbits were known to be ellipses and the force to the centre was believed to be an inverse square force. He also says that such a force 'truly makes out all the Appearances of the Heaven . . . not that I believe there really is such an attraction to the very centre of the Earth'.[35] Here was another source of either forgetfulness or dissimulation by Newton. In 1686, when he was protesting his priority against claims by Hooke, he wrote to Halley, 'what he [Hooke] told me of the duplicate proportion was erroneous, namely that it reached down from hence to the centre of the Earth'.[36] Hooke had clearly and explicitly told Newton that this was a view he did not hold.

Hooke had by now passed on to Newton everything he firmly believed was necessary to reduce 'all the Cœlestial Motions to a certain rule'. He (Hooke) could not do it analytically, neither could Halley or Wren, but Hooke knew it had to be done for the sake of natural philosophy and he hoped Newton would do it, which of course Newton did, but in his own time and in his own way, intensely, privately and silently until he was ready to present to the world what he now knew would be a magnificent achievement. He would allow nobody, especially not Hooke, to take any credit for what he had done. He ignored Hooke's letter of 6 January 1680, and another of 17 January. Their correspondence was at an end. When Halley went to see Newton in Cambridge in the summer of 1684 to find out how far he had gone towards finding the connection between a planetary orbit and an inverse square law of gravitational attraction, Newton replied, much to Halley's astonishment, that around 1680 he had found that the orbit was elliptical, but had set aside his calculations. A search of his papers did not bring them to light, so Newton promised Halley to repeat his calculations and send them to him.[37]

On 10 December 1684 Halley told the Royal Society that he had again visited Newton in Cambridge and had seen his 'curious treatise *De Motu*' (On Motion) which Newton wished to be entered in the Society's Register Book to establish his priority in its contents.[38] Newton then produced a series of greatly expanded versions of *De Motu*, culminating in the manuscript of *Principia* which was received by the Royal Society (the book's dedicatee) on 28 April 1686. Halley was given the task of reporting to the Council on its contents.[39] It is a treatise on the mathematical principles of natural philosophy (as its full title explains) and defines the relationships between force and motion, from which it is possible to explain planetary orbits and countless other phenomena.

Hooke was incensed that Newton had not given him the credit he deserved in *Principia* and he made his feelings known publicly in coffee house and tavern. Evidence that, before the publication of *Principia*, Hooke had shown geometrically that under a central linear force the orbit of a planet would be elliptical comes from a document in Hooke's hand in which he describes and illustrates the construction of a polygonal orbit by incremental combinations of tangential and central motions according to the principle he had proposed twenty years earlier (Figure 31).[40] The resultant path, made up of discrete steps, is circumscribed by an ellipse. One would expect to find a similar construction by Hooke of the orbit of a planet under a central inverse square force, but none has been found.[41] Although Hooke's treatment is graphical not analytical, it is the first demonstration based on mathematical principles that the orbit of a planet moving under a central force is an ellipse. It was done two years before the publication of *Principia*.[42]

When Halley wrote to Newton on 22 May 1686 at the Royal Society's request to tell him that they appreciated the honour he had done them by dedicating *Principia* to the

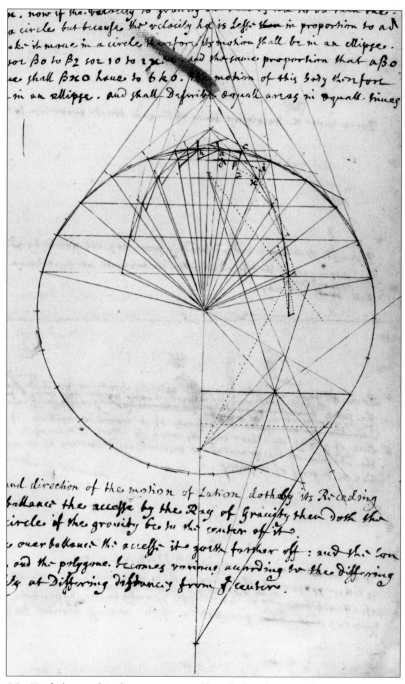

31. Hooke's graphical construction (detail) dated September 1685 of the trajectory of a body attracted to a centre by a linear force. He creates a polygonal trajectory by combining motion tangential to the path with motion towards the centre at discrete intervals. (*MS O.11a.1, f.16r: The Master and Fellows of Trinity College Cambridge*)

Royal Society, and that the Society intended to have the book printed at its own expense, he added:

> There is one thing more that I ought to inform you of, viz. that Mr Hooke has some pretensions upon the invention of the rule of decrease of gravity being reciprocally as the squares of the distances from the center. He says you had the notion from him, though he owns the demonstration of the curves generated thereby to be wholly your own. How much of this is so, you know best; as likewise what you have to do in this matter. Only Mr Hooke seems to expect you should make some mention of him in the preface, which it is possible you may see reason to prefix. I must beg your pardon that it is I, that send you this ungrateful account; but I thought it my duty to let you know it, that so you might act accordingly, being in myself fully satisfied, that nothing but the greatest candour imaginable is to be expected from a person, who has of all men the least need to borrow reputation.[43]

On 2 June 1686 Council ordered *Principia* to be printed. Halley was ordered to 'undertake the business of looking after it, and printing it at his own charge; which he engaged to do',[44] and soon discovered that the process required much 'looking after': he occupied a calm temperate zone between the chill winds of intellectual vanity from Newton and the passionate gusts from the hurt feelings of Hooke. Halley deserves great credit for saving *Principia* from being blown apart in the storm and guiding it safely to publication in 1687; although Halley expected 'the greatest candour imaginable' from Newton, it was not forthcoming.

In a letter to Halley dated 20 June 1686 Newton accused Hooke of plagiarising the ideas of Borelli on the causes of planetary motion (ideas which Hooke had specifically rejected), and then went on to say:

> He [Hooke] has done nothing, and yet written in such a way, as if he knew and had sufficiently hinted all but what remained to be determined by the drudgery of calculations and observations, excusing himself from that labour by reason of his other business, whereas he should rather have excused himself by reason of his inability. For 'tis plain, by his words, he knew not how to go about it. Now is not this very fine? Mathematicians, that find out, settle and do all the business, must content themselves with being nothing but dry calculators and drudges; and another, that does nothing but pretend and grasp at all things, must carry away all the invention, as well of those that were to follow him, as of those that went before.[45]

Hooke had not 'done nothing but pretend and grasp': he had given Newton the key to calculating orbital motion based on an inverse square law.[46] But *Principia* was much more than a discovery of the relationship between planetary motion and gravity. Newton's achievement was to set that particular explanation in a coherent system, which integrated new concepts of force and mass with motion, time and geometry to produce Newtonian mechanics – the foundation for thought and action in science, technology and engineering for more than 200 years. Hooke, at least, deserves recognition for goading Newton towards that achievement. By his persistent experimenting and deep intuitive understanding he constructed his 'System of the World', which had much in common with Newton's. Hooke could not have written *Principia*; but perhaps without Hooke's hints and goading and Halley's cash and moderating influence on both men, Newton might not have bothered with it.

CONTRIVANCES

Although the Royal Society did not give Hooke much time to complete one set of experiments before setting him off in another direction, he must bear some responsibility for not publishing a corpus of his experimental work. He knew that recording what he had done was an essential part of Baconian natural philosophy, but his impetuosity made it hard for him to stop doing experiments and start writing full accounts of them. He always preferred experimenting, lecturing and debating. He took on heavy responsibilities as City Surveyor between 1666 and 1674, a post which occupied much of his time. However, I think there is another important reason why he did not finish many of the experimental investigations he had started and which promised so much.

Hooke's intuition and prescience in the design of scientific instruments to investigate many of the natural phenomena that interested him were so exceptional it was impossible for him, or for anyone else at the time, to make the instruments to the high standards necessary to give reliable measurements of sufficient accuracy. Some of his most ingenious instrumental designs could not be made properly until metallurgy, opto-mechanical engineering, electrical power and even electronics had been sufficiently developed. When instruments he had designed were eventually made and used in the twentieth century, it was forgotten that he had originally set out the design principles 300 years earlier. His frustration at being unable to make what he knew was needed did not blunt his optimism that one day it would be done. Of course, nobody believed him and he could not substantiate his claims by demonstration; his reputation as a braggart grew accordingly. I shall look at only two of his experimental designs to show that his ideas needed more than two centuries of technological development before they could be realised. Each of the instrumental designs came out of the work he had done at Durdans during the plague of 1665. One instrument was for making angular measurements in astronomy, the other for measuring terrestrial gravity.

An Astronomical Quadrant

The angle-measuring instruments Hooke took to Durdans during the plague year of 1665 were the forerunners of his great equatorial quadrant, an astronomical instrument in which he incorporated some of Wren's ideas on telescopes and the optical and mechanical know-how he and his craftsmen had developed over many years in his workshop at Gresham College. In promoting his idea for such an instrument, Hooke entered into a quarrel with another scientist. The astronomer Johannes Hevelius (1611–87), who worked in Danzig, was compiling a catalogue of star positions using measurements taken with open (i.e. non-telescopic) sights as Tycho Brahe had done before him. In 1668 the Royal Society wrote to Hevelius recommending that he should use telescopic sights for his measurements because they were more accurate than open sights. Hevelius disagreed and gave his reasons in *Machina Cœlestis*, published in 1673. He claimed that with the unaided eye he could measure angles to an accuracy of a fifth or a tenth of a minute of arc and that measurements to the accuracy of one second of arc ($\frac{1}{3600}$ of a degree) were feasible using open sights. In a Cutlerian Lecture Hooke explained why Hevelius was wrong, and described some simple practical demonstrations to show that the accuracies claimed by Hevelius were impossible to achieve with the unaided human eye, which was incapable of resolving anything less than about a minute of arc ($\frac{1}{60}$ of a degree). Hooke went on to criticise Hevelius's painstaking astronomical observations made over many years, saying that if he had used telescopic sights as he had been advised to do, his results would have been much more useful and a great improvement on those made earlier by Tycho Brahe. To show exactly what he had in mind for significantly improving the accuracy of astronomical measurements, in 1674 Hooke published his Cutlerian Lecture *Animadversions on . . . Hevelius*.[47] It included a scintillating design for a telescopic quadrant in which optics, mechanics and horology were integrated to enhance the capacities of the human hand and eye in a remarkable and unprecedented way. His illustration of the complete quadrant (Figure 32) contains what is probably a representation of himself using the instrument in his rooms in Gresham College, although there is no evidence that he made a complete instrument. He published detailed graphical and verbal descriptions of all the components and how to make and assemble them into a working instrument.

A mechanism controlled by a timepiece regulated by a conical pendulum continuously moved the graduated arc and two telescopes (one fixed and one movable relative to it) around an axis directed towards the north celestial pole. The rate of rotation was synchronised with the apparent rotation of the stars so that they would seem to be stationary when viewed through the telescopes. This meant that an accurate pointing to a star could be made without having constantly to adjust the direction of sight to keep pace with the star's apparent motion. It was, of course, the stars that were still and the Earth that was in motion on its axis. Moreover, by bringing the fields of

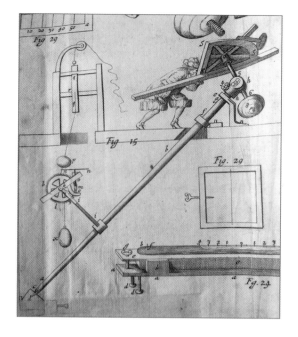

32. A telescopic quadrant for measuring the relative positions of stars was Hooke's most ingenious optical-mechanical instrument. He published detailed design drawings and verbal instructions for making it in *Animadversions On . . . Hevelius* as part of his censure of Hevelius for not using telescopic sights in place of open sights to increase the accuracy of astronomical measurements. (*Hooke 1674b, Tab 2a: © The Royal Society*)

view through both telescopes into one eyepiece, the observer, by moving one telescope relative to the other, could carefully bring the image of one star seen through one telescope into exact coincidence with the image of a second star seen through the other telescope. The angular separation between the two stars could then be read against the graduations along the arc of the quadrant. Convenience and accuracy were built in to the instrument.

In the design of his equatorial quadrant Hooke introduced a synthesis of applied optics and mechanics which was to characterise scientific instruments for the next 200 years, until electrical and subsequently electronic devices replaced many optical and mechanical components. He said he knew it would be possible to make instruments small enough to carry in one's hand and which could measure angles to an accuracy of one second or better, although it was not until the 1920s and later that materials and manufacturing techniques made the realisation of Hooke's vision possible: opto-mechanical theodolites reading directly to one second of arc and less were then routinely manufactured by Wild in Switzerland, Zeiss in Germany and Hilger and Watts in the UK.[48]

Gravimeters

When Hooke returned to London in 1666 after his time in Durdans during the plague, he lost no time in reporting to the Royal Society on his experiments into the Earth's gravitational attraction. On 21 March 1666 he presented and read a paper on gravity[49] in which he first justified his experiments by saying, 'though [gravity] seems to be one of the most universal active principles in the World, and consequently ought to be the most considerable, yet has it had the ill fate, to have been alwaies, till of late, esteemed otherwise, even to slighting and neglect'.

He then summarised all his attempts to measure changes in gravitational attraction at Westminster Abbey, old St Paul's and the chalk wells at Banstead Downs near Durdans. He claimed that 'in the making of [the experiments], I endeavoured to be as accurate as the way was capable of', but external conditions such as vibration or 'some other unheeded accident, might intervene in the Experiments, which might much contribute thereunto', and concluded 'that nothing of Certainty could be collected from these Tryals; save only, that if there were any Difference in the Gravitation of the Body, it was but very small and inconsiderable'. We now know that over the height range of 21.6 metres used by Hooke at Westminster Abbey, the proportional change in gravitational attraction is only about 1 part in 150,000, so Hooke's apparatus had to be about 150 times more sensitive than it was in order to detect the difference in gravitational attraction he was looking for. He knew he had to do better, deciding that 'if therefore there be any such inequality of Gravity, we must have some waies of tryal much more accurate than this of Scales'. His ideas for measuring gravity and its variation by timing falling bodies and by accurate weighing, or balancing, were put into practice throughout the world nearly 300 years later, when at last it became possible to make, in accordance with the principles he outlined, portable instruments (gravimeters) which were adequately robust and accurate.

The first successful experiments which verified the inverse square law of gravitational attraction were made by independent groups in the 1980s. One team of scientists worked down a mineshaft and another in high buildings. They were concerned about the stability of their observing platforms, calibration of their instruments and the effects of wind vibrations on their observations, each of which had been identified by Hooke 300 years earlier as an 'accident' which might 'much contribute' to the outcome of his experiments at Westminster Abbey, old St Paul's and Banstead Downs. Subsequently experiments down a borehole in ice seemed to show evidence of gravity which did not follow the inverse square law. However, after re-examination of the results from these earlier experiments and a new experiment carried out on a high tower, confirmation within the limits of experimental error that gravity did follow an inverse square law was achieved.[50] The procedure was the same as Hooke had suggested, to measure gravity at different positions between the base and the top of a high building.

A meteorological tower, some 300 metres high, at Erie in Colorado was chosen. The gravimeters were based on the principle of a vertical elastic spring and hanging weight proposed by Hooke, but a simple mechanical spring would have to be very long and very weak to register the minute changes in weight brought about by changes in

Observation height (m)	Measured Δg (10^{-5} m s^{-2})	Predicted Δg		Measured − predicted average (10^{-5} m s^{-2})
		Model 1 (10^{-5} m s^{-2})	Model 2 (10^{-5} m s^{-2})	
8.198	-2.556 ± 0.009	-2.550 ± 0.010	-2.553 ± 0.010	-0.005 ± 0.013
21.912	-6.789 ± 0.010	-6.782 ± 0.010	-6.783 ± 0.010	-0.007 ± 0.014
48.568	-14.986 ± 0.010	-14.994 ± 0.011	-14.992 ± 0.011	0.007 ± 0.015
97.323	-30.000 ± 0.010	-29.990 ± 0.012	-29.983 ± 0.012	-0.014 ± 0.016
149.136	-45.908 ± 0.011	-45.913 ± 0.015	-45.904 ± 0.015	0.001 ± 0.019
197.896	-60.892 ± 0.012	-60.888 ± 0.018	-60.876 ± 0.018	-0.010 ± 0.022
249.718	-76.800 ± 0.013	-76.800 ± 0.021	-76.785 ± 0.021	-0.008 ± 0.025
295.438	-90.816 ± 0.014	-90.835 ± 0.023	-90.817 ± 0.023	0.010 ± 0.027

TABLE I. Comparison between measurements and Newtonian predictions.

33. Results of measurements verifying the inverse square law of gravitational attraction. The table closely resembles one published 338 years earlier by Boyle and Hooke (Figure 12). The second column showing measured changes in acceleration corresponds to column D and the third and fourth columns, showing what those values would be if the inverse square law holds, correspond to column E. (*Speake et al. 1990, 1968: © The American Physical Society*)

gravity. Such an unwieldy mechanism would be subject to influences that would completely mask the effects of changes in gravitational attraction. By designing a new kind of spring, with a twist in it, before making it into a coil (the so-called 'zero-length spring'), it was possible to make a gravimeter with adequate sensitivity and robustness for use outside laboratory conditions.[51] Moreover, it is interesting to note that the numerical results of the experiments to test the hypothesis that gravitational attraction followed an inverse square law were published (Figure 33) in a manner resembling very closely the way Boyle and Hooke had published their results to test the hypothesis that the pressure and volume of a given mass of air are in inverse proportion (Figure 12).[52]

Hooke's foresight can also be seen in his attempts to time a freely-falling body in order to measure the Earth's gravitational attraction. Hooke's contrivance for timing the freely-falling body was used by the Royal Society at Gresham College for ballistics, and Hooke later used it in old St Paul's. It worked for a short while but it broke during the trials and was set aside. No diagram of it by Hooke has been found, but when William Croone[53] wrote on 15 September 1664 to Henry Power, his fellow physician and member of the Royal Society, he included a sketch of it suggesting that Power should make a similar instrument and use it for timing the fall of bodies down the mineshafts near Halifax.[54] The sketch is very crudely drawn (Figure 34), with little attempt to show clearly how the components worked or the locations where they would work.[55] Croone knew he had not made things very clear when he wrote rather abruptly 'If you cannot understand my rude description, you may designe a better yourselfe'. Hooke failed in his attempts to use his timing device effectively inside old St Paul's because he could not find useful universal standards for measuring time and distance, and the materials and methods available to him for making the instrument were grossly inadequate. It was

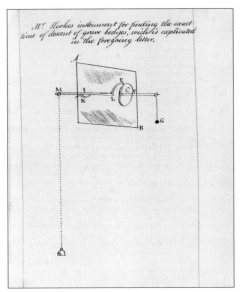

34. John Ward's copy of Hooke's timing device in a letter dated 15 September 1664 from William Croone to Henry Power (the original letter has not been found). (*Add. MS 6193, f. 60r: British Library*)

35. The Micro-g FG5 portable gravimeter and controlling computer. The vertical cylindrical dropping chamber is 200mm long. (*Micro-g Solutions, Inc*)

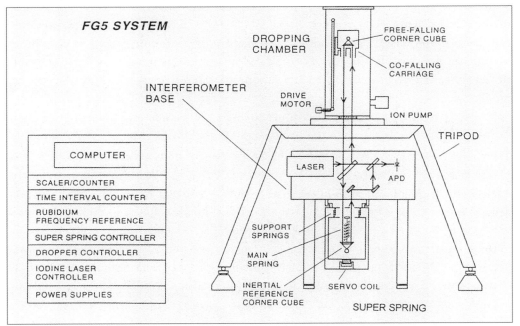

36. Schematic diagram of the Micro-g portable gravimeter showing how Hooke's idea to measure terrestrial gravity by timing a freely-falling body has finally been realised. The use of springs, an evacuated chamber and Boyle's Law (used in calculation of the drag coefficient for the near-vacuum) are further echoes of the experimental investigations of Boyle and Hooke. (*Micro-g Solutions, Inc*)

only about twenty years ago that both problems were finally resolved, and Hooke's idea was realised in the portable FG5 gravimeter (Figure 35).[56]

The FG5 owes much to Hooke and to Boyle: it measures time intervals and distances travelled by a freely-falling body – the same principle Hooke tried in old St Paul's – but distances in the FG5 are measured by laser interferometry and time is measured by an atomic clock. In the FG5[57] the 200mm-long dropping chamber (Figure 36) is evacuated to a very low pressure, about one billionth of atmospheric pressure.[58] Even at such a low pressure there are enough molecules in the FG5 dropping chamber to retard motion significantly. Boyle's Law, revealed by Hooke and Boyle, is used to calculate by how much the remaining molecules slow down the otherwise freely-falling body.[59] Springs having particular properties deriving from Hooke's Law of Elasticity insulate the dropping chamber from short and long period vibrations.[60] The gravimeter is also used for general scientific purposes such as calibration of instruments for measuring force and pressure. Accurate measurements of the Earth's gravity field and its variations in space and time have many uses, particularly in geophysics and oceanography – such as for monitoring sea level change, vertical crustal movements arising from melting glaciers and changes in sub-surface cavities and aquifers, and for understanding processes that lead to earthquakes, and the dynamics of ocean currents which are now thought to drive long-term global weather systems. They are also used in conjunction with satellite positioning systems to define a global reference framework for geodesy and aircraft navigation. These applications were of interest to Hooke in their seventeenth-century contexts, when he was trying to understand the multitude of changes in what he referred to as the 'Terraqueous Globe', and to devise instruments for more accurate navigation, predicting the weather and automated surveying.

REPUTATION

When Conrad von Uffenbach visited the Royal Society from Germany in 1710, only seven years after Hooke's death, he was appalled to see the parlous state of the Society's instruments, most of which had been made by Hooke over a period of thirty years. He found:

> the finest instruments and other articles . . . not only in no sort of order or tidiness but covered with dust, filth and coal-smoke, and many of them broken and utterly ruined. If one enquires after anything, the operator who shows strangers round . . . will usually say: 'A rogue had it stolen away', or he will show you pieces of it, saying 'It is corrupted or broken'; and such is the care they take of things![61]

Hooke's science began to emerge from Newton's shadow into the public eye when R.T. Gunther began in 1930 to publish a series of books on his life and work, which included his earlier diary. Andrade also wrote a few reviews and articles on Hooke and his science between 1935 and 1950 when he made Hooke the subject of a lecture at the Royal Society which was followed by a broadcast talk.[62]

However, Hooke had not been completely neglected before 1930. A long article on him (in the category 'Isle of Wight') was published in Diderot's *Encyclopédie* in the eighteenth century. Moreover, a few scientists of note had gone to his writings and had been surprised at what they found. Thomas Young (1773–1829), whose experiments on the interference of light showed that it had a wave-like character, wrote, 'there was nothing that could have led to [a wave theory of light] in any author with whom I am acquainted, except some imperfect hints in those inexhaustible but neglected mines of nascent inventions, the works of the great Dr Robert Hooke'.

Joseph-Jérôme Lalande (1732–1807), astronomer and Enlightenment *philosophe*, wrote of Hooke's *Micrographia*, the *Cutlerian Lectures* and *Posthumous Works*: 'In these works one finds ideas for most of our modern instruments: this was the Newton of mechanics.'[63] The *Encyclopaedia Britannica*, unenthusiastic about Hooke in the third edition of 1797, had become almost adulatory by 1801, after the addition of footnotes and a new account of him by George Gleig was published in supplementary volumes.[64]

Andrade's claim in his 1950 Wilkins Lecture at the Royal Society that 'all those who have gone direct to Hooke have conceived the highest admiration for his astonishing industry, his whole-hearted devotion to science, his inventiveness, his ingenuity, his fertility and his brilliant theoretical insight . . .'[65] has been substantiated by many who have, for the first time, 'gone direct to Hooke' in the last fifty years. Signs that Hooke's scientific reputation today is still undergoing a restoration can be found in Bud and Warner's book about scientific instruments, where his name appears more often than those of other famous scientists such as Lord Kelvin, Carl Zeiss, Jesse Ramsden, Isaac Newton and James Clerk Maxwell.[66]

PART TWO
BUILDING A
NEW CITY

8

A GREAT CONFUSION

Panoramic views of London appeared from a high point on the south bank of the Thames before the Great Fire generally show a layer of steeply pitched roofs and pointed gables of common houses, through which some of the prominent buildings and the towers and spires of the parish churches rise up (Figure 37). Above all looms the great bulk of St Paul's Cathedral, with or without its spire, depending on whether the view was made before or after 1561 when it was struck by lightning and burnt down. Visible from Hampstead and Highgate in the north and from Blackheath in the south, old St Paul's epitomised the fabric of London, which was shortly to disappear in flames. Old, decrepit, structurally unsound and in need of extensive and costly repair, the cathedral was of great concern to those responsible for it. William Laud, Bishop of London during the reign of Charles I, raised a fund of more than £100,000 with the patronage of the king, whose architect Inigo Jones was given a free hand to repair the building in 1633. After ten years the scaffolding was removed to reveal five black marble steps leading to a new west front, which resembled a

37. Detail from Anthonis van den Wyngaerde's 'Panorama of London' (c. 1544) showing St Paul's Cathedral looming over the huddled tenements and warehouses down the slope to the Thames. The church of St Benet, Paul's Wharf rebuilt by Hooke after the Great Fire can be seen midway between the south transept of St Paul's and the river. (*Ashmolean Museum, University of Oxford*)

Roman temple; Portland stone facings and pilasters applied to the external walls of the nave and transepts replaced soot-impregnated stonework and Norman buttresses (Figure 23).

The severely damaged Gothic tower was next in line for repair, but political and social upheavals, as so often in London's history, foiled a plan for improving the fabric of the city. Charles I and William Laud were executed, Inigo Jones joined the court in exile, Parliament replaced the Dean and Chapter with a committee which stripped St Paul's of its ornaments and allowed large-scale vandalism and desecration by the Army and the mob to take place. Land adjacent to St Paul's was sold for houses, which were built against the cathedral walls. Shopkeepers set up their stalls under the roof of the west portico. So much damage was done during the Commonwealth period to Inigo Jones's decorative new work and to the exterior and interior that major repairs were once again needed in all parts of the cathedral.

Soon after the Restoration in 1660 the choir at the east end was repaired so that Anglican services could again be held. A Royal Commission was appointed in 1663 to organise a survey of the fabric of the whole cathedral, approve a plan for repair and oversee the new work. It soon became apparent that the state of the structure was so poor that expert technical advice would be needed. Accordingly, Hugh May, Roger Pratt and Christopher Wren were brought in to advise the commissioners. Hugh May, courtier and friend of the portrait painter Sir Peter Lely, was Paymaster of the Works to Charles II and as such had overseen the extensive overhaul of the royal palaces and other buildings since 1660; but he was more of a competent financial administrator than an imaginative architect or planner. The lawyer Roger Pratt, a friend of John Evelyn, was also a connoisseur gentleman architect, having travelled widely to make a serious study of buildings in France, Italy and the Low Countries. He built houses mainly for gentlemen rather like himself, and a few grand mansions, including one for the Lord Chancellor (Lord Clarendon) in Piccadilly, which, according to Sir Howard Colvin, was 'one of the most influential buildings in the history of English domestic architecture'.[1] He was knighted in 1668 for his services to the rebuilding of the city. Christopher Wren was more than ten years younger than either Roger Pratt or Hugh May, and at the time he had less experience of practising architecture than they.[2] But he was Savilian Professor of Astronomy at Oxford, a Fellow of the Royal Society and one of the world's leading mathematicians and scientists. Robert Hooke wrote in the Preface to *Micrographia*:

> I first set upon this Enterprise, [microscopical examinations] yet still came to it with much Reluctancy, because I was to follow the footsteps of so eminent a Person as Dr. Wren, who was the first that attempted anything of this nature; whose original draughts do now make one of the Ornaments of the great Collection of Rarities in the Kings Closet . . . since the time of Archimedes, there scarce ever met in one man, in so great a perfection, such a Mechanical Hand, and so Philosophical a mind.[3]

Clearly Wren had a reputation for both practical skill and scientific and mathematical knowledge of a high order. The king had personal knowledge of his intellect and ingenuity and knew that his advice on repairing old St Paul's would be useful. Evidence has recently been presented which strongly suggests that Wren's royalist and Anglican connections led to an invitation as early as 1661 to advise Gilbert Sheldon, who was appointed Bishop of London soon after the Restoration.[4]

The cathedral was by then a dilapidated confusion of styles. The consultants to the commissioners had different views on what should be done. Roger Pratt favoured a series of low-cost patchwork repairs. Hugh May retreated into the background by concentrating on his administrative work as Paymaster. Only Wren had the enthusiasm, ideas and ambition to make extensive repairs that would be worthy of London and in accord with the ambition of the new Dean of St Paul's, William Sancroft. Inigo Jones's portico was repaired. Wren and Roger Pratt wrote their conflicting reports and proposals to the commissioners. To settle the matter and recommend which plan should be adopted, the commissioners appointed a committee consisting of the Bishop of London, the Dean of St Paul's, the consultants May, Pratt and Wren, and three independent advisers, men of taste and discrimination, well-known at court: John Evelyn, Fellow of the Royal Society and active in its affairs; Thomas Chicheley, a well-connected, staunch Anglican *bon vivant* with a reputation as a good judge of buildings; and Henry Slingsby, Master of the Mint, probably chosen for his technical knowledge.

Their meeting at St Paul's on Monday 27 August 1666, with workmen in attendance, has been vividly described by Jane Lang.[5] Wren pointed out evidence of structural weakness in the main pillars supporting the nave roof and the irregular spacing and cracking of the columns supporting the tower. He used a plumb-line to show that some of the main pillars were leaning outwards at the top by more than six inches from the vertical. Pratt, supported by Chicheley, claimed it was a deliberate act by the medieval builders to give an illusion of added height. Wren argued that the outward lean was caused by the weight of the roof and said what he would do to counteract it. Evelyn backed Wren, saying that the original Norman builders did not employ such classical subtleties. Wren also produced his plans for a double dome, the inner made of brick and the outer of timber and lead, supported on a tall drum with columns around its circumference. Less than a week later their deliberations became irrelevant. For the third time St Paul's Cathedral was destroyed by fire.

The city, huddled below the cathedral's looming bulk, was also in need of reformation. Arguably as many as 100,000 people could have been living within the city's walls at the time of the fire of 1666 (Figure 38).[6] Rich and poor lived in a random conglomeration of narrow streets and alleyways, constricted by shop fronts and hanging signs built out from their owners' houses. In some of the wider streets markets were set up, either along one side or in the middle, forcing carts and pedestrians to pass by on one side or the other. Overhead, as each storey jetted out further than the one below, frontages on opposite sides of the street converged towards one another, sometimes leaving only a foot or two between them through which light and air could enter. The

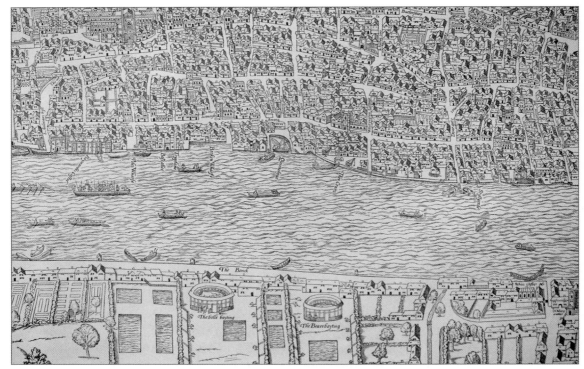

38. Detail from a 1980 facsimile of the 'Agas' woodcut map of the 1560s showing the density of building fronting the quays and wharves along the north bank of the Thames. The mouth of the Fleet Ditch is at the extreme left. (*Guildhall Library, Corporation of London*)

more important streets, made of cobbles embedded in gravel, sand and the detritus from the multitude of activities all around, were poorly maintained. Lesser streets, alleyways and courtyards were often deep in mud. Neither pedestrians nor houses were protected from the traffic and filth which passed along their streets.

Narrow alleys and crooked passageways led from the streets, passing between and under the upper storeys of tenements to give entry to enclosed inner courtyards. Despite regulations governing noxious trades, too many tradesmen practised their crafts – baking bread, smelting metals, burning lime, brewing beer, curing leather, making soap and so on – in workshops close to or even adjoining the places where they lived with their families and apprentices. Houses and clothes bore the stains and stinks of manufacturing. Raw materials and fuel were stacked in corners or stored in lean-to timber sheds, protected from the weather, as were many of the houses, by coverings of timber coated in pitch. Waste products, animal, vegetable and mineral, from furnaces, stables and the crowded tenements either escaped through chimneys into the pall of smoke which hung in the air or were thrown into the street where they lay until carried away by rainwater along open channels (or 'kennels').

Scavengers went round collecting rubbish, dumping what even they had no use for at laystalls near the edges of the city or throwing it down the steep banks of the Fleet River. Lying just outside the city's western wall, the Fleet had become a squalid ditch after centuries of receiving London's rubbish. The flow from upstream had dwindled as more water was diverted by the New River Company into its pipes in the north of the city to supplement water from natural springs and wells. Inhabitants in the south used water noisily pumped up from the River Thames by waterwheels set in the 'starlings', or footings, of London Bridge and carried through lead pipes over the steeple of St Magnus's Church at the Bridge Foot.

Nearly all the buildings were timber-framed, with laths and plaster filling the wall spaces between, and wooden floors set on joists at the higher levels. Uncontrolled building, rebuilding and repairs over the centuries had resulted in a structural confusion of adjacent properties, with rooms or a staircase of one tenant at a higher level resting in part upon the rooms of a neighbour. Below ground too, encroachment was not uncommon. A neighbour sometimes extended a cellar beneath the foundations of an adjoining property. Party walls were not always regular throughout the height of the building, but displaced to one side or the other at different floor levels. A house could have up to five storeys, each one or two rooms deep, built as need, opportunity or ambition determined. Cellars were used for storage of materials and goods, or to provide dark and damp accommodation for poorer tenants. The ground floor was often used as a shop or workshop, or as a room for doing whatever other business the owner or occupier of the house was engaged in. The dining-room was on the first floor, a bedroom or two on the second. An attic or garret, often poised precariously against a crumbling chimney, was used to house other tenants, apprentices or family.

In contrast, the houses of wealthy merchants, built of brick or stone, stood among the wooden houses but usually set back from the noisome street and with a courtyard or garden behind to give some privacy. One of the grandest of the merchants' houses had become Gresham College, stretching from Bishopsgate Street to Broad Street. At the beginning of the seventeenth century aristocrats and gentry and other wealthy inhabitants began to move away from the noise and filth of the walled city to Southwark or to the new squares of Covent Garden, Westminster and St James's, but most of the wealthy merchants remained close to the places where their wealth was created.

Before 1666 four prominent buildings or groups of buildings, made from stone or brick, signified to the citizens the different ways in which the complex and crowded city was governed and socially organised. First, the Royal Exchange, built by Sir Thomas Gresham in 1566 with the Bourse at Antwerp as his model, was the driving force behind London's financial and commercial activities for creating wealth through trade in goods and services both at home and overseas.

The halls of the livery companies formed the second group of prominent buildings. Almost nobody could practise a particular trade or craft in the city (or even keep a shop) until they had served a seven-year apprenticeship working for a member of the appropriate livery company and living in his employer's family home. When the apprenticeship was completed satisfactorily, the apprentice became a 'freeman', which meant he had the freedom of the city to work for someone else or to set up on his own and be eligible for election to a livery company.[7] Standards of workmanship and the weights and measures used for selling goods were monitored and maintained by the livery companies through fines, or expulsion and consequent loss of livelihood for unsatisfactory standards or excessive charging.

The third group of prominent buildings was formed by the 110 parish churches.[8] Many were as ancient as the livery company halls, but more were either built or repaired in the seventeenth century than has been thought.[9] The lower tier of government was the parish, and its church was the centre of parish life, similar in many ways to village life at the time. Parish officers were responsible for maintaining the church, keeping law and order, scavenging the streets and providing charitable aid to the poor who lived within the parish boundary. Guildhall, the fourth significant building and seat of the city's government, was not prominent, but lay in a roughly triangular area of ground between Basinghall Street to the west and Aldermanbury to the east, hidden from view behind a tumble of houses along Cateaton Street to the south.[10] At the upper level of government the city was divided into twenty-six wards. Each ward nominated an alderman to a seat on the City's Court of Aldermen for life, and sent its representatives (from four to ten) to the City's Court of Common Council, the City's legislative body sitting in Guildhall with the Lord Mayor at its head. The Court of Aldermen acted as a sort of executive committee. Each alderman had a deputy, usually the senior common councilman of the ward, who acted as his administrative assistant. The durability of the prominent buildings was an indication of the durability of the institutions which created them, a social structure which was soon to withstand and recover from the catastrophe of the Great Fire.

Fire was part of the daily lives of the inhabitants of London. In their houses and yards they used fire not only for domestic heat and light, but for their work. Many craftsmen, such as silversmiths, glass-makers and bakers, kept their fuel and lit their fires inside and up against the walls of the places where they lived. Outbreaks of fire were usually quickly noticed and speedily put out by the cooperative efforts of neighbours and parish officials. The fire that began in Thomas Farriner's bakery in Pudding Lane in the south-east of the city in the early hours of Sunday 2 September 1666 was no different, but it quickly developed into such an exceptional fire that it has become known as the Great Fire. The hot dry summer, a strong wind from the north-east and a mass of combustible stores and buildings separated by narrow alleyways on the slope down to the Thames all combined to set the fire on a destructive course. The pump which supplied the east of the city with water from the Thames was one of the first civic amenities to be destroyed. In the London of 1666, however, an exceptional fire had to have an exceptional cause. The way in which the high steeple of St Laurence Pountney Church burst into flame was a clear indication to Dr Thomas Middleton that this fire was not simply an accident, like most of the others: 'I saw the fire break out from the inside of Laurence Pountney Steeple, where there was no fire near it. These and such observations begat in me a persuasion that the Fire was maintained by design.'[11]

What that design might be was soon discovered by a resident at Temple, in the south-west of the city, then far from the flames, when he went outside at 9 o'clock that Sunday morning to find the streets:

> . . . full of people, and those of fears: first it was already imagined the design of the French and Dutch in revenge for what our forces had lately done at Brandaris upon the island of Schelling: and the riding of a hot-headed fellow through the street (with more speed and fear than wit) crying 'Arm, Arm!' had frightened most of the people out of the churches.[12]

Pepys of course was soon busy. Having told the king of what he had seen and heard, he went to find the Lord Mayor Sir Thomas Bludworth to pass on a message from the king. Despite the resonance of his name, the Lord Mayor on reading the king's message telling him to pull down houses in front of the fire to make a fire-break:

> cried, like a fainting woman 'Lord! what can I do? I am spent: people will not obey me. I have been pulling down houses; but the fire overtakes us faster than we can do it.' That he needed no more soldiers, and that, for himself, he must go and refresh himself, having been up all night. So he left me, and I him, and walked home, seeing people all almost distracted, and no manner of means used to quench the fire.[13]

The Temple resident went to see how things were in the east of the city:

> walking towards the Fire, we were stopped in Cannon Street by the abundance of goods and carts with which it was filled. Here we met my Lord Mayor on horseback with a few attendants, looking like one frightened out of his wits . . . I was that evening a second time on the water; and it was then it appeared with all the horror and dreadfulness imaginable: the flames afforded light enough to discover themselves, the black smoke and the buildings they so imminently threatened.[14]

It was a time of fear and confusion as people tried to save themselves and their livelihoods. For four days and nights a 'bow' of flame passed westwards and northwards through the city leaving widespread destruction in its wake.[15] The Lord Mayor's authority was inadequate to organise the usual procedure of pulling down or blowing up buildings ahead of the fire to create a fire-break. By the time assistance came from the Army under the command of the Duke of York the fire was unstoppable. Water pumps could not be manoeuvred through the narrow and crooked streets to places where they were needed, and transportation of water by hand was futile. When an inhabitant could see that the loss of his or her house was inevitable, it was possible only to flee by road or river by whatever means were available,

39. Marcus Willemsz Doornick's 1666 print (engraver unknown) shows clearly the burnt area of the City of London. Probably the first of many similar prints published by English and continental cartographers and engravers in the years following the Great Fire, it contains a verbal description of the damaged and undamaged areas. (*Guildhall Library, Corporation of London*)

taking as many belongings or stores as possible and trying to find a safe place to hide what could not be taken. The booksellers around St Paul's hastened to place their stocks in the crypt for safety, but the roof of St Paul's collapsed and molten lead flowed through the debris, and the dense stock of paper underneath smouldered for more than a week.

The fire statistics, though arguable, are stark. Less than 20 per cent of the area inside the city walls (about 440 acres, or 180ha) remained untouched by the flames. About 13,000 houses were destroyed, making at least 65,000 people homeless, but the number might have been as high as 80,000. Ninety parish churches, six chapels, fifty-two livery company halls, Guildhall, the Royal Exchange, the Custom House, compters[16] at Wood Street and Poultry, the gaol for malefactors at Newgate, Bridewell workhouse for vagrants, the Sessions

House[17] and three city gateways, Aldersgate, Ludgate and Newgate, were all destroyed (Figure 39). We do not know how many people died as a consequence of the fire because the bills of mortality were of course not published at the time and the first parish records to be published after the fire showed that fewer people had died in the three previous weeks than in the week before the fire began. We can only conclude that although a few eyewitnesses recorded seeing individual fatalities, the total cannot have been more than a few hundred, otherwise they would eventually have been recorded in some way.[18]

The great confusion of huddled buildings had been reduced to a layer of rubble and ashes. For the first time it was possible to see east–west across the city from one wall to the other, and the Thames could be seen from as far north as Cheapside. The shells of parish churches and other prominent masonry buildings stood high above the debris, giving points of reference for the streets and alleys once so familiar to Londoners but now hidden beneath the still-smoking charred timber and grey-white powdery ash. The stink of dense insanitary human occupation had been replaced by the acrid smell of wood-smoke. Old St Paul's still stood high above everything, signifying by its ruinous gothic bulk the enormity of the task of renewal which now confronted the rulers of the city and its citizens (Figure 40). The civic, religious, commercial and domestic lives of the city's inhabitants had been catastrophically damaged, but already rebuilding was being planned.

40. Thomas Wyck's pen and wash drawing (*c.* 1673) of the burnt and partly demolished St Paul's Cathedral. The view is from the site of the choir, looking south-west towards the nave and south transept. (*Guildhall Library, Corporation of London*)

9

❧❧❧

WITH ALACRITY AND CHEERFULNESS

As soon as the fire had died down, though with the ruins still smouldering and likely to flare up again in the wind, the Privy Council returned to the City its authority to govern, which had been temporarily taken away during the fire. On 6 September the king wrote to the Lord Mayor directing him to call the aldermen together and resume governing the city. Twelve members of the Court of Aldermen met the same day, despite the general exodus from the chaotic ruins. It was soon clear to them that Guildhall was so damaged internally by the fire that it would be impossible for the City's rulers and administrators to meet and work there. An alternative place had to be found quickly. The stone-built Gresham College in Bishopsgate Street stood in the north-east corner of the city which had escaped the worst effects of the fire. The Gresham Trustees were in no doubt that occupation of the college by the City was not only necessary but proper. During the last days of the fire orders were sent out to members of the City's Court of Aldermen that they would soon be called upon to meet in the college. So on Thursday 6 September they were able to make a start on the daunting tasks of restoring the confidence of the citizens in the ability of the City to deal with the immediate problems and facing up to the arduous business of rebuilding a ruined city. The Gresham Trustees commandeered Gresham College.

At this first meeting the Court of Aldermen issued a series of orders intended to show the citizens that the City was in control and working to re-establish trade, the lifeblood of the city, and to provide shelter, albeit temporary, for the homeless. The Lord Mayor issued a proclamation that markets were to be continued 'streightly charging' and that market officers were to see that trading was carried on 'according to the Lawes and Usages of this Citty'. The Court further ordered that rubbish be cleared from the bridge and from roads leading to it on the Southwark side. All freemen who had lost their premises were permitted to erect temporary sheds in which they could resume their businesses on 'void' land on each side of the bridge, with the agreement of the bridgemasters. Void land not used in this way was to be fenced in by the bridgemasters for the security of passengers crossing over the river. Representatives of the City were ordered to wait upon the king to acknowledge his 'expressed regard and affection' for the City, 'to beg his continued grace and favour for recovery' and to entreat him to send tents into Finsbury Fields for the 'poor people who remain there' without habitation. Aldermen were ordered to appoint in each ward 'honest and able persons' to ensure the fire did not re-kindle. The last order of the day was that the Lord Mayor and sheriffs whose houses had been consumed by the fire shall make use of rooms in Gresham College for lodgings and accommodation.[1]

Unfortunately the City was temporarily diverted from its task of relieving the suffering of the citizens by a little domestic difficulty within the college. Not all Gresham Professors were willing to forgo their privileged lives. Those, like Hooke, who lived full-time in the college rather than illegally letting out their accommodation to tenants, were faced with eviction. Those who had let their lodgings lost that income. Despite being told that they would continue to be paid their £50 annual salaries,[2] at least one of them had to be forcibly removed by the City. On 7 September the Court of Aldermen ordered the City Chamberlain to use Dr Jonathan Goddard's lodgings for his office and the rooms 'formerly used by' Dr Horton[3] for his accommodation, which he was to share with the Deputy Town Clerk Mr Avery and the City Swordbearer (all three of them had lost their houses) 'for better service to the City and security of the records'.[4] Dr George Gifford, Gresham Professor of Divinity, should have been in the lodgings formerly occupied by his predecessor Thomas Horton, but they were locked.[5] The next day, Saturday 8 September, the City records state:

> This Court conceiving the Lodgings Lately held by Doctor Horton to be most comodious in severall respects for the placing of the Records, and other writings of daily use & necessity to this Court, Doe order that the same bee cleered against Munday Morning and the Records & Bookes then removed and brought thither And that the Lodgings at the end of the Gallery bee in Like manner and with Like speed cleared for the accommodation of Mr Godfrey with the goods in his charge belonging to the Company of Mercers, And in case of any contempt or neglect of this Order the Citty Artificers are to break open the Doores and see it executed accordingly.[6]

The City did not need to issue more orders of this kind. George Gifford was removed, albeit temporarily.

Before the weekend further orders were issued by the Court of Aldermen to clear rubbish from inside the walls of Guildhall, preserve melted lead and iron and other materials of value and then board up all passages to Guildhall to secure it from vandals.[7] Freemen were allowed to erect more sheds and tents for business, this time on four areas of land – two against the City wall (outside from the postern near Broad Street to Moorgate and inside from the postern to Coleman Street); in the Artillery Ground; and at Smithfield. The City Surveyor Peter Mills was ordered to set out the sheds and tents in agreement with the Lord Mayor and sheriffs. In response to requests from traders, who before the fire had places in the upper pawne[8] of the Royal Exchange, they too were allowed to set up sheds, which were to extend no more than four feet from the wall, provided the work was done as required by the Lord Mayor and sheriffs with the assistance of Peter Mills, the City Surveyor. Any trader formerly at the Royal Exchange who was prepared to pay his share of the cost of paving the quadrangle at Gresham College could erect a shed there and continue trading.[9]

At the meeting on Monday 10 September of the unwieldy Court of Common Council, the first after the fire, it was ordered

> that all the Streetes Lanes & Common Passages in every Ward be presently cleared & voided of all Rubbish & other Obstructions by the late Inhabitants every one before his owne Premises And that noe other Labour be permitted upon the Ruines of the said late dwellings till this worke be finished That thereupon such further proceedings & Councells may be followed for the Cityes Welfare and Recovery As shall be convenient And that his Lordship doth forthwith issue out precepts for performance of this Order.[10]

The City was fearful that unregulated building would become widespread. In less than a week since the flames had died down, practical steps had been taken to continue administration, re-open some markets, provide shelter for the homeless, allow temporary premises to be built in an orderly fashion so that freemen of the city and traders from the Royal Exchange could continue their business, legislate for the streets to be cleared and for all rebuilding to stop until long-term plans could be drafted and put into effect. When it is realised that most of the aldermen and City officials were themselves homeless and many had lost goods and personal belongings, their detailed attention to the needs of the city as a whole is admirable. Moreover, they and their deputies, as freemen, were expected to take on the responsibilities of their roles voluntarily and without payment.

The City had made a good start – an opinion shared by the king. On 13 September 1666 Charles II issued a proclamation in which he set out his views and intentions in relation to rebuilding the city. It is a mixture of the visionary, the pragmatic and the impossible, but it was an important statement which largely determined, if not explicitly, what was done on the ground. He began by expressing his hope that God will

> give us life, not only to see the foundations laid, but the buildings finished, of a much more beautiful city than is at this time consumed; and that as the seat and situation of it is the most convenient and noble for the advancement of trade of any city in Europe, so that such care will be taken for the re-edification of it, both for use and beauty, and such provision made for the future against the ordinary and casual accidents by fire, as may, as far as human wisdom can provide, upon the sad experience we have had, reasonably secure the same, and make it rather appear to the world, as purged with the fire (in how lamentable a manner soever) to a wonderful

beauty and comeliness, than consumed by it: and we receive no small encouragement in this our hope, by the alacrity and cheerfulness we observe in those who have undergone the greatest loss, and seem the most undone; who, with undaunted courage, appear to desire the same as we do, and resolve to contribute their utmost assistance thereunto . . .

He went on to proclaim that the necessary 'rules and directions' for rebuilding would take time to prepare, so he made known his 'thoughts, resolutions and intentions' now to prevent 'hasty and unskilful building many may purpose to erect for their present conveniences, before they can know how the same will suit, and consist with the design that shall be made'. His intentions were 'to provide for the just right and interest of all', but if:

> some obstinate and refractory persons will presume to erect such buildings as they shall think fit, upon pretence that the ground is their own, and that they may do with it what they please, such their obstinacy shall not prevail to the public prejudice: but we do hereby require the lord mayor, and the other magistrates of the city of London, in their several limits, to be very watchful in such cases, and speedy to pull down whatsoever such men shall presume to set up, so much to the disturbance of public order and decency; and that they forthwith give notice to us or our privy council of such their proceedings, and return the names of such refractory persons who presume to contemn this our injunction, and we shall give order for their exemplary punishment, without the violation of the public justice.

To reassure citizens who expected to be prevented from rebuilding as quickly as they would wish – a suspicion likely to be shared by many – the proclamation said the 'whole design' of the new city would be made 'in a short time, with the assistance and advice of the lord mayor and court of aldermen'. Even a short delay needed justification. Some indication of the forthcoming benefits to the city as a whole had to be given to the citizens. The proclamation announced that houses in the beautiful new city were to be made of brick or stone, not timber which 'hath sufficiently convinced all men of [its] pernicious consequences'. Main streets would be straightened and widened so that traffic could pass more freely along them and fire could not pass across from one side to the other. Access to the waterside would be made easier. A 'fair key or wharf' would be built along the north bank of the Thames and 'no house shall be erected within so many feet of the river, as shall be within few days declared in the rules formerly mentioned'. Moreover, the houses to be erected fronting the river would be 'fair structures, for the ornament of the city' and any houses to be occupied by 'brewers, or dyers, or sugar-bakers' which 'by their continual smokes, contribute very much to the unhealthiness of the adjacent places' were to be built in a place to be decided by the

Lord Mayor and aldermen where 'all those trades which are carried on by smoke [can] inhabit together'. The king wanted London to have the grand buildings and fine streets worthy of its importance as a great port and city for trade and finance.

In order to put his 'great and glorious design into practice', the Lord Mayor and Court of Aldermen were directed to:

> cause an exact survey to be made and taken of the whole ruins occasioned by the late lamentable fire, to the end that it may appear to whom all the houses and around did in truth belong, what term the several occupiers were possessed of, and at what rents, and to whom, either corporations, companies, or single persons, the reversion and inheritance appertained; that so provision may be made, that though every man must not be suffered to erect what buildings and where he pleases, he shall not in any degree be debarred from receiving the reasonable benefit of what ought to accrue to him from such houses or lands; there being nothing, less in our thoughts, than that any particular person's right and interest should be sacrificed to the public benefit or convenience, without such recompense as in justice he ought to receive for the same: and when all things of this kind shall be prepared and adjusted, by such commissioners, and otherwise, which shall be found expedient, we make no doubt but such an Act of Parliament will pass, as shall secure all men in what they shall and ought to possess.
>
> By the time that this survey shall be taken, we shall cause a plot or model to be made for the whole building through those ruined places; which being well examined by all those persons who have most concernment as well as experience, we make no question but all men will be pleased with it, and very willingly conform to those orders and rules which shall be agreed for the pursuing thereof.
>
> In the mean time, we do heartily recommend it to the charity and magnanimity of all well-disposed persons, and we do heartily pray unto Almighty God, that he will infuse it into the hearts of men, speedily to endeavour by degrees to re-edify some of those many churches, which, in this lamentable fire, have been burned down and defaced; that so men may have those public places of God's worship to resort to, to humble themselves together before him upon this his heavy displeasure, and join in their devotion for his future mercy and blessing upon us; and, as soon as we shall be informed of any readiness to begin such a good work, we shall not only give our assistance and direction for the model of it, and freeing it from buildings at too near a distance, but shall encourage it by our own bounty, and all other ways we shall be desired.
>
> Lastly, that we may encourage men by our own example, we will use all the expedition we can to re-build our custom-house in the place where it formerly stood, and enlarge it with the most conveniences for the merchants that can be devised; and upon all the other lands which belong unto us, we shall depart with our own right and benefit, for the advancement of the public service and beauty of the city; and shall

further remit to all those who shall erect any buildings according to this declaration, all duties arising to us upon the hearth-money for the space of seven years.[11]

The promise in the last sentence to suspend a hated tax for those who rebuilt according to the proclamation was a strong incentive to comply. The overall intention to create a new and more beautiful city, safer and healthier than its predecessor, was accompanied by an exceptional idea for administering it. A map of the city would be made, based on accurate measurements of the boundaries of each individual property. For each toft, or parcel of land, a written record would be compiled of the nature and purpose of the present (or lost) buildings and of all matters relating to ownership, including rents, reversions and inheritances. A register of such records used in conjunction with the map showing the surveyed boundaries of each property, now known as a cadastre, would allow compulsory purchase of ground for widening streets and other improvements to be more efficiently carried out. It could also be kept up to date and used in the future. An accurate map and the associated register would codify the complexities of land tenure in the city and provide information about the size, shape, position and use of individual parcels of land which would be useful for valuation, taxation, civic planning and conveyancing. In effect, the proclamation proposed the creation of what would now be called a 'parcel-based land information system and cadastre' for London.

The proposed systematic collection and recording of information for the benefit of London and its citizens closely resembles the Baconian plan for collecting and recording observations of natural phenomena which was being vigorously pursued at the time by members of the recently formed Royal Society in order to understand more about the natural world for the benefit of mankind as a whole. The two approaches to collecting and using information for public benefit have much in common. Both the natural scheme and the civic scheme demonstrate an intention to clarify what is obscure or complicated, whether created by nature or by man, for the general good. It is reasonable to suggest that the ideas for an information system for London came from like-minded scientists, members of the Royal Society who had influence both at court and in the City, men such as Sir William Petty, Sir Robert Moray and John Evelyn (particularly) at court and Wren and Hooke in the City. John Evelyn's *Fumifugium, or the Inconveniencie of the Aer and Smoak of London Dissipated* (1661) is a damning essay on the way smoke and other noxious waste products from activities such as soap-boiling and lime-burning were allowed to pollute the air of London. It was approved of by the king, who commanded Evelyn to draw up a bill for Parliament prohibiting pollution, but nothing came of it. Given Evelyn's long and practical interest in horticulture and his belief in the importance of all land as a national asset to be properly managed, it is likely that the idea in the proclamation for a register and map of land ownership had much to do with him.

Although measurement of every toft in the city and the collection of information about each one could have been done simultaneously, the tasks could not possibly have been completed within a year. The plot would have had to be more accurate than was possible with routine land-surveying methods in use at the time. Documents relating to tenure would have to be brought in and assessed, but some had been lost in the fire and many citizens had left London to live elsewhere until the spring and were unavailable to provide the necessary information. Witnesses would have to give evidence in cases of dispute and judgments made. If the city were to be completely rebuilt on new foundations, the boundaries of all the new tofts would have to be staked out, measured and certified and all re-conveyances recorded. The idea was far-sighted but utterly impracticable. A new plan showing the streets in the ruined areas of the city was produced soon after the fire (Figure 44) and was useful for planning street widening and locations for new markets. When most of the rebuilding had been completed, a large-scale plan of the whole city was made using new methods of urban land surveying and cartography (Figures 53, 80 and 81). The plan symbolised the city's remarkable recovery, but it was not the basis of the parcel-based land information system that had been proposed.

The proclamation was an inspiring vision of a new and more beautiful city, cleaner, healthier and more ordered than the city that had been destroyed. It was not a scheme for building such a city, but it set most people's minds at rest. Although the king and the City at the outset both wanted to build anew, the impracticability of such a vision was soon recognised by the men who advised the king and indeed by the king himself.[12] To begin with, there was no money for buying land from thousands of landowners: the City had none to offer and the commons were debating the raising of funds for the war against France and Holland throughout the last three months of 1666 and had no time to consider London's needs. As soon as the first practical steps were taken to start building, they could lead only to a city rebuilt on old foundations, but with some new and widened streets and other useful improvements. Even if the money were available to buy the thousands of land parcels, the delay in measuring and valuing them and then reallocating them on a completely new ground-plan would be too great. The clearly stated prohibition of unregulated rebuilding (and promise of punishment within the law for such acts) in Proclamation 48 suggests that the king knew the prospect of delay would alarm and anger many citizens and set at risk London's future as a great centre for finance and trade. If rebuilding in London could not start soon, it would take place somewhere else. But with winter approaching, some delay was inevitable. Large-scale rebuilding could not start until the spring. If the plans and rules for rebuilding could be completed in the next few months, irrevocable damage to London and the nation would be avoided. Swift and decisive action was needed.

10

❧❧

THE MIDDLE WAY

Never a tranquil place, nor one suitable for quiet contemplation, Gresham College in late September 1666 was London's hub, the location where those who governed the city lived, met and had their administrative offices. It was also the place where the business of the Royal Exchange and its tenants was carried on while rebuilding took place. Hooke was allowed by the City to remain in his rooms where he had lived continuously (except for a spell in Surrey and the Isle of Wight during the time of the plague in 1665) since his appointment by the City as Gresham Professor of Geometry in March 1665. He was already well known to leading figures in the City through his Royal Society, Cutlerian and Gresham appointments. Now living and working among them as they began the task of rehabilitating the citizens and creating conditions for the resumption of normal trade and commerce, he was ideally placed to put himself forward as somebody who could be useful to them in their endeavours. He seized the first chance that came his way by putting forward a layout plan for rebuilding London.

Ideas for a new city had been around since at least 1662, when a Royal Commission was set up to reform London's buildings and streets. Although Wren and Evelyn were not formally appointed as commissioners, they took part in their debates.[1] The topic would easily have fitted into informal conversations between Wren, Evelyn, Hooke and other members of the Royal Society, who thought London was in great need of reformation. New and regular buildings made from brick and stone were needed, the whole laid out on a street pattern based on reason, proportion and efficiency rather than chance, which had led to the present confusion. It is therefore not surprising that within a few weeks of the fire detailed plans for new layouts were presented by Wren, Evelyn, Hooke and two others.[2] In the years between 1662 and 1666 they had been working on their designs in the expectation that rebuilding would take place. Wren was first off the mark after the fire, showing his plan (or 'model') to the king on 11 September 1666. Oldenburg wrote to Robert Boyle on 18 September 1666 telling him he had complained to Wren that the Royal Society had lost an opportunity to be looked on with favour by the king by not having an early sight of Wren's layout plan so that they could promote it as their own preference. Wren's response to Oldenburg was he had been 'so pressed to hasten it, before other desseins came in that he could not possibly consult the society about it'. All chance of the Royal Society receiving recognition was not lost, however. Oldenburg went on to tell Boyle that he hoped, when Wren's plan 'comes to be presented to the parliament, as the author will be named, so his relation to the society will not be omitted'.[3]

Evelyn presented his plan two days later than Wren, on the day of the proclamation, when he spent an hour or so discussing his ideas for a new city with the king and queen and the Duke of York. Wren's proposal included a detailed argument against rebuilding on the old foundations, asserting that to do so would be 'a Shame to the Nation' if it now let the City 'slide into Its old Barbarity, for which when it is irreparable our posterity will blame[4] the ill and untractable Humours of This Age'.[5] Wren's whole argument against rebuilding on the old pattern was so forceful that it implies he feared such an event was more than possible, despite the king's proclaimed desire for a city of 'wonderful beauty and comeliness'. Such a city was what Wren and Evelyn were now showing the king.

Hooke, on the other hand, showed his plan first to the City, probably with the encouragement and support of Sir John Lawrence, who had been Lord Mayor in 1665 and chairman of the meeting of the City Side of the Gresham Trustees which had rectified the improper election of Dacres instead of Hooke as Geometry Professor.[6] He then showed it to the Royal Society at its meeting on 19 September 1666, held in the lodgings of Walter Pope, Gresham Professor of Astronomy and member of the Royal Society.

Mr. Hooke shewed his model for rebuilding the city to the society, who were well pleased with it; and Sir John Laurence, late lord mayor of London, having addressed himself to the society, and expressed the present lord mayor's [Sir Thomas Bludworth] and aldermen's approbation of the said model, and their desire, that it might be shewn to the King, they preferring it very much to that, which was drawn up by the surveyor of the city [Peter Mills]; the president answered, that the society would be very glad, if they or any of their members could do any service for the good of the city; and that Mr. Hooke should wait on them with his model to the King, if they thought fit to present it: which was accepted with expressions of thanks to the society.[7]

Hooke's layout plan is now lost. Richard Waller wrote in 1704 that he was told it was in the form of a rectangular grid of streets.[8] The plan commonly attributed to Hooke, similar to the plan described by Waller, can be seen, truncated, in the upper left-hand corner of a printed sheet by Marcus Willemsz Doornick, published in Amsterdam in 1666 (Figure 39). In the top left-hand corner of the print is an unattributed and rather crude truncated layout plan entitled 'NIEW MODELL om de afgebrande Stadt LONDON te HERBOUWEN' (Figure 41).[9] Another printed sheet with illustrations similar to Doornick's was published a year later in Amsterdam by Jacob Venckel: like Doornick's print, in the top left-hand corner there is the same unattributed layout plan for

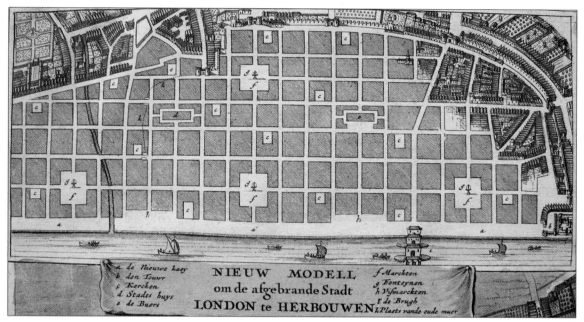

41. Detail from Marcus Willemsz Doornick's 1666 plan (Figure 39) showing a new layout plan for London. The plan has been attributed to Hooke, but without convincing evidence in support. (*Guildhall Library, Corporation of London*)

rebuilding London, but it is not truncated.[10] Doornick's and Venckel's layout plan and other versions of it published in Amsterdam in the aftermath of the fire have been attributed to Hooke,[11] even quite recently.[12]

It is possible that the small plans shown in the Dutch prints of 1666 and later were based on Hooke's designs. They show a rectangular street layout, the form which Waller in 1705 said he had heard was what Hooke proposed, but it is none the less very difficult to accept that they can be anything more than stylised representations of Hooke's original plan. They show no provision, for instance, for a new St Paul's Cathedral. The site of old St Paul's is to be used for general building; the closest proposed church lies to the west, outside the city wall, on the slope down to the Fleet River. Both Wren and Evelyn in their layout plans placed the new St Paul's more or less on the site of old St Paul's and made it an important intersection. It is very likely that Hooke would have given similar prominence to the new cathedral. Although a new 'de Buers' is shown close to the site of the burnt Royal Exchange, as might be expected, a new Guildhall, shown as 'Stadts huys', is shown just to the north of the site of old St Paul's, and a new piazza, market and fountain shown on the site of the old Guildhall are unlikely innovations. Hooke was by this time a man experienced in civic affairs and was acquainted with London's rulers. He knew about the pre-fire intentions of the commissioners and his friend Christopher Wren to repair old St Paul's and to make other improvements to the city as a whole. It is very unlikely that his new layout plan would show new locations for such important buildings, and even if it did it is inconceivable that it would have been approved by the City. The small plan shown on prints by Doornick, Venckel and others is more of a fanciful decorative invention (possibly loosely based on Hooke's plan) by a draughtsman working on the main map. The plan seems to have been attributed to Hooke only because it differs from all the other known plans and shows a rectangular street layout.

Although the king's proclamation had ruled out the possibility of allowing rebuilding to take place haphazardly on the old foundations, some citizens had already started to do so, despite severe warnings from the City and the king. The Privy Council and the City, working independently and in cooperation, had to act quickly and forcefully to stop a growing number of infringements of the proclamation. On 2 October 1666 the Court of Common Council had to take action against the perpetrators of two new outbreaks of fire caused by craftsmen secretly pursuing their trades: a plumber who was melting lead in a cellar and a brewer working in a small room that was accessible only by a narrow passage through which the fire-engine could not pass. Had the fires not been quickly quenched, the consequences would have been serious. Allegations that some people already starting to rebuild were encroaching on neighbouring land and making use of inadequate foundations were investigated.[13] A citizen named William Jones reported to the Court of Aldermen on the same day that people were rebuilding in Castle Yard (just outside the city wall, to the west of Smithfield Bar) 'contrary to the tenor of his Majestyes Late proclamation'. The City Chamberlain's yeomen were ordered to forbid further rebuilding at the site. Orders also went out to several citizens who had built sheds encroaching into Long Lane (running north-east out of Smithfield into Aldersgate Street, also outside the city wall) to cut down and remove the sheds themselves.[14] There was high demand for the services and goods of such tradesmen as plumbers and brewers and high prices could be charged for accommodating goods or people in unburnt areas, even in rough wooden sheds. Inevitably some inhabitants attempted to supply the demand, despite the proclamation. Throughout the winter months of 1666–7 the City had to deal with an increasing number of allegations of infringement. It was only through the sense of civic responsibility possessed by most citizens, and the vigilance of officials in the parishes and wards, that such transgressions were reported and acted upon. By responding speedily and efficiently where necessary the aldermen and councilmen were able to keep excessive contraventions at bay and so leave the city more or less ready in the spring for rebuilding, if not to the 'great and glorious design' which the king and the City hoped to see, then at least according to 'rules and directions' which 'provide for the just right and interest of all'. Given the extent of the catastrophe, that was the most that could reasonably be achieved.

On 27 and 28 September 1666 the House of Commons held a general debate on rebuilding the city, but could not decide which of the plans should be adopted. They did, however, reach general agreement that speed was necessary and unregulated rebuilding should not be allowed, but they gave no indication of how the incompatibility between speed in rebuilding and the drafting of new regulations should be reconciled. They ignored the matter for three months while they debated how to finance the current war against Holland and its new ally France for maritime supremacy in support of English foreign trade, a war which was indecisive and probably brought more damage than benefit to England's trade. Parliament left the matter of rebuilding London to be decided by the Privy Council and the City.[15]

Henry Oldenburg, secretary of the Royal Society, made it his business to know what was happening in politics as well as in science. He wrote to Boyle on 2 October 1666 to give him an idea of how Members of Parliament were thinking about the way London should be rebuilt:

> The rebuilding of the citty, as to the model, is still very perplext, there appearing three parties in the house of commons about it. Some are for a quite new model, according to Dr. Wren's draught; some for the old, yet to build with bricks; others for a middle way, by building a key, and enlarging some streets, but keeping the old foundations and vaults. I heare, this very day there is a meeting of some of his majesties councill, and others of the nobility, with the leading men of the city, to conferre about this great work, and to try, whether they can bring it to some issue, before the people, that inhabited London, doe scatter into other parts. The great stresse will be, how to raise money for carrying on the warre, and to rebuild the citty at the same time.[16]

Oldenburg's intelligence network, as usual, was in good working order. His account reveals an acute early understanding of the problems lying in wait for all those with a vested interest in, or responsibility for, how London would be rebuilt, which would soon take up much of their time and energy.

At the 4 October 1666 meeting of the City's Court of Common Council, a report of the Privy Council meeting was presented by Sir Thomas Adams who led the City delegation. He declared they had

> attended the right honorable the Lord Chancellour & other Lords of his Majesty's most honorable privy Councell & received from their Lordships his Majesty's pleasure That for the better and more expedition of this worke he hath pleased to appoint Dr Wren Mr May & Mr Pratt to joyne with such Surveyors & Artificers as should be appointed by the City to take an Exact & speedy survey of all Streetes Lanes Aleys houses & places distroyed by the late dismall Fire That every particular Interest may be assertained & provided for & the better Judgment made of the whole Affaire This Court doth therefore Order that Mr Hooke Reader of the Mathematicks in Gresham Collidge Mr Mills and Mr Edward Jermyn do joyne with the said Dr Wren Mr May &

Mr Pratt in taking the said Surveigh And that the Deputy & Common Councellmen have notice of the Surveighs when the same shall be taken in every Ward to the End they may be in readinesse to take Care for the Interest of themselves and the Inhabitants of their respective Wards.[17]

Just as Parliament had left its decision on how the rebuilding should proceed to the Privy Council and the City, so they, in turn, now passed the responsibility to these six men. Although they were nominated at first specifically to oversee the survey of all the city streets and foundations, they were in effect given the responsibility to decide on behalf of the Privy Council and the City all the most important technical matters about the form of the rebuilt city. It is appropriate therefore to look a little more closely at the men who were given such an important task.

The king's three representatives, referred to as 'His Majesty's Commissioners for Rebuilding' or the 'King's Commissioners' for short, were Christopher Wren, Hugh May and Roger Pratt, each of whom had been nominated before the fire to advise on repairing old St Paul's. The City nominees were referred to as 'Surveyors of New Buildings' or simply as 'City Surveyors', although their duties were much more demanding than those of the single City Surveyor before the fire. One nomination was City Surveyor Peter Mills, whose plan for rebuilding had been rejected by the City in favour of Hooke's. Mills had been City Bricklayer (1643–60), Master of the Tylers' and Bricklayers' Company (1649–50 and 1659–60) and since 1644 a Governor of St Thomas's Hospital.[18] He owned and leased property in London and designed new buildings for himself and others after the fire.[19] He also designed the triumphal arches for the entry of Charles II to London at the Restoration and organised on behalf of the City the celebrations and pageants on the Thames to welcome the king and queen to Whitehall.[20] He died in 1670. Another City choice, Edward Jerman,[21] had followed a family tradition going back to Elizabethan times when he was appointed City Carpenter (1633–57). Jerman did not accept the City's nomination as one of their representatives, preferring instead to work on private architectural commissions. He was engaged to design the Royal Exchange and some of the new halls for the livery companies, but died in 1668 before many of his post-fire buildings were completed.[22]

The nominations of May, Pratt, Mills and Jerman are clearly appropriate. Between them they had many decades of experience in the finance, design and technical construction of a wide range of public and private buildings in London – exactly what was necessary for the task ahead. The choices of Wren and particularly Hooke are at first surprising, if only for the relative youth of the two men, and suggest that the king, through his Privy Council, and the City thought that the experience of the other four men, although necessary, was not sufficient for the task. Wren's nomination is perhaps less surprising than Hooke's: he had already come to the notice of the authorities as a very clever and able young man, and had been chosen to advise on the pre-fire repair of old St Paul's. Hooke had no significant experience of surveying, building construction or architecture, but his plan for rebuilding had been approved by the City. Even so, it hardly seems enough to have warranted his nomination. With highly educated men like Wren and Pratt on the king's side, the City probably thought that they should nominate someone of similar intellectual standing. Mills and Jerman were fine craftsmen with respectable social positions in the City, but their knowledge and vision were relatively limited. It was probably Sir John Lawrence who suggested that Hooke would be a suitable City nominee. He knew of Hooke's scientific work and his Cutlerian and Gresham Lectures. He also knew that Hooke and Wren had scientific interests in common and that they shared the essentially optimistic and rational view of the future held by most of their fellow scientists. Furthermore, they had high technical expertise and the ambition and ability to use these qualities for personal profit and public benefit. In nominating Hooke, the City showed a foresight that was later justified, as Reddaway has said about the king's nomination of Wren.[23] The Royal Society's astute secretary Henry Oldenburg could see that cooperation between Wren and Hooke would serve the City well. In a letter to Boyle in October 1666 he wrote:

> The other grand affair about the rebuilding of the Citty, is not neglected neither; Strict injunction being now issued by the Lord Mayor, in the Kings name, wch done, the Survey and admeasurement of all such Foundations is to be forthwith taken in hand, and tht by the care and management of Dr Wren and M. Hook: wch survey is to be exactly registred; for the better stating thereafter everyones right and propriety: And then the method of building will be taken into nearer consideration, and, 'tis hoped, within a short time resolved upon.[24]

Although John Evelyn recorded only a week after the fire that the king and the City expected it would be feasible to rebuild London on a completely new ground-plan,[25] the idea was gradually abandoned as the consequences of Parliament's failure to decide or give guidance on matters relating to the rebuilding became apparent. There were too many unanswerable questions. How could thousands of land parcels be acquired so that a new pattern of streets could be staked out? Then it would be necessary to allocate thousands of new land parcels to those who had lost their pre-fire ground. How could these transfers be made equitably? Although some arrangement could be made to make the gain or loss of ground equitable, it was impossible to say how long the process would take, or how to account in each transaction for a better or worse location, or how to compensate for loss of trade or business during the whole process. Above all was the question of where the money for such an ambitious project could come from.

During the six months after the fire the sub-committees appointed by the City and the Privy Council to plan the rebuilding met separately and together to decide how to proceed, but only scanty records of the meetings have survived.[26] The questions were also debated informally at court and in the city, private papers giving a few glimpses of the way arguments were going. Sir William Petty, an early economic statistician,[27] considered how to estimate the time and costs involved, and how the rebuilding might be financed by taxation over seven years, later to be repaid with interest; however, even he could not come to any definite conclusions.[28] When Captain Valentine Knight presented his layout plan he suggested a means of raising more than £200,000 annually, which would not only pay for the rebuilding, but finance the Army and Navy as well: he proposed that each person allocated land for rebuilding should pay rent annually to the king in proportion to the area of ground. He also suggested a toll on barges using his proposed canal, which would run northwards from the Thames at Billingsgate and then westwards to meet the Fleet River. But Captain Knight seriously misjudged the king's mood. Far from approving his suggestion, the king ordered his arrest, announcing 'as if his Majesty would draw a benefit to himself from so public a calamity of his people, of which His Majesty is known to have so deep sense, that he is pleased to seek rather by all means to give them ease under it'.[29]

The survey was intended to be the basis of a new land information system could not start until all the rubbish had been cleared away from the streets and sites of the former houses to reveal the old alignments and foundations prior to measurement. Attempts to clear the streets failed. The difficulty was made worse by the growing number of citizens who erected sheds and other temporary structures which made the survey harder, not easier. In October the City tried once more to get the streets cleared and the survey started. On 9 October 1666 the Court of Common Council ordered every proprietor of a house or other building to clear the rubbish away from their foundations within the next fourteen days and place it in orderly piles clear of the roads and building lines. The proprietors were to pay 18*d* (1*s* 6*d*) to the City Surveyors for each of their foundations which was measured.[30] Other difficulties had to be dealt with. On 3 November 1666 each alderman was required 'for the due punishing according to Law of Vagrants Sturdy Beggars loose and idle Persons who greatly abound wandring in & about the Streetes & Lanes & amongst the Ruins of this City . . . to erect a substantiall paire of Stocks and Whipping Post to be made and set in Convenient place within your Ward And herein not to faile.'[31]

The plague in 1665 and the press-gangs roaming the ruins had removed a number of men from the streets who might otherwise have found themselves in trouble with the City as vagrants. Civic disorder such as there was consisted mainly of contravention of the City's orders banning the erection of temporary buildings. Many sheds continued to be built by people intending to resume their business or trade. Most such cases were dealt with by ward officers, and some good progress was made, especially in moving the traders and their businesses from the Royal Exchange to Gresham College. Shopkeepers who traded in the quadrangle of Gresham College were ordered to pay £46 5*s* to John

Stanley, carter, for the carriage of 254 loads of bricks and 354 loads of rubbish from Guildhall to Gresham College for paving the quadrangle for their convenience.[32] Trade amid the ruins had started. The Court of Common Council met again on 17 October and agreed on various measures, including clearing the streets so that information such as the size, ownership and rents of individual tofts could be collected and registered, and the form of punishment for non-compliance, all of which would be taken to the Lord Chancellor for his opinion and advice about preparing a bill.[33] Other matters then arose which first delayed and finally put paid to the idea of a parcel-based land information system for London.

When the City sub-committee members took their proposals for this to the Lord Chancellor they were given a draft of a more urgent bill for the City to discuss, this time relating to the manufacture of bricks and lime, vast quantities of which would soon be needed. They considered this new bill at their meeting on 31 October, calling on the King's Commissioners and the City Surveyors to advise them.[34] The prospect of a parcel-based land register was receding. The Royal Society, in their pursuit of useful knowledge, began at this time to discuss materials that could be used for building, including the different sorts of clay which were good for making bricks. Various members reported their observations. One said that when in Holland he had noticed that the nearer the bricks known as 'klinker' were to the source of heat in firing, the harder they became; another reported that Mr Wylde[35] 'had a way, by mixing several sorts of earth together, to make hard and lasting bricks', and yet another reported that the diplomat Sir George Downing had commended the bricks made in the Isle of Ely as 'being equal in goodness to any of the Dutch klinkers'. Hooke added that earths which vitrified made the most lasting bricks, whereupon he was ordered to 'make trials of several earths by burning them in a wind-furnace to see which kind would yield the best brick'.[36] Such enthusiasm for useful knowledge characterised the Royal Society in its early years, but members were impatient for results:[37] their ambition outran the resources available to undertake the necessary scientific research.

The Royal Society put many pressures on Hooke. In the week he was given the task of finding by experiment how to make the best bricks he was experimenting with dogs' blood, asked to read the observations made in Madrid by the Earl of Sandwich and report on them to the Royal Society, and also to perform some experiments he had devised using a conical pendulum.[38] The City then placed another heavy burden upon him when its Court of Common Council decided to

> nominate & appoint Mr [blank] Hooke of the Mathematicks in Gresham House Mr Peter Mills & Mr Jermyn from time to time to meete & consult with Mr May, Dr Wren & Mr Pratt Commissioners appointed by his Majesty concerning the manner forme & highth of Buildings in this City the Scantlings[39] of Timber removeing of Conduits[40] and Churches and Alteration of the Streets And it is ordered that from time to time

they report such their Consultation to this Court and give noe Consent or make any Agreement therein without the speciall Order of this Court.[41]

The latter proviso was a formality. The City's three nominees were left to decide matters on its behalf. In effect, this meant Hooke alone, as Jerman seems to have played no part and Mills was becoming infirm and would soon become ill. Within a period of less than four weeks Hooke had been given the tasks of supervising the compilation of a parcel-based land information system and cadastre for London, of finding out by experiment how to make the 'best' bricks (tasks which are still incomplete more than 300 years later) and of planning with three other men the form and content of the new city. These tasks were additional to all his other weekly experiments for the Royal Society and his lectures for Gresham College and Sir John Cutler. When it is remembered that at this time the only regular payments he was receiving were for his least onerous work, the Cutlerian and Gresham Lectures (he was owed at this time more than £100 arrears of salary by the Royal Society),[42] his optimism and willingness to accept the great demands placed on him can be seen as exceptional qualities, matched by his self-confidence that he had the energy and talent to do what was expected of him. Only two days later he was given a formidable experimental programme to perform for the Royal Society and an order to represent the City in the drafting of the new building regulations, he was given even more work to do.

The Gresham Trustees, who were fully aware of Hooke's other commitments, also needed his expertise for an urgent rebuilding project. The City's Court of Common Council and the Company of Mercers gave full powers to the Gresham Trustees to rebuild the Royal Exchange – the main source of income for Gresham's estate (Figure 42). Having earlier arranged for the site to be cleared, the Gresham Trustees decided on Friday 2 November 1666 to get an estimate of the cost of rebuilding. They ordered that Hooke, Peter Mills and Edward Jerman be asked to view the Exchange and report in writing and in person a week later on the condition of its foundations and what materials remained that could be re-used, and give detailed estimates of the cost of rebuilding upon the old foundations.[43] As experienced City craftsmen, Mills and Jerman could each expect a sizeable private income in the coming years. They were reluctant to become jointly involved in the Royal Exchange either with one another or with Hooke, who was significantly younger and had no experience of working as a building craftsman, in what they could see would be a complicated task. It would also be less rewarding financially in comparison with the fees they, particularly Jerman, could receive as independent consultants to citizens and institutions desperate to rebuild. Moreover the Gresham Trustees had no authority over them. Mills's orders as City Surveyor came from the City's Court of Common Council and Court of Aldermen, and Jerman at this time was independent of the City, and by keeping his distance from all activities the City had offered him was giving every indication that he intended to

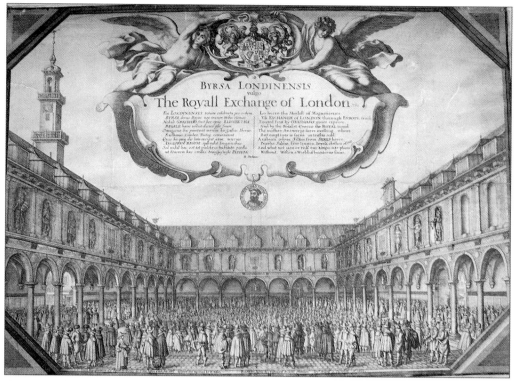

42. Wenceslaus Hollar's 1644 engraving of the courtyard of the first Royal Exchange. Although damaged in the Great Fire, Hooke found it to be structurally sound and recommended that it should be economically repaired using recycled materials. However, the Gresham Trustees decided to build a much more expensive new Royal Exchange on an enlarged site (Figure 43). (*Guildhall Library, Corporation of London*)

remain so. Thus Mills and Jerman were not prepared to do what the Gresham Trustees had asked. Hooke, on the other hand, held a Gresham appointment and probably thought it was the right thing to do, in his own and the Gresham Trustees' interests. The Trustees were responsible for maintaining income to Gresham College from the Royal Exchange rents and he saw a chance to demonstrate to anyone who might doubt his competence that he understood the methods and materials used in building well enough to be able to estimate costs of construction and assess the workmanship and rates of pay of City craftsmen. Judging that there was some distaste by Mills and Jerman for the work they had been asked to do at the Royal Exchange, the Gresham Trustees gave them another week to prepare their report. At the same time the Trustees

Ordered that Mr. Hooke by himselfe be againe desired to prepare a Draught and an Estimate of the totall Charge of Rebuilding the Exchainge betweene this and Fryday morneing next and that hee bee made acquainted with the Comittees conception of building the pillars with a Kinde of Marble found in the West Countrey of which they Conceive Sir John Frederick can give him an Account both of Stone and price thereof.[44]

When the Gresham Trustees met again on 16 November 1666 Mills and Jerman asked for even more time to prepare their report but Hooke had his ready in writing:

Upon Examining the Foundation of the Royall Exchainge and considering the former structure of itt as well as I canne Recollect itt from my memory, and by the helpe of the partes now standing, I doe finde that by makeing a particular Estimate of the severall thinges to bee done in Order to the Rebuilding of itt anew in the same forme as itt was of heretofore (abateing onely the statues of the Kinges in the Nieches, and the Arched roofe of stone over the walke which I thinke would be better if made a plaistered seeleing whereby all the Crosse irons might be spared) to make the pillars Arches Architrave freez and Cornice, and the Borders of the Nieches and the Fower windowes, of Portland Stone, and to pave the walkes with squared Purbeck stone. That the wholle Charge will amount to betweene Fower and Five Thousand pounds supposeing all the Matterialls weare to bee new bought but the paveing for the most parte seemes good the pedestalls of all the Pillars are very little damnifyed by the Fyre. There are more than halfe Bricks enough to Rebuild it. There is a greate Quantity of Stone which may bee made use of for makeing the Arches. The Pillars and Arches and fronts at both the Entryes are little hurt. And there is a good Quantity of Lead etc. which lying yet confused I cannot soe readily make an Estimate of.[45]

Hooke's report is a remarkable achievement, bearing in mind it was his first attempt to present his findings on the state of a building, propose how it should be rebuilt and estimate how much it would cost. It reveals a knowledge of architecture, building materials, techniques and their costs which would normally have been gained only with experience following a long apprenticeship. Hooke had observed carefully and experimented for the Royal Society on the strengths of different kinds of wood,[46] and tried to find the best way of making bricks. He had also looked at Kettering-stone as a building material with Wren, evidence that their common interests were established before the fire.[47] Such scientific activities illustrate very well the extent to which Hooke had made use of John Wilkins's ideas, which he had come across as a schoolboy at Westminster School and in 'the dark shops' of London's mechanics, about the importance of practical skills. Hooke's unusual abilities are early evidence of the wisdom of the City in nominating him as someone who could come close to matching the King's Commissioner Christopher Wren in intellect and scientific interests. The burgeoning friendship between the two men was recognised by the City as important for good working relations with the king and necessary for the speedy reconstruction of the city's buildings and resumption of its trade and commerce.[48]

Evidence of the close association in Hooke's mind between building a new natural philosophy and building a new city can be seen in his uncompleted *General Scheme* in which he wrote that the method of collecting a philosophical history (his term for a systematic record of observations, questions and opinions about nature)

> shall be as the Repository of Materials, out of which a new and sound Body of Philosophy may be raised. This is to comprize a brief and plain Account of a great Store of choice and significant Natural and Artificial Operations, Actions and Effects, ranged in a convenient Order, and interwoven here and there with some short Hints of Accidental Remarks or Theories, of corresponding or disagreeing received Opinions, of Doubts and Queries and the like, and indeed until this Repository be pretty well stored with choice and sound Materials, the work of raising new Axiomes or Theories is not to be attempted, lest beginning without Materials, the whole Design be given over in the middle, for out of this are to be taken the Foundation Stones, on which the whole structure should be raised, and those ought to be proportioned according to the rest of the Materials; for otherwise there may follow Great Inconveniences, in prosecuting of it, here therefore ought to be laid up the more substantial Parts: But as for the most curious and precious things which may serve for the finishing or compleating this grand Structure, they are to be sought for as occasion shall require and prompt. For as in any great building, none can be so perspicacious as to foresee every particular thing he shall need, for the compleating of it, but leaves the Care of providing them till occasions call for them, as being then best able to judge which of that kind of Material which is wanting will be most fitting for his purpose and so with that proceeds till other occasions call for other Requisites and Helps: And so from time to time furnishes himself with those more choice things, as the Occasions require; so there is none but before he sets upon such a Design, will be sure to provide himself of a sufficient store of such Materials as he knows altogether necessary, nor will he neglect to lay hold of such things, as offering themselves by chance, put him in mind that he shall have occasion for them before he can finish his Design; and certainly much better it were, if the Architect were so skilful as to foresee to provide all kinds of Materials before he begins; for thereby his Work would be carried on the more compleatly and uniformly, without necessity of pulling down, or altering, or piecing, or transforming any part, or staying or interrupting.[49]

This proposal for a philosophical history is firmly based in the material world of building and architecture, both in terms of its language ('Repository of Materials', 'Foundation Stones', 'grand Structure' etc.) and in its intent. Although *A General Scheme* is undated, the above passage shows that when writing it Hooke had in mind his new responsibilities given to him by the City on 31 October 1666 for planning the rebuilding of London.[50] Strong resonances can be detected between his ideas for a philosophical

43. Robert White's 1671 engraving of the second Royal Exchange. Angels on clouds of glory brandish trumpets carrying banners of the City (left) and Mercers' Company (right). (*Guildhall Library, Corporation of London*)

history and his November 1666 report to the Mercers' Company on the materials for rebuilding the Royal Exchange.

Despite Hooke's obvious competence the Gresham Trustees did not welcome his recommendation to make use of many of the former materials for rebuilding the Exchange. They preferred Jerman's ambitious plan to rebuild anew, a task which he performed with extravagant gusto, despite failing health, until his death in November 1668.[51] His responsibilities were then taken over by Edward Cartwright, who had been contracted as Jerman's Master Mason on the project. Cartwright saw the rebuilding through until trading started again in September 1669. Hooke's original estimate of the cost (£4,000–£5,000 or less if, as he recommended, materials from the old Exchange were recycled) was in the end exceeded nearly twelvefold.[52] A magnificent building (Figure 43) had been built quickly, but even allowing for increased costs of land, materials, transportation and workmen in response to demand, the final sum of nearly

£60,000 is astonishing.[53] The continuing burden of servicing the debt taken on to pay its share almost bankrupted the Mercers' Company.[54]

The idea of rebuilding a completely new city gradually faded, along with attempts to make a survey of every site for land registration. A beadle's booth was set up in each ward, where a clerk was ready to record all particulars for registration. Attempts to persuade occupiers to take to their local booths documentary evidence of all the rights and terms of their possessions as well as certified accurate plans and areas of their ground soon failed. People were living away from London, or could not afford to have the ground measured, or had lost their documents in the fire, or were unable to locate their former boundary under the rubble. Fewer than 10 per cent of more than a thousand residents in one ward registered their interests. There is no identifiable point at which a formal decision to abandon the plan to rebuild London on a completely new street pattern was made. It is almost certain that the King's Commissioners (Wren, May and Pratt) and the City's Surveyors (Hooke and Mills) soon saw that the intended survey for land registration was impossible to carry out in a reasonable time and so they persuaded their respective committees to accept a limited amount of piecemeal improvements in place of wholesale rebuilding. They did this despite three of them (Wren, Mills and Hooke) having a personal interest at stake in the form of their own new layout plans. No evidence has been found that any one of the three tried to promote his own scheme against what was becoming accepted as the public interest. In October 1666 the King's Commissioners and the City's surveyors decided on the new widths of certain existing streets, a plan they presented to a joint session of the Privy and Common Councils' sub-committees for rebuilding. The agreed new street widths were approved by the Lord Chancellor on 31 October 1666 and defined by royal proclamation.[55]

During the winter of 1666/7 the Privy Council and the City, with their advisors the commissioners and surveyors, prepared details for the Rebuilding Act. That winter was particularly cold in January and again in March. Journeys to and fro across the bleak snow-covered landscape of ruined London between Gresham College in the north-east of the city and Westminster were commonplace for the City's Aldermen and Surveyors as they hastened to agree with the Privy Council. Recognition by the King's Commissioners and the City's Surveyors of the need to rebuild mainly on the old foundations was confirmed, again by implication, when the City's Court of Common Council on 30 November 1666 made a list of twenty-three items, or 'Heads thought requisite to be inserted into the Act for rebuilding'. They specified, among other things, materials, the sorts of buildings allowed, responsibilities for party walls, raising of wharves, paving, balconies, drainage, sewers, conduits, scantlings and rules for building and arching of cellars. Hooke had played a significant part in drafting these specifications and would spend the next few years seeing that they were complied with.[56]

Plans for a completely new city on new foundations were not included, nor was a survey of the existing foundations. In December 1666 the City began to clear away

44. Part of John Leake's 1666 compilation of plots of six areas of the ruined city surveyed by himself, John Jennings, William Marr, William Leybourne, Thomas Streete and Richard Shortgrave. Some pre-fire street and lane widths are written in red. (*Add. MS 5415.E1: British Library*)

rubbish from the streets, but it was done not with the intention of surveying the old foundations for the proposed register of land but to ease movement around the city and expose the old streets so they could be surveyed and a map drawn up to assist in planning the rebuilding largely on the old foundations. The clearance work was carried out by contractors under the supervision of Edward Tasker, Keeper of the City's Greenyard.[57] The cost was £103 15s 4d, £100 of which was paid by the king.[58] Six competent land surveyors (John Leake, John Jennings, William Marr, William Leybourne, Thomas Streete and Richard Shortgrave)[59] working under Hooke's supervision quickly made a survey of the burnt area of the city. Each surveyor was responsible for plotting his work on a map sheet. John Leake compiled a manuscript map from the six separate sheets in December 1666. This map (Figure 44) was very different from the one intended to show the boundaries of all existing land parcels for land registration purposes. Although given the title 'An Exact Surveigh' by Leake, the plan shows only simplified street alignments.

This is to be expected, given the speed with which the map had to be made and the general planning purposes for which it was needed. A new waterfront is roughly indicated by a colour wash. Some other proposals for rebuilding are lightly drawn in. It has the appearance of a working copy that was used in the months following the fire when discussions about rebuilding were taking place.[60]

It was essential that legislation be passed by Parliament in time for rebuilding to start as soon as winter gave way to spring. Neither the City nor the king could delay once the weather changed for the better. The City's Court of Common Council ordered its sub-committee for rebuilding 'doe meete weekely on Mundays Wednesday & Fridays at Eight of the Clock in the Fore noone and shall be constantly warned by Ticketts and attended by the Officers thereunto appointed'.[61] These meetings were in addition to joint meetings with the Privy Council's rebuilding sub-committee at Westminster, and others where members of the City's Court of Common Council and Court of Aldermen met formally and informally for debate and argument in the crowded passageways, rooms and courtyards of Gresham College.

The sequence of meetings, questions and messages between the Privy Council and the City continued in January. The contents of a parliamentary bill for governing the rebuilding were hastily agreed and assembled into a draft acceptable to the king and the City. Many of the proposed improvements were responses to long-held views about the defects of the old city, some of which had been included in the act of 1662,[62] but with little consequence. The severe criticisms of the condition of the old city by John Evelyn, one of the leading members of the Royal Society, in his 1661 publication *Fumifugium* were influential in the drafting of the new bill, but there was no time to agree on how many of the defects he had described (such as the intermixture of manufacturing and residential properties and the way in which waste products were freely dispersed in and over the city) should be rectified by the act, but they were taken account of during rebuilding when specific complaints arose. Other suggestions made by Evelyn, such as paved streets and replacing spouting gutters with down-pipes for disposing of rainwater from roofs, were incorporated into the act. The City had to spend much of its time deciding how to legislate for producing and regulating the prices of the enormous amounts of material (stone, bricks, lime and timber) and personnel (craftsmen and labourers) which would be needed by a variety of interests – individual citizens, institutions such as livery companies and hospitals, parish churches, St Paul's Cathedral and the City's own buildings such as Guildhall, gateways, gaols and the Royal Exchange.

The City's twenty-three 'Heads thought requisite to be inserted into the Act for rebuilding' were modified more by addition than reduction in the weeks before the first Rebuilding Act was passed by Parliament and received the royal assent on 8 February 1667.[63] There had been a continuous rush to agreement, first within the City, then between the City and the Lord Chancellor as head of the Privy Council's Rebuilding Committee, then within the House of Commons and finally within the House of Lords.

Delays and obstructions occurred, but were overcome by the cooperative effort of many men loyal to the interests of London and its citizens. The King's Commissioners and the City's Surveyors were in almost continuous attendance at the meetings of sub-committees and Parliament to advise and answer queries. London's Common Councilmen and their advisers argued their case and compromised when necessary. Members of the Royal Society with influence at court or in Parliament, including John Evelyn and Samuel Pepys (who had been admitted to membership two years previously), urged agreement on the main clauses in the bill. The king showed his concern for the citizens' welfare by delaying the prorogation of Parliament until the bill had been passed.

Another bill, relating to the laws of property ownership rather than to the form and content of property, which were addressed by the Rebuilding Act, was passed in January 1667.[64] The responsibility for bearing the cost of rebuilding each individual house had to be determined each time a dispute arose. Landlords, tenants and sub-tenants all had an interest in rebuilding, but disputes over who should pay had to be settled quickly and with equity. Repairs were normally the responsibility of the tenant, but rebuilding was not the same as repairing, especially when legislation required expensive brick or stone to be used to replace timber, lath and plaster. The act made provision for a Fire Court specifically to settle disputes between landlords and tenants as to rebuilding. At least three judges drawn from the King's Bench, Common Pleas and Exchequer Courts adjudicated in each case. No appeal was allowed, except to a larger Fire Court than the one which made the decision being contested. The bill proved very difficult to draft and the resultant act was prolonged three times, as wholly beneficial to the rebuilding programme. As Reddaway has said, 'Thanks to the Judges who conducted [the Fire Court] it became the most valuable of the means given to the City by Parliament to help on the rebuilding.'[65] One of the reasons for its success was that the drafting of the bill which led to the Fire Court was largely the work of the men who had the responsibility for making the court judgments.

The first Rebuilding Act left many details to be sorted out by the City and the king and by a second Rebuilding Act of 1670.[66] It was, however, complete enough to allow rebuilding to take place as soon as the spring weather arrived. It provided a clear but broad set of rules, although it was left to the City Surveyors (Peter Mills and Hooke, to begin with, Edward Jerman was elsewhere) to make decisions on the ground when disputes arose during and after the rebuilding, whether between the City and a citizen or between citizens. Although Peter Mills and Hooke had to make many hundreds of such decisions in the next decade,[67] their close involvement in the long process of drawing up the provisions of the act qualified them beyond all others in the city to undertake that onerous task speedily and effectively. Their participation in the drafting of the legislation they would later enforce was similar to the way the judges prepared the legislation they later enforced in the Fire Court to such good effect.

11

TO THE BEST OF MY SKILL, KNOWLEDGE AND POWER

Hooke and Mills now had what they needed to begin their important task of surveying and supervising the building of the new city. The Rebuilding Act of 1667 was the legal framework within which the City Surveyors would begin work. The overall intention of the act was to build a city more regulated, uniform and graceful than its predecessor and much less liable to suffer from 'great and outrageous fires'. Rebuilding for habitation was banned, unless it conformed to the rules and orders of building prescribed by the act. Anybody putting up an irregular building would be 'committed to the common gaol till he shall have abated or demolished the same'. In order to prevent irregular building the act required the City to elect 'one or more discreet and intelligent person or persons knowledgeable in the art of building to be the surveyors or supervisors to see the said rules and scantlings duly observed'. Before any private rebuilding could begin, the surveyors were required to stake out, measure and certify the foundations. Only four sorts of new building were allowed to be built for habitation: the first were the smallest, those fronting 'by-lanes'; the second were those fronting 'streets and lanes of note'; the third those fronting 'high and principal streets'. The roofs of each of the first three sorts had to be uniform. The fourth and largest sort were 'mansion houses for citizens or other persons of extraordinary quality not fronting the three former ways'. For each of the first three sorts of building, the number and heights of storeys (including cellar and garret) and the scantlings were specified.[1] Only the scantlings were specified for the fourth sort of building, but no more than four storeys were allowed. The rest of the design was left to the good taste and wisdom of the owner and architect, who would know that everyone else of taste and influence would be keeping a watchful eye on what they were up to. However, to avoid extravagantly dominant buildings the City later decided to produce some design guidelines for houses of the fourth sort. The exterior of all classes of buildings had to be made of brick or stone, except for timber breastsummers,[2] which had to be made of oak. Walls had to be entire and built up vertically from the ground. Party walls had to be set out equally on each party's ground. The neighbour who built the party wall first ('the first beginner') was ordered to leave 'convenient toothing' in the wall 'for the better joining of the next house'. When the second party was ready to build, they had to pay half the cost of the party wall to the first builder, plus interest at 6 per cent. This regulation was an important factor in allowing the rebuilding to take place speedily as it meant the first party could start work before his neighbour was ready. The act specified that all houses of the third sort 'shall have balconies 4 foot broad with rails and bars of iron' and that rainwater falling from their roofs 'be conveyed into channels by pipes on the sides and fronts of houses'. No jetties, windows or 'anything of the like sort' were allowed to extend beyond the ancient foundation line of any house (except for temporary stall boards set against an open shop window).

The Lord Mayor was required by the act to 'define and declare' by 1 April 1667 at the latest which and how many streets 'shall hereafter be deemed' by-lanes, streets or lanes of note, or high and principal streets. All the streets to be rebuilt had to be marked and staked out so that 'they shall be better known and observed'. The penalty for moving or removing a surveyor's stake was three months' imprisonment or a fine of £10, or, if the offence was committed 'by a person of low and mean condition', he was to be whipped in public close to the place where he committed the offence 'till his body be bloody'. Other penalties were physically less severe. If any person who formerly had a house (or houses) which was burnt or pulled down had not within three years rebuilt on the same ground, then the Lord Mayor was required to give notice for the building to be completed within nine months. If the owner still refused or neglected to rebuild, the Lord Mayor was empowered to sell the property. In order to encourage the citizens to rebuild quickly without undue expense, two judges of the King's Bench were to be appointed who could set the prices of materials such as bricks, tiles and mortar. To avoid a chronic shortage of craftsmen and labourers, and immoderate wage rates, men from outside London who were not freemen of the city were permitted to work for seven years (or as long as the rebuilding lasted) and enjoy the same privileges as freemen.

Some regulations devolved the settlement of disputes to the aldermen of the wards where the buildings were situated. Differences or disputes arising over the stopping up of lights, windows, watercourses, gutters and so on were to be settled locally in this way. Other regulations removed the authority from the ward aldermen and placed it in the hands of the City. The number and places for all common sewers, drains and vaults and the manner of paving and pitching the streets and lanes would now be designed and set out by persons appointed by the Lord Mayor. Provision was made for those trades and occupations judged noisome or perilous in respect of fire to be prohibited in the high and principal streets, and for conduits now standing there to be removed and erected in other public places.

The act empowered and required the Lord Mayor to enlarge specific streets, including: Fleet Street; the street from the east end of St Paul's Cathedral into Cheapside; from Cheapside into Poultry; from Poultry to the west end of Cornhill; Blowbladder Street; Newgate Street (where the shambles lately stood); Ave Marie Lane; from St Martin's le

Grand to Blowbladder Street; from St Magnus Church to Gracechurch Street; the north end of Gracechurch Street; Thames Street; and Old Fish Street. He was also empowered to enlarge any other street or narrow passage less than 14 feet in breadth and was required to open and enlarge several streets leading down to the Thames for the convenience of trade and the better passage of carts to and from the river. In order to prevent inundation at spring tides and to make the ascent from the Thames easier for traffic, the act ordered that Thames Street and all the ground south of it to the river be raised by at least 3 feet above the existing ground levels. No buildings were allowed to be constructed within a distance of 40 feet from the Thames between the Tower and Temple Stairs. Buildings were also prohibited within a distance of 40 feet from the middle of the Fleet River, on either side, between the Thames and Clerkenwell before 24 March 1668.

So that the Lord Mayor could perform and accomplish the work ordered by the act, all coal brought into London sold by the chaldron[3] or tun would be taxed at a rate of twelve pence (one shilling) for every tun and the revenue paid to the mayor. The money raised was to be used in the first place 'for the satisfaction of such persons whose grounds be taken for the enlarging of the streets and for the making of wharves and quays on the North side of the Thames, on each side of the sewer called Fleet ditch and also for the building of prisons in the City', and books had to be 'kept in the Chamber of London . . . in which all monies thereupon received shall be set down'. The second day of September was designated to be observed for ever as a day of public fasting and humiliation within the City and Liberties of London 'to implore the mercies of Almighty God upon the said City to divert the like calamity for the time to come'. Another form of memorial was specified, 'The better to preserve the memory of this dreadful visitation': a column or pillar would be erected on or as near the place where the 'said Fire so unhappily began, as conveniently be made in perpetual remembrance thereof'.[4]

The act left the City with much to do, but its officials were given a lot of freedom to decide what to do and how to accomplish it. On 25 February Sir John Lawrence was appointed to lead a City committee, with the surveyors in attendance, to meet with the king's representatives to discuss and seek approval of the City's decisions on the enlargement of the streets.[5] Over the next two days they listed the streets under the three classifications defined by the act and decided on eight different widths ranging from 60 to 14 feet, the latter width being the minimum for straight lanes and passageways. They drew up the design guidelines of buildings, with courtyards to the rear, which would be acceptable as 'buildings of the fourth sort' to front the Thames and the new Fleet Canal. In order to improve water flow along the Fleet River, new levels for Fleet Bridge and the surrounding ground were defined. If approval were given, Sir John was to order the streets to be staked out.[6] The meeting took place at Berkshire House[7] on 13 March 1667:

His Majesty haveing heard the two Acts of the Comon Councell read distinctly to him, of the 26th and 27th of February last, the Map[8] of the Citty lying before him, his

Majesty lookeing upon the lines drawne out in the said Map according to the Orders
mentioned & deliberating & discoursing much thereupon; his Majesty doth fully
approve & commend all the Particulars mentioned in the said Orders with these
Animadversions upon some of them.[9]

Responses to the animadversions, or critical comments, by the king were not all feasible
under the Act of Parliament, but the City did what it could to meet them. The king wanted
the markets to be moved out of the streets, particularly from Newgate, Leadenhall Street
and Cheapside, where they had for centuries blocked the traffic, and relocated on sites
away from the streets. It is surprising that the City had not thought of such an obvious
improvement. Some of the king's other animadversions which were feasible under the
parliamentary Rebuilding Act, such as the additional widening of some streets, the
addition of Lombard Street to the list of high streets and the very practicable idea to use
rubble from old St Paul's to raise the approach to the Bridge so that the first arch could be
raised by three feet, giving greater clearance for river traffic, were incorporated into the
City's Act of Common Council dated 29 April 1667,[10] which was confirmed by the Lord's
Committee on 8 May 1667.[11] The king also appointed his commissioners Hugh May, Roger
Pratt and Wren to be ready at all times to assist the City and its surveyors.

The City's act gave the surveyors the heavy responsibility for enabling, directing and
controlling the rebuilding. The mass of recommendations, decisions, orders, directions
and acts arising from countless formal and informal meetings between representatives of
the City, the king, Parliament and their official and unofficial advisers finally devolved to
Peter Mills and Hooke (later to Hooke and John Oliver). As the City Surveyors of New
Buildings it was now their joint responsibility to see that rebuilding on the ground, face-
to-face with the citizens whose livelihoods were at stake, was done according to the
Rebuilding Act. Peter Mills was an old City hand, but Hooke had only recently (at the
Royal Exchange) had any experience of the sort of work he would now be required to do
almost every day for the next seven years, his Royal Society, Gresham and Cutlerian
duties notwithstanding.

The City's confidence and trust in Hooke during the hectic months between its
approval in September 1666 of his plan for rebuilding and the publication of the Act of
Common Council in April 1667 is remarkable. A man with as yet no formal connection
with the City (except indirectly through his appointment as Gresham Professor of
Geometry) was trusted effectively to determine on the City's behalf important technical
matters relating to the rebuilding of the city and to take charge of surveys for a new
map of the existing streets. On the other hand Hooke trusted the City to treat him fairly
in matters of remuneration. Although Mills and Jerman, who had already held City
appointments for many years, were formally involved in the City's activities during the
winter of 1666/7, Mills's uncertain health and Jerman's indifference to the City's
requests (other than in connection with the Royal Exchange) indicate that Hooke played

the major role for the City, despite holding no office. This state of affairs was finally rectified at a Court of Common Council on 13 March 1667 when, in accordance with the requirement in the Rebuilding Act for the City to appoint 'one or more discreet and intelligent person or persons knowledgeable in the art of building to be the surveyors or supervisors to see the said rules and scantlings duly observed' the Court of Common Council decided that

> Mr Peter Mills Mr Edward Jarman Mr Robert Hooke & Mr John Oliver are chosen to be surveyors & supervisors of the houses to be new built in this Citty & destroyed by the late fire according to the late Act of Parliament in that behalfe
>
> And it is ordered that the said surveyors doe forthwith proceed to the stakeing out the streets as is ordered & directed by this Court in pursuance of the said Act
>
> The Aldermen Deputies & Common Councell men of the severall wards of this Citty destroyed by the late fire are desired to be present in their severall wards at the stakeing out of the streetes.[12]

At a meeting of the Court of Aldermen on the following day only Mills and Hooke were sworn in as City Surveyors. Jerman was absent, as usual. When the City had earlier proposed an appointment to the glazier John Oliver (*c.* 1616–1701) he asked to be excused but offered to assist the ailing Peter Mills gratis, which the City readily accepted.[13] Following the death of Peter Mills in 1670 Oliver and Hooke shared the duties of City Surveyor. Oliver went on to become Master Mason to the Crown and succeeded Edward Woodroffe as assistant surveyor to St Paul's Cathedral.[14] Hooke, who received no similar offer of assistance from Oliver, took his full burden with no apparent objection:

> This day Robert Hooke Master of Arts and Mr Peter Mills two of the Surveyors elected by Common Councell in pursuance of the Late Act of Parliament for rebuilding for the purposes in the same Act mentioned and declared, were here sworne for the due Execution of the said place in form following viz:
>
> You shall sweare that you shall well and duly see that the Rules and Scantlings sett downe and prescribed in an Act of this present Parliament for building within the Citty of London and Libertyes thereof bee well and truly observed And that in all other things you shall truly and Impartially Execute the place or office of Surveyor or Supervisor within the said Citty and Libertyes as by the same Act of Parliament is directed and intended according to the best of your skill knowledge and Power Soe helpe you God.[15]

Six days after the swearing-in, the City sealed an instrument authorising Mills and Hooke to stake out the streets.[16] Hooke mentioned in passing to the Royal Society at its meeting on the following day that because the air had been for a good while so thick about London he had not been able to see the new star 'in collo Ceti' or the other 'in Cingulo Andromedae', a typical example of his incessant interest in and observation of all things around him, whether amid the rubble on the streets or in the heavens.[17]

On 27 March 1667 Hooke and Mills began staking out the streets, starting with Fleet Street. Peter Mills wrote in his survey book: 'Wee began to stake out the streets in Fleet street the 27th of March 1667.'[18] An account[19] written by the City's Clerk of Works lists expenses incurred in the week ending 30 March 1667. It shows that workmen were paid for each of the seven days and that six carpenters and seven labourers used 1,220 feet of timber for stakes. In subsequent weeks a carter was engaged to carry the timber around the City. The major part of staking out the streets was completed in about nine weeks, but work continued intermittently for the next few years as the Court of Aldermen continued to implement the City's orders and responded to specific requests from individuals, groups of neighbours and corporate bodies, provided the work was within the act.[20]

A very rough estimate of the total length of the streets staked out by Mills and Hooke in the nine weeks beginning 27 March 1666 can be made from the records of the Clerk of Works for that period.[21] They show a weekly average of 670 feet of timber used for stakes, equivalent to about 6,000 feet over nine weeks. If the stakes were each 5 feet long and they were set out along both sides of the streets, on average every 100 feet apart, there would have been enough stakes for a little over 11 miles of streets. We do not know the procedure used by Mills and Hooke to stake out the streets, nor what apparatus or instruments they used, but two clues have been found which hint at how the work was done.

Among the Clerk of Works' accounts is the item '1 whole deale used for sights' at a cost of 1s 6d.[22] The cost of timber used for the stakes was only 2d per foot, so the item is clearly a superior piece of timber, probably planed all round, which was used for sighting along and across the streets to align the stakes. Despite Hooke's genius at designing optical instruments, he would not have bothered to devise a telescopic sight for the purpose of staking out streets: open fore and back sights would serve the purpose well enough. The second piece of evidence is in the record of the Royal Society's meetings around the same time which were held in Arundel House, a collection of buildings on the south side of the Strand, with gardens down to the Thames. The Society had transferred its meetings there on 9 January 1667 at the invitation of its owner Henry Howard, later the 6th Duke of Norfolk, to make more space in Gresham College for the use of the City. In April and May 1667 Hooke was experimenting and reporting on different ways of making bricks and designing a geometric curve which the string of a conical pendulum could wrap itself round as the bob rotated and so keep more regular time. Then, at the meeting on 25 April 1667:[23]

Mr. Hooke produced a level, almost the same as that of the French, of which an account had been lately published in the 'Journal' des Scavans. He was ordered to give a scheme and description of it in writing.

He proposed a way of measuring the circumference of the earth with a twelve foot glass and three stakes to be practised in St. James's Park in a calm day. It was ordered to be put in execution as soon as might be.[24]

This is strong evidence that when Hooke was staking out the streets, aligning the stakes through a wooden sighting device, he realised that, because the Earth is not flat but more or less spherical, when looking through a horizontal sight at a stake a hundred feet away, the downward curvature of the Earth's surface would mean the stake would appear to be very slightly lower (about 1mm over a distance of a little over 100m) than it would be if the Earth were flat. If this apparent decrease in height could be measured (it would require a telescopic sight which could be accurately set horizontal, and three stakes at different separations would give a more accurate result than two) the Earth's radius could be simply calculated using the geometry of the circle. Hooke knew that refraction of the line of sight through the atmosphere would have a significant effect on his observations, and would have to be allowed for in some way. Characteristically he made many attempts to understand atmospheric refraction in order to make more accurate measurements. His earliest published account of his work on the refraction of light rays by air and other media is in *Micrographia* (see Figure 11).[25]

The staking out of the streets was the first major action taken by the City under the Rebuilding Act, so they were alert to a deluge of objections and appeals from individuals, neighbourhoods and even parishes. Once the stakes were in place, it was obvious to all where the most ground had been lost and which amenities were being taken away. When Pepys saw the staked lines he recorded 'if ever it be built in that form, with so fair streets, it will be a noble sight'.[26] One source of grievance arose when owners on one side of a street being widened thought that more ground had been taken from them than from the owners on the opposite side. Anyone having a grievance could appeal to the City and even to the king in Council. The City had its procedures for dealing with the many complaints and petitions that were made, but they were time-consuming and required much attention from the aldermen, deputies and councilmen who were unpaid for their pains and had their own livelihoods to look after. The surveyors, too, were fully engaged in the procedures to deal with complaints and petitions. They were frequently called upon by the aldermen and deputies to accompany them on their investigations at the places where the complaints arose, there to advise them on technical matters and recommend what action should be taken to settle the disputes. The City had no money to pay compensation except for the specific loss of ground defined by the Acts. They had to negotiate, arbitrate, compromise and even amend their former decisions in the face of the many objections. But they had no absolute power to enforce their decisions: if their rulings were not acceptable to the plaintiffs, then the grievances would be taken to the courts or to the king in Council. The City's actions would then be subject to direct external influence on matters which its officials, as the traditional internal rulers of

London, had been responsible for. The new circumstances were hard to accept, but Parliament had no intention of intervening in the matter, and the king, although generally sympathetic to the City's problems, could only encourage it in its endeavours. The repertories and journals of the City covering the months following the staking out of the streets record many complaints and petitions arising from the consequences. For instance, when neighbours who objected to their street being widened on the grounds that it would attract much more traffic than before the fire and petitioned for it to be made narrow again, the City agreed.[27]

Two petitions, typical of many which Hooke had to investigate and report on, relate to the widening to 20 feet of Water Lane, leading south out of Tower Street to Thames Street and beyond, to meet the Thames at the western end of the Custom House. Water Lane was in the eastern part of the City where Hooke did most of his surveying at this time, Mills dealing generally with surveys in the west. The first petition, which came before the Court of Aldermen on 14 May 1667, was by William Wheatley, grocer. It showed

> that before the Fire hee had the Inheritance of severall houses on the East side of Water lane whereof 7 foote of ground by the Length of 180 foote is staked out for enlargement of the passage, which renders the remainder unfitt for building; And that the staking out of more ground on the West side the said Lane will make the said passage more uniforme and the prospect better to the Thames, and sufficient ground left for the Owners to build upon It is thought fitt and ordered by this Court that a review bee taken by the Surveyors of the premises, and consideration had of altering the same to the petitioners accommodation if the matter appear to be as is reported in his said petition.[28]

Hooke would have visited Wheatley's property and decided on his recommendations to the City, probably on 17 May 1667 when he went to stake out the northen section of Water Lane to a width of 20 feet in accordance with the order of the Court of Aldermen the previous day.[29] Wheatley's property was in the southern section of Water Lane which Hooke had staked out earlier. No record has been found to show whether or not Wheatley succeeded in his petition. If he had failed, we would expect to find a record of payment of compensation for loss of his ground, but none has been found. In Ogilby and Morgan's map of the rebuilt city,[30] Water Lane is shown to be about 13 feet wide, certainly closer to 10 feet than to 20 feet, which suggests that Wheatley regained his ground after Hooke's visit.[31] Other evidence confirms this conclusion. After Hooke had staked out the northern section of Water Lane on Friday 17 May 1667, Robert Wakelyn, citizen and ironmonger, was moved to petition the Court of Aldermen four days later.[32] As with Wheatley's petition, no evidence of the City's decision for or against Wakelyn has been found, but when on 20 July 1670 Hooke measured and certified the area of ground lost by Wakelyn from his group of three properties at the north-east corner of the junction between Thames Street and Water Lane (which Hooke himself had staked out on 23 July 1667)[33] he accounted only for the ground taken away for widening Thames Street,[34] which seems to confirm that Wakelyn, like Wheatley, had lost no ground on the east side of Water Lane.

The City hastened to devise a procedure for rebuilding private houses in time for work to begin as soon as most of the important new street alignments had been staked out. When disputes arose over who was responsible for rebuilding a particular property, the matter was decided by the Fire Courts. Two hundred copies of the Act of Common Council dated 29 April 1667[35] were printed by James Flesher, the City's Printer,[36] to advertise the procedure to be followed by each builder.[37] The sum of 6*s* 8*d* for each foundation was paid by the builder into the City Chamber. The builder's name, number of foundations and their locations were entered into the Chamberlain's day books (Figure 45).[38] The builder was then given a receipt for the money paid to the Chamber and told the name of the surveyor responsible for certifying foundations in that area. The builder and the surveyor then negotiated and agreed the surveyor's fee for his work and arranged a date and time when they could meet at the site. The builder had to remove all rubbish from the area to reveal what was left, if anything, of the old foundations.

When the surveyor arrived at his client's site, he first tried to locate the old foundations by examining the ground. If the evidence of where they had been was unclear, he sought the opinions of his client, neighbours and other residents of the parish. Sometimes he examined old deeds to see if they contained any record of the dimensions of the property. After taking all the evidence presented to him (making a return visit if additional written evidence could be produced) and satisfying himself that the foundations had been located, the surveyor staked out the building lines, party walls and piers, allowing for the effects of any street widening, and measured the lengths of the boundary lines. He recorded in his survey book information such as the date, client's name, location and dimensions of the site, number of foundations, names of neighbours and sometimes a sketch. Soon afterwards he wrote a certificate from information recorded in his survey book, and handed it to the client, who then paid his fee in cash. Only then could rebuilding on the site begin. The City had no plan for the rebuilding of private houses to take place in any particular sequence, since that would have been impossible to implement. Instead, the surveyors were free to respond as quickly as they could to the requests for staking out and certifying foundations as soon as they were recorded in the Chamberlain's day books.

With his satchel containing measuring rods, chalk, survey books and writing materials, Hooke must have been a familiar sight in the years after the fire as he stood amid the ruins, surrounded by a small group of neighbours and passers-by, some interested in just watching and listening, others with evidence or opinions to offer. His surveying was performed on a public stage, his measurements and staking out determined by justice and fairness. Disagreements were settled by the surveyor there and then on the basis of evidence clear to all, subject always to approval by the Court of Aldermen. The buildings

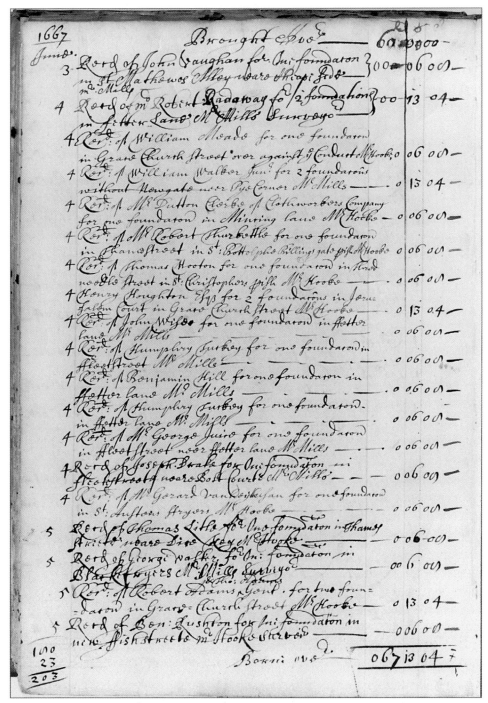

45. A folio from the Chamberlain's day book used for recording payments of 6s 8d to the City for each foundation survey and certificate. A clerk usually recorded the name of the surveyor for each survey. The number of foundations and the money paid are carried forward from one folio to the next. (*ex-Guildhall Library MS 275 f. 4v: Corporation of London Records Office*)

where citizens lived were also the places where they made their living. After six months with only temporary homes and sheds for their livelihoods, most were desperate to rebuild quickly. Mills and Hooke could not keep pace with the rate at which payments were coming into the Chamber, and inevitably delays of one or two months built up. The backlog became worse at the end of July 1667 when Mills fell ill for a few weeks. Oliver then helped Hooke with the onerous task,[39] but either Oliver or the City delayed a formal appointment until 28 January 1668, when Oliver was sworn in as the third City Surveyor.[40] Mills, Hooke and Oliver then shared the work which the City had intended to be undertaken by four surveyors, but Mills's health was failing. He carried out his last survey on 19 July 1670[41] and died within the next three months.[42] He was not replaced. Thereafter Hooke and Oliver together shared the duties of City Surveyor. Hooke was the only City Surveyor who worked throughout the whole of the rebuilding period, but the magnitude of his contribution has not been recognised. He himself was partly responsible for this neglect, particularly in relation to his foundation surveys.

The Chamberlain's day books are an orderly and continuous record of the progress of private house rebuilding over three decades. The first entry is dated 13 May 1667, when Mills was nominated to certify the foundation; the last was allocated to Hooke on 28 July 1696, but 95 per cent of the foundations had been staked out and certified by the end of 1671. The day books show that 8,394 foundations were staked out and that £2,798 was paid to the City for the surveyors' services. This money is often referred to in the City's records as 'The Foundation Cash'. It was used to pay the salaries of the surveyors and some other costs arising from the rebuilding, such as Counsels' fees. It has been generally thought that Mills and Oliver staked out most of the foundations, but recent evidence has been brought to light which shows that Hooke staked out more foundations than either of them. We know about the foundations staked out by Mills and Oliver from the records they made in their survey books which they handed in to the City. Although these twenty manuscript books are now lost, they were transcribed in the eighteenth century into four volumes, which have been published in facsimile, with an introduction and index.[43]

There is no evidence that Hooke handed in his survey books to the City, despite being ordered to do so, as the following diary entry shows: 'with committee of City Lands all the afternoon till almost 7 at night, they enquired concerning my books and concerning Certificatts, would have my books Deliverd'.[44] Hooke's survey books too are now lost, but we do not have transcriptions of their contents as we do for Mills's and Oliver's. It is not difficult to find a reasonable explanation for Hooke's refusal to hand in his survey books to the City. We have already seen how he was thinking about his science when he was staking out the streets, so it is likely that he made notes in his survey books that were not solely related to his surveying duties. He carried his books with him when he was out and about in London from around 1667 to 1672, by which time most of the staking out of streets and foundations was finished. Although he used the books on site for recording measurements and other surveying details, he also used them when he was in the city coffee houses and inns, writing out certificates for citizens and his reports to the City. It would have been convenient to write notes in the survey books about the fees he received, ideas for experiments or new apparatus and other *aides-mémoire* relating to the weather or to the many incidents, conversations and people he came across during his hours away from Gresham College. If the contents of his survey books went beyond the records of his surveying and included also some scientific ideas or sketches, or matters of a more personal nature, it would explain why he was very reluctant to hand them to the City. Some evidence to support this explanation comes from the fact that he began his diary as a memorandum book at around the time he ceased to have his survey books regularly to hand. Staking out streets and foundations had decreased in frequency and intensity by that time.

Even though Hooke's survey books are lost,[45] we know from other evidence that they were an orderly and efficient record of his surveying. From time to time he was called upon by a client to issue a duplicate certificate to replace one he had written many years earlier but which the client had lost. Hooke was able to meet these requests because of the highly organised and thorough way in which he had kept all his surveying records over many years. When writing a duplicate certificate he was always able to find in his books not only the values of his measurements, but also neighbours' names and the locations of their property relative to his client's ground.

Despite the lack of evidence in his own hand of how many foundation certificates he issued, it has been possible to compile evidence from other sources of what he did and to make a reasonable estimate of the number of foundations he set out and certified. His diary gives very little indication of the magnitude of this work because entries do not begin until 1672, by which time more than 95 per cent of the foundation surveys had been completed. The Chamberlain's day books do not give a surveyor's name for each foundation, but more than 1,582 of the 8,394 are definitely allocated to Hooke. Of the rest, nearly 4,000 are unallocated to any surveyor, but it has been estimated that Hooke staked out more than 1,400 of these. For example, on 8 February 1673 John Oliver and Joseph Anis paid in £1 to the Chamber for their three foundation surveys at Fleet Bridge.[46] Hooke noted in his diary for 27 March 1673 'set out Oliver and Anis'.[47] From many such similar examples it has been shown that Hooke staked out, measured and certified about 3,000 foundations.[48]

For six or seven years after the fire Hooke spent most of his mornings working as City Surveyor. This period was the busiest time of his life, and it was lucrative. At the start he was mostly engaged on foundation surveys. From a study of the transcriptions of Mills's and Oliver's survey books, thirty minutes seems a reasonable average time for staking out, measuring the boundary perimeter lengths and recording all the details of the measurements, location of the site and neighbouring properties. Time spent in locating the old foundations, listening to witnesses, examining deeds, clearing lines for measurement (which was not always done before the surveyor arrived), travelling from one site to another and writing a foundation certificate can only be guessed at – say another thirty minutes. So time spent on a single foundation was about an hour, possibly less. Time spent on multiple contiguous foundations was not in direct proportion to the time spent on a single foundation. For contiguous foundations only one certificate was usually issued, giving measurements of the perimeter of all foundations staked out, not of each foundation separately. During the months of March, April and May 1669 Hooke's share of the foundation surveys was about ninety each month, not counting any backlog. By working six days a week, he would have spent at least three hours each day on foundation surveys alone.[49]

Salaries were paid to the City Surveyors from the Foundation Cash. Initially £100 *per annum*, beginning at Michaelmas 1666, they were increased to £150 from Lady Day 1667 and paid regularly each quarter until Christmas 1673, at which time payments to the City for foundation surveys had almost ceased. In all, Hooke received £1062 10s from the City in salary, but after 1673 he was paid occasional gratuities for specific services. In addition to receiving a salary, the surveyors were paid negotiable fees from citizens for their services. The amount Hooke received in fees for his foundation certificates has been assessed from evidence in his diary. When Abraham Jaggard paid 6s 8d to the Chamberlain on 8 September 1673 for a foundation certificate of his property in Pudding Lane,[50] he arranged for Hooke to stake out and certify the foundation eight days later and paid him a fee of £1.[51] Samuel Defisher paid Hooke a guinea (£1 1s) on 22 November 1672 to stake out and certify his foundation in Newgate Street for which he had paid 6s 8d to the Chamberlain a week earlier.[52] These two examples suggest that the usual fee for a foundation certificate was about one pound, but sometimes it was ten shillings or less. The size of the fee does not seem to be related to the number of foundations certified at one time. If the average fee for Hooke's 3,000 foundations was ten shillings, then he would have received about £1,500 in fees for this service alone, most of it in the years 1667–72. This was a high income when about £80 would be adequate for an educated professional, and one of £300 capable of maintaining a gentleman in the expected degree of luxury.[53]

12

❧⁓❧

CALCULATING THE LOSSES

Legislation was in place for the great rebuilding. Requests for staking out foundations of private houses were coming in faster than the City Surveyors could deal with them, but construction work was going ahead much more slowly. Building materials were in short supply. Bricks, tiles and lime had to be made, stone quarried and timber seasoned. Craftsmen such as bricklayers, carpenters and masons were still relatively few in relation to the demand. Even though non-freemen had been allowed under the Rebuilding Act to work in the city for up to seven years, they had not come in sufficient numbers by the spring of 1667 to ease the shortage. The Fire Court judges were busily engaged in adjudication between owners, lessees and tenants on such matters as who was responsible for the costs of rebuilding, and what rents, if any, were payable for burnt and uninhabitable buildings. People were finding that rebuilding was going to be expensive and difficult. The Fire Court records show just how expensive rebuilding could be. A corner house of the third sort in Lombard Street would cost £900 and one in a prime position in Cornhill, £700. A mansion house, or building of the fourth sort, was expected to cost £3,000.[1]

Rents for accommodation in buildings which had escaped the fire had risen to three or four times their original value. Outside the wall, properties in Bloomsbury and Covent Garden were in particular demand for housing the families and apprentices of tradesmen and craftsmen. A royal warrant was granted for shops to be erected in the grounds of St Bartholomew's Hospital, a move which benefited both the shopkeepers and the Hospital Trustees who received rents from their new tenants. Other traders set up temporary shops in the form of booths or sheds on the sites of their burnt properties, some finding that significant stock stored in their cellars had escaped the fire. The poor found accommodation at first under tarpaulins erected in fields around London, but later moved into nearby villages. In place of their tents at Moorfields some quite substantial accommodation was built.[2] Charitable funds were collected and dispersed through the normal procedures for such relief in wards and parishes.

Gradually, as house foundations were staked out, it became apparent how much or how little ground had been lost. Citizens whose ground was taken away to make space available for general improvements were entitled to compensation for their loss. The City not only had to decide on the amount of compensation and the procedures for paying it, but also had to ensure that the procedures were properly carried out and generally accepted by the citizens. On 22 January 1668 the Committee for Letting the City Lands (commonly called the City Lands Committee) was empowered[3] by the Court of Common Council, according to the Rebuilding Act, to reach agreement on compensation with owners and tenants of ground taken away and used for making new streets or for enlarging old ones, taking into account any melioration of loss. The 1667 and 1670 Rebuilding Acts allowed for compensation for private land taken by the City to be paid from monies raised by the tax on coal (often referred to as 'the Coal Monies' in City documents) levied specifically to pay for rebuilding. The City Lands Committee was also empowered to call on counsel and other assistance, and to pay for such services from the Foundation Cash. The City Surveyors were ordered to attend the City Lands Committee from time to time.[4]

The chain of empowerment was becoming familiar. Beginning with the king and Parliament it passed to the City's Court of Common Council, then to one of its sub-committees and once again ended up literally in the hands of the City Surveyors whose measurements of the dimensions of lost ground, calculation of area and certification of the loss were necessary in each individual case before any compensation was paid. A claimant paid a negotiable fee to one of the surveyors for an area certificate. The claimant then took the certificate to the City Lands Committee, where the claim was registered to be heard. At the hearing the Committee treated with the claimant and reached agreement on the rate of compensation (sometimes taking into account melioration of the loss of ground by improvements by the City such as easier access to buildings or a better prospect), always based on the certified area of ground lost. When the City and the claimant agreed on compensation, the claimant was given a signed warrant instructing the Chamberlain to pay the agreed sum at the end of six months from the date of the warrant. This delay was intended to allow time for any other person who had a lawful interest in the compensation money to lay a claim. Upon receiving the money, a conveyance of the ground to the City was made and the payee was required to indemnify the City against any further claims in relation to the certified ground.

Although Mills and Hooke had staked out the majority of the widened and new streets by the end of May 1667, the City did not start paying for ground taken away until almost a year later, when agreement was reached with Richard Hodilow on a sum of £600 to be paid from the coal monies for the loss of his ground in Cheapside for the making of the new street.[5] However, no record of a surveyor's area certificate or any record of the area of ground taken away has been found, so this settlement is exceptional. Two weeks later, on 18 March 1668, the Court of Common Council repeated its order made on 22 January empowering the City Lands Committee to satisfy claimants for loss of ground, but added that compensation was to be paid by the Chamberlain from the coal monies, thus rectifying an omission from the earlier order.[6] The earliest recorded area certificate is by Mills, dated 4 April 1667.[7] Hooke was occupied in dealing with claims for compensation for nearly twenty years. His earliest recorded area certificate is dated 16 July 1668;[8] his last is dated 11 March 1687.[9]

Each area certificate gives the claimant's name, the location of the site, a statement of the dimensions and aspects of the boundary lines and the area of ground taken away. When the old foundations could be clearly identified and measured, as in the following example (Figure 46), the certificate was straightforward:[10]

> These are to certify that I have admeasurd the ground taken from two foundations as they are now built[11] belonging as I am informd to M^r. Trotman being the 4th. & 5th. foundations from Great east cheap on the west side of fish street hill. and I doe find that there is now layd into the said street of the aforesaid foundation twelve foot and ten inches In depth at the north end, and eleaven foot seaven inches in the middle, and twelve foot and fowr inches at the south end thereof and the whole bredth of ye said houses fronting the street is fowrty foot the superficiall content whereof is fowr hundred eighty and three foot & fowr Inches In testimony wherof I have hereunto set my hand this 14th. Day of November 1670.   Rob: Hooke

```
    40 .
    11 . 7
    23 . 4
    44
    20 .
   483 . 4[12]
```

Hooke's measurements were always made and recorded in feet and inches, and he wrote areas in square feet and fractions of a square foot. However, he did not use the now commonplace decimal fractions (0.5 is five-tenths, $\frac{5}{10}$ or $\frac{1}{2}$). Instead he used twelfths, or duodecimal fractions, where 0.5 means $\frac{5}{12}$ and 0.6 means $\frac{6}{12}$ or $\frac{1}{2}$. Using the calculation above as an example, the area of 483.4ft² means 483$\frac{4}{12}$ft², not 483$\frac{4}{10}$ft² where the fractional part is in the more usual decimal form. One reason for using duodecimal fractions in this way is that it makes the calculation of compensation easier when payment is made in pounds, shillings and pence. Compensation was usually paid at 5s per square foot, which is equivalent to 5d per $\frac{1}{12}$ of a square foot. By expressing an area as a duodecimal fraction, the calculation of compensation for the fractional part is simplified.[13] However, it seems as if the City's clerks who calculated the amount to be paid did not make use of this simple method. Instead they sometimes used a ready-reckoner to find the amount, but more often they calculated it in long-hand at the bottom of the surveyor's certificate.

It might be thought odd that Hooke gives no plan, sketch or other graphical representation of the foundations in this certificate. Unlike the other two surveyors, Mills and Oliver, Hooke rarely chose to do so, relying instead on written information alone. It has been said that his area certificates were therefore less careful and detailed than Oliver's,[14] but it can be argued that Hooke was more scrupulous in not including a plan

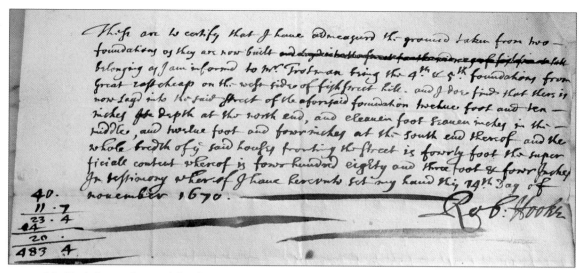

46. Hooke's certificate of the dimensions and area of ground taken by the City from Mr Trotman for widening Fish Street Hill at its west side. In the left-hand margin Hooke has calculated the area from the dimensions using duodecimal notation. (*Comptroller's Deeds Box K, T/12: Corporation of London Records Office*)

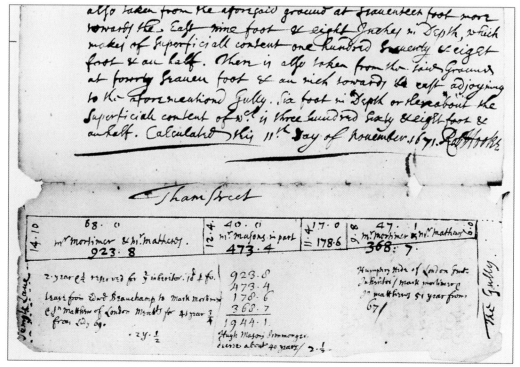

47. Part of Hooke's certificate of the dimensions and area of four parcels of land taken for widening the south side of Thames Street. Hooke used a sketch in his certificates only when he thought it would clarify the verbal description, as he did here where four contiguous foundations are certified. (*Comptroller's Deeds Box K, M/42A: Corporation of London Records Office*)

in his area certificates because the measurements he and the other surveyors routinely made were insufficient to define the shape of the lost ground and it would be impossible to make a true-to-scale graphical representation of the ground from them. A verbal definition was unlikely to be misinterpreted in the way a necessarily erroneous graphical definition could be. However, Hooke almost certainly drew a dimensioned sketch of the ground in his survey books for his own convenience, and when he thought a sketch would help to clarify a certificate for multiple owners he duly provided one (Figure 47).

Although Hooke's experimental genius lay in his ability to integrate the concept of an experiment with the design and performance of new instruments for observation and measurement and to present measurements in an innovative and critical way, he made no innovations of any kind in instrumentation for surveying measurements in rebuilding London. Although his equatorial quadrant (Figure 32) shows that he had a genius for instrument design, he chose not to exercise it when there was no need. Open sights and the resolution of the human eye were quite adequate for staking out streets and foundations. It was not necessary to use telescopes or graduated circles to measure the angles required to calculate the shape of each piece of ground taken away by the City. It was sufficient to assume that each area was made up of four sides, two of which were at right-angles to the street, even though that condition was unlikely to be found in practice, given the irregularities the rebuilding was intended to remove. Each plot of ground taken away was assumed to be trapezoidal, or capable of being made up of trapezia. Its area could then be found by measuring the length along the street and the two depths at right angles to it, and multiplying the length by the average depth. Measuring angles would have slowed up the site work and the calculation of area of lost ground, but would have added nothing of significance to the calculated area and the amount of compensation paid for the loss. Surveying was a civic duty, where it was necessary to work quickly to provide measurements which met a social need. It was unlike science, where the most accurate feasible measurements are usually necessary. Hooke had an appreciation that instruments and methods had to be 'fit for purpose'.

Problems often arose that required more than simple linear measurements and calculations to find the area of ground taken away. Sometimes on arriving at a site he found that the old foundations had been obliterated by new building, or had been taken up or covered over when a road was widened or a new one made, so it was impossible to measure them. He then had to resort to other sources of evidence, such as old leases, for his certificate. On 16 May 1671 Hooke had to refer to a lease of 1663 in order to write a certificate for a Mr Hogsflesh of Fish Street Hill:

> These are to certify that I find the Dimensions of the Remainer of a certain toft of Ground belonging to Mr. Zachary Hogsflesh upon which Mr. Gamblin hath built to contein in front to fish street hill twenty three foot & eight inches and in depth at the south end eleven foot & seaven inches and in depth at the north end six foot three inches and an half. And I find by a Lease of the said Ground from Mr. Hogsflesh to Mr.

Love made in the year 1663. that the Dimensions of the house then were twenty five foot & eight inches in Length and [s]eaven [foot &] six inches in bredth the Difference of [. . .] tofts is eighty two foot or th[e]rabout [. . .][15]

On another occasion Hooke had to take dimensions (in ells) from a charter written in the reign of Edward VI to calculate an area in Bearbinder Lane. He added the following statement to his calculation of the area as 1012 square feet: 'And I have examined the foundations as far as I could And conceive that the Said dimensions are very near the said content of the said Ground, and it seemeth to be rather more than what is here expressed.'[16]

He took dimensions from the 'survey book of the Hospitall of Christchurch' to certify another area of ground taken away at Fish Street Hill.[17] Anthony Tanner ('Citizen & Tyler and Bricklayer of London') surveyed a nine-sided toft in Black Horse Alley near Fleet Bridge and drew a plan at a scale of 1in to 8ft for a Mr Henry Dixon. Tanner swore an oath that the measurements were made by him and are as shown on the plot. Hooke then used Tanner's dimensions to calculate and certify the area on the reverse side of the plot. He calculated the area to be 'one thousand and fifty foot or thereabouts' which is only 3 per cent less than Tanner's value. The magnitude of the discrepancy is insignificant (given the scale of the plan and the indeterminate shape of the ground – all of which is covered by Hooke's 'thereabouts'), but it shows that Hooke took the trouble to recalculate the area and did not simply accept Tanner's value.[18] In March 1676 he had to refer to an entry made in April 1669 in Mills's survey book in order to write a certificate for ground taken from two houses on the west side of Foster Lane belonging to Lady Alice Viner, having found no record in his own books.[19]

Hooke was sometimes asked by a claimant to write a new area certificate because the original was said to be lost. He had then to take care that the replacement certificate did not result in a duplicate payment of compensation, either in error or by design. When he wrote a certificate to replace one he had written earlier for a Mr Howland of Grant's Key in Thames Street, now said to be lost, he thought it pertinent to add a note for the Comptroller 'pray take notice Least it [the original certificate] be brought in by some other hand into whom it may have fallen'.[20] The detailed and accurate records kept by the City, and by the surveyors in their survey books, ensured that payment twice for the same ground was very unlikely, even after an interval of some years, as the following example shows. Hooke certified an area of ground lost in New Fish Street Hill for Arthur Wind Esquire on 31 January 1671.[21] Following Wind's death, the parishioners of St Margaret's, New Fish Street Hill, asked Hooke to write a repeat certificate. He did as requested, making use of 'my book of surveys' and stating clearly that the certificate he had written for Wind was lost 'as is affirmed', adding that he had been asked to write the new certificate because interest in the 'said Lost ground' was now being claimed by the parish.[22] In due course this new certificate was handed in to the City, but no payment to the parish was authorised. A clerical addition to the certificate states that a warrant for payment had been issued to Wind on 15 February 1671.

Discrepancies between the two area certificates written by Hooke for the same lost ground in New Fish Street Hill, one written almost six years after the first, give a clue to how Hooke recorded his measurements in his (now lost) field books. The areas he certified are not identical, but the measurements he recorded are.[23] The discrepancy shows that Hooke did not record the area in his survey book, but calculated it later from the dimensions he measured and recorded at the time. The certified written descriptions in the two certificates of the positions and aspects of the boundaries of the ground lost are quite different, revealing that Hooke had recorded the layout and dimensions of the site in his survey book in the form of an annotated sketch, which he later used as the basis for the slightly differing verbal descriptions.

Through his intimate knowledge of the drafting of the Rebuilding Acts, Hooke was able from time to time to make compensation payment more efficient for the City and for a claimant. When he had to write a certificate for the loss of four separate foundations belonging to a Mrs Merrick, he concluded his certificate with a note to the Chamberlain pointing out that payment for the loss from only two of the four foundations was covered by existing legislation: 'The 162 foot and the 127 foot are to be paid for by the Act of Parliament already past but the preceding quantitys of ground cannot be payd for till the additional act passe.'[24] The Additional Act would not be passed for another ten months, but Hooke was aware of its contents, recognised that it would be relevant to the particular survey he was working on and gave warning of the effect it would have on the compensation to be paid.

When foundations could not be measured because they had been substantially lost or buried, and no satisfactory written evidence about their dimensions could be found, Hooke required appropriate and reliable witnesses to give sworn evidence of what formerly stood at the site. When called upon to certify an area of ground taken away for widening St Michael's Hill, he could not find the old foundations because they had been removed, so he 'could not certainly Measure the depth of the lost ground'. He used an affidavit[25] sworn by George Hodgkin, citizen and carpenter, to certify the area of the lost ground. After writing down the area sworn to by Hodgkin, Hooke added 'which I judge to be very probable'.[26] When old foundations belonging to a Mr Parsons at the corner of St Clement's Lane and Cannon Street had been removed by workmen when the streets were cleared immediately following the fire, Hooke's detailed knowledge of the city street widening was again used to smooth the compensation. In writing the area certificate for Parsons, Hooke judged the dimensions given in an affidavit by the bricklayer and carpenter who rebuilt Parson's house in 1669 to be acceptable because they corresponded to the ground he knew had been taken away from the opposite side of the street.[27]

Large areas of lost ground brought large sums of money in compensation. In such cases the usual approximate method of calculating area by assuming the sides of the lost ground to be perpendicular to the street was no longer appropriate. Measurements all round the perimeter were needed, but sometimes they were difficult or impossible to carry out. Other evidence was crucial. When preparing to write an area certificate for the parishioners of St Andrew Hubbard to compensate them for the loss of their church,[28] Hooke was able to measure the south and west sides of the old foundations as 85½ft and 44½ft respectively, but he could not measure the other two sides:

> . . . but the old foundations being Pluckd up at the North east Corner I could not certainly find the the length of the North & east sides, but by the testimony of many of the Antients of the Parish & by a ground platt of the said church and churchyard made by Mr. Street an accurate measurer whilst the walls were yet standing I find that the church & churchyard[29] had Square corners and that the north side was very neer equall to the south & the east side very neer equall to the west. Whence the superficiall content of the whole must be three thousand eight hundred and fowre foot.[30]

For such a large area the shape of the ground was very important. As the three preceding examples illustrate, Hooke was generally scrupulous in stating in a certificate his opinion of the reliability of oral and other evidence, but not always. When certifying an area of lost ground for Sir George Waterman, who had been Lord Mayor two years earlier, Hooke accepted and used without comment Sir George's affirmation of one dimension that could not be measured.[31] Sir George was said to be 'a person almost voide of understanding, but not of will. He is very weake in the one and very perverse in the other.'[32] Hooke might have thought it unwise for him to comment on the reliability of his client's evidence. In any case the missing dimension was affirmed by Sir George to be only 18 inches.

In very rare cases Hooke recognised that a claimant was suffering undue hardship. He would then add a sentence or two to his area certificate pointing this out to the City Lands Committee and suggesting ways in which it might be alleviated. A Mr Martindale owned land adjacent to the Fleet Channel, part of which was taken away to make the new wharf. Hooke visited the site and reported that Martindale showed him where the ground lay for which he was seeking compensation, but it was buried so deep in rubbish that its dimensions could not be taken. Hooke wrote two inessential but helpful statements in the certificate. He suggested that Martindale's deeds and sworn statements by his tenants might suffice as evidence, adding that it would be a great expense for Martindale to clear the ground so that it could be surveyed.[33] He wrote similarly sympathetic words in a replacement certificate for the parishioners of All Hallows Church, Barking:

> Whereas I did formerly make a certificat[34] of the[35] quantity of Ground taken of from the Parish houses & the Churchyard of St. Alhallows Barking. and did not therein expresse the Great & extrao[r]dinary Expense the said Parish have been necessitated to be at first[36] for the taking Downe a wall which was substantiall and next[37] for the Rebuilding the same in another place for the Inlargement of the street, which they would otherwise not have been necessitated to doe, and thirdly for the Removing a great quantity of

earth for Reducing the same to the Levell of the street the charge of all of which as I am credibly informed doth amount to one hundred pounds or thereabouts. whereby they have susteined a Double losse to what any other person hath susteined whose buildings being burnt, the ground only is taken away. Being now upon the humble addresse of the Parishioners of the said Parish to this Committee[38] orderd to view and consider of their complaint and certify this Honourable Committee I doe hereby certify that they have been necessitated both to pull downe the old wall of their churchyard which might otherwise have served a long time, and to Rebuild the same anew and Also to Remove much earth wherein severall corps had been not long before buried which hath been a great & extraordinary charge to the said Parish and I humbly conceive the same may be taken into consideration by this Committee and the said Parish allowd soe much more for their Ground then what is ordinarily[39] allowed, having been doubly Damnifyd by the aforesaid Inlargment of the street and noe wise at all ameliorated.
Feb:4:167⅔

Rob: Hooke.[40]

It was not necessary for Hooke to write such comments in his reports. The fact that he did so from time to time shows that he saw examples of hardship which, in his opinion, went beyond what most citizens suffered from the fire. Evidence of whether or not the City acted as he requested in the two cases cited has not been found, but it is unlikely that Hooke would have troubled to report these matters if he expected that nothing would come of it. In any case, he showed compassion to those whom he thought were suffering unduly and did what he could to alleviate their hardship.

More than 650 area certificates were written by the City Surveyors Mills, Hooke and Oliver, of which roughly half were Hooke's. His diary has many entries which might refer to area certificates, but his usual terse style makes it difficult to be sure. In any case, by 1672 when he began his diary he had already written more than half his area certificates. Some diary entries can be related to a known area certificate. When he wrote for example on 4 February 1673 'Lems certificate guinny. Hauslopes 10sh. St. Peters cornhill 20sh.' he was referring to the area certificate dated 3 February 1667 for ground lost by Joseph Lem at the south-west corner of Suffolk Lane and Cross Lane and another of the same date for ground lost by the parishioners of St Peter's Church at the corner of Cornhill and Gracechurch Street.[41] However, his reference to Hauslope has no corresponding entry in the City's records. Hauslope was a coal merchant – Hooke paid him 18s on 9 March 1675 for a load of coal[42] – so the diary entry could refer to a payment of 10s Hooke made to Hauslope in settlement of a bill during the exceptionally cold winter of 1666/7. Hooke had visited Hauslope at his wharf only three days before, on 1 February 1667.[43] These diary entries are examples of the minutiae in the life of an exceptionally able and busy man as he engaged in continuous collection, assessment and reporting of evidence both for understanding the natural world and for meeting the needs of his fellow citizens.

13

WE HAVE MET UPON THE PLACE

Procedures to ensure that private houses were built in their proper places were working well. By 1674 the foundations of more than 80 per cent of the 8,000 private houses that were rebuilt after the fire had been staked out and certified. In 1672 a backlog of applications had built up, but it did not hinder the rate at which houses were rebuilt. Disputes about who had to pay for the work, the shortage of skilled craftsmen and the high cost of materials had more effect on the rebuilding of private houses than the backlog of foundation surveys. Having arranged for their surveyors to stake out the new streets and ensure that private houses were rebuilt in the right places, the City now had to decide who should monitor the buildings as they were constructed to ensure that the proper materials were being used and that the houses conformed to one of the four kinds allowed by the Rebuilding Acts.

For more than 150 years preceding the fire of 1666, the City had a procedure for investigating allegations of irregular building. It was known as 'taking a view' or 'viewing'.[1] About five or six City Viewers were appointed from among the master craftsmen to assist with technical aspects of each allegation.[2] City Viewers were allowed to continue with their regular work, so the appointment was part-time. Any citizen or institution who thought that a building was irregular, or causing a nuisance, could lodge a formal complaint with the Court of Aldermen. The court usually considered the matter at its next meeting and would order at least three viewers to investigate, sometimes in the company of the alderman and deputy of the ward where the cause of the complaint was located. The party of at least five men would go to the site, examine the evidence, speak to witnesses as well as to the plaintiff and the alleged offender, and then report their findings and recommendations to the Court of Aldermen, who would decide what should be done. The phrase 'we have met upon the place' was commonly used in introductions to the viewers' reports.

The City Viewers were also called upon to report on the quality and costs of materials and workmanship for the City's own building work. By 1654 the City's building programme had increased to the point where the traditional five or six part-time viewers could no longer provide adequate supervision of the City's own works. Accordingly, Peter Mills and Edward Jerman were then appointed City Surveyors to take views for an annual salary of £60. Sometimes referred to in City documents as the City's 'Surveyors General', they were required to forfeit all other employment and work full-time viewing the City's works.[3]

In the aftermath of the fire it was clear to most people of authority in the city that the traditional City Viewers and City Surveyors would not be up to the task of dealing with the matters that now had to be settled against a background of technical building regulations of far greater complexity and rigour than they were accustomed to. The City decided that Mills, Hooke and Oliver, the City Surveyors they had appointed after the fire, should be given the additional responsibilities of viewing private houses and the City's new building works. Although no specific decision by the City was recorded, the traditional City Viewers ceased to be given orders to view in the aftermath of the fire, only gradually resuming their role after 1674, when most of the new building had been completed.

The first view by the City Surveyors after the fire was ordered by the Court of Aldermen on 12 November 1667. A dispute between Nailor and Beane about an unspecified matter at a site near Basing Lane was ordered to be viewed by Mills and Hooke.[4] The last view by City Surveyors for which evidence has been found was ordered on 14 December 1693 by the City Lands Committee. Five days later Hooke, Oliver and John Freeman, deputy of the ward of Bishopsgate Without, went to view the buildings complained of by the ward officers. Hooke wrote the report, part of which is transcribed below:[5]

> . . . we . . . have met upon the place and viewd a certaine building near rose ally in Bishops gate street in the Parish of St Buttolph without Bishops Gate now erecting by Ralph Hardwick Esq or some other whereof complaint hath been made to this Court by the Grand inquest of the ward, and we do find that the said Building is wholy irregular and as we conceive very insufficient and it is therefore our opinions that the same ought to be reformed and amended and built according to the Directions and Scantlings prescribed by the Act of Parliament for Rebuilding this City. And whereas we find there are divers other houses building adjoyning so the same, which we find to be likewise irregularly built, we are of opinion that the same[6] ought to be amended also.[7]

During the twenty-five years between the first and last views taken by Hooke almost every conceivable complaint was passed to him for his attention. Imposition of the new building regulations for the good of everyone too often took away or diminished the rights of an individual who decided to recover what had been lost by rebuilding contrary to the Rebuilding Acts. The old city had many narrow passageways and small inner courtyards where occupiers had rights of light and passage and the use of gullies and watercourses for draining waste and storm water. Many citizens lost rights when the small spaces were regularised. Upper storeys of some former houses had been 'jetted-out' (extended, sometimes without support, beyond the old timber-framed load-bearing walls) into and above the streets and small yards. Opening up the streets and yards to air and light by banning jetting out meant that people lost floor space for housing family, apprentices and tenants. Fires and furnaces necessary for some trade practices, such as metalworking, had long been a source of nuisance to neighbours. In some specific places they were forbidden by the Rebuilding Acts and if rebuilt they had to be taken down. People who formerly lived near churches sometimes claimed when rebuilding that their new properties and even their lives were in peril from collapsing masonry and so they asked for damaged spires and towers to be inspected and, if found dangerous, to be taken down.

Encroachments, party walls and intermixtures of interests gave rise to many complaints. Although the surveyors had to stake out and certify party walls before rebuilding could begin, it was always tempting for the person who built first to try to gain a little ground by encroaching on to the neighbouring property or an adjacent alleyway or lane. Sometimes an encroachment on to a major street was attempted. The cost of a party wall had to be shared equally between the adjacent occupiers, but this was not always done without one or the other complaining. The first to rebuild had to pay the full cost and recover the neighbour's moiety later. Holes had to be left in the brickwork on the neighbour's side for the joists and beams of the adjoining building. Before the fire occupants of adjoining properties sometimes lived in rooms lying partially above or below their neighbours' accommodation. Such an intermixture of interests had usually been brought about when a house was extended upwards and partially over the adjacent house. Later, the house which had been built over might have been extended upwards and back across the other. Intermixtures of interests were not possible under the new building regulations because party walls had to be built 'vertical and entire upwards' from the ground. The nett loss or gain by each party had to be compensated for by payment from or to the other – another cause for complaint.

Complaints were brought to the Court of Aldermen in different ways. The surveyors had to look out for and report weekly in writing to the Lord Mayor any irregular building whether or not neighbours had made a complaint.[8] They were also ordered by the City Lands Committee to send in lists of names of persons who had built against the city walls, and to stop them from proceeding until the City had considered the matter.[9] The many hundreds of views of private rebuilding which Hooke and the other City Surveyors were ordered to undertake generally arose as a result of a formal complaint by a citizen to the Court of Aldermen that a neighbour's new building was not in accordance with the Rebuilding Acts, or was in other ways dangerous or detrimental to the property or life of the complainant or others in the neighbourhood. Once the Court of Aldermen had judged that there were good grounds for the complaint and that it was not being made for spurious reasons, at least two of the surveyors (after Mills's death,

Hooke and Oliver worked jointly on nearly all views) and sometimes the alderman and deputy of the ward were ordered to view the complaint, taking with them anyone else they thought could add to their knowledge and experience.

Taking a view of private rebuilding was much more complicated and time-consuming than staking out and certifying foundations and areas of lost ground. The City could not afford to have claims lodged against it for damages and loss of income. To enable the City's response to a complaint to be quick, decisive, equitable and enforceable the viewers had to agree unanimously on their verdict and present clearly the reasons for their conclusions. We find that in almost every case Hooke wrote the report of each view he took part in. Most complaints turned out to be justified, with consequences ranging from minor alterations and payments of compensation to taking down nearly complete buildings and starting again from the foundations. Viewing private rebuilding was an additional burden for the surveyors, but they were rewarded financially in the form of a negotiable fee paid to them directly by each complainant. Some examples follow to illustrate the diversity of the hundreds of cases which Hooke investigated and the manner in which he reported them over a period of about twenty-five years.

In July 1671 Hooke was called upon to view an intermixture of interests between Mr Edward Harvey on the one hand and Mr John Jackson and Mr John Neave on the other at their adjoining properties just south of Goldsmith's Hall. The complexity inherent in resolving complaints about the removal of intermixture of interests is seen in the following transcription of Hooke's report. The traditional strict formality in the opening sentences was gradually reduced by Hooke after his first few views, probably to save time. His efficient drafting of the reports can be seen from the small number of alterations and corrections he made (described in the notes):

Whereas the Right honourable S[r]. Rich: Ford K[t]. Lord mayor of the City of Lon[don] was pleased by an order bearing Date Jul.5.1671 to summon the surveyors of the City of London to view An[10] intermixture between the[11] interests of M[r]. Edward Harvy, M[r]. John Jackson & M[r]. John Neave situate on the south side of Goldsmiths hall & on the north of Kerry lane;[12] and to act and doe therein as in and by the Additionall Act[13] of Parliament for building the City of London[14] is limited & appointed. we the said Surveyors having accordingly mett upon the place and viewd the said Interests and understood from the severall partys concerned their severall intermixtures[15] upon the whole matter w[e] doe order and appoint that M[r]. Harvy shall build the Remaining part of the ground that is left in the first story intire and upright making use of the walls[16] built by M[r]. Neave and M[r]. Jack[son] as party walls. he the said Harvy paying unto them the said p[artys] truely the moyety of their said[17] party walls. and further that M[r]. Harvy shall carry the[18] party wall between the outlet of M[r]. Jacson N[ew] made and his own grownd upright upon the same foundations that are now set; returning the same at the west end thereof upon a sqare to the party wall now built by M^r. Jacson. and that M^r. Jackson shall have liberty to come home to the said wall with that part of his house where he hath now placed windowes. but whether he shall soe think fitt or not yet that he shall pay the said Harvy for the moyety of the said party wall[19] being about five foot in length east west[20] & two foot north & south[.] And further that all differences touching any former intermixtures between the said Harvy & the said Jacson[21] shall cease. Moreover we doe order that M^r. Neave shall pay unto M^r. Harvy in Compensation of the washouse and part of the yard built upon by him the said Neave the summe of three pounds, and that all Differences between the said partys touching any former intermixtures or yards shall cease in testimony whereof we have hereunto set our hands this 8th. of July 1671.[22]

The document is signed 'Rob: Hooke Jo. Oliver'. Reports like this were hardly ever accompanied by a sketch or diagram: as with Hooke's area certificates, these were liable to be misconstrued as being more accurate than was feasible, or to be poorly copied by clerks, so he generally excluded diagrams and sketches from his reports of views.

When an occupier formerly had possession of a chimney or staircase next to an adjoining property, and was the first to rebuild the new party wall, he had an opportunity to re-establish ownership of the former facility, often to the detriment of the neighbouring occupier. On the other hand, the second to rebuild often exploited to his own benefit a neighbour's facility, thereby damaging the neighbour's interests. When Mr Linch complained that his neighbour Mr Harford had pulled down his stairs and broken into his chimney, Hooke found that the matter was much more complicated, as his report shows:

. . . we whose names are underwritten have met upon the place and have viewd all the matters Complayned of by M^r. Linch against M^r. Harford about pulling down as he alledges a whole pair of Stairs belonging to his the said Linch his house and for breaking holes into one of his chimneys. And upon the whole matter we find that the said Hartford in the repairing of a flight of stairs from the ground into the 2^d story hath set the same contiguous to the back side of a chimney[23] belonging to the said Linch and we find that the old stairs which he tooke away had a bearing into the said chimney but the workmen in setting up the new ones hath not put the Bearers into the same holes but into some new ones they have made whereby we find that they have loosned some of the brick on the back side of the chimney of the said Linch. we find also that the said Linch had a flight of stepps from his second story into his 3^d. which flight of steps did appear in the second story of the said Hartford. and we upon examination of all particulars doe find that the said flight of steps was two foot and two inches broad between the main timbers[24] and that the

lowest step of the said[25] flight was 8 inches above the floor of the 2d. story. and was
so Raysed as to leave the headway of the Door case towards the east full 7 foot high
and two foot & half wide. how the same came to be pulled down we know not but it
is our opinion that the said Harford doe againe put up a flight of steps in the same
place & of the same dimensions as before, and likewise that he doe take Care to stop
up any breach or crack that may have been made in the back of the chimney and to
take care that there may not be any danger of fire caused[26] thereby. We further find
that the said Hartford complaineth against the said Linch fi[rs]t for putting in a
watercourse into the[27] said Harfords sink where he hath no right to any. and
secondly for[28] removing and taking quite away an old post placed in the street
ranging to the party partition between the entry and the shop. and hath layd and
inclosed all the said Room into his own shop and hath thereby inlarged the same
and hath also inlarged his shop by making the said party partition thinner than it
was before, for which complaint we find the said Harford had good Reason. But we
find that the said Linch hath declared that he will remove the said watercourse, and
It is our opinion he[29] the said Linch ought to set up the post in the place where it
was before, and that the said hartford doe forthwith satisfy himself about the
substantiallness of the partition and pay the said Linch the money due upon
[re]wa[r]d. All which &c
Dated the 14th. of June 1686.[30]

As well as Hooke and John Oliver, Joseph Titcombe and George Hatton took part in
the view. Titcombe and Hatton were two of the four City Viewers who in the 1680s were
increasingly involved in viewing at a time when the matters to be viewed were no longer
exclusively related to new buildings.

When a Mr Weightwick in 1676 began to rebuild his house adjacent to that of his
neighbour Mr Reynolds, the amount Weightwick should pay to Reynolds as his moiety
of the cost of building the party wall was complicated by the fact that Reynolds had
built the party wall nearly nine years earlier. Hooke had to draw on his knowledge of
how costs of construction had changed during that time in order to calculate an
equitable settlement:

. . . we whose names are underwritten have met upon the place and have viewd the
Party walls built by Mr. Reynols between his house and the house of Mr. Weightwick
and we have measured and computed the same and finding the same to amount to
five rod three quarters & 15 foot, which being built in the year 1667 we estimate at
seaven pounds & ten shillings per Rod and thereby finde it to amount to one and
twenty pounds and having been built eight yeares and eleaven months the interest of
the same according to the Act of Parliament[31] amounteth to Eleven pounds 4
shillings which together with the aforesaid summe amounteth to thirty two pounds

four shillings. which we conceive the said M^r. Weightwick ought forthwith to pay to the said M^r. Reynolds. All which neverthelesse we humbly submitt to your Lordship & worships.

Dated the 12 of July 1676.[32]

Hooke rarely showed any arithmetical working on his documents. He might have written his sums in his survey books, but he often used mental arithmetic and there is some indication that he did so in this case when calculating the amount of money to be paid to Reynolds. The dimensions he cites are in superficial measure (square rods and square feet). One rod is $16\frac{1}{2}$ft long. In his mind he takes the area as $5\frac{3}{4}$ square rods and multiplies it by the cost per square rod (£7 10s, or £$7\frac{1}{2}$) as follows: $5 \times £7 = £35$; $\frac{3}{4} \times £7 = £5$; $5 \times £\frac{1}{2} = £2$; giving a total cost of £42, ignoring all fractions. The moiety is half this amount, i.e. £21. The interest on £21 @ 6 per cent per annum for 8 years and 11 months is $£21 \times 6$ per cent $\times 8\frac{11}{12}$, or $£21 \times \frac{6}{100} \times \frac{107}{12}$, which he thinks of as $£10\frac{1}{2} \times 1\frac{7}{100}$ or $£(10 + \frac{1}{2})(1 + \frac{7}{100})$ which is approximately $£(10 + \frac{1}{2} + \frac{7}{10})$ or $£11\frac{1}{5}$ which is Hooke's £11 4s. The value of the work is thus £32 4s, which Hooke writes. Of course, there is no evidence that Hooke worked out the amount in this way, but he was capable of it. If fractions are not ignored at the start of the calculation, and the amount is calculated to the nearest penny, it comes to £33 8s 4d which is £1 4s 4d less than Hooke's approximate value. The discrepancy is less than 4 per cent of the total, but the calculation of the more accurate value would have taken much longer. We have here another example of approximation warranted by expediency. The fact that the accurate amount in this case is more than the approximate amount actually paid is not significant. Other examples can be found which show the opposite, but approximation by ignoring fractional parts usually led to slightly less being paid than was strictly due.

Encroachment by building across the centre line of a party wall was another irregular practice, intended to gain some advantage over a neighbour. On a few occasions the matter in dispute was alleged to be an error in the staking out of a party wall by one of the surveyors (Hooke in the following example). As with many views, it was found that infringements other than the one which instigated the view were discovered. When a Mr Conyers complained that his neighbour Mr Hawkes had encroached on his ground, a view by Peter Mills, Hooke and John Oliver dated 13 June 1668 found a different explanation, as Hooke's report shows:

. . . we find that the north Howse of Mr Hawks is built upon the walls that were errected before the fire and according to the setting out thereof by Mr Hooke And whereas there is some dispute about a parte of the said ground whether it were Mr Conniers ground or Mr Hawkes's It being a matter of title we leave it to the determination of the law. As for the incroachment complained off by Mr Conniers to be made by Mr Hawkes upon the south parte of his said grounds Wee find it to have proceeded from a mensuration made of the ground of the said Mr Coniers by Mr Jones Bricklayer Which mensuration we find to have beene made by guesse before the cleering of the said ground as it is confirmed to us by the said Mr Jones who doth affirme also that he doth imagine notwithstanding that it was pretty neere the truth.[33]

The report illustrates that disputes about ownership were decided by the Fire Court, whereas surveyors were concerned with settlement of disputes about boundaries. Hooke and the other City Surveyors were sometimes ordered by the Fire Court to undertake a specific survey relating to a case and report their findings. As part of a judgment made on 30 May 1667, Peter Mills and Hooke were required to find the dimensions of a courtyard off Cheapside and report on the effects on a party's rights to light if some of the yard were taken for building in lieu of the cost of surrendering a lease. The Fire Court Calendar records:

All the parties appearing Peter Mills and Robert Hooke certified that the yard on the east side of the house was 40 feet N. to S., 18 feet wide at the S. end and 12 feet wide at the N. end, that the petitioners had a slip of ground on the east side of the yard which was too narrow for building, and that Archer without damage to his lights might spare 3 feet at the S. end and 1 foot at the N. end, which land they valued at £10.[34]

From time to time Hooke faced physical danger when viewing buildings, generally because of their dilapidated condition. He was sometimes called upon to climb up the steeple of a ruined church to inspect its structural stability in response to complaints from people building nearby who feared it would fall down. He was equally in danger when investigating allegations of irregular excavations for cellars and vaults, as we see from the following report written by Hooke:

. . . we whose names are underwritten have mett upon the place and viewd the matters complaind of by Mr John Davys against a building of Mr Nathaniell[35] Stanton in Love Lane in Aldermanbury and have Discoursd with both the said partys and have examined the foundations. and upon the whole we find that the[36] wall[37] of Mr. Davys house is set upon an old chalk wall which is about two foot and a half Dee[p][38] and noe more whereby upon the building of Mr Stanto[n] on the east side thereof and his Digging of a celler we find that he hath dugg below the bottom of the same soe that the said wall is much indagerd. thereby it is therefore our opinion that the said wall ought to be forthwith underpinn'd and sufficiently secured at a party charge. All which notwithstanding we humbly leave to your Lordship.
Dated Aug 30. 1671.[39]

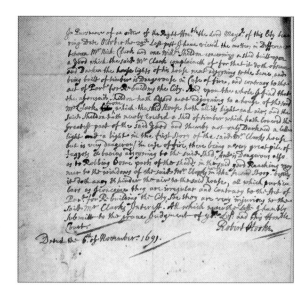

48. Hooke was still working for the City
25 years after the fire. This manuscript
is his report of a view in November 1691
of allegations that a shed built in a yard
was a fire hazard and infringed rights to
light. (*Misc. MS 93.129: Corporation of
London Records Office*)

Complaints from occupiers or owners that their contractors had used illegal materials
were regularly made. In July 1673 Marmaduke Rogden complained that his carpenter,
Henry Reeves, had built several houses for him in Watling Street which were irregular and
contrary to the Rebuilding Acts. A clerical copy of Hooke's report tells us that Hooke found

> the said Henry Reeves hath erected eight severall houses for the said Mr Rogden in
> Watling Street three whereof are fronting towards the street and five backwards, all of
> them irregular in diverse particulars, as followeth, to witt wee finde three party walls
> wanting in the Back houses, Three Lintells throughout all the said houses of Firr,[40] A
> greatest part of all the roofes of firr, Severall of the Mantletrees and some of the
> windowes of Firr, The Cellar floores genrally insufficient and severall of the Joysts of
> firr being lesse also in scantlings then they ought, As also deficient for that Most of
> the boarding of the floores [are] unperfected and ill layd, Severall of the Stayre-Cases
> & doores not finished, the windowes of the Back Cellars without Iron barrs, And three
> houses of Office wanting, which ought to have been made according to Articles
> between the said partyes.[41]

For such extensive use of illegal or inadequate materials and poor workmanship, the
only thing that could be done was to rebuild again at Henry Reeves's expense, even
though it might ruin him and his business.

Twenty-five years after the fire old practices that had contributed to the speed
with which the fire spread were returning, as Hooke discovered during one of his
last views (Figure 48). He went to investigate a complaint by a Mr Nicholas Clark

that a timber shed being built by William Sheldon in a yard took away some of the light to his (Clark's) house. As we see from Hooke's report, the matter was more serious:

> . . . I have view'd the matters in Difference between Mr Nich: Clark and one Willm Sheldon concerning a shed built upon a Yard which the said Mr Clark complaineth of for that it doth obscure and Darken the house lights of his house next adjoyning to the Same, and being built of timber is Dangerouse in Case of fire, and contrary to the act of Parlt. for Rebuilding the City. And upon the whole I find that the aforesaid Sheldon hath a yard next adjoyning to a house of the said Mr Clark from[42] which the said House hath all its light and air; and the said Sheldon hath newly Erected a shed of timber which hath covered the Greatest part of the said Yard and thereby not only Darkned a Cellar light and a light in the first story of the said Mr. Clarks house but is very dangerous in case of fire, there being a very great pile of faggots & bavins[43] adjoyning to the said shed. And is Dangerous also as to Robbing Some parts of the shedds in the said yard Reaching very neer to the windows of the said Mr. Clarks house[44] in the second story. besides it doth anoy & hinder the air to the said house, all which particulars as I conceive they are irregular and contrary to the Act of Part. for Rebuilding the City, Soe they are very injurious to the said Mr. Clarks Interest. All which neverthelesse I humbly submitt to the grave Judgment of your Lop. and this Honourable Court.   Robert Hooke
>
> Dated the 6th. of November 1691.[45]

Even though this was almost Hooke's last view, he was still taking trouble to report on matters that were not strictly forbidden by the Rebuilding Acts, but were nevertheless likely to lead to inconvenience or even to crime.

Hooke's conscientious attention to detail and his knowledge of the Rebuilding Acts were attributes often needed by others. The report of a view of rights of light and an ill-placed gutter taken on 5 December 1673 by the alderman and deputy of Tower Ward, Sir John Robinson and Henry Williamson, was signed by both men but was written by Hooke although he was not officially required to take part (Figures 49 and 50). Pepys thought Robinson was 'a talking, bragging Bufflehead' a 'loggerhead' and 'a vain, prating, boasting man . . . as if the whole city and Kingdom had all its work done by him'.[46] John Aubrey said '[Robinson] was not so wise as King Salomon'.[47] Hooke usually was in attendance when Robinson was ordered to view, but his diary records of these events are strictly factual, for example 'at Sir J. Robinson's, at Peaks view'.[48] Ward officials found it useful to have Hooke's advice and skills at writing reports, especially when measurements and calculations were required, as illustrated by another report written by Hooke of a view by John Moore and John Sexton, alderman and deputy of Walbrook Ward, on Saturday 14 July 1677:

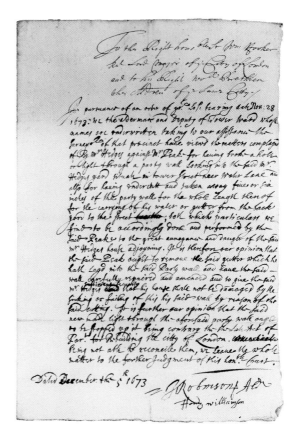

49. Report of a view by Alderman Sir
John Robinson (Figure 50) and Deputy
Henry Williamson, but written by Hooke.
The City ordered Robinson and
Williamson, not Hooke, to view the site,
so Hooke did not sign the report. The
nominated viewers called on Hooke's
expertise because measurements were
needed, even though they were of the
simplest kind. (*Misc. MS 92.170:
Corporation of London Records Office*)

. . . we the Alderman and Deputy of the Ward of Walbrook have met upon the place
and have[49] viewed a small wall built by Mr. Bell next adjoyning to the Interest of
Captain Pierce and find the same to be made use of as a party wall[50] for the said
Captain Pierce for which the said M^r. Bell affirmeth he hath not Receiv'd satisfaction
according to the direction of the Act of Parliament for Rebuilding the City the
measurement of which we have Receivd from the said Mr. Bell attested under the
hand of James Rollesson[e] to be three rod a quarter and eight foot which at 7^L. 10^s
per rod he hath computed to amount to 24^L: 11^s: 0^{dd} And the Interest for the
forbearance of the same for 9 years and an half amounting to 14: 00: 00 The summe
of both which added together makes 38: 11: 09 We have Indeavoured to compose the
Difference between them, but being not able to end the same we humbly submit it to
the Grave Judgment of this Honourable Court.[51]

Although Hooke's name does not appear on the document and he was not required to
take part in the view, he was asked by the alderman and deputy to accompany them. He

50. John Michael Wright's portrait (*c.* 1662) of Sir John Robinson, Lord Mayor 1662–3 and Lieutenant of the Tower 1660–79, whose report (Figure 49) was written by Hooke. (*Guildhall Art Gallery, Corporation of London*)

was at Deane's coffee house that Saturday morning with Moore and Sexton where he wrote the report of the view before going to meet Wren for 'much discourse' about the work of the mason Joshua Marshall at St Stephen's Church, Coleman Street.[52]

'View' has been used indiscriminately by most writers on Hooke in connection with all or any of the surveying tasks he undertook for the City,[53] but it now is seen to refer to a site visit and written report to the City on a particular dispute between inhabitants arising during rebuilding. It is in this sense that he used 'view' in his diaries.[54] Archival evidence of the views of private rebuilding undertaken by Hooke is abundant, but incomplete.[55] Hooke's diaries have many typically terse references to places, people and sums of money, many of which could be related to views, such as 'Rossington, Smither lane, 10sh. Bland and Taylor, Mincing Lane . . . Meynell 13*s* 6*d*'.[56] Occasionally he is more explicit: 'Capt. Looks view at the Bridge. . . . to Committee at Guildhall. View at Laurence Lane 10sh,'[57] but even here he does not give the name of his client in Laurence Lane. From all these sources it has been found that Hooke made at least 500 views of new buildings.[58]

Such a large number is an indication of the great effort Hooke put in to this important activity to ensure that rebuilding went according to the new regulations. Although he shared the responsibility with Mills and Oliver, and sometimes with the alderman and deputy of the ward where the view was taken, he took the dominant role in all the 500 or more views he was involved with. This is evident from the fact that

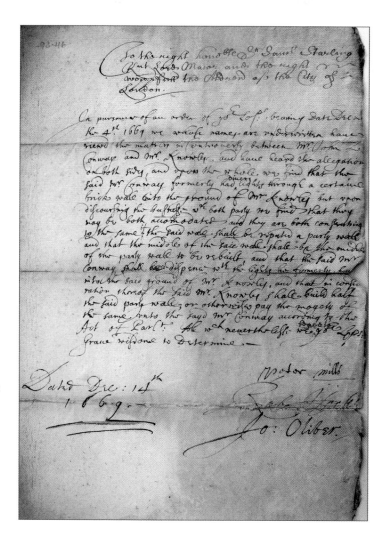

51. A report of a view of a dispute about a party wall and rights to light. The view is written by Hooke and signed by him and by the other two City Surveyors, Peter Mills and John Oliver. (*Misc. MS 93.116: Corporation of London Records Office*)

every existing original report of a view in which he took part was written by him. Although a strict hierarchy was observed in the order of signatures on a report – Mills, Hooke, Oliver, according to their first appointments by the City – Hooke always wrote the report, even when Peter Mills, his senior, was also involved (Figure 51). In an unusually verbose diary entry Hooke gives us a glimpse of his professional relationship with John Oliver when they were together at Jonathan's coffee house on 6 May 1693: 'At Hublons View 1 G⊙[59] I paid J. Oliv. for yesterdays View 10.[60] Viewed it again with J.O. I drew Report at Jonathans,[61] we both signed it.'[62] Hooke collected the fees, wrote the reports and paid Oliver his share. Hooke was the dominant surveyor, doing more than anyone to ensure that the location, structure and form of new houses were regular, legal and in much more congenial surroundings than they were before the fire.

14

UNEXPECTED PRESSURES

A CANAL

Hooke's responsibilities as City Surveyor in staking out streets and in ensuring that private rebuilding was carried out in the proper places and in accordance with the new regulations were only part of what the City wanted him and the other surveyors to do. When the king and the City came to accept that the visionary ideas for a magnificent new city were not realistic, they did what they could to ensure that the Rebuilding Acts allowed as much as possible of the vision to be realised. A new broad quay along the Thames from the Tower to Temple Gardens with an array of buildings of the fourth sort facing the river was a grand ambition which was included in the legislation. So too was the proposal to canalise the Fleet Ditch and transform it into the tidal channel, navigable at high tide from the Thames to Holborn Bridge, it once had been, but this time to build broad quays either side with warehouses beneath and houses of the third sort behind. Plans were also made to improve public health by relocating street markets to new sites, re-laying a new system of paved streets with sewers, water pipes and conduits, and relocating laystalls and houses of common easement in more suitable places. A monument to the ability of the king and the City to recover quickly from the dreadful disaster was planned and some gateways had to be rebuilt. It fell to the City to ensure that all these public works were done, using the coal tax to pay for them. Both Hooke and Oliver[1] had a great deal of responsibility for these building works, but once again Hooke's contribution was by far the more important.

The interests of the City and the king coincided when the canalisation of the Fleet Ditch came to be considered. Those interests were taken care of and put into effect through the friendship and common intellectual pursuits of Hooke and Wren, with the political and moral support of Sir John Lawrence, to whom Hooke had first presented his layout plan for a new city. The technical problems of canalisation were so great that they could not have been overcome without the close cooperation of those three men. The City's involvement in transforming Fleet Ditch into the navigable Fleet Channel according to the second Rebuilding Act of April 1670 began in November of the same year, when the City Lands Committee ordered Hooke to meet with Wren, as one of the King's Commissioners for New Buildings, and make a written report to the Committee on what work should be done.[2] The order was nothing more than the City giving an early recognition of its obligations in the matter. It was in no hurry to start work, having to wait for income from the tax on coal to accumulate sufficiently to pay the first contractors. In early February 1671 Hooke and Oliver were ordered to attend every meeting of the committee,[3] but within a month they had to be reminded of the orders they had already been given. The City Lands Committee decided to meet every Wednesday afternoon and it was 'ordered that Mr Hook & Mr Oliver fail not to be present at every meeting of this Committee according to the summons given to them in that behalfe'.[4] At the same committee meeting Hooke was ordered to 'attend Dr Wren to obtain the King's directions and approbation for the manner of wharfing on Fleet Ditch, whether with timber brick or stone'.[5] There is an intimation here of difficulties to come. The Committee met every Wednesday afternoon. The Royal Society at that time met on Thursday afternoons, but it changed to Wednesday afternoons in April 1672,[6] so Hooke would soon be faced with a direct conflict of interests. He usually worked for the City in the mornings, leaving the afternoons and evenings for his many other activities. Oliver, too, had private work which he attended to mostly in the afternoons.

The report by Wren and Hooke originally ordered in November 1670 was presented to the City Lands Committee at the end of the winter, on 22 March 1671.[7] It starts with a detailed technical specification for the construction of timber wharfing at least 12 feet high, rising gradually to 24 feet at Holborn Bridge. It specifies the dimensions of timber piles, mudsills,[8] puncheons,[9] campshots,[10] and the types of iron cramps and ground ties to be used. The written description is not easy to comprehend, which perhaps explains why Wren and Hooke said it would be necessary to have a model at a scale of 2 inches to 1 foot (whether drawn and/or made from wood is unclear) of the whole structure to refer to when negotiating and supervising contracts between the City and its contractors. Wren and Hooke also suggested that a 100ft length of wharf at full scale should be built under their supervision at a cost of £6 per square foot to serve as a prototype; even a scale model might be ambiguous in places.

The report then went on to recommend a scheme for removing from the ditch the centuries of accumulated mud and other detritus which had so badly affected the health of people living nearby. Wren and Hooke suggested 'an agreement be made for 14 Lighters to attend the digging, 7 to goe off every Tide & 7 to lye till the next Tyde to be filled at Ebbe & during the Tyde to carry on the dry digging'. They then approved the proposals of four men, John Simpson, John Rooke, Green & Edward Maybank to

> digg the dry worke att 5*d* per yard & the wett worke att 8*d*. To fill in & ramme to the land tyes at 12*d* per piece, & to the back side of the wharfing at 2*d* per foot running. To keep at worke 120 men. To find all tooles wheelbarrows basketts & planks to run in. To dispose of

all stones & bricke as shall be directed. To take up the old stone wharfing at 12*d* per yard. To preserve all found piles above 3 foot long. To be paid according to measure weekly.

The final recommendations were that

. . . some Ingenious Carpenters doe attend the direction of the Surveyors for making & placing of Pumps where necessary & conveyances for the land water & sewers, and a person to take Exactly the levells & direct the diggers in the orderly carrying on of the worke, which must be estimated according to the occasion.[11]

In March 1671 the City Lands Committee enthusiastically accepted all the recommendations made by Wren and Hooke. They ordered workmen to be employed forthwith to dig the channel. Thomas Fitch and John Ball were appointed as initial contractors for the whole project, although Ball's contract was not renewed. One of the two major projects for improving London was about to begin, but nobody involved in it had any notion of the severe technical and other problems that lay in wait. The work was eventually completed three-and-a-half years later, in October 1674, after patient trial and error on the part of Wren and Hooke when faced with a series of frustrating failures, and the forbearance of the City, particularly Sir John Lawrence, in trusting the judgement of their two advisers and the expertise of their main contractor despite alarming increases in costs.

One of the problems Wren and Hooke faced was the magnitude of the lateral pressures that would be exerted on the timber walls of the wharf by the adjacent ground. The valley sides of the Fleet were much steeper than those bordering the Thames (where timber wharves had been used for more than a thousand years) and much steeper than they are today. Groundwater added to the pressure on the timber wharfing, whose scantlings were soon discovered to have been quite inadequate to withstand unprecedented lateral forces.[12] Each time the water flowing in underground springs from catchment areas upstream in Clerkenwell and beyond broke through the wharfing, Wren and Hooke had only trial and error to guide them. They redesigned new sections with increased timber scantlings, or with brick in place of timber. In either case, work was delayed and costs went up.

The technical problems brought about by natural processes were made worse by human activity. The removal of existing rubbish from the old ditch to make a navigable channel was straightforward. Use was made of the tidal variations to dig out material at low tide and carry it away by water at high tide. But surface water flowing down the sides of the valley carried with it a mass of refuse dumped in the streets together with rubbish left over from the fire, all of which was deposited either on ground being prepared for quays or in the channel itself. In both cases the work of digging and carrying away was increased. Attempts were made to reduce this added burden by constructing sluices and drains, but they were overwhelmed by the next heavy downpour of rain. A spit of mud into the Thames had accumulated at the mouth of the Fleet. It was very difficult to remove without hindrance to normal river traffic, but it interfered with the movement of the lighters engaged in transporting the mud dug out from upstream. A far more serious threat to the project came from people living in Middlesex, outside the jurisdiction of the City, who used Turnmill Brook in Clerkenwell and other headwaters of the Fleet River to carry away their domestic rubbish, offal and waste from various trades and crafts downstream into the city. Above Holborn Bridge the City arched over the stream as far north as its jurisdiction reached and installed 15ft-high vertical gratings across the arch to keep out the rubbish, but they were not cleaned out regularly and were frequently breached by the weight of garbage from slaughterhouses borne down from upstream by strong currents after heavy rain, all of which then had to be cleaned away by the contractors.

Throughout the three-and-a-half years of the project, Hooke spent many hours, often with Wren, and sometimes with Oliver, at the Fleet Channel dealing with countless technical and administrative matters relating to the construction works. Hooke and Wren had frequent formal meetings with the main contractor Thomas Fitch, with workmen and citizens and with members of the City Lands Committee. Hooke himself had frequent informal meetings and proposed detailed redesign and construction procedures for the Fleet Channel, its quays, wharves and bridges. He drew up new or revised articles of agreement between contractors and the City; specified new gradients for the channel bed and supervised levelling surveys; examined built walls and wharves and the damage to them caused by excessive lateral pressure; redesigned piles, footings and retaining walls in the channel; decided to change from predominantly timber to mainly brick construction; chose locations and specified the structure of new vaults for use as warehouses; gave instructions for removal from the river bed by lighters of mud and rubbish dumped by citizens and coming down from places outside the jurisdiction of the City; investigated and recommended resolution of conflicts between City workmen and traders wanting access to bring goods up the river; checked the quality of all workmanship and materials; certified bills of quantity and wage rates; and reported, often at length, on all these matters for the City.[13]

Even though Hooke investigated incidents with Wren, Oliver and others, Hooke always drafted the reports himself. He would not have signed a report written by Oliver, and Wren only wrote a report to the City in exceptional cases when he personally, as the King's Surveyor-General, was called upon to do so. However, Wren signed reports that were written by Hooke; they met and cooperated so frequently about the Fleet that Hooke knew what Wren would agree to sign. The report below shows Hooke again going among the citizens, talking to them, taking note of what they said, and presenting as evidence what he himself had heard and seen. It was written on 18 April 1674 after one of the most severe breaches of the gratings above Holborn Bridge and the consequent deluge of silt and rubbish into Fleet Channel:

In pursuance of an Order of this Committee dated the thirteenth instant wee whose names are subscribed, have viewed the floor of Fleet channell between Holborne bridge and Fleet bridge, and have discoursed with severall of the neighbouring inhabitants, who are of opinion that since Xmas last, when the said Channell was cleared; the soil and Rubbish which hath descended thereinto from Turnmill brook by Reason of and since the last great floods, hath filled up the floor thereof so as to raise it three foot high, at the least, as all of them, and more as some affirme, particularly Mr Jordan and Mr Middlemore who dwell in the two next houses to the west side of the said Channell next Holborn bridge, who affirming that they had very often taken exact notice thereof and being demanded the Reason that moved them so to doe told us that about Xmas when the said Channell was cleared, the foundations of their houses were[14] discovered so low that they feared their sinking or impairing by the said clearing, but after the said Floods, there came in so considerable a quantity of dirt and soil, that rose up to the heighs aforesaid. One other Mr Harris a Goldsmith, informed us that he observed that the top of a Barge, which is now in part covered with the said soile was before the said floods about three foot[15] above the floor of the said Channell, and those that were present affirmed that others of their neighbours had taken notice of the filling the said Channell to the height aforesaid. Wee have also taken notice of the severall parts of the said Channell between the said Bridges, which wee find all raised tho' with some inequality, some more, and others lesse than three foot as near as we can judge, and finding the length thereof to be three hundred and threescore yards and thirteen yards wide which computed amounts to[16] about four thousand six hundred and fourscore yards[17], which is also[18] the number of yards solid, which according to the best accounts wee can make comparing one place with another, wee judge, hath since the last clearing, by Reason of and since the late great floods, descended into the said Channell, and without the speedy Removall whereof there can be no effectual progresse in the worke.[19] And finding that Mr Fitch by his Covenants is allowed two shillings per yard solid for earth dug out and carried away for the making the wharf[20] at the said Channell wee are of opinion hee may Reasonably deserve so much for carrying away the Rubbish and soile aforesaid. All which wee Certify and submit to this Honourable Committee. Dated the eighteenth day of Aprill 1674.[21]

As early as 1672 the City realised that the cost of building the Fleet Channel was going to be very much more than expected. The City Lands Committee had to be satisfied that everything possible was being done to achieve the aim of the Rebuilding Act and that nothing improper was taking place. The regular participation of Sir John Lawrence in the business of the Fleet Channel was of great importance in gaining the support of the City in the face of seemingly endless disasters and delays. A lengthy report (Figure 52) recommending greatly increased payments for new work and a new contract for Thomas Fitch signed by Wren, Hooke and Oliver (but almost certainly drafted by Hooke) was followed by a reasoned endorsement of the recommendations signed by Lawrence, William

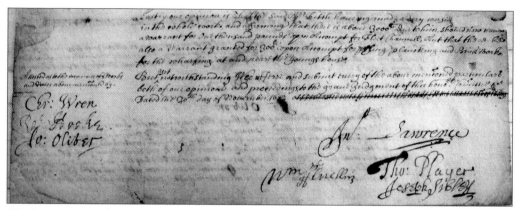

52. Signatures at the end of a clerical copy of a report recommending the City Lands Committee to continue the work on canalising the Fleet Ditch despite greatly increased costs (detail). Hooke spent many days drafting and seeking the signatories' agreement to the report which was crucial to the completion of the whole scheme. (*City Lands Committee Papers MS 57: Corporation of London Records Office*)

Flewellen,[22] the City Chamberlain Sir Thomas Player, and Joseph Sibley.[23] The endorsement praised Fitch, Wren (particularly) and Hooke for their continued diligence on behalf of the City. The report relies heavily on the authority of Wren, the King's Surveyor-General, as a reason for continuing to pay more money to the present contractor Thomas Fitch, and for revising the existing contract. Fitch was present at the committee meeting on 20 November 1672 when the full report was well received by the City Lands Committee which ordered new articles of agreement for the work in and about Fleet Channel to be drawn up as recommended by Wren, Hooke and Oliver, and in the manner of the former articles.[24] An early crisis in the rebuilding programme had been avoided, but the part played by Hooke in the affair has, as so often in the past, been obscured by Wren's reputation. It is possible to look behind the formal report, in which Wren's name was used to such good effect, to see how important were Hooke's activities behind the scenes in the weeks before the City Lands Committee decided to continue with the Fleet Canal.

Sir John Lawrence had been a supporter of Hooke at least from the time Lawrence was chairman of the Gresham Trustees when Hooke was appointed Professor of Geometry at Gresham College in 1665. It was Lawrence to whom Hooke first showed his layout plan for rebuilding the city in 1666 and who approved it in preference to Mills's. Hooke regarded him as 'my good and sure freind'.[25] Lawrence was an important figure in the City. His installation feast in 1665 was attended by the king and queen and an unusually grand array of courtiers for a Lord Mayor's installation. According to John Evelyn, who was present, the feast was said to have cost one thousand pounds,[26] which was about half Lawrence's annual income at the time of the fire.[27] Lawrence was a courageous and respected member of the City. As Lord Mayor in 1665, at the time of the plague, he remained in the city throughout and urged his aldermen to do the same. His reputation in the City can be judged from the numerous positions he held, often for more than one period. He was Master of the Haberdashers' Company and a committee member of the East India Company (each three times), and Governor of the Irish Society and President of St Thomas's Hospital (each twice), Father of the City in 1690 and Alderman of Queenhithe Ward from 4 February 1658 until his death on 26 January 1692, except for the period of suspension of the City's Charter.[28] A leading City Whig, in his friendship with Hooke he shared a common purpose of civic duty and responsibility. He was one of four City merchants proposed by Seth Ward and elected Fellow of the Royal Society on 27 November 1673, exempt charges, at a time when the Society's fortunes were declining; perhaps the Society was looking for some support from the City. Described as 'slightly active' (judged by the number of times his spoken contributions at meetings were recorded in the Society's minutes), he was none the less elected to the Council of the Royal Society in 1674, 1678 and 1680.[29]

Hooke and Lawrence met regularly, often dining together at the latter's home, usually on a Saturday. In the frequency of their meetings and the apparent amiability of their relationship there is a resemblance to the relationship between Hooke and Wren. Although Hooke often made disparaging remarks in his diary about colleagues in the Royal Society and in the City with whom he worked closely, Lawrence and Wren hardly ever received such obloquy. Hooke's congenial relationships with each of them and the mutual trust and respect which they engendered were important factors in the efficient rebuilding of London.

Hooke's efforts were crucial in overcoming the first major crisis in building the Fleet Channel.[30] He realised in early October 1672 how serious the situation was. From that time until the crucial meeting of the City Lands Committee nearly two months later he was in an almost continuous flurry of one-to-one meetings with Wren, Lawrence, Fitch (who is referred to as 'Fitz' in Hooke's diary), the craftsmen involved in the construction work and the surveyors who assessed its quality and the quantities and costs of materials used. He met them all over the city in places where they and he went about their other tasks – in Gresham College, at various sites alongside the Fleet, at St Paul's, in Guildhall and at dinner with Wren or Lawrence. From time to time he met the City Lands Committee to report progress and present a formal proposal. On the morning of 14 November 1672 he carried out two commissions (probably views) in Crutched Friars, receiving 10s for each, met Dr Ralph Cudworth, author of philosophical books, and a divine, dined in his own rooms at Gresham College, staked out a foundation in Sherbourne Lane, and then went to the Rose Tavern at Fleet Bridge where he met Sir John Lawrence, Sir Thomas Player, William Flewellen, Wren, Sir William Hooker,[31] Joseph Sibley,[32] and Thomas Fitch and his younger brother John. Oliver's name is not mentioned. They all viewed the work and agreed on the recommendations to be presented to the City Lands Committee six days later. Following the meeting Hooke went to Garraway's coffee house near the Royal Exchange where he met Richard Shortgrave (the Royal Society's Operator, who assisted Hooke not only with his scientific experiments but also with his duties for the City), probably to arrange for a final set of measurements to be made and included in the report.[33]

There is no doubt that Wren, Lawrence, Hooke and Thomas Fitch all made essential and complementary contributions to the successful completion of the Fleet Channel despite contrary views which have so far prevailed about Hooke's contribution. Reddaway has written that as far as Hooke's planning of the scheme is concerned, 'Hooke's *Diary* . . . is disappointing . . . its curt jottings, though they show that he was actively concerned in the work of supervision, give no indication of how much he contributed towards the planning of the scheme. The only entries which can be construed as bearing upon the latter are those of October 1st and of November 2nd, 1673, and they are too slight to build anything upon'.[34] Although it is true that Hooke in his diary seldom wrote even a word or two to indicate why he went to a particular place or met a particular person, and that any one diary entry is too slight to build anything upon, the accumulation of names and places he recorded in the few weeks preceding the City Lands Committee meeting on 20 November and the many references to his name in the City records are strong circumstantial evidence of his involvement in all aspects of the Fleet Channel. In the winter of 1666/7 he was engaged with the King's Commissioners in the conceptual design of the transformation of a ditch into a canal. Although the design of structural elements such as piles, piers, wharfing, quays, bridges and cellars was led by Wren at the start of the project, the redesign found to be necessary was done by Wren and Hooke in cooperation. It was Hooke who ensured through many site visits that the design was properly understood and executed by Fitch and his sub-contractors. He was trusted by Wren and Lawrence not only to draft the detailed and lengthy formal reports to the City on the progress and costs of the work, but also to meet often and informally with the City's committees to allay their fears about rising costs. It is hard to see which other individual did more.

The Fleet River became a ditch through long neglect and was transformed into a navigable canal by design at a cost of £51,307 6s 2d,[35] a sum far in excess of anything that might have been expected when Wren, Hooke and Oliver presented their detailed designs to the City in the spring of 1671. Its successful completion in autumn 1674 meant the City had to find ways of maintaining it. The second Rebuilding Act allowed the City to set and receive tolls for navigating the canal and dues from using the wharfs and cranes, but the idea that maintenance costs could be offset by income was not realised. By 1679, after three years of collecting tolls and dues, less than £200 had been received as income. The main reason for such a low figure can be seen in Ogilby and Morgan's map (Figure 53), which shows a cluster of lighters at the mouth of the canal, but very few along its length. It was more convenient and cheaper for goods arriving on the Thames to be transported inland by cart than by boat along a tidal canal. Illegal entries into the vaults beneath the quays (Figure 54) were made from the basements of the houses fronting the canal, which contributed to the shortfall in the City's income and made it impossible to maintain the channel. The quays were increasingly used for wheeled traffic because there were no similarly broad and direct

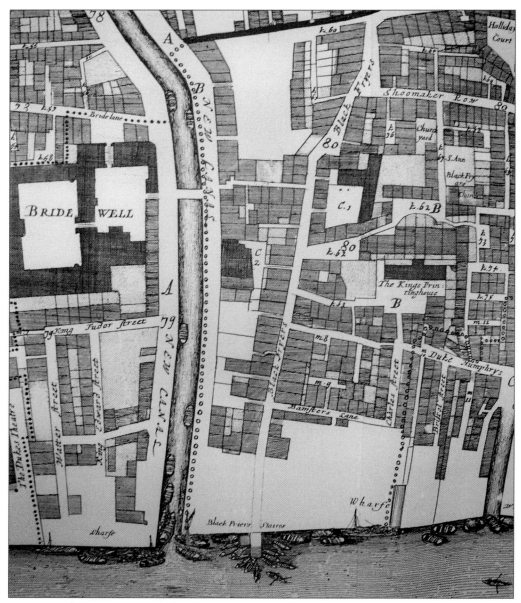

53. Detail of Ogilby and Morgan's 1/1200 scale map (1676) of the largely rebuilt city. The area of open ground on the quay immediately north of Blackfriars Stairs was the site where Sir Thomas Fitch, the main contractor for the construction of the Fleet Canal, would later build his house (Figures 54 and 83). (*Guildhall Library, Corporation of London*)

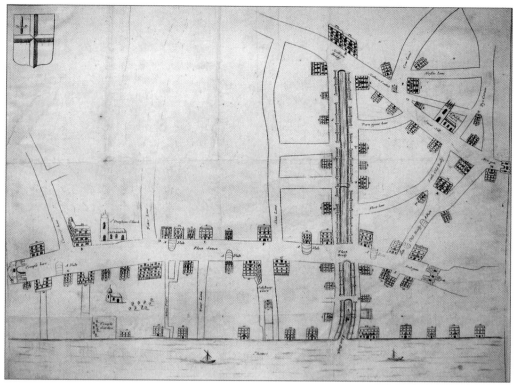

54. A sketch plan (1681) of the Ward of Farringdon Without by Andrew Yarranton, former officer in the Parliamentary Army and a manufacturer of tin plate. It shows buildings along Fleet Street and the new canal having vaults and balconies which could be used for defence in the event of a Papist invasion. Also shown is Sir Thomas Fitch's house on the quay at Blackfriars adjacent to the east side of the canal. (*Guildhall Library, Corporation of London*)

north–south streets nearby. Various traders used the quays for storing goods, parking carts, repairing carriages, sawing masonry and serving food and drinks. Inevitably the local inhabitants resumed their custom of dumping rubbish in and at the sides of the Fleet. Silt continued to be deposited in the upper reaches of the canal to such an extent that by around 1730 it was no longer navigable above Fleet Bridge. In 1733 the stretch between the Holborn and Fleet Bridges was covered over and used for a market, the quays either side serving as roads. Thirty-three years later the lower reaches were covered over. When the first Blackfriars Bridge was built in 1769, the canal was completely covered by a road. It now flows into the Thames from beneath Farringdon Street and New Bridge Street, hidden from view.

A QUAY

The construction of a new broad quay along the north bank of the Thames from the Tower to Temple Gardens with an array of houses of the first sort behind presented different but even more difficult problems to the City. John Evelyn expressed the views of many in Charles II's court when he compared London's appearance very unfavourably with the views of other cities he had seen during his visits to Holland, Belgium, Italy and France.[36] He found the rotting timber wharves and stairs along the north bank of the Thames (Figure 82) particularly disagreeable in comparison with the waterside at Genoa or at Constantinople. Visitors from overseas coming to London by water were confronted by a scene of mercantile activity amid noisome laystalls and a disorganised mass of warehouses, heaps of coal and stacks of timber. Narrow winding lanes ascended the steep ground leading away from the river, crowded with carts taking goods to and from the lighters clustered around the landing places. The king and the City thought a new Thames quay was an essential feature of a rebuilt city, and apart from John Evelyn other members of the Royal Society thought so too.

The project was hardly mentioned in the first Rebuilding Act, when the City had more urgent rebuilding work to do than starting on a new quay. The second Rebuilding Act passed by Parliament in April 1670 gave more details of the quay, but the City, still busy seeing to the needs of the citizens to rebuild their houses, did not begin to plan what might be done to meet the requirements of the act until a year later. The City Lands Committee then decided that from the bridge upstream to the Temple a broad quay, clear of all buildings and varying from twenty to eighty feet in depth should be built by extending the bank of the river southwards. The rubble excavated for the Fleet Channel would be used to build up the new quay to five feet above high-water mark. The encroachment into the Thames was the City's idea, but the act specified that the quay should be kept free of all buildings. To save expense, the City decided that the areas of ground would remain in private ownership, with boundaries marked only by denter stones.[37] The owners would be responsible for clearing their sites, but would later receive income from levies on the use of their portion of the quay for merchandise brought ashore.

In a manner resembling his instruction to consult with Wren at the start of the Fleet Channel scheme, Hooke in May 1671 received the following order from the City Lands Committee:

Whereas this Committee intend speedily to sett about & perfect the Water line upon the River of Thames according to the Prescription of the Act of Parliament, Itt is therefore ordered that Mr Hooke doe attend upon Dr Wren his Majesty's Surveyor for his concurrence & advice therein And further that he would bee pleased to consider what designe may be most apt & convenient for that purpose And acquaint this Committee with his Opinion.[38]

At the same time it was 'ordered that Mr Hook doe treat with some good & able workman for building of a substantiall payre of stayres at the old Swan & report to this Committee his proceedings That an Agreement may bee thereupon made for the same & The same out of hand performed'.

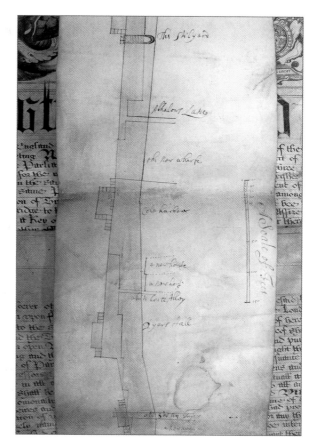

55. Detail from the 1/600 plan on parchment (Charter 98) of the Thames Quay (1671). Letters Patent lie behind the plan. Over 8 feet (2.5m) in length, it was plotted by Richard Shortgrave from his survey measurements. The existing shore line at high tide is shown as an irregular line running through a shaded area bounded at the north by a line representing the limit of the area to be kept free of buildings and at the south by the proposed new shoreline and stairs. (*Corporation of London Records Office*)

Within three weeks a survey of the waterline had been made, a scale plan drawn and the proposed new alignment drawn upon it (Figure 55). The stairs at the Old Swan mentioned by the City were among many proposed to be built at intervals along the new quay. The ground shown on the plan used for the design of the new waterline was surveyed and plotted by Richard Shortgrave under Hooke's supervision.[39] The City Lands Committee

> . . . ordered that the City Surveyors doe attend Dr Wren – his Majesty's Surveyor with the designe or draught of the Waterline by them prepared for his approbation That the same may be ascertained and the Wharfe to bee thereupon made according to the late Act of Parliament speedily undertaken Which worke will bee the better & more easily accomplished by imploying the soyle & rubbish to be taken up at Fleet ditch for that purpose.[40]

Hooke was ordered to accompany members of a City sub-committee to Billingsgate Dock to negotiate a contract with workmen for taking down old stairs and building new ones according to his design. By 5 July 1671 the City was eager to proceed as quickly as possible.[41] Five days later the City ordered work to start as soon as the king could be persuaded to agree to their proposals and authorise letters patent,[42] which were issued on 4 December 1671[43] (Figure 55).

The vigorous and confident start soon slowed through lack of money to pay for the scheme. The City had become apprehensive at the growing cost of the Fleet Channel, where technical problems kept cropping up. In building the Thames Quay, however, the main problems were not technical but derived from the many interests that could not be reconciled without payment and the unclear wording of second Rebuilding Act on the matter. The occupants and owners of the wharves and warehouses ('wharfingers') were to have their buildings cleared and ground taken for making a quay. The second Rebuilding Act was unclear on how compensation should be paid. It seemed that the coal tax would be inadequate – and it had already been increased by the Act to cover the cost of rebuilding the parish churches. The owners were unwilling to give up their ground and income without compensation, in cash or by warrant. The prospect of an income in the future from the use of their ground for landing goods, even though it would be marked in the new quay by denter stones, was not enough for them to give up what they already had.

In the second half of 1672 and the first half of 1673 the City Lands Committee made a few attempts to move ahead with the work, but nothing came of their efforts. Caught up in the actions of the Lord Chancellor (the Earl of Shaftesbury) and the City to get agreement from the owners, Hooke spent time on fruitless attempts to make progress on the quay, going back and forth between Guildhall, Westminster and the owners' properties. Typically terse diary comments such as 'Dougate dock . . . Guildhall about water line with Dr Wren' appear from time to time,[44] but he soon became more deeply involved in the muddle. After meetings with the Lord Chancellor and Wren on Wednesday 21 May 1673, Hooke went with a bricklayer to take a view at the quay.[45] Two days later Hooke was in the presence of the king on what appears to have been a visit by members of the Royal Society. He recorded in his diary:

Lord Chancellor, Sir P. Neile, Sir R. Moray, Mr. Lock, &c. (in the councell chamber King smild on me) Lord Chancellor rattled for nothing. fetchd map. met him on water. to Whitehall with Chancellor. at Sir R. Morays. walkd in park with Dr. Wren. King seeing me cald me told me he was glad to see me recoverd asked for degre by water. home. Garways.[46]

The Chancellor had apparently urged upon Hooke the need to get on with making a detailed map of the riverside so that the ground to be taken for the new quay could be identified on it and the areas to be taken from the wharf owners or 'wharfingers' could be marked out and cleared. On the following Monday, after meeting the Lord Mayor at

Guildhall, Hooke went again to see the Lord Chancellor who ordered a map to be made of the section of the quay between London Bridge and Dowgate.[47] Within a week Hooke had taken the measurements, assisted by Harry Hunt, a young man who would become Hooke's constant companion in later years,[48] and had drawn the map.[49] The Chancellor then issued orders to clear all buildings from the waterside except for a stretch between Dowgate and Whitefriars. The orders were ineffective. The Chancellor apparently held Hooke personally accountable for the delay, although neither the City nor Hooke had any authority to do what the Chancellor required. In August 1673 the matter came up at a meeting of the Council attended by Isaac Barrow and Prince Rupert, both prominent members of the Royal Society and well known to Hooke. It was through them that Hooke learned of the Chancellor's anger. He received an order to attend the Council at its next meeting.[50]

On 3 September, the day of Hooke's attendance at the meeting of the Council, he prepared himself for what he expected to be a difficult discussion. He went first to see the Lord Mayor and then on to Westminster where he called on Wren at his official house in Scotland Yard before facing the Chancellor's anger. He seems to have been well prepared, for he recorded in his diary 'Councell table. The Lord Chancellor accused me with great bitternesse and craven but grew milder . . .'. Hooke reported back to the Lord Mayor who '. . . Warnd the wharfingers to take downe'.[51] The following day, after Hooke dined with the Lord Mayor and Chamberlain, the wharf owners were summoned; some of them were then bound over to clear their ground.[52] The next day Hooke was back with the Lord Chancellor until 1 p.m., reporting on the actions he and the City had taken.[53] They seemed to have resulted in at least some clearance taking place because three weeks later he visited the wharf owners again and told them to start paving.[54]

While attempts by the City and Privy Council to persuade the owners to clear the ground had started to have an effect, they soon began to lose interest in the project. Hooke continued to view the wharves, certify ground taken away and report from time to time to the Council, only to find on occasion that his report was not needed.[55] On 7 November 1673 Shaftesbury was removed from office and little more was done to proceed with the grand scheme.[56] By the mid-1670s the places where goods were transferred between land and water were moving downstream to wharves below the Bridge. The owners who had complied with the Chancellor's orders and vacated their ground, expecting to receive an income from its use for bringing ashore merchandise, could see their hopes fading. They petitioned the City for compensation, but with its rebuilding programme running at an alarming deficit the City could only express sympathy and an intention to seek a means of paying. The clamour for compensation increased so much that in 1681 the City Lands Committee decided to seek counsel's opinion on what the City should do under the terms of the second Rebuilding Act to meet the claims. Counsel's opinion was that the main purpose of the act was to restore London's trade and commerce: only when that had been achieved could an assessment be made as to whether or not the owners who had vacated their ground had suffered a loss. Although claimants were still not content (and at least one claimant, Sir Henry Tulse, was a member of the City Lands Committee), the Committee was seen to have done all it could to meet their needs. The Thames Quay described in the king's patent was never to be fully built but parts of it were, particularly at the mouth of the Fleet Channel, Blackfriars, Dowgate Dock and Puddle Dock. Hooke played his usual part in designing and supervising the rebuilding at these places. He had helped to draft the technical details of the Rebuilding Acts and he knew of the great problems the City faced in going ahead with the Thames Quay and that it was unlikely it would ever be completed. This did not deter him from conscientiously performing his duties in relation to it, which were often onerous and sometimes unpleasant.

GATEWAYS

The city's damaged gateways were much less prominent than the Fleet Channel and the Thames Quay in the vision of the more beautiful city. Substantially built, mainly of stone, they could still serve their original purposes for a few years after the fire, but they were symbols of the City's authority. When their repair was begun in 1672 Hooke was involved in work on Newgate and Moorgate. On 17 July 1672 the City Lands Committee ordered the surveyors to assist in designing and estimating the cost of rebuilding Moorgate, to value Little Moorfields and decide how it could be disposed of for use as a hay market, and to view the work in progress at Newgate, which had been patched up after the fire and continued to be in use as a gaol.[57] The design of Moorgate and estimates of the cost of building ordered by the City Lands Committee to be made with the assistance of the surveyors[58] were presented to the Committee on 9 October 1672. The estimate was £2,013 12s. The Committee decided that the design was ornamental and useful and agreed that the charge was necessary and reasonable.[59] The work was approved by the City Lands Committee on 16 October 1672, when it was ordered to be undertaken.[60]

The report of the Newgate view was presented on 14 August 1672, when the Committee decided that the west front should be taken down and rebuilt according to a design by Hooke, who recorded 'Sir Will. Peak. Committee City Lands for the repair of Newgate'.[61] No mention is made of Oliver in the minutes, so it can be assumed that he did not work on the design. The committee members who, with Hooke's advice, had reported on the view were made responsible for overseeing the building construction, dealing with the workmen and preparing the accounts for repair work done at Newgate since the fire.[62] They were referred to as the 'Newgate Committee'. At a meeting on 27 August 1672 the Newgate Committee decided to delegate its responsibility to the City Surveyors.[63]

Unpaid repair work had been in progress at Newgate for at least two years, and it was only now that the City decided to pay for the repairs and go ahead with rebuilding the

more severely damaged parts. Hooke
responded by submitting the estimate for
rebuilding to the Newgate Committee on 5
September 1672,[64] and was with the
Committee again on 11 September when the
carpenter Roger Jerman and the tiler and
bricklayer Anthony Tanner were ordered to
erect a shed to house the cistern to be located
at Newgate, with a small lodging room above
and 'in all things' to observe the directions
and appointments of Hooke and Oliver. It was
also recorded at the meeting that the bill
proposed by Hooke for the rebuilding
amounted to £2,279.[65] On the orders of the
City Lands Committee, Hooke continued
working on Newgate and other gateways. He
was ordered to view the work at Newgate
with Oliver and two of the City's master
masons and to investigate the source of stone
being used, following a complaint to the City
that it was of poor quality.[66] One of the
surveyors (un-named) was ordered with
Shortgrave to measure Tanner's work at
Newgate.[67] Hooke continued to supervise the
construction works: he was there with the
City Chamberlain on 13 June 1673,[68] and he

56. A print (*c.* 1750) of Newgate, by an
anonymous artist and engraver. The
gateway was designed by Hooke after the
Great Fire and rebuilt 'much more
commodious and strong' according to the
adjoining caption. (*Guildhall Library,
Corporation of London*)

made many views of adjacent tofts as the rebuilding progressed. By the time it was
completed the cost had risen to £9,484, so it seems as if Hooke's design was too modest
for the City's taste. The finished Newgate (Figure 56) bore Caius Cibber's carvings of the
king's arms and the City's arms either side of the top of the portal.[69]

Hooke's work on Newgate was similar to his work on the more important Fleet
Channel and Thames Quay. No other individual was engaged in those projects as
widely as he was from design to completion. Hooke dealt almost daily with technical
problems, measuring, advising, discussing, appraising and reporting. He faced up to
and mitigated the unjustified wrath of the Lord Chancellor over the Thames Quay and
he reconciled differences between the City and its contractors when construction costs
increased alarmingly. He did all he could to make progress even though he knew the
quay could not be completed in the way originally intended. He worked hard to
alleviate discord whenever he thought it was likely to hinder the work, and performed
his duties with conscientious efficiency.

15

FOR THE WELL-BEING
OF ALL CITIZENS

GETTING RID OF THE WASTE

When Hooke was staking out streets and working on the canalisation of the Fleet Ditch, building the Thames Quay and rebuilding gateways, he was helping to realise the vision of the rulers of London and of the nation for a more beautiful city. He served the needs of householders when he staked out the foundations of their dwellings and certified for compensation areas of their ground taken away by the City. All who lived in the city also benefited from his engagement in the tasks of laying sewers and water pipes in paved streets, siting and building conduits, relocating markets and rebuilding churches.

City wards and parishes managed local facilities such as watercourses and drainage gullies for the physical health of parishioners, while the churches administered their spiritual life. As City Surveyor Hooke was called upon by the City Lands Committee to advise them on what would now be called public health engineering, in particular the laying of sewers and water pipes and the siting of houses of common easement. The rebuilding of sewers was overseen by the Commissioners for Sewers (and Paving), whose members included aldermen and deputies appointed by the City. In the spring of 1667 Hooke, with Mills and Oliver, worked with the commissioners to produce rules and directions for gradients of the streets and lanes under the supervision of the common councilmen of the wards. The City's instrument for setting up the Commissioners for Sewers in accordance with the Rebuilding Act is dated 16 May 1667:

> This day one writing dated this present day authorizing my Lord Maior and Aldermen and diverse Commoners of the Common Councell in each ward to designe and sett out the Numbers of all Common Sewers Dreynes and Vaults and the order and manner of paving and pitching the streetes and Lanes within this Citty and Libertyes according to the late Act of Parliament for rebuilding the Citty and an order of Common Councell in pursuance thereof was here sealed with the Common Seale of this Citty.[1]

A few months later, following meetings between the City Surveyors and the commissioners, the City printed a document prescribing the rules and directions for setting gradients of streets and lanes for better drainage.[2] The commissioners were authorised to levy rates on the inhabitants living in the areas served by new sewers and paving, and to remove trade practices that were dangerous or noxious. With the advice of the surveyors, the commissioners were officially responsible for administering the sewers and paving, but in effect they relied on the surveyors to direct all the technical aspects of the work, taking them on views of work in progress and of disputes between neighbours. The surveyors directed the construction work and supervised the levelling surveys, the setting out of gradients of streets and sewers and the construction of drains. The City's instrument setting up the commissioners also set in motion an enterprise intended to make a considerable improvement to the health of the inhabitants, but some people who lost their livelihoods by it through construction work alongside or through their property raised objections that had to be dealt with by the City, again with the advice of the surveyors. Hooke did not simply go along with what the City decided, but put forward suggestions for greater efficiency.

Much of Hooke's work on new sewers centred around the Fleet Ditch, and was closely related to the arduous and costly task of making it navigable. He and Wren had included a proposal about building sewers (which was accepted and implemented by the City) among their first detailed technical proposals for the Fleet Channel to the City Lands Committee on 22 March 1671, recommending that

> . . . some Ingenious Carpenters doe attend the direction of the Surveyors for making & placing of Pumps where necessary & conveyances for the land water & sewers, and a person to take Exactly the levells & direct the diggers in the orderly carrying on of the worke, which must be estimated according to the occasion.[3]

The proposed sewer design turned out to be as unsatisfactory as the design for the wharf, and for the same reasons – exceptionally steep side slopes to the ditch, unprecedented lateral pressure on the walls of the wharves, and rubbish and silt brought down from upstream. As early as June 1671 Sir Jeremy Whitchcot wrote to the City Lands Committee complaining that the cellars of his houses by the Fleet Channel had become flooded by sewage as a result of blocked drains.[4] The committee was exceptionally busy at this time and responded that they were proceeding as quickly as possible in accordance with the Rebuilding Act and had engaged workmen solely to deal with the sort of complaint that Whitchcot had made. They ordered the City Surveyors to view and report on any damage Whitchcot had suffered and suggest what redress should be made to him.[5] No record of the surveyors' report has been found, but two years later the City paid £800 to Whitchcot for 2,508 square feet of ground taken away on the west side of the Fleet Channel in front of his twenty-two tenements.[6] The compensation rate paid by the City was rather higher than the 5s normally paid and probably includes compensation for the damage done earlier to Whitchcot's property by blockage of drains. Hooke charged Whitchcot 5 guineas for the area certificate.[7]

Hooke's many responsibilities for detailed supervision of the construction of new sewers included directing craftsmen and monitoring the materials they were using. He had to ensure that the construction materials were safely transported to the site and securely stored at a time when they were in great demand. The large brick-lined sewer from Aldgate to Crown Hill was built by the bricklayer John Fitch. Once the trench had been excavated and the specified gradients set out, Fitch was ordered to

> . . . doe the Brickework thereof good lyme and sand and hard burnt bricks and noe Rubbish. To bee made two bricks thick at the least and four foot broad below & seaven foote high for which he shall be paid after the Rate of six pounds per Rod to be reduced to a brick & an halfe solid measure. And Mr Shortgrave is desired to Admeasure the same Worke as it shall be performed every 14 days and give account thereof to this Committee. And in order to the said Worke that a Breach be made in the Cities wall for a cart passage to carry in earth for that purpose and Labourers imployed to digge & prepare the same who shall be paid after the Rate of 5d per yard. Agreed further that for what timber shall bee imployed there for plancks & pyles the said Fitch shall be paid after the rate of 4d per foot running measure.[8]

A week later Hooke was authorised, with Fitch's assistance, to make a gate or postern at a convenient place in the city wall near Crutched Friars for easier transport of building materials for the sewer and of fill for raising the base of the trench to the appropriate levels. Tenants living nearby were ordered to comply if any part of their ground was needed for temporary storage of construction materials.[9]

Another matter of public health was the siting of houses of common easement (latrines). Hooke contributed in many practical ways to ameliorating the worst effects of these necessary, but noxious, public facilities. Their location near inns often led to objections from neighbours, which Hooke had to investigate, as he did on 10 November 1674 when the widow Mrs Pattarell objected to one such place close to Richard Cannon's inn.[10] The surveyors were also ordered to find a way of removing the noxious consequences of unregulated public usage as a latrine of a place against the south wall of Guildhall.[11] This area was a chronic nuisance. A cleric about to move with his family into the parsonage of St Lawrence Jewry complained that the nearby house of common easement in a narrow passage at the end of Guildhall Yard was unwholesome and prejudicial to himself and his family; the surveyors (that is, Hooke, since it was in his area of the city) were ordered to relocate it in a place where it would be less offensive.[12] When the citizens of Queenhithe asked the City Lands Committee for a house of common easement to be erected in their parish, the City Surveyors were ordered to decide on the site and method of construction.[13]

Laystalls were places where all kinds of rubbish, including sweepings from the streets, refuse and ashes from houses, dung and straw from stables and waste from trade practices, were stored until their contents could be taken by barge to market gardens along the Thames outside London. It was the City's responsibility to find and stake out sites for laystalls, paid for from the coal money.[14] Following the usual procedure the City passed on the task to Hooke and Oliver, who had difficulties finding places where the inevitable objections could be more easily dealt with. Slaughterhouses were also sources of nuisance. The responsibility for siting them in places permitted by the Rebuilding Act, but with minimum offence or annoyance from the organic waste, was also given to the surveyors, who had to reach agreement on the location with the Master and Wardens of the Company of Butchers.[15]

SUPPLYING CLEAN WATER

Containment and removal of waste from sewers, houses of common easement and laystalls was necessary for the improvement of public health, but so too was the supply of clean water throughout the city. Hooke was involved in repairing existing water pipes and building new ones. Before the fire the City had difficulties repairing broken underground pipes because their exact route through the city was not known. On 22 June 1669 the Court of Aldermen decided that all pipes and aqueducts should be shown on a map and that Hooke should organise the survey:

> And it is referred to Mr Hooke by assistance of . . . Mr George [the City's Plumber] to draw a Line or plott of the severall pipes or Aqueducts by which it may readily & plainly appear how & where the same lye for better finding & discovery thereof from time to time as Occasion shall require.[16]

Nothing was done until a month later. Hooke probably made it known that what the City had proposed was far too much for him or anyone else to complete before construction could begin. The Court of Aldermen made minor concessions by changing its former order. John George, the City's Plumber, was now ordered to undertake the mapping, supervised by Hooke. The specification was also changed slightly.[17]

The idea for such a map was far-sighted, but it is not surprising that there is no record of one having been produced, or even begun. A new survey of the whole city would have been necessary in order to represent accurately the positions of water services. It would have been an impossibly difficult undertaking for John George, and Hooke would not have found time to organise such a survey. Three years later the City Lands Committee made another attempt to have an accurate map made of the supply of fresh water throughout the city, when Richard Shortgrave and the City Plumber were ordered to 'make an Exact plott or map of the Pipes which convey Water from all conduits belonging to this Citty and all branches from the same with the severall places where they lye in the streets of this Citty or other places. And give an account thereof unto this Committee.'[18] The Committee also agreed to pay Shortgrave for his pains, and nearly four months later it again ordered him to deliver the map, but none was forthcoming.[19] It was for this sort of use that a map of the kind Hooke later designed (and Ogilby and Morgan published) would serve; but that was still five years away.

In June 1671 the City Surveyors staked out a site (formerly occupied by the church of St Pancras in Soper Lane) prior to constructing there a general cistern intended to be of use to the whole city. It was to replace the conduit near the Royal Exchange, which was to be replaced by stop-cocks. The surveyors were ordered to design the cistern and the City Plumber instructed to make it, according to the directions and under the supervision of the surveyors.[20] The work had been completed by March 1672 when the surveyors were ordered to advise and direct the City Plumber, John George, in laying an underground pipe (protected by a timber casing specially treated against borers) through Bird in Hand Alley to the cistern. Hooke continued from time to time, at the City's request, to work on water pipes and conduits. In 1677 he was involved in designing a new conduit at the bottom of Snow Hill (as part of widening the approaches to Smithfield) and in solving the associated problem of water distribution across the steep ground leading down to the Fleet Channel.[21] When in 1680 it was decided to replace the old conduit at the west end of Cheapside near Foster Lane, Hooke was asked to design its replacement. In consultation with Wren he produced a design in the form of an obelisk. Although the City approved the design, they wanted certain changes, which Hooke incorporated.[22] The conduit was not completed, but served as a meeting place for the city's chimney sweeps until it was demolished in 1727.[23] As late as 1683 the City was still calling on its surveyors to take views of water supplies. Hooke and Oliver presented a detailed report of a view they made of the water supply from Albemarle House in Piccadilly to the Thatched House in the Strand to discover why the water that was formerly plentiful at the conduit in the Strand was now much less. They found several reasons. Labourers digging for bricks along the route had removed some from the lining wall, thus letting out the water, which had collected into ponds or just drained away. Many feeder channels had decayed or were broken by new building works, and leaked profusely. The need for an accurate map to manage the water supply could not have been more clearly seen. The surveyors recommended the rebuilding of the whole supply.[24]

SUPPLYING FRESH FOOD

Another task confronting the City in its endeavours to make the streets healthier and easier for traffic was to find new locations for street markets. Inhabitants who lived in close proximity to the markets before the fire suffered from the smells and rubbish left behind on market days. Pedestrians, pushers of handcarts and people making use of the increasing number of coaches were all hindered in their passage by stalls set up in the streets. Petitions against the markets were regularly presented to the City. When a market was moved in consequence, the petitions continued in much the same way – only the petitioners were different. The fire provided an opportunity to reduce the detrimental effects of market trading while at the same time continuing to make dairy produce, meat, poultry and garden produce fresh from the countryside available to London's inhabitants. The city's markets were intended to be used on dates and at times regulated by the City for the sale of food grown and brought in by people living outside London. The market traders were different from city shopkeepers, who were freemen, having served their seven-year apprenticeships and been admitted to one of the livery companies. For centuries there had been competition or collaboration between the two groups, with freemen sometimes selling from the markets and people from the country ('foreigners') selling their produce illegally to shopkeepers, often through middlemen.

After a first, unsuccessful, attempt in October 1667 to find suitable sites for permanent markets, the City's Markets Committee presented its proposals to the Court of Common Council on 12 February 1668.[25] Four sites were proposed: Leadenhall market, south of the western end of Leadenhall Street; the Stocks or Woolchurch market in the former churchyard of St Mary Woolchurch Haw, south of the junction of Poultry and Cornhill; Honey Lane or Milk Street market, north of Cheapside; and Newgate market, between Newgate Street and the west end of St Paul's.

The surveyors had much to do, especially Hooke who was often nominated alone to undertake work at the market sites. Mills and Oliver were nominated individually much less often. They measured and certified ground taken away from citizens at the market sites for which the compensation rates paid from the coal tax were a matter for bargaining between the owners and the City. The surveyors were ordered to supervise the preparation of level ground for the market house at Newgate and agree rates with workmen for paving the area.[26] Three weeks later they reported that they had agreed a rate of seven pounds per (square) rod.[27] On 1 September 1669 they were ordered to do similar work at Woolchurch market and Hooke was specifically ordered to stake out ground for one of the markets at Leadenhall, and to measure the dimensions of an area of ground bought by the City from a Mr Farrington with the intention of including it as part of the market. The leaseholder of Leadenhall markets was Miles Temple, a grocer. Hooke and Oliver were ordered by the City Lands Committee to consult with him on designs for the Leadenhall markets and then present them to the Committee.[28] Temple had been granted the lease by the City for thirty-one years at £2,100 per annum. In return he was allowed to take the profits and dues from trading. He spent money on preparing the markets which, it was later discovered, should have been paid for from the coal tax. He surrendered his lease two years later after a series of disputes with the City.[29]

All this work went ahead as quickly as it could at a time when the demand on the surveyors' time to stake out and certify the foundations of private houses was reaching its peak. But the demands were unrelenting. On 10 February 1670 the surveyors were given many more tasks relating to the markets, including drawing the design for a piazza on the south side of Woolchurch market and advising the clothworker Francis Burton and the fishmonger Robert Weddell of the Markets Committee on how to contract for the piazza to be made; measuring the dimensions and examining the workmanship of cellars being dug at Leadenhall to see if they were fit for use by the market people and if so, determining their lease value; considering and reporting on Miles Temple's plan for a building above the piazza at Leadenhall market; and deciding what should be done to prepare Honey Lane market for trading. The surveyors were finally ordered not to fail to report in writing to the Committee on all these matters within six days.[30] The winter was coming to an end and the City was eager to get the markets ready for trading as quickly as possible.

The new sites for markets were accompanied by new City legislation intended to make them more manageable than they were before the fire. Large-scale surveyed plans of the markets and surroundings showing individual stalls would help in the management of such tasks as allocation of space, assessment of rents and making improvements. On 19 November 1672 the City Surveyors (that is, Hooke and Oliver – Mills had died) were ordered to make surveys of Newgate, Honey Lane and Woolchurch markets and draw plans showing the bounding streets, the houses fronting them, names of their inhabitants, whether unoccupied or unbuilt, and the details of the owners. In effect a 'spatially related market information system' was being thought of, a much smaller version of the visionary parcel-based land information system and cadastre for London which had been abandoned. It is unlikely that any such surveys were carried out by Hooke, although he was as capable as anyone of doing the work. His own abilities went far beyond routine measuring and plotting. There were many other surveyors (such as the men who in 1666 quickly produced the six plots which John Leake compiled into a map of the streets of the burnt city) who were experienced in making accurate surveys and plots. Hooke's role would have been mainly supervisory, yet in the months following the order he gives some indications that he might have done a little measurement himself, perhaps to check the work of others. He was at Newgate market in the morning of the day after the plans were ordered, but does not say why.[31] On 7 February 1673 he recorded 'measured woolchurch market'.[32] He was at Newgate market for an unspecified purpose on 29 May 1673,[33] and again on 23 September 1673 but with John Wise, clockmaker, specifically to view the market clock.[34] At none of these visits could he have made anything other than a few measurements for a specific purpose. The work ordered by the City Lands Committee would have taken a few days at each market to complete.

Unfortunately the 'spatially related market information system' was delayed too long. There is no evidence that any plans of the kind ordered by the Committee in 1672 were made before 26 June 1677 when William Leybourne presented a plan he had made of Honey Lane market and was then ordered to make similar plans of all the city's markets.

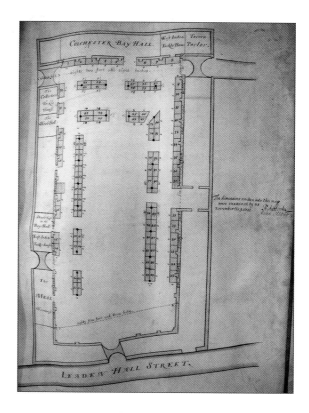

57. Leybourne's 1677 parchment plan of Leadenhall beef market shows the locations of 94 stalls in the piazza with 23 dots marking the positions of oak columns on stone bases which supported the slate roof. Two more columns and twelve more stalls were added later. North is at the bottom of the plan. (*Plan Drawer 92.c: Corporation of London Records Office*)

The Committee were impatient. Only a week after the order was given the Committee's clerk entered a memorandum 'to hasten Mr. Leybourne about the plotts of the markets'. The City then threatened Leybourne that if he did not 'finish the severall plotts of the markets' within a fortnight he 'would have nothing for his paines'. The threat worked. Leybourne was paid £20 in August 1677 and another £12 at the end of the year for six plans: the beef market (Figure 57), the Greenyard and the herb market at Leadenhall; the Stocks market at Woolchurch; Honey Lane or Milk Street market; and Newgate market.[35] These plans omit much of the detail originally specified for, but they are accompanied by Leybourne's dimensions of each stall and other information such as whether a stall is covered or not and its weekly and annual rents (Figure 58). The tables and associated plans are a greatly simplified example of the register of land which the City intended to set up and use for managing the rebuilt city. The plans were later annotated with the inscription 'The dimensions written into this Mapp were examined by us. November the 3. 1692.' followed by what purport to be the signatures of Hooke and Oliver, but Oliver's name is not his signature and Hooke's name is very probably a careful copy of the form of his signature at that time.

The new markets were among the more successful improvements after the fire. Their locations were well chosen, set back from the main thoroughfares yet accessible by carts

THE BEEFE MARKET,
IN
LEADEN-HALL.

The Marks or Signes of the Stalls.

58. William Leybourne's parchment table of data concerning the lettings of the stalls at Leadenhall beef market, identified on his plan (Figure 57). Dimensions, areas and numbers of each kind of stall are listed in columns at the left; rents are at the right. The 94 stalls shown on the plan would yield an annual rent of £57 19s 2d. (*Plan Drawer 92.c: Corporation of London Records Office*)

through the lesser streets and lanes. They were much better managed than before and the 'foreigners' who sold goods there were pleased with them. The land bought by the City specifically for the new markets provided the vendors with more secure and less dangerous sites than they had ever had in the days when blows, accidental and intentional, delivered by passing traffic upset their street stalls and damaged their produce.

A BUILDING PARTNERSHIP

The walls of many of the parish churches, mostly built of stone, were still standing after the fire, some protruding only a little way above the general level of the ground, others standing as high as before, but now supporting a damaged steeple. They were the main landmarks after the fire, giving some reference to the streets, lanes and alleyways hidden beneath rubble. Inside, many had been gutted, their roofs collapsed on to the floor in a confused heap of burnt timber, tiles and melted lead and bell-metal. Of the 110 parish churches before the fire, only 20 survived; 55 were destroyed and rebuilt. The remaining 35 were destroyed and not rebuilt.[36] They had remained in ruins during the first few years after the fire, but from time to time Hooke assessed the structural stability of walls or steeples which threatened to collapse on to the new building going on around them.

In the winter months of 1666 when the City was busily working with the Privy Council to decide on legislation for rebuilding, they gave little attention to rectifying the loss of four-fifths of the parish churches. The parishioners erected small wooden sheds called 'tabernacles' on cleared church ground, or put a timber roof over an area of their damaged church so that services could continue.

The enormous cost of rebuilding, and the huge amount of material and workmen needed to carry it out, presented difficulties which the City had no time to deal with at formal meetings, until it became necessary to do so in January 1667. The Commons Committee, after consulting with the Archbishop of Canterbury and the bishops of London and Exeter about rebuilding St Paul's and the parish churches, sent their draft order to the City, asking to be informed of how far the City had gone in the matter. On Saturday 12 January 1667 the Court of Aldermen ordered some members of the City's Court of Common Council and the City Surveyors to attend the Commons Committee daily to report on progress. We see here another example of the way in which members of the Royal Society were closely involved in the policy and detail of rebuilding the city. The Bishop of Exeter was Seth Ward FRS, Savilian Professor of Astronomy at Oxford in the 1650s. As his pupil, Hooke had made improvements to the pendulum clock Ward was then using for timing his astronomical observations. Ward had been at the meeting of the Royal Society on 19 September 1666 when Hooke showed his layout plan for the city,[37] in the presence of Sir John Lawrence, whom Ward successfully proposed for election to the Royal Society on 27 November 1673.[38]

The 1670 Rebuilding Act provided for an additional tax of 1s 1½d on each chaldron of coal to pay for the cost of rebuilding London's parish churches. It also identified the thirty-five burnt churches which would not be rebuilt. Evidence that Hooke had an important role in the rebuilding of the churches comes from the City's 'The Accompt of Sallerys Paid unto Officers and Servants Emploid in Building Parochiall Churches',[39] which shows that between 1671 and 1693 he was paid a total of £2,820 – about the same amount as he received in his lifetime in combined salaries from Gresham College and the City.[40] Exactly what he did in return for such a large and specific charge on the 1s 1½d tax on a chaldron of coal is much harder to assess in the absence of direct evidence.

The Archbishop of Canterbury, the Bishop of London and the Lord Mayor of London had been given the responsibility by the second Rebuilding Act for rebuilding the parish churches. Soon known as the Commissioners for Churches (although not designated as such by the act) they quickly nominated Wren to take charge of all design and construction matters, assisted by Hooke and Edward Woodroofe, a master mason and Wren's assistant at St Paul's. Woodroofe died in 1675 and was replaced the following year by John Oliver.[41] Although Hooke was referred to by the Commissioners for Churches as one of Wren's two assistants, the relationship between the two was more complex than that between master architect and assistant. Wren trusted Hooke in all technical matters relating to rebuilding the city. He knew of Hooke's extravagant claims for his scientific instruments, but he also understood that they were not simply the boastings of a vain man but true insights into what could be done when optical and mechanical technology was freed from its contemporary limitations. The City had recognised the importance of their friendship and common intellectual interest in science and its uses when they nominated Hooke in 1666 to work with Wren and the king's other commissioners in drafting technical specifications for Parliament. Since that time they had seen complete justification of their trust in Hooke to do all that was asked of him. However, Wren did not authorise such a large sum to be paid to Hooke simply because they were good friends.

A detailed study of the relationship between the two men in connection with explaining planetary motion[42] has shown that each gained from the ideas of the other. It is probable that a similar interaction in relation to the properties of structural materials and structural design, if not in architectural design, took place during their frequent meetings in Wren's office at St Paul's, or at Scotland Yard, or at any of the dozens of construction sites in the city where they were working. But they could have worked together on rebuilding the churches at almost any time and at any one of the many places where they met, drank coffee, dined, sketched diagrams for arches or orbits, or just talked. The difficulty of identifying Hooke's specific contributions amid a welter of meetings is illustrated by the following typical extract from Hooke's diary:

> To Sir Ch: Wren with Mr. Hill and Aubery. Mr. Henshaw and Dr. Holder there.[43] Discoursed about petrifactions of Bodys, about plaisters, about framing glasse, form of arch light gold statues, Staining marble, Filligreen sodering with bran, about printing stuffs and guilding stuffs, about Dr. Moors notions, about ghosts and spirits. By coach home. 1sh. Eat sturgeon vinegar and sugar. Agreed not.[44]

The extent and particulars of Hooke's contribution to the architecture of the city churches are matters still to be fully investigated and argued over. Scant archival evidence is very difficult to corroborate independently, but it is now generally accepted that Hooke's architecture shows Dutch influence and it has been argued that of three city churches clearly influenced by Dutch architecture, two were designed by Hooke: the churches of St Benet, Paul's Wharf, at the junction of Victoria Street and White Lion Hill (Figure 59), and St Edmund the King on the north side of Lombard Street (Figure 60). The broad outlines of Hooke's architecture were made known after long neglect when his earlier diary was published in 1935,[45] nearly seventy years ago, but which of London's parish churches can be attributed to Hooke is still a 'prickly question . . . which seems set to run and run'.[46] A recent discussion of the extent of Hooke's contribution to the architecture of the city's parish churches[47] has been criticised as unsatisfactory because the criteria used for attributing churches to Hooke were not specific enough.[48]

There is, however, evidence of Hooke's considerable contribution to the management and direction of building work on the church sites. In the year and a half from the time

59. The church of St Benet, Paul's Wharf, in 2003, hemmed in by St Benet's Hill on the east and south, Queen Victoria Street on the north and White Lion Hill on the west. Generally attributed to Hooke, it is built of brick on a square plan and shows Dutch influence in such external decorative features as festoons and contrasting stonework in the quoins and modillioned eaves. (*Author's collection*)

60. The church of St Edmund the King and Martyr, Lombard Street in 2003. The original steeple was replaced in the early eighteenth century at which time the festoons which ornamented the neck-shaped gable on the façade were removed. (*Author's collection*)

he began his first diary in 1672, Hooke recorded more than sixty visits to twenty-four different churches,[49] but in his usual terse style – nothing more was necessary for *aides-mémoires* except when he needed to record a specific detail, as he did when he agreed a contract price with the mason Joshua Marshall: 'At Sir Ch. Wrens. Agreed with Marshall for St Stephens, Coleman Street, for £770 for east and south sides. Dind with Marshall.'[50] Sometimes he visited a church alone, sometimes with Wren. The reasons for many of these visits can only be guessed at, but if he was accompanied by Wren it was almost certainly related to church building works. When he gives the names of ward aldermen and deputies, the visit was possibly a view by Hooke as City Surveyor to examine and report on matters such as damaged and allegedly dangerous church walls, towers and steeples. In any case, accompanied or not, Hooke's participation in the rebuilding of the city churches was extensive. It followed the pattern of his views of the City's own rebuilding programme, except that his conclusions were not reported formally as written reports, but given directly to craftsmen working at the site (and later to Wren if necessary) where he would have been able to give directions by sketches or orally about how the work should be done, or improved upon. Hooke made an important contribution to the efficient management of day-to-day site procedures, calling in at sites where the churches were being rebuilt on his daily journeys through the city, checking that materials of proper quality were being delivered from the store, monitoring the progress of rebuilding and deciding on alterations to the design when circumstances demanded. Because Wren trusted him to do what was necessary he relieved Wren of a great burden, although in doing so he added considerably to his own.

During the rebuilding of London Hooke gained a reputation as an efficient architect and supervisor of construction works. The technical and scientific knowledge of building procedures and materials which he had already gained by the early 1660s were greatly enhanced by his experience as City Surveyor and in particular by his close professional association and friendship with Christopher Wren. Hooke was soon in demand as a private architect. He brought to his private work the methods of construction management that Wren and he had begun to use for building St Paul's and the parish churches. At the beginning of the seventeenth century it was usual for master craftsmen to consult with the client and agree on a design which the craftsmen were responsible for building, using their materials and labour. Such arrangements, which had generally worked well since medieval times, became irrelevant after the fire, when most of London had to be rebuilt. The huge amount of materials and personnel necessary called for careful management of the work and control of costs. The beginnings of modern construction management can be seen in the way Wren's office was organised. The complementary roles of architect, engineer, surveyor and contractor emerged. Hooke and Wren were quite capable of taking on the first three roles, which have subsequently evolved into separate professions, each sub-divided into more specialised areas of practice.

BUILDING FOR INSTITUTIONS AND INDIVIDUALS

The medieval Bedlam Hospital for the insane, situated a little to the west of where Liverpool Street station now stands, was not destroyed by the fire but by 1674 it was in a decayed state. Sir William Turner, President of the Court of Governors of Bridewell and Bedlam, commissioned Hooke to design a new Bedlam Hospital to be built in Moorfields. Turner was Lord Mayor from 1668 to 1669, during which time he had worked closely with Hooke and had recognised, as many had before him, that Hooke was exceptionally able, energetic and eager to please and had already engaged him in the rebuilding of Bridewell Prison. The depth of Turner's trust in Hooke's ability can be judged from the hugely ambitious scheme he was given. The old Bedlam had accommodated 25 patients,

61. Robert White's 1677 engraving of Bedlam Hospital, Moorfields, viewed from the north. Although the generous and airy spaces of Upper and Lower Moorfields fronted its north elevation, its south wall lay very close to London Wall. The building shows the influence on Hooke's architecture of French monumentality and Dutch detail. (*Guildhall Library, Corporation of London*)

whereas the new Bedlam was to accommodate 120, both men and women. Hooke's startlingly original design included single airy rooms for the inmates and an impressive façade, more than 500 feet long (Figure 61). Construction work began in 1674 when the design was approved by the Board of Governors. Hooke chose as the main contractor the bricklayer John Fitch who had worked on the Fleet Channel. Under Hooke's direction the work was quickly completed at the reasonable cost of about £17,000. Hooke asked for a fee of £200, but the Board of Governors voted that he should have as much as £300.[51] The king's inaugural visit took place on 29 August 1676. Hooke recorded the important formal event in his diary in the same matter-of-fact way that he wrote about a welter of other lesser details of his life: 'King at Bedlam on Tuesday 29th of August. Committee at Bedlam the day before.' He had not only designed the building and supervised its construction, but had designed and directed the making of its sewers, the garden wall and railings, turrets, sculptures for the gateway (Figure 62) and other decorations.

Bedlam's splendour attracted both praise and criticism at the time. Jokers said it was so magnificent that those responsible for it must have been mad. After discussing the building itself and many contemporary and present-day opinions of it, an architectural historian has recently concluded that it 'was meant to evoke . . . magnificent beauty, charitable hospitality, good and healthful order' stimulated by 'the sight of the architecture, of carved stone fronts, great galleries, and tidy rows of airy cells'.[52] It is possible to find resonances of the natural philosophy of Hooke and some of his Royal

62. Detail from Robert White's 1677 engraving (Figure 61) of Bedlam Hospital, Moorfields, showing the frontispiece and entrance gateway, topped by Caius Gabriel Cibber's life-size statues representing melancholic and raving madness, now on display in the museum of Bethlem Royal Hospital. (*Guildhall Library, Corporation of London*)

Society colleagues in the beauty, order, geometry and airiness of the hospital. On 18 April 1678 John Evelyn 'went to see new Bedlam Hospital, magnificently built & most sweetely placed in Morefields'.[53]

As an asylum it changed the way mentally ill patients were cared for by allowing air and light into living spaces where previously darkness and squalor were normal. It influenced the design of similar institutions for more than a century, including Wren's Chelsea Hospital in the following decade and George Dance's St Luke's Hospital in the 1750s. Around 1810 it was discovered that the building was no longer safe, so Hooke's Bedlam was demolished. Even Fitch's experience and Hooke's technical knowledge were inadequate in the seventeenth century for designing and building the foundations of a large building on the site of an ancient ditch sufficiently well to last for more than 150 years. The eventual demolition of Hooke's Bedlam Hospital was a fate shared by all his other privately-commissioned buildings in London.

In the years following plague and fire, gentry and aristocrats moved westwards out of the city to St James's Fields, between Pall Mall and Piccadilly. Speculative developments by financiers and master builders were producing ready-built houses, but prospective buyers needed someone to advise them on such matters as the prices being asked and the quality of materials and workmanship. They also sometimes needed advice on the design, cost and progress of additional work. Although Hooke's reputation as an architect and surveyor had been made among merchants and tradesmen as a result of his work as City Surveyor, it soon came to the notice of gentry and aristocrats, mainly through his connections in the Royal Society, particularly with Boyle's sister, Lady Ranelagh. By early 1676 he was accepting a number of varied commissions in the new West End, including one from Boyle's sister-in-law Lady Burlington to design a garden and advise on a water supply by lead pipes to Burlington House on the north side of Piccadilly.[54]

Hooke was also engaged by John Harvey, Treasurer of the Queen's Household, to negotiate a price for a house built by the mason Abraham Story. In his dealings with Story, whom he knew well from the time they worked together a few years earlier on the city church of St Edmund the King, he showed he was a tough negotiator, capable of striking a bargain on behalf of his client. Story was asking £5,500 for the property, but Hooke calculated the cost of building, went over the house with Story, discussed the matter with him at Garraways (where he bought him chocolate) and told Harvey that in his opinion £5,000 was an appropriate price to pay. Harvey delayed a decision for a few weeks, but following a visit with Hooke to the house he instructed Hooke to offer Story £5,000. Hooke dined at Story's two days later and put the offer to him. Story rejected it, but said he would do more work which would be included in the asking price. Hooke reported Story's decision to Harvey, saying that the extra work Story had offered to do was worth only £200. After a few more meetings with Harvey and with Story in the following weeks, Harvey gave Hooke power to agree a price of £5,150 'all things being

COLLEGIUM REGALE MEDICORUM LONDINENSIUM

63. David Loggan's drawing and 1677 engraving of the Royal College of Physicians in Warwick Lane. The viewpoint is at the entrance to the College from Warwick Lane, looking east. Steps on the right lead to the residence of Dr Daniel Whistler (1619–84) who negotiated with the Physicians' benefactor Sir John Cutler and Hooke on the placing of the entrance to the College and the theatre above it. The door at the end of the courtyard led to a hall where the poor could receive advice. (*Guildhall Library, Corporation of London*)

done'. Hooke thought he could do better. Two days later he recorded 'Agreed with Story for £5,000 for house completed. He would bring me a paper with a blank to fill. Met Mr. Harvey and told him. He liked it well.'[55]

Harvey had so well liked what Hooke had done that he gave him further similar commissions in his purchases of more houses in St James's. Hooke soon had many more offers coming his way from other wealthy clients to work for them as architect or negotiator and consultant in the West End and the city.[56] In addition to Bedlam Hospital he was responsible for the (later Royal) College of Physicians (Figures 63 and 64) in Warwick Lane (1672–8, theatre demolished 1866, remainder destroyed by fire in 1879); Merchant Taylors' School in Suffolk Lane (1674–5, demolished 1875); Montagu House in Bloomsbury for the courtier and diplomat Ralph Montagu, on a site now occupied by the British Museum (1675–9, gutted by fire 1686); and Haberdashers' Aske's Hospital, Hoxton (1690s, rebuilt 1826), with a long façade resembling Bedlam,

65. *Above*: The church of St Mary Magdalene, Willen, Buckinghamshire (*Gentleman's Magazine Supplement* 1793, 1165 plate 2). It was built *c*. 1680 by Hooke for Richard Busby, his former Head Master at Westminster School. The cupola has been removed and an apse built at the west end, but otherwise the structure is original. (*Willen Church Council*)

64. *Left*: David Loggan's drawing and 1677 engraving of the Physicians' Theatre and College entrance. Tiers of steeply raked benches encircled the demonstration area, daylight entering at three higher levels all round. Hooke based his design on the theatre at Leiden, but he knew from the anatomical experiments at the Royal Society that light and clear views of the dissection table were essential. (*Guildhall Library, Corporation of London*)

but more Italiante than Dutch. The one important Hooke building which does still stand in London has been generally thought of as Wren's: the Monument in Fish Street Hill has stood for more than 300 years as an unrecognised Hooke memorial.

Outside London, Hooke's buildings include Escot House in Devonshire (1677–8, or 1680–8); almshouses at Buntingford, Hertfordshire, for his former astronomy teacher at Oxford, Seth Ward (1689 or later); Ragley Hall, Alcester, Warwickshire (1679–83); Ramsbury Manor, Wiltshire (1681–6); Shenfield Place, Essex (1689); and, for his former Head Master at Westminster School Richard Busby, the parish church of St Mary Magdalene (Figures 7 and 65) at Willen, near Milton Keynes in Buckinghamshire (1680).[57] Busby also commissioned Hooke to 'repair and beautify' the chapel at Lutton in Lincolnshire, Busby's birthplace.[58]

16

❧

A PERPETUAL REMEMBRANCE

The first Rebuilding Act empowered the Lord Mayor and Court of Aldermen to erect a column or pillar to be a permanent memorial of the fire, the pillar to be sited as close as possible to the place where the fire had started. The idea for a memorial originated less than two months after the fire, when the City's Court of Common Council listed twenty-three 'heads' they thought should be included in the Rebuilding Act. Head 14 was 'That the second day of September yearly be kept as a day of public Humiliation within this City & Liberties in Memoriall of this sad Desolation by Fire And that a Columne be erected upon the place where the Fire began as a perpetuall Remembrance of it.'[1]

In January 1669 the City ordered Hooke to stake out the foundations of a toft in Pudding Lane belonging to Thomas Farriner,[2] the owner of the bakery where the fire had started. When Hooke heard that Farriner had paid the fee of 6s 8d for a foundation survey, he informed the City. Just over a week later, on 28 January 1669, the City Surveyors were ordered to view Farriner's ground and report their findings because the toft where Farriner was about to rebuild was at the site of the proposed pillar.[3] No surveyors' report on the view has been found, but they probably said that the toft was too small, surrounded by other domestic buildings and unsuitable as a site for a monument. Another site had to be found.

A rare example of Hooke's use of a sketch is in an area certificate of 1677 (Figure 66).[4] The document is extensively damaged and large sections of manuscript are lost. The certificate deals with several contiguous foundations already taken by the City from St Margaret's Church for building the pillar and adjacent piazza. The certificate would be far too verbose and difficult to understand without the sketch:

> These are to certify that I h[ave. . .] foundations of [. . .] fish street An[v. . .] from the front [. . .En]largement of F[is]h street hi[ll. . .] at the lower end and one foot & [. . .] at the north end of the Pedestall of the Column and the Bredth of the said front is fifty eight foot & eight inches which makes of superficia[ll] content two hundred and ten foot. Sep. 1st. 1677. Robert Hooke.
>
> I have also taken the Dimensions of the Ground up[on which . . .][5] the[6] said Pedestall standeth and find the same to be twenty seaven foot square which maketh of superficiall content seaven hundred & twenty nine foot.

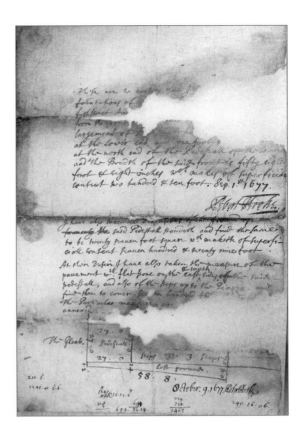

66. Hooke's certificate of the dimensions
and area of ground taken by the City
from the church of St Margaret, Fish
Street Hill for making the piazza and
pediment of the Monument.
(*Comptroller's Deeds Box K, M/37A:*
Corporation of London Records Office)

At there Desire I have also taken the measure of the pavement with flat stone on
the east & south[7] sides of the said pedestall, and also of the steps up to the Piazza. and
find them to cover se[av]en hundred thi[rty four. . .] The Particular measure are [. . .]
annexed.[8]

    October.9.1677 Robert Hooke

210. 5ˢ

1245. at 2ˢ.6[9]

The construction of the pillar and piazza in a widened Fish Street Hill was under the
direction of the City Lands Committee, which had been ordered by the Court of
Aldermen on 10 June 1669 to consider where the pillar should be located and to make
arrangements for building it.[10] St Margaret's Church in Old Fish Street would not be
rebuilt, the parish merging with the adjacent parish of St Magnus the Martyr to the
south. The chosen site was close to Pudding Lane and seemed suitable for building a
pillar. However, a new development of private houses to be built on adjoining land might
obstruct views of the pillar. On 3 August 1670, when the churchwardens of St Magnus
were given permission to take down the wall and steeple of St Margaret's Church, the

City Surveyors were called upon to view the buildings which Nicholas Barbon[11] was proposing to erect on land adjoining the site chosen for the pillar, and to certify whether or not they would obstruct the view of the memorial. The City Lands Committee could then decide whether to allow Barbon to go ahead or to purchase the ground from him.[12] Some months later the Committee received the surveyors' report and allowed Barbon to go ahead and rebuild on foundations to be set out by Hooke.[13]

On 26 January 1671 the Court of Aldermen considered Hooke's general design for the pillar:

Upon view of the draught now produced by Mr Hooke one of the Surveyors of new buildings of the Pillar to be erected in memory of the Late dismall Fire the same was well Liked and approved, And it is referred to the said Surveyors to estimate and certifye unto this Court the charge of the said Pillar.[14]

About two weeks later the Court of Aldermen approved the cost and recommended the City Lands Committee proceed 'with all expedition' to build the pillar according to Hooke's draft.[15] Although other designs for the column were made by Wren and by Woodroofe, it was Hooke's design, approved by Wren's signature on behalf of the king, that is closest to what was built. The column stands where Hooke set it out, 202 feet high and allegedly the same distance from the source of the fire in Pudding Lane. A 28ft square plinth supports a pedestal about 21 feet square and 40 feet high surmounted by a fluted Doric column 15 feet in diameter and 120 feet high. The abacus carries a railed balcony and supports a domed cylinder topped by a flaming gilt urn (Figure 67).

There is no doubt that Hooke and Wren worked together on the structural design of the pillar to ensure that it would serve not only as a proper monument to London's recovery from disaster but also as a zenith telescope and dropping chamber for scientific investigations. It was particularly important in this context that the foundations of the pillar were adequate, a reason for Hooke's discovery of a 6ft-deep bed of gravel at the site.[16] Hooke's uncompleted experiments with the zenith telescope protruding through the roof of his rooms at Gresham College and with pendulums, barometers and falling weights in old St Paul's could be continued inside the pillar. Recently a chamber beneath the ground-level floor has been rediscovered (Figure 27).[17] This space was used for the main scientific purpose of the pillar – the telescopic observation of the changes in position of a star directly overhead at different times of the year (the star's 'parallax') in order to calculate the radius of the earth's orbit around the sun. The telescope objective lens was mounted somewhere near the top of the pillar, inside the dome, but below the hinged doors to the flaming urn above. The telescope eyepiece was fixed about 200 feet below, inside the underground chamber where Hooke or whoever was taking the observations would be seated, or more probably lying, looking up through the telescope. The success of the experiment depended upon keeping the line of sight throughout the

67. A print (*c.* 1676) by P. Tempest of a drawing and engraving by William Lodge of the Monument, Fish Street Hill, seen from the west. The shadows are imaginatively shown as if the sun were high in the north-west. (*Guildhall Library, Corporation of London*)

200 feet from eyepiece to objective lens in the vertical direction not only when observations were being made but for months at a time. Unfortunately, as so often was the case with Hooke's ingenious instruments for measuring variations in natural phenomena, the differences he was trying to measure were so small that the methods and materials available to him prevented him from making instruments accurate enough to do what he wanted. At the pillar, conditions were not stable enough. The effects of vibrations caused by air currents passing down the core column and changes over a longer period in the relative positions of the objective lens and eyepiece brought about by vibrations from passing wheeled traffic were much greater than the changes in the star's parallax he was trying to measure.

Hooke worked on the detailed design of the pillar and the acquisition of land for construction. On 9 October 1672 the City Surveyors (only Hooke and Oliver by this time) were ordered to set out and enclose an area of ground adjoining the pillar at Fish Street Hill to be used for scaffolding and carving the base panels, taking care for the convenience of the passage of carts.[18] On 6 November 1672 the City told the parishioners of St Magnus that they would have a warrant granting payment for loss of their ground as soon as Hooke had completed and certified the certificate they had presented to the City.[19] Hooke

68. Caius Gabriel Cibber's sculpture on the west panel of the Monument pedestal. The assembly, laden with allegory, invites speculation that the two craftsmen working at the top of the building on the right and the hunched hod-carrier below them are more than they appear to be. (*Guildhall Library, Corporation of London*)

frequently called at the site as he passed by on his other business for the City, certifying wages and bills of quantity, checking workmanship and generally keeping an eye on the work, sometimes making brief notes in his diary. He was at the site on 8 August 1673; on 11 September he discussed the pillar with Sir Thomas Player, the City Chamberlain; and by 19 October he had completed a detailed design of the ornamental stonework. On 28 March 1674 he discussed it with Abraham Story the master mason and others, probably including Wren, and on 1 June he visited the site and recorded that the pillar was 210 steps above the ground. He visited again on 7 August and recorded that the pillar was 250 steps above the ground. On 8 September he dined at the pillar with Joshua Marshall, master mason (and son of the King's Mason), who was in charge of the pillar stonework, and on 6 November he visited the Lord Mayor to discuss the iron railings for the pillar balcony. On 16 December he went first to the Lord Mayor's parlour with Caius Gabriel Cibber and later to the pillar to arrange for sculpting the bas reliefs on the west panel at the pillar base (Figure 68).[20] The king, shown as a Roman emperor accompanied by Science, Architecture, Liberty, Justice, Victory and Fortitude brings relief to the languishing City and despairing Citizens supported by Time, Manual Skills and Industry. Plenty and Peace soar above, while fuming Envy is imprisoned in a vault beneath the King's feet.

As the construction of the column neared completion, the City Lands Committee thought a statue of the king would be an appropriate ornament to place at the top, so they asked Wren for his opinion. A statue of that sort would make it very difficult to see straight up through the column to the sky: the idea of the column as a zenith telescope was in jeopardy. In a careful reply to the City dated 28 July 1675 Wren sent some ornamental designs for the top of the pillar he had made and shown to the king. He began by saying that the king had found a large ball of gilded metal to be 'most agreeable' and 'an Ornament to the Town at a very great distance'. However, if the City preferred a statue of the king, then that too would be appropriate. Although Wren did not say so directly, he made it clear that a statue of the king would have to be very large (at least 15 feet high) so that when seen from afar or from ground level it did not appear to be puny and offensive to the king. A large statue would be extremely expensive (at least £1,000) and difficult to raise. Wren said that on second thoughts he had rejected his original idea of a phoenix because 'it will be costly, not easily understood at that Highth and worse understood at a distance; & lastly dangerous by reason of the sayle the spread winges will carry in the winde'.[21] On the other hand a copper ball 9 feet in diameter, made in sections and decorated with gilt flames would cost only £350. It would be large enough to be entered and used for setting off fireworks. The City took all the hints and rejected the idea of a statue. Through his subtlety Wren had ensured that the pillar would remain a zenith telescope. Hooke was soon engaged in commissioning the metal ball. Less than a week after Wren had written his letter to the City, Hooke recorded: 'Walkd with Sir Christopher in Privy Garden and Discoursd of the Ball for the Columb.'[22] It was made by the brazier Robert Bird, but not without difficulties, as Hooke noted in his diary: 'To Birds the urn bungled'; a month later 'At Bird's, saw half the urne made'; and after another month 'to Birds, Bath Lane, he had finishd urne'.[23] It consisted of a wooden frame covered in copper, brass and gilt, but the problem of mounting it had to be solved. In early April 1676 Hooke discussed the problem with John Oliver and the City Lands Committee, eventually deciding to use an iron frame, which he designed on 7 April.[24]

The main structure of the pillar was completed by the middle of October 1676 when the scaffolding was taken down.[25] A month later members of the City Lands Committee and the City Surveyors visited the site to see if anything more had to be done to finish it.[26] Apparently everything was finished; two days later on 17 November 1676 there was what seems to have been some kind of official, but low-key, opening of the pillar when Hooke recorded in his diary: 'At Piller the laying it open reported with Sir Chr. Wren.'[27]

By December 1676 Hooke and Oliver had certified the audited accounts as reasonable.[28] A month later Hooke took them to Sir Francis Chaplin (who would become the next Lord Mayor) and discussed them with him the same day.[29] Hooke continued to work at the pillar. In 1677 he certified two areas of ground taken from the parishioners of St Magnus as a site for the pillar and piazza (Figure 66). It seemed as if the matter was now finished. But the City Lands Committee was not satisfied by what it had seen in the audited accounts. Hooke and Oliver were ordered to look further into some of the bills paid by the main contractor, the stonemason Joshua Marshall. In some cases there was no evidence that the work or materials paid for had been done or delivered. A year later, in December 1677, the accounts were still being argued over, with Hooke trying to find the truth about incidents that had taken place years earlier. The sort of problems he

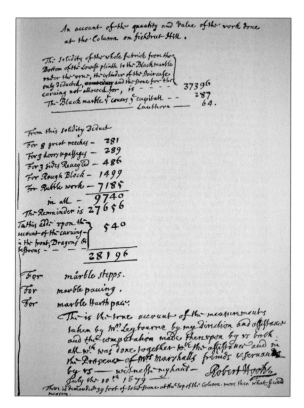

69. Hooke's account of the quantity of stone (excluding black marble) used in building the Monument. The measurements, made by William Leybourne under Hooke's supervision and in the presence of Joshua Marshall's widow, show that 28,196 cubic feet of stone were used, only 39 cubic feet less than the quantity in Marshall's bill which the City Lands Committee had queried. (Gunther 1930b, 527)

was dealing with and the attention he gave to them are illustrated by his report dated 19 December 1677:

In pursuance of an order of this Committee of the 15th. of this Instant we whose names are underwritten have inquired concerning the quantity of stone & Rubble used by Mr. Marshall in and about the column at Fishstreet hill. and we find that Mr. Shortgrave was imployed by the city for taking the measurements of the Block & Rubble used in the foundations and pedestall of the said Column upon every course of stone there set.[30] But Mr. Marshall affirming that he hath not hitherto had any account of any such admeasurements though he doth remember that such were taken by him, And Mr. Shortgrave being since Dead, we were not able to make an exact computation and estimate of the whole work; It Requiring much more time then we had allowed to doe the same. But we are of opinion that the said Mr. Marshall hath Given an account of the same such as he can make out upon oath by the persons he hath employed about the work he having (as he affirmes) kept a constant account of the stone & Block that hath been Deliverd into and used about the said work.[31]

Joshua Marshall's death in 1678 did not bring an end to Hooke's investigations into the accounts for the pillar. The quantities of stone actually used were at issue between the City and Marshall's widow. To resolve the dispute Hooke took the surveyor William Leybourne to the pillar, where they re-measured the dimensions of nearly all the stonework in the presence of Mrs Marshall's friends and servants. Hooke calculated the quantities of Portland stone and black marble and wrote his report to the City (Figure 69).[32] Through Hooke's endeavours the Monument accounts were finally approved. Disbursements to November 1675 amount to £12, 347 12s, but an unidentified sum of £1,102 19s 9d is added. This could represent the final payment by the City as a result of Hooke's later investigations. The total cost, paid from the coal tax, was £13,450 11s 9d.[33]

70. The view in 1996 looking north up Fish Street Hill from above the gilded flames at the top of the Monument. The aperture at the top of the final ladder (see Figure 27) is wide enough to permit a person to stand and work on assembling a mount for the objective aperture of a zenith telescope. The tall building to the right of centre ('Tower 42', formerly 'National Westminster Tower') stands on the site of Gresham College. (*Author's collection*)

For about 300 years the Monument has been generally attributed to Wren, usually on the basis of the contents of *Parentalia*, but we now know that Hooke was primarily responsible for its design and construction, although Wren's agreement was necessary (and readily given). The report on quantities is clearly in Hooke's hand, not Wren's, which must have been clear to the author of *Parentalia*, who nevertheless presented it as Wren's.[34] The City expressed its gratitude to Wren for his services during the rebuilding when on 6 June 1672 they decided to make an ex-gratia payment to him, but the decision was made during the committee's meetings about the Fleet River and the Thames Quay, not the Monument. It was moved at a meeting of the City Lands Committee that its officials take into consideration the 'many and great Services which Christopher Wren Esq. his Majestys Surveyor hath performed for the benefit and on the behalfe of the Citty of London'. They forthwith agreed, ordered and signed a warrant for the Comptroller to draw 100 guineas from the Coal Account and take them to Wren's lodgings 'as a Testimony for the present of their kind resentment of his good inclinations and Services towards the Welfare of the said City'.[35] The Monument was intended to be a symbol of London's resurgence from fire (Figure 70), but it also symbolises the growth of experimental science and the cooperation between the friends Wren and Hooke in the pursuit of knowledge and the well-being of the inhabitants of London.

17

A FULL AND GLORIOUS RESTORATION

It took a little longer for Hooke to emerge from Wren's shadow than from Newton's. Unlike Newton, Wren did not position himself to obscure Hooke from our view: his son Christopher and grandson Stephen did it for him. In 1750 Stephen Wren published *Parentalia*, written by Christopher Wren Jnr. Although *Parentalia* has been judged a fairly accurate record of primary sources, its biographical details must be treated with great suspicion. Christopher Wren was uncritical in his account of his father's life and was anxious for his father's memory.[1] Unfortunately for Hooke the result is that *Parentalia* shows Wren as having rebuilt the whole of London almost single-handed. Hooke's architectural and surveying work is either presented as Wren's or ignored. The importance of *Parentalia* as a source of details about Wren's life kept Hooke in the shade until the recovery of his reputation in architecture which began with M.E. Batten in 1935 when his diaries were published.[2] Recognition of the extent of his surveying came relatively recently.[3]

It was not only *Parentalia* and misfortune that hid Hooke's surveying for 300 years: Hooke contributed to his own obscurity by his stubborn refusal to hand in his survey books. Had he done as the City had asked, his contribution would have been recognised earlier, as Mills's and Oliver's were. We see here the intransigence which also overshadowed his scientific achievements. He never made claims for his surveying or architectural achievements as he did in science. The former he considered as services to citizens and clients, but science meant even more to him – it was his passion, and he cared very much about what his contemporaries wrote and said about him in this field. But until recently nobody seems to have written anything about his surveying, even though he must have been a familiar figure, measuring, staking out and interviewing inhabitants in the streets of London after the fire.

Apart from the Monument, there is nothing in London to commemorate his life and work, most of which took place within the walled city. A nineteenth-century memorial window in St Helen's Church, Bishopsgate, depicted Hooke carrying his surveyor's measuring rod. It was one of a group known as 'London Worthies', but they were all destroyed when the Baltic Exchange was bombed by terrorists in April 1992 and have not been replaced. However, there is one more silent memorial to Hooke, which has existed since 1674.

When London was rebuilt after the fire, the City needed an accurate and complete large-scale map for managing its resources and planning new works. All main features such as buildings, streets, lanes, alleyways, quays, gateways, the city wall and environs would have to be individually measured and plotted to produce a homogeneous topographic map. Such an accurate survey and topographic map of London was very much in Hooke's mind in the mid-1670s, but he knew it would require new methods in surveying, cartography and engraving, with an efficient team to do the work. Hooke knew two capable men who could do what was necessary, so he found opportunities to sound them out.

John Ogilby (1600–76) was a dancer, born in Kirriemuir, whose career ended when he

71. John Ogilby. An engraving by William Faithorne based on a portrait by Sir Peter Lely. (*C.L. Ogleby's collection*)

broke a leg performing in a masque for James I. Before the fire he ran a dancing school, owned a theatre, translated Virgil and Aesop into English and wrote lines for the orator at the procession on the eve of the coronation of Charles II. He lost his house and possessions in the fire and was left with assets of only £5. Responding to the growing interest in foreign lands he began to publish an *English Atlas* in five volumes (Africa, America, Asia, Europe and Great Britain). In the early 1670s he presented some atlases to the City, in return for which he was paid gratuities of £20 each. He dedicated *Africa* to the king and was appointed His Majesty's Cosmographer in 1671.[4] Ogilby and Hooke often met informally in London's coffee houses, where they talked about new techniques for compiling, engraving and printing maps and atlases and the difficult problem of financing the preparatory work, which could take years. Ogilby used Garraways coffee house near the Royal Exchange for selling lottery tickets to raise money for his projects. Hooke was very interested in the making of *Britannia*, Ogilby's road atlas of England and Wales. He offered Ogilby some new ideas for measuring road distances and suggested different ways of depicting hills. Hooke's technical advice and promotion of Ogilby to the City were vital to the eventual publication in 1675 of the road map volume of *Britannia* and related products, which we would now call spin-offs.[5] Ogilby would be the man to oversee compilation of the separate surveyed plots, the engraving of the plates and the printing of the map sheets.

An° Salutis 1674. *GULIELMUS LEYBOURN* EFFIGIES Año Ætatis 48.

72. William Leybourne, drawn and engraved by Robert White, 1674. (*Royal Institution of Chartered Surveyors Historical Collection*)

The second man Hooke identified to work on the surveying for the new map was William Leybourne (1626–1716). He had been contracted by the City for ad hoc land and quantity surveying throughout the rebuilding programme, and had been supervised by Hooke. He was a teacher of mathematics and author of several books, the most famous of which was *The Compleat Surveyor* first published in 1657, a book of great importance to the practice of surveying in England for nearly a hundred years. The fifth edition was published in 1722, six years after the author's death. Leybourne and other surveyors and measurers, including Richard Shortgrave, sometimes joined Hooke and Ogilby in Garraways. They sat around a table, discussing their ideas for mapping London anew, sketching different measurement schemes on papers laid in front of them, dividing the city into areas for each individual surveyor, and working out how the city should be partitioned into separate map sheets. There was at the time no better group for deciding how all this should be done and for seeing the project through to completion. Leybourne's years of practical land surveying, Shortgrave's skills in mechanics and Ogilby's experience in cartography, printing and publishing all came together under Hooke's guidance.

The traditional methods of land surveying were inadequate for making the accurate large-scale map that was needed. At the time of the fire the most common equipment for measuring land and making a plot comprised the plane table, chain and circumferentor. A plane table was used for surveying areas of open ground. The surveyor plotted the details on a sheet of paper mounted on the plane table as he moved around the site (Figure 73). Chaining with offsets could be used in places where it was possible to measure with a chain along survey lines close to the detail to be shown on the plot. A circumferentor, based on a magnetic pointer and similar to a surveyor's compass, was used to find the magnetic bearings of the survey lines measured by chain. The method was particularly useful for surveying long and narrow stretches of land, such as a length of road or river.

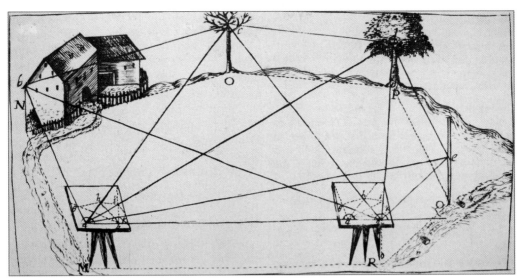

73. Early seventeenth-century plane tabling. Base stations M and R were plotted to scale on a sheet of paper fixed to the table which was set up first at R and oriented on M. Rays to features such as P, O and N were drawn from R using a sighting rule, or 'alidade'. The table was then set up at M, oriented on R and rays drawn from M to P, O and N. The intersections of these rays with the corresponding rays drawn from R are the plan positions of the features. (*Austellungskatalog, Deutscher Verein für Vermessungswesen, Weisbaden, 1971, 83*)

The two editions of William Leybourne's book published before the fire[6] contain descriptions of how to use plane tables, chains and circumferentors for measuring land in rural areas for owners of estates and manors, but it contains no evidence that urban surveying was an important specialised activity. In fact, the subject is hardly mentioned at all. A plane table and chain could be used to survey and plot streets and houses in a small block of ground, but when a hundred or more small blocks had to be surveyed, plotted and fitted together to make a map of the whole city, the errors inherent in measuring and plotting would mean that unacceptably large gaps and overlaps would be inevitable. The circumferentor could improve accuracy, but in city surveying its magnetic needle would be deflected by local magnetic attraction by iron artifacts, producing undetected errors as large as several degrees in bearings. Hooke and his team had to devise new methods of surveying.

At the time Leybourne was working on the survey of the rebuilt city he hastily wrote a description of the method he was using for inclusion in the third edition of *The Compleat Surveyor*, published in 1674.[7] He also included in the book for the first time a fulsome dedication (Figure 74) to Sir Thomas Player, the Chamberlain of London, through whose offices payments of fees were made to Leybourne and the City's other contractors. Leybourne praises Player's 'excellency of . . . mature Judgment in Arts and Sciences' and says with little subtlety that he has been further persuaded to dedicate his book to Player

To the Right Worſhipfull
Sir THOMAS PLAYER, Knight,
Chamberlain of *London.*

SIR,

AS the excellency of your mature *Judg-*
ment in Arts and Sciences hath
over-perſwaded me, ſo the wonted
goodneſs of your natural Diſpoſition
doth farther invite me, to ſhelter
theſe enſuing Tractates under the *Tutelage of your*
Worſhip's *Patronage , whereof* GEOME-
TRY *is the Subject; a matter of that worth and*
eminency, that Philo (*the* Jew) *termed it the*
Princeſs and Mother of all other Sciences;
receiving its originall Name *from* Meaſuring the
Earth : *for when* Nilus *by his* Inundation
drowned and confounded the Ægyptian Banks,
by help of this Geodæticall Art (after the Fall of
the Waters) every man had his *portion of Land*
reſtored to him again. *And how much occaſion we*
have had to make uſe hereof in the late London
Ruines, your Worſhip *cannot be inſenſible, and*
my ſelf *(being ſeveral times by the Citie's favour*
employed therein) *can eminently witneſs.* Now how
neceſſary Geometry *is, not only in* Civill, *but in*
Military *Affairs alſo,* I refer to your Worſhip's
                                                    * 2   Cenſure,

74. The first page of William Leybourne's dedication of the third edition of *The Compleat Surveyor* (Leybourne 1674) to the Chamberlain of London. He associates his gratitude for commissioned surveys and the Chamberlain's mature judgment with praise for geometry, the queen of sciences, which enabled surveyors to restore each parcel of land to the rightful owner following flooding of the Nile in ancient Egypt. (*Royal Institution of Chartered Surveyors Historical Collection*)

because 'these few years since London's dreadful Conflagration, I have been employed in the Admeasurements of the Publick Works belonging to this Honourable City, in which your Worship is so deservedly dignified both in Place and Person'.[8]

Leybourne's hastily cobbled together description of the innovative urban surveying procedures used for Ogilby and Morgan's map is not very clear. It is hard to think a novice surveyor could understand what was being described. Another surveyor working for Ogilby, John Holwell (1649–86), later published a much fuller and clearer account of a new method for mapping cities (Figure 75).[9] Holwell surveyed about half (200 acres, or 40ha) of the city, experience which he made good use of when writing his book. He tells us a lot about how the work was done. He, Leybourne and a third surveyor, Gregory King,[10] used a semicircle (or graphometer) to measure angles between the chain lines in polygons to improve the overall accuracy of their survey (Figures 76 and 77). The measuring chains were 50 feet long, each one made up of fifty links. Corners of buildings and other features were surveyed by measuring perpendicular distances from the chain lines to the features using 5-foot or 10-foot rods. First, each surveyed polygon was plotted from the measured angles and distances, using protractor and scale. Surveyed features were then plotted using long and short scales to replicate the chain line and offset lengths.

75. Title page of John Holwell's *A Sure Guide* (Holwell 1678). The contents of the second part of the book describe the surveying procedures devised by Hooke for Ogilby and Morgan's 1676 map of the rebuilt city. (*Graves 124.c.2: image reproduced courtesy University College London Library Services*)

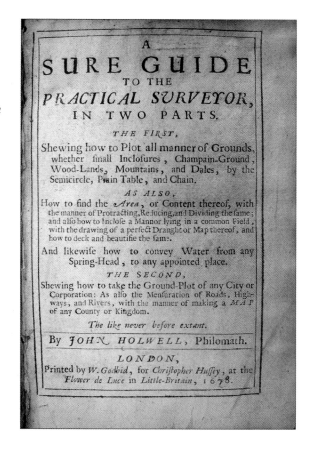

A
SURE GUIDE
TO THE
PRACTICAL SURVEYOR,
IN TWO PARTS.

THE FIRST,

Shewing how to Plot all manner of Grounds, whether small Inclofures, Champain-Ground, Wood-Lands, Mountains, and Dales, by the Semicircle, Plain Table, and Chain.

AS ALSO,

How to find the *Area*, or Content thereof, with the manner of Protracting, Reducing, and Dividing the fame; and alfo how to Inclofe a Mannor lying in a common Field, with the drawing of a perfect Draught or Map thereof, and how to deck and beautifie the fam:.

And likewife how to convey Water from any Spring-Head, to any appointed place.

THE SECOND,

Shewing how to take the Ground-Plot of any City or Corporation: As alfo the Menfuration of Roads, High-ways, and Rivers, with the manner of making a *MAP* of any County or Kingdom.

The like never before extant.

By *JOHN HOLWELL*, Philomath.

LONDON,

Printed by *W. Godbid*, for *Chriftopher Huffey*, at the *Flower de Luce* in *Little-Britain*, 1678.

Overleaf: 77. The semicircle (Figure 76) on its original wood tripod. Each tripod leg has an iron foot and comprises two sections of roughly equal length joined together by a metal sleeve. The instrument is fixed to its mount by a screw collar bearing onto a ball and socket joint with a pad of soft leather between the surfaces. The semicircle on its tripod stands a little over four feet (1.2m) above the ground. (*Inv. no. 17420: Museum of the History of Science, University of Oxford*)

Holwell reveals by implication that he and the other surveyors adopted for the first time three principles, which ever since have been applied in land surveying: first, carry out a full reconnaissance and decide what measurements are needed (Holwell describes reconnaissance as making an 'Eye draught' of the site);[11] then work from the whole to the part, which means measure, plot and check the positions of only a few points (selected during reconnaissance) over the full extent of the area to be surveyed before surveying all the other details in the spaces between; and finally make independent checks at important stages in the work.[12] The introduction of these principles into the survey for the map of rebuilt London probably came out of the informal meetings between Hooke and the surveyors in Garraways coffee house. They are characteristic of Hooke's scientific viewpoint of observations and measurements as unavoidably subject to human error, and therefore to be guarded against by vigilance on site and at the drawing-board. Holwell shows (Figure 78) a polygon ABCDEFG enclosing groups of buildings and streets. He explains how the measurements of internal angles at A, B, C, D, E and F should be made with a graphometer and recorded in a survey book with other observations (Figure 79).

76. An English semicircle, or 'graphometer', c. 1700. Instruments like this one were used for measuring horizontal angles in surveys for Ogilby and Morgan's 1676 map. The four-inch (100mm) radius brass arc, subdivided into degrees, was read by interpolation to the nearest ½ degree. The two alidades are each about 14 inches (350mm) long, the fixed one being slightly shorter than the movable one. (*Inv. no. 17420: Museum of the History of Science, University of Oxford*)

Ogilby planned the new map of the city as part of his *English Atlas*. Having received Hooke's support and the City's approval of earlier volumes, he had little trouble in getting the City to agree to fund his map. Although Ogilby was responsible for financing the whole project and he sub-contracted Leybourne to manage the surveying, Hooke's presence was in the background throughout and sometimes to the fore, as when he was one of those nominated by the City's Court of Aldermen to approve Ogilby's survey. He was involved in the early informal debates in Garraways and other London coffee houses and at Gresham College.[13] His diary has the usual laconic remarks such as 'At Garaways with Ogylby and Shortgrave',[14] but sometimes he gives a clue to what took place: 'Mr. Ogylby left sheets'[15] and 'at Garways designd sheets for London'[16] refer to the need to decide how to divide the map into a number of separate sheets for printing. A related decision was made two days later when Hooke informed Wenceslaus Hollar[17] that the scale of the printed map would be 1 inch to 100 feet (or 1/1,200).[18]

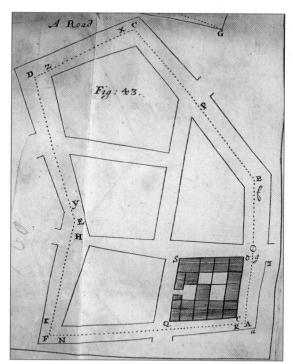

(180)

The Table of Observations taken when you went about the High Streets.

Station	Angles		Dist.		Off-sets	
	d.	m.	Feet		Feet	Feet
					R.	L.
1 ⊙ A	95	30			5	00
at —			6	from A	00	7
at —			47	from A		
—				a Street R.& L.	10	6
at—			52	from A	0	5
at—			100	from A	12	00
2 ⊙ B	140	00	100	from A	11	8
at —			61	from B a Street		
—				to the R. & L.	9	9
at —			120	from B	0	8
at—			127	from B	8	00
3 ⊙ C	100	00	127½	from B	8	00
at—			8	from C	00	9
at—	00	00	64	from C	00	4
at—			75	from C	12	00
4 ⊙ D	100	00	75	from C	9	11
at—			41	from D a Street		
—				to the R. & L.	5	00
at—			92	from D	00	7
5 ⊙ E	210	00	100	from D		
at—			9	a Street R. & L.	7	12
at—			70	from E	7	7
6 ⊙ F	74	30	83	from E	7	5
at—			8	from F		
at —			67	a Street R. &L		7
at—	00	00	123	from F	4	5

Having

78. A diagram (Holwell 1678, fig 53) of a typical polygon ABCDEF surveyed for Ogilby and Morgan's map. The lengths of the sides were measured by chain and the angles in the polygon by semicircle (Figures 76 and 77). Offsets were measured from the chain lines to corners of buildings and other features to be shown on the map. (*Graves 124.c.2: image reproduced courtesy University College London Library Services*)

79. A table (Holwell 1678, 180) showing how to record the measured angles (in degrees and minutes) and sides (in feet) of the polygon illustrated in Figure 78. Offsets to corners of buildings and other features to the left and right of the chain lines are shown recorded in feet in the two right-hand columns. (*Graves 124.c.2: image reproduced courtesy University College London Library Services*)

More decisions on cartographic design were made in October 1673. Hooke's diary entry 'at Garways with Ogylby. Shewd him the way of Letters for marking his map and also the way of shadowing' tells us that he had decided on the styles and sizes of lettering to be used for names and references and on the hachures and stipples to distinguish between different types of buildings and ground.[19] On 8 December 1673 Ogilby picked up the first printed sheet from Wenceslaus Hollar and took it to Hooke who recorded, 'with Ogylby at Dr. G/odderds he brought me his 1st sheet of London from Hollis'.[20] The project was not without its difficulties: 'to Ogylby, Shortgrave and he squabbled'.[21] Ogilby showed the second sheet to Hooke on 9 January 1674 and they went to see the Lord Mayor twice before the end of the month.[22] Although in the early months of 1674 Hooke helped Ogilby write applications to various livery companies and other institutions in the city asking for sponsorship of his atlases, the printing of the sheets of

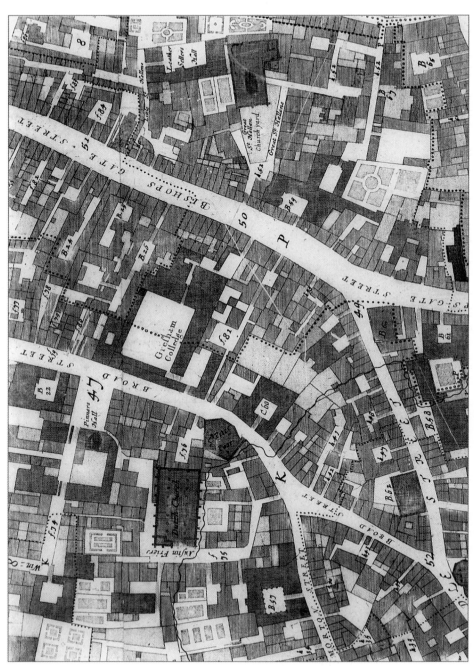

80. Detail (at reduced scale) of Ogilby and Morgan's 1676 map of the largely rebuilt city showing Gresham College and the entrances to it from Bishopsgate Street and Broad Street. The church of St Helen, where Hooke was buried, is opposite Gresham College on the east side of Bishopsgate Street. (*Guildhall Library, Corporation of London*)

the city map progressed slowly. Hooke checked the engraver's work for the title and borders surrounding the format of the map on 29 January 1675,[23] and a few days later told Ogilby and Gregory King, one of the land surveyors who worked on the map, about his ideas for reducing the size of the sheets and folding them to make a more portable map,[24] which would have been the prototype of the 'A to Z' city guides. Eventually, Ogilby published a notice in the *London Gazette* for 20–4 April 1676 saying that the map of London would be 'suddenly finished' and warning against forgeries (Figure 80).[25] It shows many cartographical features devised by Hooke for the purpose: different shading for domestic and institutional buildings; delineation of ward and parish boundaries; a system of letters and numerals for finding the names of parishes, courts, yards, alleys, churches, livery halls, and houses of note in an accompanying table; and conversely a grid reference system for finding the locations on the map of places listed in the table. An explanation of how to use the map was published and sold with it at a total price of £2 10s.

John Ogilby did not live to see his map presented to the City. He died on 4 September 1676, only six weeks before it was formally received by the Court of Aldermen. His step-grandson William Morgan took over his projects. Clients' nervousness about their investments in *Britannia* were probably alleviated when the City paid Morgan £100 for the map and he put a notice in the *London Gazette* in January 1677 stating that the map would be sold at various places in the city.[26] The title of what is now known as Ogilby and Morgan's map is

A Large and Accurate Map of the City of London.
Ichnographically Describing all the Streets, Lanes, Alleys, Courts, Yards, Churches, Halls and Houses, &c. Actually Surveyed and Delineated, by John Ogilby, Esq; His Majesties Cosmographer.

As with his surveying, Hooke's contribution to urban mapping has gone largely unrecognised, but 'Ogilby and Morgan's map' was a great leap forward.[27] Before the fire, all maps of cities in England, with possibly only one exception,[28] showed buildings in the form of a bird's-eye view, such as the 'Agas' map (Figure 38).[29] Orthographic representations of individual or small groups of buildings were common, some of which were beautifully drawn and coloured, such as those of Ralph Treswell (*c.* 1540–1616).[30] Although attractive to look at, bird's-eye maps do not show the parts of buildings facing away from the observing bird, and what is shown is geometrically inaccurate. Hooke decided a plan view of the city was needed,[31] and devised a new method for urban mapping without losing positional accuracy across the full extent of the city. Triangulation from a baseline in London's streets would have been impractical. Hooke was quite capable of making and using angular instruments for urban surveying if they were necessary, but here they were not. Existing instruments could be used in new ways.

81. Detail of Ogilby and Morgan's 1676 map of the largely rebuilt city reproduced here at approximately the original scale of 1/1,200. It shows the frontage between the east side of 'the Gully opposite to Harp Lane' (n41, or Sabb's Quay, which is entered through a passageway beneath the first storey of the houses) and the east side of 'Temple Lane' (n38, or Ralph's Quay) which Hooke had measured on the ground as 172 feet 1 inch (Figure 47). (*Guildhall Library, Corporation of London*)

The scale of the map is 1 inch to 100 feet (1 in 1,200); but how accurate was it? Given the way it was surveyed, with the main polygonal framework of chain lines running along the streets and lanes, the plotted frontages of the buildings are likely to be more accurate than their backs, which would have been more difficult to measure (if they were measured at all) because they were further from the chain lines. The dimensions of enclosed courts might have been measured, but locating their positions and orientations relative to the chain lines would have been generally impossible, except by eye or by reasonable guesswork. These inaccuracies, deduced from the way the surveys were carried out, have been independently confirmed.[32] Although locally there may be significant errors in positions of party walls and enclosed yards and deficiencies in content, overall the accuracy of positions is remarkably high.[33]

We can use some of Hooke's own measurements to check the accuracy of one very small part of Ogilby and Morgan's map. On 11 November 1671 he wrote an area certificate for four contiguous foundations along the south side of Thames Street between what he called 'Temple Lane' and 'The Gully'.[34] It can be seen (Figure 47) that his measurements show the combined length of the four foundations was 172ft 1in. The length of the frontage of buildings from 'Temple Lane' to 'The Gully' measured on a modern reproduction of Ogilby and Morgan's map[35] (Figure 81) is 1.73 inches, which at the scale of the map corresponds to 173 feet. The discrepancy (11 inches, or 0.28m) is insignificant at the scale of the plot (about ⅛mm) given the inevitable small errors in measuring and plotting and the unstable material on which the map is printed.

The complete map, made up of twenty sheets, backed by linen, mounted, framed and hanging on a wall, was (and still is) an impressive sight, about 5 feet high and 8 feet broad. The innovative technical procedures used in taking survey measurements for the map demanded a new way of managing the surveyors. The men whom Hooke had earlier directed to undertake the survey work for John Leake's map of the streets in the burnt city had necessarily to work quickly as a team. Surveyors at that time were proud of their own independent authority and gave directions to their assistants. Working as part of a team would not have come easily to them, but under Hooke's authority they clearly achieved the cooperation necessary to produce Leake's map so quickly. Similar cooperation was needed for Ogilby and Morgan's map, but the surveying was much more demanding than before.

The interests of any individual surveyor could not be allowed to conflict with the interests of the project. When one surveyor's measurements were plotted, they had to be not only internally consistent but also externally consistent with the work of others. If they were not, then checks had to be made on the conflicting data to determine which were in error and so had to be measured again: a surveyor's authority through age, social position, appointment or experience was not sufficient justification for preferring his measurements. There are similarities here between surveying and scientific professional criteria. What is right, or acceptable, is not determined by personal authority, but by measurement, mathematics and peer agreement. In bringing together the group of individuals who made the map, Hooke showed that he could organise an efficient collective effort, something he was often prevented from doing for the Royal Society because of lack of money. The map is a collaborative and scientific achievement, accurate enough for its purpose. Compared with the previous bird's-eye maps of London, it is austere and lacks immediate appeal, but it is a result of the application of science to the civic life of London and was the first map of its kind to be made in England.

There is no sign of Hooke's name on the map itself, but he designed the framework and detail measurements of the land survey, the cartography and printing, and oversaw

82. Painting from the School of Samuel Scott (*c.* 1750) of the mouth of the Fleet Channel. (*Guildhall Art Gallery, Corporation of London*)

83. Wenceslaus Hollar's drawing and engraving (*c.* 1660) of the Thames waterfront by Milford Stairs, east of Arundel House in the Strand. It shows the pre-fire decaying timber wharfing and general dereliction of this busy tidal area. (*Guildhall Library, Corporation of London*)

all technical processes through to publication. Moreover it depicts the city he did so much to bring into existence, the structure of which can still be seen today. The map and the city it shows are memorials of his technical knowledge, managerial skill and fervour for accuracy in civic life, all of which entitle him to be regarded as the first professional surveyor in the modern sense.

As for the city shown on the map, it was not, and could never have been, a completely new city, but it was 'a more beautiful city' (Figures 82 and 83). Despite the rather idealised view of river traffic, Figure 83 in comparison with Figure 82 shows the great improvements which were made after 1666 to the Thames Quay, despite the difficulties. The comparatively little use of the canal for water traffic compared with the Thames seen in Ogilby and Morgan's map (Figure 53) can also be seen in Figure 83. One difference however is at Blackfriars steps where a large house is seen in Figure 83 to occupy what was open ground at the time of the surveying for Ogilby and Morgan's map. The house was built before 1681 (Figure 54) and after 1676 (Figure 53) by Sir Thomas Fitch as his own residence. Fitch was the main contractor for canalizing the Fleet Ditch who received a knighthood for his work. The City was not only more beautiful, but easier to walk through. By 1668 the steepness of the slopes from the Thames northwards had been reduced, as Pepys noticed with satisfaction as he walked home one afternoon from the Royal Exchange: 'So I home, and took London-bridge in my way, walking down Fish-street and Gracious-street[36] to see how very fine a descent they have now made down the hill, that it is become very easy and pleasant.'[37]

John Woodward, physician and member of the Royal Society, thought that however disastrous the fire might have been to the inhabitants, the reconstruction

> . . . had prov'd infinitely beneficial to their Posterity; conducing vastly to the Improvement and Increase, as well as the Riches and Opulency, as of the splendor of this City. Then, which I and every Body must observe with great Satisfaction, by means of the Inlargements of the Streets; of the great plenty of good Water, convey'd to all parts; of the Common Sewers, and other like Contrivances, such Provision is made for a free Access and Passage of the Air, for Sweetness, for Cleanness, and for Salubrity, that it is not only the finest, but the most healthy City in the World.[38]

Hooke had shown exceptional industry and efficiency, a strong sense of duty and rectitude in his work. He brought air, light and beauty to London. But in his view, it was an imperfect beauty, the work of man. What Wren and Hooke saw revealed through their microscopes and telescopes was an intricate natural beauty – the work of God. It was brought to light by artifice – optical and mechanical instruments designed to improve the imperfection of human eyesight. By observation, reason and practical mechanics they and their colleagues in the Royal Society had institutionalised experimental science to reveal hitherto unknown beauty, both simple and complex. A new natural order had been revealed, which Hooke could aspire to create by artifice for the inhabitants of London. The laws and regulations he helped to devise and then put into effect through design, craftsmanship and meticulous management over the course of ten years were intended not to produce the perfect working city, but one that was more orderly, healthier and much more beautiful than what had gone before. Hooke's unique conceptual and practical skills as scientist and surveyor were highly important in the realisation of that aspiration.

NOTES

Introduction

1. In the seventeenth century 'science' (from the Latin *scientia*) was used to describe any body of knowledge organised in a systematic manner. What we now call 'science' was then referred to as 'natural philosophy' – the seeking of truth about the natural world through observation, experiments and reason. The word 'scientist' did not come into use until the nineteenth century. Here, 'science' and 'scientist' are used interchangeably with 'natural philosophy' and 'natural philosopher' respectively. 'Experimental philosopher' is used to describe a natural philosopher who is particularly engaged in experimental science.
2. Pepys 1970–83 vi, 36–7.
3. Birch 1745–6 ii, 13–16.
4. Pepys 1970–83 vi, 37.
5. Formerly known as the National Westminster Bank (or NatWest) Tower.
6. 'Espinasse 1956.

Chapter One

1. Or 'Cecellie Giles'.
2. Hooke 1705, i–xxvii.
3. On 14 October Hooke recorded 'Lent Aubery 20sh., he promised to repay it' (Hooke 1935a, 65). A little over a month later Hooke 'Lent Mr. Aubery 20sh. more' (Ibid., 71, entry dated 25 November 1673)

but this was not enough to save Hooke's friend. On 5 March 1674 Hooke recorded 'Mr. Aubery arrested for £200' (Ibid., 90).

4. Aubrey 2000, 393–7.
5. Hooke's elder brother John left school in 1644 to start a seven-year apprenticeship to a Newport grocer in the same town. John Hooke was Mayor of Newport when he hanged himself in 1678. Financial and family problems seem to have contributed to his suicide.
6. Much of this information about Hooke's early life in the Isle of Wight has recently been brought to light by Lisa Jardine (Jardine 2002, 14–23).
7. Aubrey 2000, 393–7.
8. Hooke 1705, ii.
9. Drake 1996, 60–8 and *passim*.
10. Hooke 1705, 279–450. Ellen Tan Drake has produced a new transcription of *A Discourse on Earthquakes* with new annotations and an introduction (Drake 1996, 153–371).
11. Hooke 1665, 93–100 and Schem. IX, Fig. 1.
12. Hull 1997, 49, Figs 2 and 3.
13. Nakajima 1994.
14. Any craftsman or tradesman wishing to profit by practising his craft or trade in the City of London had to become a freeman of the City, but first it was necessary to be admitted to membership of the relevant trade or craft guild. This could be done either through a seven-year apprenticeship or, in

the case of a practitioner accepted by the members as properly skilled, by purchase (Lely was admitted through purchase). As a freeman, a craftsman had the advantage of trading privileges and civic rights that were denied to others. For particulars of present-day guilds (known as 'Worshipful Companies') and membership (known as 'the Livery') see Corporation of London 2001.

15. Hooke 1705, iii.
16. Aubrey 2000, 394. It was generally thought that Hooke's legacy amounted to £100 until evidence was found that it was only £50 (Nakajima 1994). Aubrey also says that he thought Hooke had instruction in painting from the miniaturist Samuel Cooper as well as from Lely, but cannot say whether it took place before or after Hooke was with Lely. Cooper's technique would have been useful to Hooke when he prepared his illustrations for *Micrographia*.
17. Barker 1895, 77–85.
18. Aubrey 1949b, xc. Aubrey cites what is supposed to be John Dryden's opinion, shared by John Locke, both of whom had been taught by Busby (Hill 1988, 195).
19. Barker 1895, 60.
20. Sargeaunt 1898, 78. A few years before Hooke arrived at Westminster, a benefaction of £27 6s 8d annually was sufficient to maintain four scholars at the school.
21. Barker 1895, 146.
22. Aubrey 1898, 411.
23. Hooke 1705, iii.
24. Aubrey 2000, 395.
25. Aarslef 1970–80, 368–70.
26. Hunter 1994a, cvi.
27. Hooke 1705, iv.
28. Hooke 1705, iv.
29. Aubrey 2000, 395.
30. Hartley 1960, 53–4.
31. Rostenberg 1989, 197.
32. Quoted by Aarslef 1970–80, 366.
33. Hooke 1665, sig. g2r.

34. Hooke 1665, sig. g1v.
35. At least two well-known figures who shared Hooke's interests in instruments for navigation and surveying had set out along the well-marked path from Westminster to Christ Church: Richard Hakluyt in the 1560s and Edmund Gunter in 1599.
36. Aubrey 2000, 395.
37. Hooke 1705, iii.
38. Nakajima 1994, 15.
39. Kent 2001, 11–12.
40. Hartley 1960, 91–2 and Jardine 2002, 116.
41. Mach 1960, 141–7. The enthusiastic von Guericke later trained teams of up to eight horses to try to separate even larger hemispheres.
42. Bennett 1982, 17, 40 and 74.
43. Hooke 1705, iii.
44. Perhaps Greatorex learned from Hooke some new techniques in mechanical engineering that enabled him in 1664 to be involved in making a diving machine intended for use in the construction of the Tangier mole (Taylor 1954, 229).
45. Boyle 1999 iii, 57.
46. Davis 1994, 157–75.

Chapter Two

1. Birch 1756–7 i, 7.
2. The amanuensis's annual salary was to be 40s (Birch 1756–7 i, 7), but the Royal Society Treasurer's Accounts Book 1660–72 shows that on 28 August 1661 the amanuensis was paid a half-year's salary of £2.
3. The salaries and other costs were to be paid for by the levy of a joining fee of 10 shillings and an annual subscription of a shilling a week (£2 12s annually) from each member on being elected to the Society as a Fellow.
4. Birch 1756–7 i, 21.
5. Hooke 1661.
6. Birch 1756–7 i, 21.
7. Birch 1756–7 i, 123.

8. Moray and Wilkins probably spoke to Boyle about releasing Hooke.
9. Birch 1756–7 i, 124.
10. Birch 1756–7 i, 124.
11. Royal Society Council Minutes (Copy) i 6.
12. 'Mr Hook was Elected a Fellow of the Society by the Council, and Exempted from all Charges' (Royal Society Council Minutes (Copy) i, 11 and Birch 1956–7 i, 250, dated 3 June 1673). Others elected Fellow were also exempt from charges for many reasons, usually connected with the benefit their membership was thought to bring to the Society through their wealth or position (Hunter 1994c, 89–92).
13. Birch 1756–7 i, 125.
14. Birch 1756–7 i and ii, contain, *passim*, many examples of such diversity.
15. Birch 1756–7 i, 485–6, dated 9 November 1664.
16. Hooke to Boyle, 10 November 1664 (Boyle 2001 ii, 398–400).
17. Birch 1756–7 ii, 54.
18. Hooke 1665, sig. g2r.
19. Hooke 1665, sig. A2r.
20. Pepys 1972–86 vi, 18.
21. Cooper 2003, 20. Hooke continued to receive his salary, not always promptly, until 1688 when the office of Curator of Experiments effectively disappeared.
22. Studies of seventeenth-century science and the social background of people involved in it have revealed interesting and useful social aspects of Hooke's relationships with his technicians and the kinds of places where they worked, exchanging technical information and preparing and testing instruments for Hooke's performance of experiments in front of the Royal Society (Shapin 1988 and 1989, Pumfrey 1991 and Iliffe 1995).
23. Hooke noted their names in his lecture manuscripts (Hunter 2003, 111).
24. Jardine 2003a, 181–97.
25. Michael Hunter gives a detailed

examination of the Royal Society's varying fortunes in Hunter 1994, 35–49.

Chapter Three

1. 'City' on its own is used here and in what follows to denote the rulers and administrators of the City of London and their committees; 'city' is used to denote the geographical location of the City of London and its Liberties.
2. Ward 1745 gives details of Gresham's will and biographies of the earlier Gresham Professors. Featherstone 1952, Chartres and Vermont 1998 and Ames-Lewis ed. 1999 give details of the subsequent history and present activities of Gresham College.
3. John Wilkins had much to do with Isaac Barrow's appointment as the first Lucasian Professor of Mathematics at Cambridge in 1664, a post from which Barrow resigned in 1669 in favour of his brilliant pupil Isaac Newton (Ward 1740, 160–1).
4. A footnote by Thomas Birch states that the Society was eager for Hooke to be appointed Gresham Professor of Geometry (Birch 1756–7 i, 435).
5. Dacres had been a candidate when Barrow was elected in July 1662, only to withdraw at the suggestion of Sir Richard Browne, a coal merchant who had been Lord Mayor in 1660–1 and MP for various constituencies (Woodhead 1965, 39–40). Barrow was elected unanimously by the City Side (Mercers' Company Gresham Repertory ii, 209).
6. Mercers' Company Gresham Repertory ii, 215.
7. Birch 1756–7 i, 435.
8. Mercers' Company Gresham Repertory ii, 218.
9. It is highly likely that the member of the City Side Hooke was referring to was Samuel Foote (or Foot). Cutler's second wife was Elizabeth Foot, daughter of Sir Thomas Foot, who was Lord Mayor in 1642, and to whom Samuel was probably related (Woodhead 1965, 71).

10. Public Record Office C7/564/29, item 2 discussed by Michael Hunter (Hunter 1989, 287 n.25) who also (ibid., 284) points out that Pepys noted in his diary that Cutler and John Graunt (a member of the Royal Society, and friend and colleague of Sir William Petty (1623–87), a formative member of the Royal Society) were often seen together in coffee houses. Hunter goes on to say that Graunt and Petty played leading roles in the negotiations about the Cutlerian Lectureship between Cutler and the Royal Society, so Graunt might have kept Cutler informed about the Royal Society's intentions in connection with his offer to Hooke.

11. The voting at the meeting when the 'mistake' occurred had been as follows: the four who had voted for Dacres were Samuel Foote, Sir Richard Browne (who had in 1662 persuaded Dacres to withdraw in favour of Barrow), Alderman Thomas Bateman and Sir William Bateman, brothers of the Lord Mayor Sir Anthony Bateman who was present at the meeting but not entitled to take part. The five who had voted for Hooke were Sir Thomas Adams, Colonel Neville, Deputy William Flewellen, Deputy John Tivill and Nicholas Penning. Of the nine members of the City Side, William Bateman, Foote, Adams, Nevill, Flewellen and Tivill were also at the meeting when the 'mistake' was discovered (Mercers' Company Gresham Repertory ii, 217–18).

12. Hooke 1674a and b, 1676, 1677 and 1678a and b. The collected edition is Hooke 1679. If Hooke had not seen a need to publish these Cutlerian Lectures in the 1670s, they would either have been lost or remained in manuscript until the present time, together with other unpublished Cutlerian Lectures and many other Hooke manuscripts in the archives of the Royal Society and elsewhere. The collection *Lectiones Cutlerianæ* was Hooke's last work to be published in his lifetime, except for some short contributions to the seven issues of *Philosophical Collections* which he edited for publication by the Royal Society from November 1679 to April 1682 (see Keynes 1960, 46–50 and 'Espinasse 1956, 159–63, who lists the contents of each of the seven issues).

13. Hooke 1935a, 299 (dated 5 July 1677). For other spies suspected and noted by Hooke, see Hunter 1989, 307 n.98. Theodore Haak, from the Palatinate, was one of the original group of natural philosophers who met in London before the Royal Society was formed. He and Hooke often played chess together in Hooke's rooms in Gresham College. Thomas Axe was Cutler's steward.

14. Royal Society Classified Papers xx, 80, f. 179r.

15. The great confusion has been unravelled by Hunter 1989, 279–338.

Chapter Four

1. Francis Bacon (1561–1626) turned to writing about natural philosophy late in his life after having been released from imprisonment for taking bribes when he was Lord Chancellor.

2. Pepys 1970–83 v, 32–3, entry for 1 February 1664).

3. Hooke 1665, sig. b1r.

4. Hooke 1665, sig. a2r–v.

5. Hooke 1705, 1–70.

6. Hooke 1665, sig. b2r.

7. Birch 1756–7 i, 133–4.

8. Hooke here is probably referring to Bacon's idea of making use of tall buildings for experiments in *New Organon* book 2 (Bacon 2000, 163–4).

9. 'w[ch]' inserted.

10. Illegible word deleted.

11. 'to' inserted.

12. 'surface of' deleted.

13. 'same' deleted.

14. An instrument made by Boyle and Hooke for measuring changes in atmospheric pressure.

15. Hooke's device for calibrating and graduating thermometers using freezing water as the zero point is in Hooke 1665, Schem. IIII, Fig. Z. The description of the procedure is ibid., 38–9.

16. Royal Society Classified Papers xx, 7, ff. 11r–12r.

17. Boyle 1999 iii, 16 and 52–4.

18. Wren intended to make use of the south-west tower of St Paul's as a zenith telescope during the long period of rebuilding, but no useful observations were made there.

19. Gunther 1931, 151.

20. Hooke uses 'power' here in the sense that we would now use 'force' and 'tension' to mean 'stretching' or extension: the force applied to an elastic body is proportional to the extension produced.

21. Gunther 1931, 333.

22. He is considering only proportional extensions here. The extensions xo, xp, etc. of the helix are not the same as the extensions xo, xp, etc. of the spiral, but the ratios of the extensions are equal. In each case: (xo ÷ xo), (xp ÷ xo), (xq ÷ xo), . . . , (xw ÷ xo) are as 1, 2, 3, ... , 8.

23. Gunther 1931, 335.

24. Algebraically they are $pv = k_1$ and $F = k_2x$ where k_1 and k_2 are constants. Hooke was not concerned with accurate evaluation of the constants; units and standards of measurement were not defined well enough at the time for universal application and ratios were adequate for practical purposes. Furthermore he points out that in the flexing of a beam downwards the lower part is in compression and the upper part in tension.

25. Andrade made this point in his seminal 1949 Wilkins Lecture on Hooke (Andrade 1950).

26. Hooke 1678a, 9.

27. Hooke 1726, 26–8.

28. Although David Oldroyd (after reproducing the text in full) dismisses the statement as the briefest sketch of Hooke's ideas on method (Oldroyd 1987, 150), it was the first of several attempts by Hooke to set out a scheme for performing institutional experiments. Gunther reckons the undated statement 'appears' to have been written around 1662–3, without giving any further justification (Gunther 1930a, 111). Derham, editor of Hooke 1726, placed it immediately following Hooke's account (dated 11 February 1663) of the refraction of ice and crystal, which placement might have been the basis of Gunther's viewpoint. However, Derham says in a preliminary 'Address to the Reader' that he found Hooke's papers to be 'very numerous and in great confusion' and that the best he 'could do was to rank them, as near as I could, according to the order of the Time in which they were written, or communicated. (Hooke 1726, unpaginated preliminaries).

29. These sources are discussed by Mary Hesse and David Oldroyd, and cited by Michael Hunter (Hesse 1966a, 77–9, 82; Oldroyd 1972, 113, 118–19; Oldroyd 1987, 146–9 and Hunter 2003, 123).

Chapter Five

1. Birch 1756–7 i, 173, dated 7 January 1663. We should remember that Hooke was working more than two decades before the Newtonian laws of motion had been explicitly stated. Those laws are still in common usage for many daily tasks in theoretical and practical dynamics, together with differential and integral calculus and the concept of continuous motion, velocity and acceleration. When showing how Hooke was thinking and what he was writing before such laws were formulated and mathematical tools were devised to make efficient use of them, I do not use concepts

and terms such as 'force', 'mass', 'momentum', 'impulsive force' and 'power' as they are now understood, but in the way the Hooke and his contemporaries used them.

2. Birch 1756–7 i, 177, 14 January 1663. It seemed to some members as if Hooke had not rehearsed his performance well enough, so he was ordered to go away and practise until he was ready. Such an attitude at the beginning of institutionalised experimental philosophy was not uncommon among those members of the Royal Society who had been admitted more for their wealth and influence than for their expertise in science. They expected a good show, but this particular experiment of Hooke's was very ambitious. It was one of three other experiments he proposed to perform the following week: on insects living in pressurised air; on respiration; and on the different refractions of light in cold and warm water (Birch 1756–5 i, 179, dated 14 January 1663).

3. A design drawing.

4. Birch 1756–7 i, 179, dated 21 January 1663.

5. Birch 1756–7 i, 192, dated 4 February 1663.

6. Birch 1756–7 i, 193–4, dated 11 February 1663.

7. Royal Society Classified Papers xx, 12, ff. 19r–21v, dated 18 February 1663.

8. Illegible text deleted.

9. 'by [. . .] using' deleted.

10. 'it' deleted.

11. Royal Society Classified Papers xx, 12, ff. 20r–21r, 18 February 1663.

12. If we discuss the mechanics of Hooke's experiment using the concepts and definitions of Newtonian mechanics, we would use mathematical equations and concepts such as linear momentum, kinetic energy, inelastic collision, impulsive force, inertia and mass. We can find hints of all of these concepts in Hooke's account. The 'celerity' of the falling ball is its linear momentum divided by its mass; the 'force' which on collision is 'returned into the ball', makes it a 'little flatted' and so is 'lost', is the kinetic energy of the falling body; the loss of 'force' on impact means that the 'touching' of the ball and the plate is an inelastic collision; the 'very quick and sudden motion' arises from an impulsive force; and the 'great deal of massy heavy body' is the inertial mass of the balance and counterpoise which is overcome by the kinetic energy of the falling ball. If Hooke had looked for a relationship between the mass moved and the falling body's kinetic energy, instead of its linear momentum, he would have found a close correlation, especially at higher velocities.

13. Royal Society Classified Papers xx, 12, f. 21v, dated 18 February 1663.

14. Birch 1756–7 i, 443, dated 22 June 1664. I have been unable to identify 'Mr Wilson' with much confidence. Thomas Wilson is the most likely candidate. In 1671 he conveyed messages between his cousin Flamsteed and the Royal Society's secretary Henry Oldenburg (Hunter 1995, 255). Oldenburg was accused by Hooke of trafficking in intelligence and Flamsteed was vindictive towards Hooke.

15. Birch 1756–7 i, 449, dated 6 July 1664.

16. In measuring time, 1''' was the symbol for a 'third', or $\frac{1}{60}$th of a second: 60 thirds = 1 second (or 1''); 60 seconds = 1 minute (or 1'); and 60 minutes = 1 hour.

17. Birch 1756–7 i, 456, dated 3 August 1664.

18. If a simple pendulum takes T seconds to swing from one end of its vertical circular arc to the other and back again, its period is T seconds, but it was said to beat $\frac{1}{2}$T seconds.

19. Birch 1756–7 i, 460, dated 17 August 1664. Although Hooke does not say so, the measurement he made was significant. He knew from Galileo's work that the distance fallen from rest (l) and the time of fall (t) were related by $l = \frac{1}{2}gt^2$, where g is

a constant. By measuring l for t = 1 second, the value of the constant g from Hooke's experiment can be found from g = 2l to be 31. The constant g is the acceleration due to gravity, i.e. the increase in velocity of a falling body each second. Hooke's value of 31 feet per second per second was an accurate value at the time.

20. The bullet, on emerging from the gun, started the half-second pendulum of Hooke's timer by breaking a thread which held back the timer's pendulum bob. A wooden board about three inches thick was set up in the path of the bullet at a measured distance from the gun. One end of a taut thread was fixed to the board. The other end of the thread was connected to the timer in such a way that when the bullet struck the board, the breaking of the taut thread would immediately stop the motion of the pendulum. The elapsed time would then be registered at the timer and could be used to calculate the speed of the bullet. Oldenburg told Boyle:

> but it was found upon severall tryalls that the bullet pierced through the board . . . and did not break a small slender piece of white thred, which was to have stopped the pendull. Order was given, to think upon a better way of making this Experiment.

(Boyle 2001 ii, 311–12). Oldenburg's account in his letter to Boyle dated 1 September 1664 is very similar to the description in Birch 1756–7 i, 461, which was probably derived from Oldenburg's account, in his role of secretary, of the Royal Society's meeting. There is no record of where this early experiment in ballistics took place, whether in the quadrangle at Gresham College or in one of the internal galleries.

21. The repairs were paid for by a gift of money and a warrant for timber from Queen Elizabeth I and donations from the clergy of Canterbury and the citizens and clergy of London.

22. Stow 1994, 313.

23. The relationship between the period T of a simple pendulum, its length l and the earth's gravitational acceleration g, first published in 1673 by Huygens in *Horologium Oscillatorum* (Barbour 1989, 529) is $T = 2\pi\,(l/g)^{\frac{1}{2}}$. If we use the value of the gravitational acceleration that we have found from Hooke's earlier measurements (g = 31 feet per second per second, see note 19 above) together with the measured length of the pendulum as reported by Hooke (l = 180 feet) we calculate the period T to be about 15 seconds, corresponding to a half period, or 'single vibration' of 7½ seconds. In the circumstances (a reconnaissance visit to plan more careful experiments) this is in good agreement with Hooke's reported value of 'no less time than six whole seconds'. It must be pointed out that Hooke at the time would not have used the formula in the way we have done here.

24. The 'Torricellian experiment' first performed by Evangelista Torricelli (1608–47) is as follows. Fill a cylindrical glass tube at least a metre in length, open at one end, with mercury. Then, closing the open end with a finger, turn the tube upside-down and, keeping the finger in place, immerse the open end in a reservoir of mercury. After setting the tube vertical, remove the finger. The mercury in the tube will then fall somewhat, leaving a near-vacuum at the top. Torricelli found that as he carried his apparatus (or mercury barometer) carefully up and down hills or the stairs of tall buildings, the level of the mercury in the tube fell as he went higher and rose as he went lower. We would now say that the height of the top of the mercury in the tube above the level in the reservoir is a measure

of the atmospheric pressure reckoned in inches, or millimetres, of mercury, but pressure and force were not then defined in the way they are now. Furthermore, it was not generally known at the time (although Hooke noticed the effect) that mercury could contain dissolved air or water which would adversely affect the accuracy of the barometer. The content of the space above the mercury at the top of the tube was a matter for vigorous debate at the time when the scholastic viewpoint was that a vacuum could not exist (Boyle 1999 iii, 10, n. a).

25. Boyle 2001 ii, 303–4.
26. Oldenburg to Boyle (Boyle 2001 ii, 312).
27. Hooke to Boyle (Boyle 2001 ii, 316).
28. Birch 1756–7 i, 465, dated 7 September 1664.
29. Birch 1756–7 i, 466–7, dated 14 September 1664.
30. This letter, dated 15 September 1664, was the first from Hooke to Boyle marked as from Gresham College. Hooke had moved into rooms there at some time in September 1664.
31. A drachm, or dram (dr), was a unit of weight used by apothecaries. A drachm is equivalent to 60 grains, ⅛ oz, or a little less than 3.9 grams (Cardarelli 1999, 171, where the last value on the page should be '3.887. . . g' not '3.387. . . g').
32. Birch 1756–7 i, 467, dated 14 September 1664.
33. Birch 1756–7 i, 468–9, dated 21 September 1664.
34. Boyle 2001 ii, 333–4.
35. Birch 1756–7 i, 470–2, dated 28 September 1664.
36. Hooke to Boyle, 6 October 1664 (Boyle 2001 ii, 342–4).
37. Quoted by Bell 1924, 4, n. 4.
38. Birch 1756–7 ii, 58.
39. Birch 1756–7 ii, 60.
40. Hooke to Boyle, 15 August 1665 (Boyle 2001 ii, 512–13).

41. Hooke to Boyle, 26 September 1665 (Boyle 2001 ii, 537–8).
42. Jardine 2003a, 173.
43. Evelyn 1955 iii, 416, cited by Jardine 2003a, 173.
44. Hooke to Boyle, 15 August 1665 (Boyle 2001 ii, 512–13).
45. Hooke 1705, 279–450.

Chapter Six

1. Hooke 1935a, 235, entry dated 2 June 1676.
2. Inwood 2002, 10–11.
3. Pepys 1970–83 vi, 2–3, entry dated 2 January 1665.
4. Hooke 1705, xxvi–xxvii.
5. Aubrey 2000, 396.
6. Lisa Jardine has recently revealed and discussed the astonishing intensity of Hooke's pharmaceutical regime (Jardine 2003a, 181–97).
7. Hooke 1935a, 11, 15 and 55, entries dated 28 October, 2 December 1672 and 15 August 1673.
8. Hooke 1935b, 154 and 221, entries dated 6 October 1689 and 11 March 1693.
9. Hooke 1935b, 255, entry dated 2 July 1693.
10. Hooke 1935a, 124, entry dated 30 September 1674.
11. Hooke 1935a, 56, entry dated 16 August 1673.
12. Details of Hooke's Isle of Wight family connections, including Hooke's nephew Tom Gyles (the son of Hooke's cousin Robert) who lodged with him, and an account of Grace Hooke's life can be found on pages of the website of the Isle of Wight History Centre at freespace.virgin.net/ric.martin/vectis/hookeweb/
13. Bennett 1975, 55.
14. 'Bedlam', or 'Bethlem', is an abbreviation of 'Bethlehem'.
15. Hooke 1935b.
16. Hooke 1705, xxvi.
17. Inwood 2002, 438.
18. Guildhall Library MS 23894, ii, C66.

19. Hooke 1705, xxvi–xxvii.
20. PRO Prob. 20/1315, transcribed by Jardine 2002, 555.
21. Rostenberg 1989.
22. Guildhall Library MS 6884. The diary covers the period 27 May to 13 September 1892.

Chapter Seven

1. Editors' comment in Pepys 1970–83 vi, 37, n. 1.
2. Rouse Ball, 1893.
3. *Philosophiae Naturalis Principia Mathematica* ('Mathematical Principles of Natural Philosophy'), or *Principia* for short. For an important and usefully annotated modern English translation and guide see Newton 1999.
4. See Koyré 1952, 312–16, for a summary of this earlier dispute between Hooke and Newton.
5. Newton 1959–77 i, 416, letter to Hooke dated 5 February 1676.
6. His first two laws of planetary motion appeared in *Astronomia Nova* ('The New Astronomy') in 1609. Details of what we now call his third law appeared in *Epitome Astronomiæ Copernicanæ* ('Epitome of Copernican Astronomy') in 1618–20. He showed that each planet moves in an elliptical orbit around the sun which lies at a focus of the ellipse. Furthermore, as a planet travels round its orbit, a line from the centre of the sun to the centre of the planet sweeps out equal areas in equal times. He also showed that the square of the orbital period of any planet is proportional to the cube of the semi-major axis of its orbital ellipse. The simplicity of the laws hides the years of effort and error by Kepler in discovering them, and the complex manner in which he expressed and published them. See Stephenson 1987 for an account of Kepler's astronomy.
7. Ofer Gal has pointed out that the idea of an inflected motion was also used by Hooke when he was investigating the effect of atmospheric refraction on light rays (see Figure 11). A ray of light passing obliquely through the earth's atmosphere is normally refracted downwards towards the Earth as it travels through concentric layers of air which become less dense as their height above the ground increases. Hooke saw the bending of the ray of light (or stream of light particles) as an inflection from its (or their) straight-line path (Gal 1996).
8. Birch 1756–7 ii, 90–1, dated 23 May 1666. Hooke's original manuscript from which Birch's transcript was made can be found as Royal Society Classified Papers xx, 41.
9. When a pendulum bob describes a horizontal circle, the centre of which is vertically below the point of suspension, the string traces out the surface of a cone, hence the name 'conical pendulum'.
10. Birch 1756–7 ii, 92, dated 23 May 1666. See Patterson 1952 for a discussion of how Hooke and others used pendulums for mechanisms, speculations and experiments, and Patterson 1949, 1950 for Hooke's gravitation theory.
11. That is, annual motion along its orbit around the sun.
12. Hooke 1674a, sig. A4v.
13. The star γ–*Draconis* passed very close to the zenith at London. Hooke attempted to use an eyepiece micrometer in his telescope to measure the star's displacement from the zenith when the earth was at different places on its orbit. Changes in these separations could be interpreted as parallax. Unfortunately for Hooke, neither Gresham College nor the Monument provided a sufficiently stable platform, and atmospheric refraction effects, although much reduced by observing vertically upwards, are still significant. In any case his micrometer telescopes failed to give any reliable measurements because the magnitude of

the annual parallax is much too small to be detected by instruments made by using the technology and materials of the time.

14. Planetary symbols are used in the publication, not names.

15. Hooke 1674a, sig. E2r–v.

16. A further important component of celestial mechanics had been added by Huygens with the publication of his *Horologium Oscillatorum* in 1673. At the end of the book he gives a few theorems (but no proofs) on what is now called centrifugal force (Huygens used *vis* for force). When a body travels at constant speed along a circular path (such as a stone being whirled around in a sling, or the swinging bob of a simple pendulum), a centrifugal force tends to move the stone or the bob away from the centre of rotation. The tendency is resisted by the slinger of the stone, or by the fixture at the top of the pendulum string. Huygens showed that the centrifugal force is proportional to the square of the speed of the body divided by the radius of the circular path – now expressed conventionally as $F = mv^2/r$, or $F = m\omega^2 r$, where F is the centrifugal force, m the mass of the body, v its velocity and ω its angular velocity ($\omega = v/r$).

17. Edmond Halley (1656–1742) the second Astronomer Royal was a member of the Royal Society, Savilian Professor of Geometry at Oxford and a former naval captain. He urged Newton to write *Principia* and was one of the first to apply Newtonian mechanics in science when he forecast the date of the return of a comet which now bears his name. See Cook 1998 for a comprehensive biography.

18. Lohne 1960. For us, as post-Newtonians, the proof for circular motion is straightforward. Using the notation in the preceding note, the velocity v is given by the circumference of the circle divided by the time taken to complete one revolution, i.e. the period T, so $v = 2\pi r/T$,

or $v^2 = 4\pi^2 r^2/T^2$. Kepler's third law is $T^2 = k_1 r^3$, where k_1 is a constant. For circular motion, the centrifugal/centripetal force is $F = k_2 v^2/r$ where k_2 is another constant. Substituting for v^2 in the last equation we have $F = k_2 4\pi^2 r^2/T^2 r$ and substituting in this equation for T^2 from Kepler's third law we have $F = k/r^2$ where k is the constant $4\pi^2 k_2/k_1$. So the 'endeavour to the centre' is in 'inverse duplicate proportion to the distance to the centre' – an inverse square law.

19. The first of a series of seven letters between Hooke and Newton in 1679–80. Five were published in 1893 (Rouse Ball 1893, 139–53), a sixth in 1929 (Pelseneer 1929, 237–9) and the seventh in 1952 by Alexandre Koyré (Koyré 1952) who gives a thorough analysis of all seven letters.

20. Quoted by Koyré 1952, 316. Newton 1959–77 ii, 297: quoted by Barbour 1989, 542; Nauenberg 1994, 336; and De Gant 1995, 147.

21. Quoted by Koyré 1952, 322.

22. Quoted by Koyré 1952, 322.

23. Newton had written 'I am glad to hear that so considerable a discovery as you made of the earth's annual parallax is seconded by Mr Flamsteed's observations' (quoted by Koyré 1952, 322). John Flamsteed FRS (1646–1719), no friend of Hooke, was Astronomer Royal. Both Hooke and Flamsteed were mistaken in thinking they had detected and measured the Earth's annual parallax. Hooke's account of his experiments to measure the Earth's annual parallax was published in *An Attempt . . .*, which also contained his 'System of the World' where he had put his hypothesis forward. If, as seems probable, Newton had read *An Attempt . . .*, then he had either forgotten Hooke's hypothesis or was being disingenuous (or possibly sarcastic). If we admit the possibility that when Newton wrote that he had been 'endeavouring to bend' himself from philosophy to other

studies he was making an ironic reference to Hooke's idea of a 'bending' of inertial motion by an endeavour to the centre, then we should also note that Hooke did not use 'bend' in the letter to which Newton was replying, but he did use it (as 'bent') in *An Attempt . . .* which Newton claimed he had either forgotten or had not read. It is also unlikely that Newton would not have heard or read about Hooke's demonstrations with pendulums at the Royal Society in May 1666 when his hypothesis of combining tangential and central motions was first made public.

24. Cited by Koyré 1952, 322, n. 54.

25. This Galilean experiment was to let fall a heavy body from a high tower and see where it meets the ground. If the Earth does not rotate, then the falling body will meet the ground vertically below the point from which it was dropped. However, if the Earth rotates from west to east, Newton explained, the body at the top of the tower will be moving eastwards faster than the base of the tower, so when it is let fall 'outrunning ye parts of ye earth [it] will shoot forward to ye east side of the perpendicular' and meet the ground to the east of the point vertically below the place from which it was dropped. This is 'quite contrary to ye opinion of ye vulgar' who would think that in the time taken for the body to fall to the ground the rotation of the earth eastwards would move the base of the tower in that direction so that the body would be left behind and fall to the west of a point vertically below the place from which it was dropped (Newton 1959–77 ii, quoted by Barbour 1989, 542–3).

26. This is the 'unpublished' letter (a manuscript copy of Hooke's original) which was sold at Sotheby's in 1918, came into the possession of Yale University and was the subject of Koyré 1952.

27. Birch 1756–7 iii, 512–13, dated 4 December 1679, records that Newton's proposed experiment to show that the Earth rotated on its axis from west to east 'was highly approved of by the Society; and it was desired, that it might be tried as soon as could be with convenience'. The members then debated other experiments they thought of which would either confirm or deny the expected outcome of Newton's proposed experiment. The imagination and critical judgements evident from the bare record of the debate typify the way scientific investigations were discussed, but not always performed at that time.

28. Quoted by Koyré 1952, 329. Newton 1959–77 ii, 305–6, quoted by Barbour 1989, 543–4; and De Gant 1995, 149.

29. Quoted by Koyré 1952, 329.

30. He had imagined the Earth to be sliced into two halves and separated by a small distance so that the body could fall freely in the space between.

31. Nauenberg 1994d, who points out for the first time how Newton possibly distorted his diagram in order to make it difficult for anyone to discover from it the method he had used to compute the path.

32. Quoted by Koyré 1952, 331.

33. Quoted by Nauenberg 1994, 336.

34. Quoted by Nauenberg 1994, 336.

35. Quoted by Nauenberg 1994, 337.

36. Newton 1959–77 ii, quoted by Nauenberg 1994, 338.

37. A.R. Hall has shown how Newton recovered and modified his earlier demonstration and its re-emergence in *Principia* (Hall 1992, 202–24).

38. Birch 1756–7 iv, 347, dated 10 December 1684.

39. Birch 1756–7 iv, 479–80, dated 28 April 1686.

40. Trinity College Library Cambridge, MS 0.11a.1/16. See Nauenberg 1994a, 2003 for detailed discussions of Hooke's geometric representation.

41. Hooke would almost certainly have tried the construction and found that the polygonal

orbit soon diverged from an ellipse when it approached the centre, unless the incremental steps were very small.

42. Hooke's 1685 graphical method is geometrically similar to the method Newton used in *De Motu* and which became the first Proposition of the first Theorem of the first Book of *Principia*. Although Hooke had been familiar with *De Motu* since it arrived at the Royal Society in 1684, the method in his 1685 manuscript proceeds in a unique graphical way, different from the way followed by Newton (Nauenberg 1994a, 2003); in the latter place, Nauenberg takes issue with Pugliese's interpretation of the manuscript (Pugliese 1989).

43. Birch 1756–7 iv, 484–5, note t, dated 22 May 1686.

44. Birch 1756–7 iv, 486, dated 2 June 1686. The Society, as usual, was short of funds.

45. Rouse Ball 1893, 159, quoted by Koyré 1952, 320.

46. As Newton admitted to Halley, it was only after the 1679–80 correspondence with Hooke that he saw the connection between central forces and Kepler's area law.

47. Hooke 1674b.

48. Cooper 1982, *passim*. Jim Bennett has discussed Hooke's optimism and frustration in relation to improving the accuracy of scientific instruments (Bennett 2003, 88–91). Hooke's optical instrumentation and its scientific and technical contexts are also discussed by Bennett 1989, Chapman 1995, 45–9, and Simpson 1989.

49. Royal Society Register Book iii, 93–7, dated 21 March 1666.

50. Speake *et al.* 1990.

51. The La Coste-Romberg G-type gravimeters.

52. The main difference is that here the random errors in measurements are estimated statistically as standard deviations. The right-hand column shows discrepancies between each measured difference and the weighted mean value of the corresponding two predicted differences, together with the standard deviations of those discrepancies. The magnitude of each discrepancy turns out to be less than its standard deviation, indicating that the inverse square law holds to at least the limit imposed by random errors in measurement. Five discrepancies are negative, three positive, indicating that significant systematic errors do not appear to have been made.

53. William Croone (1633–84) was a physician, Gresham Professor of Rhetoric and Anatomy Lecturer to the Surgeons' Company (Hunter 1994c, 138–9).

54. British Library Additional Manuscript 6193, f. 60r.

55. The pendulum G (Figure 34) beats seconds and causes the circular disc C to oscillate through an arc. The pendulum and disc are set in motion as soon as the weight and a length of string attached to it are let fall from M, where the other end of the string is attached. When the weight reaches the end of its fall, the string acts on the lever ML (fulcrum at K) which engages via the latch LE with the disc C, and stops its oscillation. The time of fall is then found by adding the fraction of a second found from the position of the disc in its arc to the number of full pendulum beats counted. The distance fallen is of course equal to the length of the string.

56. Micro-g absolute gravimeter. www.microgsolutions.com/

57. Niebauer *et al.* 1995.

58. 10^{-4} pascals (Pa), where $1\text{Pa} = 1 \text{ N.m}^{-2}$.

59. The 'perfect gas law', derived from Boyle's Law, is used to calculate mean gas density in order to derive the drag coefficient and so correct for the effects of the remaining molecules in the dropping chamber on the speed of the freely falling body.

60. The springs are intended to provide an inertial reference for the distance measurements. Hundreds of automated records of time and distance are processed

to calculate the acceleration of the freely-falling body in gals (after galileo; 1 gal is 1 cm.s^{-2}) to an accuracy of the order of a few microgals (1 μgal = 10^{-8} m.s^{-2}). I find this accuracy astonishingly high, particularly when it is realised that the measurement accuracy of about 1 μgal corresponds to a height change of only 3 mm.

61. Cited by 'Espinasse 1956, 13, 166 and 169.
62. Andrade 1950 and 1951.
63. Quoted by Andrade 1950, 472 (my translation from French). Andrade also quotes the astronomer Mädler, the philosopher Lasswitz (both from Germany) the geologist Andrew Geike and the astronomer Herschel; all thought very highly in the nineteenth century of Hooke's experimental and speculative science.
64. Hunter and Schaffer 1989, 3.
65. Andrade 1950, 473.
66. Bud and Warner 1998 (cited by Inwood 2002, 4–5).

Chapter Eight

1. Colvin 1995, 778.
2. The chapel at Pembroke College, Cambridge, was probably Wren's first major architectural work. It was built in 1663–5 for his uncle Matthew Wren. His second was the Sheldonian Theatre in Oxford, built 1664–9 (Colvin 1995, 1088–9).
3. Hooke 1665, sig. g2r–v.
4. Jardine 2002, 219–23. Bishop Sheldon was the main benefactor of the Sheldonian Theatre, Oxford.
5. Lang 1956, 16–18.
6. Vanessa Harding 2003, personal communication, derived from her estimate of 422,000– 485,000 as the population of the whole of London.
7. Exceptions to becoming a freeman by apprenticeship were men who obtained freedom of the city by patrimony or redemption, having first been admitted to a livery company.

8. Jeffery 1996, 356–9.
9. Merritt 1998, 935–60.
10. Although Cateaton Street has been widened and now forms part of Gresham Street, Guildhall is still hidden away behind buildings fronting the surrounding streets.
11. Cited by Bedford 1966, 46.
12. Cited by Bedford 1966, 46–7. In August 1666 English sailors had landed on the island of Schelling and set fire to sixty Dutch merchant ships in harbour at Brandaris and set the town ablaze.
13. Cited by Bedford 1966, 51.
14. Cited by Bedford 1966, 51 and 56.
15. Walter Bell's book (Bell 1923, reprinted in 1994 by Bracken Books, London) is still the most detailed general account of the progress of the fire. It has been followed recently by other general accounts in book form by, for example, Gustav Milne (1986) and Stephen Porter (1996) which make use of research after Bell and give modern and contemporary sources.
16. Debtors' prisons.
17. Now the Central Criminal Court.
18. Milne 1986, 77.

Chapter Nine

1. Corporation of London Records Office Repertory 71, ff. 168r–9v, dated 6 September 1666.
2. Mercers' Company Gresham Repertory ii, 232. Only George Gifford (Divinity), Walter Pope FRS (Astronomy), William Croone FRS (or 'Croune', Rhetoric) and Hooke were in residence at the time; the rest had let their lodgings.
3. George Gifford was Professor of Divinity at the time but was absent. Dr Thomas Horton had been Gresham Professor of Divinity from 1641 until June 1661. He married in 1651, but obtained a dispensation from Parliament to allow him to retain his Gresham Professorship. The dispensation was renewed by Cromwell and by Charles II,

but revoked by the latter at the instigation of George Gifford who succeeded Horton on 7 June 1661. Horton was vicar of the church of St Helen Bishopsgate at the time of the fire (Ward 1740, 65–72).

4. Corporation of London Records Office Repertory 71, f. 170r, dated 7 September 1666.

5. Gifford was probably not far away. He was Rector of St Dunstan's in the East which had to be rebuilt after the fire.

6. Corporation of London Records Office Repertory 71, f. 171r, dated 8 September 1666.

7. Corporation of London Records Office Repertory 71, ff. 169v–70r, dated 7 September 1666.

8. Gallery of shops or other trading places.

9. Corporation of London Records Office Repertory 71, f. 170v, dated 8 September 1666.

10. Corporation of London Records Office Journal 46, f. 120r, dated 10 September 1666.

11. The preceding extracts from Proclamation 48 are taken from Birch 1887, 224–30. Other proclamations made in the preceding week were issued to allay fears of insurrection and foreign plots against the king.

12. Intimations of this recognition in John Evelyn's diary and elsewhere are cited by Reddaway 1951, 53–4.

Chapter Ten

1. Jardine 2002, 261–2.

2. Rasmussen 1960, 93–114, and Hanson 1989 and 1990 illustrate and compare the plans produced by Wren, Evelyn, Hooke, Richard Newcourt and Valentine Knight. None was adopted as the basis for rebuilding.

3. Ward 1740, 102.

4. 'blame' replaces 'curse' deleted.

5. British Library MS *Parentalia*, f. 53v, transcribed Jardine 2002, 263–6 and 534.

6. Mercers' Company Gresham Repertory II, 217–18.

7. Birch 1756–7 ii, 115.

8. Waller 1704, xii–xiii. Waller was about six years old at the time of the fire, so he is unlikely to have seen it at that time. Reddaway claimed that Hooke's plan has survived, but says nothing about its whereabouts (Reddaway 1951, 53).

9. A hand-coloured copy of Doornick's print in Guildhall Library, London, is listed as No. 17 in Howgego 1978.

10. A copy of Venckel's print in Guildhall Library, London, is listed as No. 24 in Howgego 1978.

11. Venckel's layout plan is described as 'Hooke's plan for rebuilding the city' (Howgego 1978, 57). No reason for or explanation of such an attribution is given. Despite the close similarity between this layout plan and the one in Doornick's earlier print which Howgego also lists, he does not attribute Doornick's plan to Hooke. However, a third printed sheet is listed as No. 25 and dated 1670 in Howgego 1978. It is anonymous and bears no date, but is very similar to Doornick's and it shows the same layout plan which Howgego here attributes to Hooke.

12. A recent illustration of what is probably the layout plan in Doornick's 1666 print is attributed to Hooke, but no evidence for the claim is put forward (Porter 1996, 101–2).

13. Corporation of London Records Office Journal 46, ff. 122r–v, dated 2 October 1666.

14. Corporation of London Records Office Repertory 71, ff. 177v–8r, dated 2 October 1666.

15. Reddaway 1951, 52.

16. Ward 1740, 102–3.

17. Corporation of London Records Office Journal 46, f. 123r, dated 4 October 1666. (Corporation of London Records Office Misc. MS 3.36/7 is a copy of the Order.)

18. Saunders 1997, 127.

19. London Topographical Society 1967, xx, xxvii–xxix and *passim*.

20. Colvin 1995, 655–8.

21. Various spellings (e.g. Jarmin, Jermyn) of Jerman's name appear in contemporary City documents.

22. Colvin 1995, 545–6.

23. Reddaway 1951, 58.

24. Jardine 2002, 259.

25. John Evelyn's *Diary*, ed. H.B. Wheatley 1906 iii, 345, cited by Reddaway 1951, 54, n.1.

26. Reddaway 1951, 53.

27. In 1665 Petty had estimated the value of houses in London to be £15 *per annum* at 12 years' purchase (Petty 1899 i, 105, cited by Porter 1996, 71).

28. Reddaway 1951, 70.

29. *London Gazette*, 27 September–1 October 1666, cited by Rasmussen 1960, 110.

30. Corporation of London Records Office Journal 46, ff. 123r–v, dated 9 October 1666.

31. Corporation of London Records Office Journal 46, f. 124v, dated 3 November 1666, but out of sequence.

32. Corporation of London Records Office Repertory 71, f. 180v, dated 9 October 1666.

33. Corporation of London Records Office Journal 46, f. 127r, dated 17 October 1666.

34. Corporation of London Records Office Journal 46, f. 129r, dated 31 October 1666.

35. Presumably Edmund Wylde FRS, gentleman virtuoso, of Glaseley Hall, Shropshire (Aubrey 2000, 47, 49 etc.).

36. Birch 1756–7 ii, 118–19, dated 31 October 1666.

37. We do not know whether or not any useful information found its way from members of the Royal Society into the parliamentary bill, but informal means of communication between the Royal Society and the Lord Chancellor were readily available through Petty, Wren, Evelyn and Hooke which could have been used for that purpose. The Royal Society in the next two weeks soon lost their enthusiasm for bricks when they turned their attention to observing the effects of transferring blood from a sick dog to a fit one and vice-versa, and speculating on why some unembalmed corpses that had been buried for centuries were sometimes found to be well-preserved (the dryness of the conditions was generally thought to be the reason).

38. Birch 1756–7 ii, 119, dated 31 October 1666.

39. Dimensions, or sizes, of masonry, brickwork, timber and other materials used in building.

40. 'Conduit' in the seventeenth century was generally used to refer to a street fountain where fresh water could be drawn. It was seldom used in its present sense of a pipe or duct used for the transportation of fluid.

41. Corporation of London Records Office Journal 46, f. 129r, dated 31 October 1666. (Corporation of London Records Office Misc. MS 3.36/8 is a copy of this Order.)

42. Royal Society Council Minutes (Copy) i, 140–1, dated 14 February 1667.

43. Mercers' Company Gresham Repertory ii, 257, dated 2 November 1666.

44. Mercers' Company Gresham Repertory ii, 258–9, dated 9 November 1666.

45. Mercers' Company Gresham Repertory ii, 262–3, dated 16 November 1666. The lead was later found to weigh 21 tons (ibid., 273, dated 28 January 1667).

46. The first experiments by Hooke on breaking wood took place at the Royal Society on 8 June 1664 (Birch 1756–7 i, 435–6). They are an early example of the engineering discipline 'strength of materials' and Hooke recognised their importance. In a letter to Boyle dated between 1 and 5 July he stated 'Some experiments we made of breaking wood, which were considerable, and gave occasion to hope, that this subject will afford many useful experiments' (Boyle 2001 ii, 292).

47. Hull 1997. Hooke's illustration of Kettering-stone for *Micrographia*, published in early 1665, and Wren's use of the material for Pembroke College Chapel (1663–5) show that the close personal and professional relationship between the two men began before the fire.
48. See Bennett 1982 for a discussion of Hooke and Wren in science, and Jardine 2002, *passim*, for their social relationship.
49. Hooke 1705, 1–70.
50. In *General Scheme* Hooke mentions that he discovered the rotation of Jupiter about its axis 'two years since'. He made that discovery in 1664. However, Hunter 1989, 299 and n. 70, favours 1668 as the date of *General Scheme*.
51. Saunders 1997, 128–34.
52. The total cost was £58,122 17s 4d, made up of £51,456 7s 4d for building and £6,666 10s for additional land (Saunders 1997, 134).
53. Saunders 1997, 121–35.
54. At the end of the seventeenth century the Gresham Trustees' debt had increased to a level impossible to maintain, so they petitioned Parliament to allow them to demolish the college and sell the grounds. Hooke successfully objected to the trustees' proposal, ostensibly on his own account, but actually in support of the Royal Society who would lose their accommodation if the petition succeeded. There can be little doubt that Hooke blamed the Gresham Trustees' financial difficulties on their extravagance in 1666 when they spurned his advice to rebuild the Royal Exchange for less than £5,000.
55. Reddaway 1951, 60–2.
56. Corporation of London Records Office Journal 46, ff. 132v–3v, dated 30 November 1666.
57. The City's Greenyard was an open area where the Lord Mayor's horses were stabled.
58. Corporation of London Records Office Repertory 72, ff. 25r–v, dated 6 December 1666.
59. John Jennings (1654–c. 66); John Leake (1650–86), mathematician and Master of Christ's Hospital School in 1673; William Leybourne (1626–1716?), often employed as a measurer by the City, teacher of mathematics, author of books on surveying, worked on Ogilby & Morgan's 1676 map of the rebuilt city; William Marr (1640–96), employed by Parliamentary Survey of Crown Lands, Clerk to the Kitchen of Charles II; William Morgan (*fl.*1666–90), King's Cosmographer 1675–82, grandson of John Ogilby and co-publisher of their 1676 map; Richard Shortgrave (*fl.*1658–76), instrument maker, Royal Society's Operator 1663–76; Thomas Streete (1621?–89?), mathematician. See, for example, Bendall 1997 ii, Hunter 1994c, Taylor 1954 for these and other details.
60. British Library Additional MS 5415 E.1. A reduced facsimile can be found in Reddaway 1951, between 54–5. In 1723, a print based on Leake's compilation was published by George Vertue. It has the widths of the old streets marked as well as some new, widened and straightened streets, all of which were approved for Proclamation by the Lord Chancellor.
61. Corporation of London Records Office Journal 46, f. 130r, dated 12 November 1666.
62. 14 Charles II, 2.
63. 18–19 Charles II, 8, of 8 February 1667.
64. 18–19 Charles II, 7.
65. Reddaway 1951, 91. Reddaway gives a full account of the Fire Court and how it gained the confidence of the citizens (ibid., 91–111 and *passim*). Jones 1966 gives further details of the Fire Court and a calendar to its judgments and decrees.
66. 22 Charles II, c. 11, of 11 April 1670.
67. Always subject to the City's formal agreement, which was almost always given.

Chapter Eleven

1. The act omitted to prescribe the height of a cellar in the third sort of house.

2. A breastsummer (or bressummer, bressomer, etc.) is a wooden beam placed horizontally across a wide opening, such as a shopfront, which supports the wall above it.

3. A chaldron was a measure of volume, equivalent to about 1.3 cubic metres, or about 290 gallons. It contained about a tonne of coal.

4. The quotations from the 1667 Rebuilding Act are in modern style, taken from Reddaway 1951, 80–90, Bedford 1966, 233–6 and Milne 1986, 117–19.

5. Corporation of London Records Office Journal 46, f. 146v, dated 25 February 1667.

6. Corporation of London Records Office Journal 46, ff. 146v–7r, dated 26 and 27 February 1667.

7. On the south-west corner of St James's Street, the home of Lord Clarendon at that time (Pepys 1970–83 xi, 28).

8. This map was most probably a version of John Leake's manuscript compilation made in December 1666 from the six surveyors' original sheets (British Library Additional MS 5415 E.1). It shows the proposed widths of streets and intended new works such as King Street and the Fleet Channel (Figure 44).

9. Corporation of London Records Office Journal 46, f. 147v, dated 13 March 1667.

10. Corporation of London Records Office Journal 46, ff. 151r–2r, dated 29 April 1667.

11. Birch 1887, 231–4.

12. Corporation of London Records Office Journal 46, f. 148r, dated 13 March 1667.

13. Corporation of London Records Office Journal 46, f. 147r, dated 27 February 1667.

14. Colvin 1995, 714–15.

15. Corporation of London Records Office Repertory 72, f. 80v, dated 14 March 1667. From time to time in City documents, Peter Mills, Hooke and John Oliver are referred to as 'Surveyors of New Buildings' to emphasise that their appointments were made in accordance with the Rebuilding Act and that their duties were different from those of the regular City Surveyor – the position which Mills occupied up to the time he was sworn in with Hooke.

16. Corporation of London Records Office Repertory 72, f. 81v, dated 20 March 1667.

17. Birch 1756–7 ii, 160 dated 21 March 1667.

18. Guildhall Library MS 84.1, f. 22r, reproduced in facsimile as London Topographical Society 1964.

19. Corporation of London Records Office Ex-Guildhall Library MS 322/3.

20. Corporation of London Records Office Ex-Guildhall Library MS 322/9 is the latest account of the Clerk of Works for expenses incurred in staking out the streets that has been found. It is for the seven days ending Monday 26 May 1667. Only 280 feet of timber were needed and the cart was used for only two of the seven days.

21. Corporation of London Records Office Ex-Guildhall Library MSS 322/3, 9, 10, 11, 12, 14 and 15.

22. Corporation of London Records Office Ex-Guildhall Library MS 322/10, dated 12–18 May 1667.

23. The Society had changed its meeting day from Wednesdays to Thursdays on 14 February 1667.

24. Birch 1756–7 ii, 169, dated 25 April 1607.

25. Hooke 1665, 217–23.

26. Pepys 1970–83 viii, 136, entry for 29 March 1667.

27. Reddaway 1951, 142–3, who comments in a footnote 'Anyone who has suffered from the traffic tangles in that warehouse-filled area must rue their success'.

28. Corporation of London Records Office Repertory 72, f. 105r, dated 14 May 1667.

29. Corporation of London Records Office Repertory 72, ff. 108r–v, dated 16 May 1667.

30. London Topographical Society 1992, 79.

31. On 20 May 1667 Hooke staked out for Wheatley the foundations of his property in Tower Street (Corporation of London Records Office Ex-Guildhall Library MS 275, f. 2r) but the record contains no evidence about Wheatley's property in Water Lane.

32. Corporation of London Records Office Repertory 72, f. 108v, dated 21 May 1667.

33. London Topographical Society 1967, 81.

34. Corporation of London Records Office Comptroller's Deeds Box K/W/51A, dated 20 July 1670.

35. Corporation of London Records Office Journal 46, ff. 151r–2r, dated 29 April 1667.

36. Corporation of London Records Office Printed Document 10.54(L).

37. 'Builder' is used here not to mean the bricklayer, carpenter or other craftsman who did the building work, but the person who paid for the rebuilding work.

38. Corporation of London Records Office Ex-Guildhall Library MSS 275–8 are three Day Books (MSS 275–7) and one Posting Book (MS 278). The Posting Book lists the dates, builders' names, numbers of foundations and sums paid, classified according to the locations; entries seem to have ceased in September 1679.

39. Guildhall Library MS 84.1, ff. 16–18, reproduced as London Topographical Society 1964, show entries in Mills's survey books of surveys by Hooke and Oliver. Only transcripts of the original survey books are available, so it is not possible to see whether or not other entries in Mills's books are by Hooke or Oliver.

40. Corporation of London Records Office Repertory 73, f. 62r, dated 28 January 1668.

41. Guildhall Library MS 84.2, f. 168r, reproduced in facsimile as London Topographical Society 1962a.

42. Corporation of London Records Office Ex-Guildhall Library MS 276, f. 86v, bears the signature of one of Mills's Executors for receiving Mills's quarter salary due at Michaelmas 1670. The date of the signature is 7 October 1670.

43. Guildhall Library MSS 84.1 and 84.2 are two volumes of transcripts of Mills's ten survey books and Guildhall Library MSS 84.3 and 84.4 are transcripts of Oliver's. Guildhall Library MS 84.5 is an index to the other four volumes. They have been published in facsimile as London Topographical Society 1962a, 1962b, 1962c, 1964 and 1967.

44. Hooke 1935a, 326, entry dated 7 November 1677.

45. They could still be in existence somewhere. Many of Hooke's manuscripts, including his diary, did not emerge from private ownership until 1891 and some of those were wrongly attributed at first (Hooke 1935a, v–viii).

46. Ex-Guildhall Library MS 277, f. 3r.

47. Hooke 1935a, 36, entry dated 27 March 1673.

48. Cooper 1997.

49. Cooper 1999, 51.

50. Corporation of London Records Office Ex-Guildhall Library MS 277, f. 5r.

51. Hooke 1935a, 60, entry dated 16 September 1673.

52. Corporation of London Records Office Ex-Guildhall Library MS 277, f. 2r, dated 15 November 1672.

53. Earle 1989, 17–81.

Chapter Twelve

1. Jones 1966 ii, 328, cited by Porter 1996, 117.

2. Pepys 1970–83 viii, 152 and 155, cited by Porter 1996, 82.

3. Corporation of London Records Office City Lands Committee Orders i, f. 1(a)r, and City of London Records Office Journal 46, f. 209r, both dated 22 January 1668. Each of the first three folios of City Lands Committee Orders bears the number "1" so they are differentiated here by 1(a), 1(b) and 1(c) respectively.

4. Corporation of London Records Office Journal 46, f. 209r, dated 22 January 1668.

5. Corporation of London Records Office City Lands Committee Orders i, f. 1(b)r, dated 4 March 1668 is an order for payment. An entry in the Coal Duty accounts (Corporation of London Records Office Coal Duty Account Book v, f. 43r) shows that Hodilow was paid £600 on 19 March 1668.

6. Corporation of London Records Office Journal 46, f. 219v, dated 18 March 1668.

7. Corporation of London Records Office Numerical General Index to Comptroller's Records, f. 36v, and Corporation of London Records Office Comptroller's Deeds Box K, S/1.

8. Corporation of London Records Office Comptroller's Deeds Box K, H/7A and B, dated 16 July 1668.

9. Corporation of London Records Office Numerical General Index to Comptroller's Records, H/72, dated 11 March 1687.

10. Corporation of London Records Office Comptroller's Deeds Box K, T/12, dated 14 November 1670.

11. 'and layd into the street for the widning of fish street hill' deleted.

12. This calculation in duodecimal fractions written in the left-hand margin of the manuscript gives an insight into Hooke's mental arithmetic. He calculates the area of a 40ft by 11ft 7in rectangle by first calculating (40ft $\times$ 7in) = 23.4ft^2 (duodecimal fraction) and then (40ft $\times$ 11ft) = 440ft^2. This leaves the areas of two right-angled triangles to be found. The dimensions of the perpendicular sides of the northern triangle are 20ft by (12ft 10in − 11ft 7in) so its area is ½(20ft $\times$ 1ft in). The dimensions of the perpendicular sides of the southern triangle are 20ft by (12ft 4in − 11ft 7in) so its area is ½(20ft $\times$ 9in). Hooke does not need to write these areas down, but he makes a mental note that their sum is ½(20ft $\times$ 2ft) = 20ft^2

which he then writes in his calculation and finds the total area to be 483.4ft^2 (duodecimal fraction).

13. Compensation at a rate of 3s 6d per square foot was equivalent to 3½d for ½ of a square foot – again, a simple calculation.

14. Colvin 1995, 714.

15. Corporation of London Records Office Comptroller's Deeds Box K, H/28, dated 16 May 1671. Hooke's signature and date are lost and a clerk's calculation can not be read with confidence. The date has been taken from a clerk's note on the reverse.

16. Corporation of London Records Office Comptroller's Deeds Box K, F/31, dated 10 November 1675.

17. Corporation of London Records Office Comptroller's Deeds Box K, M/22, dated 9 November 1671.

18. Corporation of London Records Office Comptroller's Deeds Box K, D/18, dated 14 December 1671.

19. Corporation of London Records Office Comptroller's Deeds Box K, V/5A, dated 2 March 1676. Corporation of London Records Office Comptroller's Deeds Box K, V/5B, is a copy, certified by the Comptroller Joseph Lane of the entry in Mills's survey book (London Topographical Society 1962a, f. 114v), on which Hooke based his calculation of area.

20. Corporation of London Records Office Comptroller's Deeds Box K, H/26, dated 6 April 1671.

21. Corporation of London Records Office Comptroller's Deeds Box K, W/25A, dated 31 January 1671.

22. Corporation of London Records Office Comptroller's Deeds Box K, W/46, dated 15 December 1676.

23. The linear dimensions in both certificates are: breadth north–south 20ft 9in; depths 6ft 10in at the south and 5ft at the north. The area is therefore 20ft 9in × 5ft 11in, which is 123.1ft^2 superficial content, to the

nearest 0.1in duodecimal notation. In the earlier certificate (Corporation of London Records Office Comptroller's Deeds Box K, W/25A) Hooke gives the area as 121.3ft² superficial content; in the later (Corporation of London Records Office Comptroller's Deeds Box K, W/46) it is given as 122ft² superficial content. This example shows the usual slight underestimate of an area through rounding errors in arithmetic. Perhaps rounding-down was deliberate; any error arising from the assumptions about the side widths being perpendicular to the street would make the calculated area too large. In any case, the methods sufficed.

24. Corporation of London Records Office Comptroller's Deeds Box K, M/5, dated 19 June 1669.

25. Corporation of London Records Office Comptroller's Deeds Box K, W/34A, dated 5 December 1671.

26. Corporation of London Records Office Comptroller's Deeds Box K, W/34B, dated 27 January 1672.

27. Corporation of London Records Office Comptroller's Deeds Box K, P/25A, dated 11 November 1673.

28. The parishes of St Andrew Hubbard and St Mary at Hill were united by the second Rebuilding Act.

29. 'were' deleted.

30. Corporation of London Records Office Comptroller's Deeds Box K, H/42, dated 17 December 1672.

31. Corporation of London Records Office Comptroller's Deeds Box K, W/45, dated 26 March 1674.

32. From a contemporary manuscript cited by Beaven 1913, ii, 188.

33. Corporation of London Records Office Comptroller's Deeds Box K, M/24, dated 14 November 1671.

34. The original certificate has not been found, but it is recorded as Corporation of London Records Office Numerical General Index

Comptroller's Records A/9, dated 10 May 1671. On 27 November 1672 the parishioners petitioned the City Lands Committee for further compensation for the loss of their church wall. On 4 December 1672 the Committee ordered Hooke and the Comptroller to consider the matter further and to examine the earlier certificate to see whether all the ground lost was contained in it or whether it was necessary to make another certificate (Corporation of London Records Office City Lands Committee Minutes, Rough).

35. 'ground' deleted.

36. 'first' inserted above the line.

37. 'next' inserted above the line.

38. 'to this Committee' inserted above the line.

39. 'all' deleted.

40. Corporation of London Records Office Comptroller's Deeds Box K, B/71, dated 4 November 1673.

41. Hooke 1935a, 26; Corporation of London Records Office Comptroller's Deeds Box K, L/17, and ibid.; C/49.

42. Hooke 1935a, 152, entry dated 9 March 1675.

43. Hooke 1935a, 26, entry dated 1 February 1673.

Chapter Thirteen

1. Loengard 1989.

2. Peter Mills and Edward Jerman had held appointments as City Viewers before the fire. Mills was a City Viewer from 1644 to 1657, having been City Bricklayer. Jerman was a City Viewer from 1650 to 1655, having been City Carpenter.

3. Jones and Reddaway 1967, x–xi.

4. Corporation of London Records Office Repertory 73, ff. 10r–v, dated 12 November 1667.

5. Hooke did not give the month date of the view, but it was the same as the month date of the order.

6. 'and' deleted.

7. Corporation of London Records Office Miscellaneous MS 93.79, dated 19 December 1693.

8. Corporation of London Records Office Repertory 73, f. 223r, dated 7 July 1668.

9. Corporation of London Records Office City Lands Committee Orders i, f. 1(c)r, dated 10 May 1668.

10. 'An' replaces '[the]' overwritten.

11. 'between the' inserted above the line replaces 'of' deleted.

12. Also known as Carey Lane.

13. 'Act' inserted above the line.

14. 22 Charles II, c.11, of 11 April 1670.

15. 'and' deleted.

16. 'of' deleted.

17. 'said' inserted above the line.

18. 'wall' deleted.

19. 'party wall' inserted above the line.

20. 'east west' inserted above the line.

21. '[or concerneing? . . .]' deleted.

22. Corporation of London Records Office Miscellaneous MS 92.73, dated 8 July 1671.

23. '[b..i. . . by the said]' deleted.

24. 'between the main timbers' inserted above the line.

25. 'fis' deleted.

26. 't[. . .]' deleted.

27. 'the' deleted.

28. 'Rais' deleted.

29. 'ought' deleted. The remainder of the manuscript is written from top to bottom in the left-hand margin of the document.

30. Corporation of London Records Office Miscellaneous MS 93.108, dated 14 June 1686.

31. 'amou' at end of line deleted.

32. Corporation of London Records Office Miscellaneous MS 93.113, dated 12 July 1676. Entered at Corporation of London Records Office Viewers' Reports ii, 27.

33. Corporation of London Records Office Viewers' Reports i, 19, dated 13 June 1668.

34. Jones 1966, i, 42–4.

35. 'Nathaniell' replaces '[Ja. . .s]' overwritten.

36. 'is a' deleted.

37. 'built by a' deleted.

38. '[. . .]' deleted.

39. Corporation of London Records Office Miscellaneous MS 92.81, f. 1, dated 30 August 1671.

40. Fir was the name for soft woods (conifers) which were forbidden to be used for supporting structural loading, where oak was required.

41. Corporation of London Records Office Miscellaneous MS 92.160, dated 15 July 1673.

42. 'from' inserted above the line replaces 'f[. . .]' deleted.

43. A faggot is a bundle of sticks or twigs held together, usually by two bands or ties, used as fuel. A bavin is a bundle of brushwood bound together at the centre by a band or tie, often used as fuel in bakers' ovens.

44. 'house' inserted above the line.

45. Corporation of London Records Office Miscellaneous MS 93.129, dated 6 November 1691. This report of a view is the last one to be found in Hooke's hand. The document was discovered laid-in at the place in Corporation of London Records Office Viewers' Reports iii where the clerk had transcribed about half of the manuscript as Corporation of London Records Office Viewers' Reports iii, 110, the concluding entry.

46. Pepys 1970–83 iv, 77; v, 12; and viii, 201.

47. Aubrey 2000, 209.

48. Hooke 1935, 73, entry for 5 December 1673, the date of the view shown in Figure 49.

49. 'as well' deleted.

50. 'wall' inserted above the line.

51. Corporation of London Records Office Miscellaneous MS 93.14, dated 14 July 1677.

52. Hooke 1935a, 301, entry dated 14 July 1677.

53. For example, the editors of Hooke's earlier diary use 'views' in connection with foundation surveys and area certificates (Hooke 1935a, xxiv). Even Margaret

'Espinasse departs from her usual accuracy
when she describes 'personal surveys . . .
of hundreds of sites which were to be built
on' as 'views' ('Espinasse 1956, 86).

54. Hooke 1935a and 1935b, *passim*.

55. The City's practice was to make clerical
copies of the viewers' reports both on single
sheets and in bound folio volumes. Many of
Hooke's original manuscripts and clerical
copies are extant, but only three of the
original four bound folio volumes remain in
the Corporation of London Records Office
whose Repertories, Journals and Minutes
contain hundreds of references to views.

56. Hooke 1935a, 23, entry dated 21 January
1673.

57. Hooke 1935a, 20, dated 8 January 1673.

58. Cooper 1999, 198–9, from Corporation of
London Records Office Viewers' Reports i,
ii and iii; Miscellaneous MSS Boxes 92 and
93; and Hooke 1935, 18–78.

59. One golden guinea (value £1 1s).

60. Ten shillings presumably, Oliver's share of
the money paid to Hooke for the earlier of
the two views reported on 6 May 1693,
but carried out the previous day.

61. Jonathan's coffee house in Exchange Alley,
near the Royal Exchange.

62. Hooke 1935b, 237, entry dated 6 May 1693.

Chapter Fourteen

1. Peter Mills had died before these public
rebuilding programmes had gone very far.

2. Corporation of London Records Office City
Lands Committee Orders i, f. 47v, dated
25 November 1670.

3. Corporation of London Records Office City
Lands Committee Orders i, f. 50r, dated
8 February 1671.

4. Corporation of London Records Office City
Lands Committee Orders i, f. 50v, dated
1 March 1671.

5. Corporation of London Records Office City
Lands Committee Orders i, f. 51r, dated
1 March 1671.

6. Birch 1756–7 iii, 42, dated 10 April 1672.

7. Corporation of London Records Office City
Lands Committee Orders i, ff. 54r–v, dated
22 March 1671.

8. Timber sills laid flat into niches cut into
the bed of the channel.

9. Upright lengths of timber, sometimes in a
wooden frame, used for supporting or
transferring loads.

10. Timber planks fixed horizontally to
puncheons to protect the sides of a
channel from the effects of the water
current and to retain the sides of the
channel in position.

11. Corporation of London Records Office City
Lands Committee Orders i, f. 54v, dated
22 March 1671.

12. Understanding of the physical processes and
interactions between water, soil and
structures has come only in the last fifty years
or so with the development of soil mechanics
and geotechnical engineering. Such
understanding is founded on the Baconian
new learning through experimental enquiries
into natural phenomena that Wren, Hooke
and their colleagues in the Royal Society were
initiating at the time the channel was being
built.

13. Abundant evidence of these activities can be
found in the Orders, Minutes and Papers of
the City Lands Committee in the Corporation
of London Records Office. Many of Hooke's
diary entries (Hooke 1935a, *passim*) show
that his involvement in the work on the
Fleet Channel took a significant amount of
his time and effort in the early 1670s.

14. 'so' deleted.

15. 'from' deleted.

16. '[. . .]' deleted.

17. 'solid' deleted.

18. 'also' inserted above the line.

19. In taking the surface area of the relevant
stretch of the channel (4,680 square yards)
to represent the volume of excess soil to be
removed (4,680 cubic yards), Hooke has

accepted the evidence that the average depth of excess soil and rubbish across the whole area of the channel brought down by the great flood was 3ft (i.e. 1 yard).

20. 'and Crosse walls' deleted.

21. Corporation of London Records Office City Lands Committee Papers MS 97, dated 18 April 1674, a clerical copy, signed by Hooke.

22. William Flewellen (or Fluellen, etc.) was Common Councilman for Bassishaw Ward and Keeper of Guildhall (Woodhead 1965, 70).

23. Deputy, Coleman Street Ward.

24. Corporation of London Records Office City Lands Committee Minutes (Rough) dated 20 November 1672.

25. Hooke 1935a, 125, entry dated 7 October 1674.

26. Bell 1924, 26.

27. Woodhead 1965, 106.

28. Corporation of London Records Office Biographical Notes.

29. Hunter 1994c, 190–1.

30. Cooper 1999, 83–6.

31. Grocer, Lord Mayor 1673–4 (Woodhead 1965, 92).

32. Tallow Chandler and Deputy of Coleman Street Ward (Woodhead 1965, 149).

33. Hooke 1935a, 13, entry dated 14 November 1672.

34. Reddaway 1951, 216, n. 6.

35. Reddaway 1951, 215.

36. A manuscript copy of John Evelyn's *Londinum Redivivum*, in Corporation of London Records Office Guildhall Library MS 94.

37. Denter stones were used to mark the corners of a property boundary. If the idea of a parcel-based land information system for London's cadastre had been put into effect, they would probably have been used all over the city to define property boundaries. A certified measured survey of the lengths of the boundary lines between them would serve to define what ground was owned.

38. Corporation of London Records Office City Lands Committee Orders i, f. 55r, dated 3 May 1671.

39. Corporation of London Records Office Charter 98. On 18 October 1671 the City ordered Shortgrave to be paid £18 10s for his work on plots and draughts relating to the waterline and wharves by the Thames and the Fleet Canal as far as Holborn Bridge (Corporation of London Records Office City Cash Account Book i, f. 144v).

40. Corporation of London Records Office City Lands Committee Orders i, f. 56v, dated 24 May 1671.

41. Corporation of London Records Office City Lands Committee Orders i, f. 59v, dated 5 July 1671.

42. The Lord Mayor, Wren and Hooke were ordered to meet with the king at Windsor (Corporation of London Records Office City Lands Committee Orders i, f. 60r, dated 10 July 1671).

43. Corporation of London Records Office Charter 98.

44. Hooke 1935a, 12, entry for 9 November 1672.

45. Hooke 1935a, 44, entry dated 21 May 1673.

46. Hooke 1935a, 44, entry dated 23 May 1673. Sir Paule Neile, Sir Robert Moray and John Locke were members of the Royal Society. The king's request in St James's Park for 'degre by water' refers to Hooke's thermometer which was based on the freezing point of water as the zero point. We do not know what scale units Hooke used for measuring temperature.

47. Hooke 1935a, 45, entry dated 26 May 1673.

48. Hooke 1935a, 45, entry for 31 May 1673.

49. Hooke 1935a, 45, entry dated 1 June 1673.

50. Hooke 1935a, 58, entry dated 29 August 1673.

51. Hooke 1935a, 58, entry dated 3 September 1673. 'Craven' here is used in its contemporary sense: to make someone give way through fear.

52. Hooke 1935a, 59, entry dated 4 September 1673.

53. Hooke 1935a, 59, entry dated 5 September 1673.

54. Hooke 1935a, 61, entry dated 24 September 1673.

55. Hooke 1935a, 64, entry dated 8 October 1673.

56. Hooke recorded Shaftesbury's dismissal in his usual laconic style, but he might have felt a little satisfaction at his departure from office (Hooke 1935a, 69, entry dated 9 November 1673).

57. Corporation of London Records Office City Lands Committee Minutes (Rough) and Corporation of London Records Office City Lands Committee Orders ii, f. 27v, both dated 17 July 1672.

58. Corporation of London Records Office City Lands Committee Minutes (Rough), dated 17 July 1672.

59. Corporation of London Records Office City Lands Committee Minutes (Rough), dated 9 October 1672.

60. Corporation of London Records Office City Lands Committee Minutes (Rough), dated 16 October 1672.

61. Hooke 1935a, 5, entry dated 14 August 1672, and Corporation of London Records Office City Lands Committee Minutes (Rough), dated 14 August 1672.

62. Corporation of London Records Office City Lands Committee Orders ii, f. 30r, dated 14 August 1672.

63. Corporation of London Records Office City Lands Committee Minutes (Rough), dated 27 August 1672.

64. Corporation of London Records Office City Lands Committee Minutes (Rough), dated 5 September 1672.

65. Corporation of London Records Office City Lands Committee Minutes (Rough), dated 11 September 1672.

66. Corporation of London Records Office City Lands Committee Minutes (Rough), dated 15 January 1673.

67. Corporation of London Records Office City Lands Committee Minutes (Rough), dated 29 January 1673.

68. Hooke 1935a, p. 47, entry dated 13 June 1673.

69. Bell 1923, 269.

Chapter Fifteen

1. Corporation of London Records Office Repertory 72, f. 108r, dated 16 May 1667.

2. Corporation of London Records Office Printed Document 10.117 (L), dated 8 July 1667.

3. Corporation of London Records Office City Lands Committee Orders i, f. 54v, dated 22 March 1671.

4. Corporation of London Records Office City Lands Committee Orders i, f. 59r, dated 28 June 1671.

5. The order was repeated on 15 November 1671, but with the instruction that the Surveyors should report their findings to the Commissioners for Sewers. (Corporation of London Records Office City Lands Committee Orders i, f. 71.)

6. Corporation of London Records Office Comptroller's Deeds Box K, W/40A, B and C, dated 20 September 1673.

7. Hooke 1935a, 61, entry dated 24 September 1673.

8. Corporation of London Records Office City Lands Committee Orders i, f. 55r, dated 3 May 1671.

9. Corporation of London Records Office City Lands Committee Orders i, f. 56r, dated 10 May 1671.

10. Corporation of London Records Office Viewers' Reports ii, 3.

11. Corporation of London Records Office City Lands Committee Orders i, f. 43v, dated 10 August 1670.

12. Corporation of London Records Office City Lands Committee Minutes (Rough), dated 23 October 1672.

13. Corporation of London Records Office City Lands Committee Orders i, ff. 66r–v, dated 4 October 1671.

14. Reddaway 1951, 295–6.

15. Corporation of London Records Office Repertory 76, f. 15v, dated 22 November 1670.

16. Corporation of London Records Office Repertory 74, f. 200r.

17. Corporation of London Records Office Repertory 74, f. 231r, dated 20 July 1669.

18. Corporation of London Records Office City Lands Committee Orders ii, f. 10v, dated 26 March 1672.

19. Corporation of London Records Office City Lands Committee Minutes (Rough), dated 5 July 1672.

20. Corporation of London Records Office City Lands Committee Orders i, f. 57r, dated 31 May 1671.

21. Hooke 1935a, 283, entry dated 3 April 1677.

22. Hooke 1935a, 438–9, entries dated 10, 16, 17 and 24 February 1680.

23. Inwood 2002, 300.

24. Corporation of London Records Office Miscellaneous MS 93.52, dated 27 February 1683.

25. Corporation of London Records Office Journal 46, ff. 210r–v, dated 12 February 1668.

26. Corporation of London Records Office City Lands Committee Minutes (Rough), dated 11 May 1669.

27. Corporation of London Records Office City Lands Committee Minutes (Rough), dated 2 June 1669.

28. Corporation of London Records Office City Lands Committee Minutes (Rough), dated 1 September 1669.

29. Masters 1974, 17.

30. Corporation of London Records Office City Lands Committee Minutes (Rough), dated 10 February 1670.

31. Hooke 1935a, 14, entry dated 20 November 1672.

32. Hooke 1935a, 27, entry dated 7 February 1673.

33. Hooke 1935a, 45, entry for 29 May 1673.

34. Hooke 1935a, 61, entry dated 23 September 1673.

35. Masters 1974, 10–11.

36. Jeffery 1996, 356–9.

37. Birch 1756–7 ii, 115.

38. Hunter 1994c, 190.

39. Guildhall Library MS 25,548, 17 and 19.

40. Cooper 2003, 61.

41. Wren and Hooke wanted their friend John Hoskins, another member of the Royal Society, to replace Woodroofe, but the Lord Mayor 'by mistake excepted him' (Hooke 1935a, 208, entry dated 4 January 1676). Perhaps it was not a mistake and the Lord Mayor wanted a man with a traditional City background to take part in the rebuilding of the churches.

42. Bennett 1975.

43. Abraham Hill, John Aubrey, Thomas Henshaw and William Holder with Wren and Hooke were all members of the Royal Society's 'Philosophical Club' which held its first private meeting on 1 January 1676.

44. Hooke 1935a, 214–15, entry dated 29 January 1676.

45. Batten 1935, 13–14 and 16; and 1936–7.

46. Geraghty 1997.

47. Jeffery 1996.

48. Stoesser-Johnston 1997, 65, who cites a review by Anthony Geraghty (Geraghty 1997) of Jeffery 1996 in corroboration.

49. 'Espinasse 1956, 178–9.

50. Hooke 1935a, 122, entry dated 19 September 1674.

51. Hooke 1935a, 265 and 267, entries dated 31 December 1676 and 11 January 1677, and Heyman 2003.

52. Stevenson 1996.

53. Evelyn 1955, entry dated 10 October 1683.

54. Hooke 1935a, 266 and 268, entries dated 6 and 16 January 1677.

55. Hooke 1935a, 268, 269, 273–5, 279–80, entries for 17, 18, 19 and 22 January, 10, 13, 16 and 19 February, 15, 17 and 19 March 1676.
56. Inwood 2002, 251–2.
57. Colvin 1995, 506–10 gives details of more of Hooke's architecture.
58. From the fifth codicil of Busby's will, undated, but not earlier than 26 February 1695, the date of the fourth codicil (Barker 1895, 146).

Chapter Sixteen

1. Corporation of London Records Office Journal 46, f. 133v, dated 30 November 1666.
2. Corporation of London Records Office Ex-Guildhall Library MS 275, f. 73v, dated 20 January 1669. The foundation was unallocated, but it was in the part of the City where Hooke did most of his staking out.
3. Corporation of London Records Office Repertory 74, f. 75r, dated 28 January 1669.
4. Corporation of London Records Office Comptroller's Deeds Box K, M/37A, dated 1 September (Saturday) and 9 October 1677.
5. 'formerly' deleted.
6. 'the' replaces 'st' overwritten.
7. '& south' inserted above the line.
8. Corporation of London Records Office Comptroller's Deeds Box K, M/37B, has a dimensioned plan of the area around the Monument and an account of sums amounting to £418 5s demanded by the rector and churchwardens for ground taken away from St Margaret's Church for building the Monument and adjacent piazza. None of these details is in Hooke's hand. On 9 October 1677 Hooke received 5s from a churchwarden for certifying the areas taken away (Hooke 1935a, 319).
9. These figures are followed by a clerk's calculations of the price of 1245ft^2 @ 2s 6d (£155 12s 6d) and the price of 218ft^2 @ 3s (£32 14s). These two areas are equivalent to the areas 729ft^2 and 734ft^2 certified by Hooke. The manuscript (see Figure 66) also shows a total price of £240 16s 6d made up from the two prices above and the price of 210 ft^2 @ 5s (£52 10s), the calculation of which is not shown.
10. Corporation of London Records Office Repertory 74, f. 189r, dated 10 June 1669.
11. Dr Nicholas Barbon, physician son of the Anabaptist and republican Praisegod Barbon, was the leading speculative property developer after the fire. He is credited with being the first to provide fire insurance for owners of London property.
12. Corporation of London Records Office City Lands Committee Orders i, f. 42r, dated 3 August 1670.
13. Corporation of London Records Office City Lands Committee Orders i, f. 46r, dated 9 November 1670.
14. Corporation of London Records Office Repertory 76, f. 58r, dated 26 January 1671.
15. Corporation of London Records Office Repertory 76, f. 72v, dated 14 February 1671.
16. Royal Society Journal Book vii, 219–20, dated 24 July 1689.
17. Jardine 2002, 315–21.
18. Corporation of London Records Office City Lands Committee Minutes (Rough), dated 9 October 1672. On 22 October Hooke made a visit to the site (Hooke 1935a, 11) when he carried out the City's order.
19. Corporation of London Records Office City Lands Committee Minutes (Rough), dated 6 November 1672.
20. Hooke 1935a, 54, 59, 66, 93, 106, 116, 120, 129 and 136, entries for 8 August, 11 September, 19 October 1673, 28 March, 1 June, 7 August, 8 September, 6 November and 16 December 1674.

21. British Library Additional MS 18,898, quoted by Jardine 2002, 317.
22. Hooke 1935a, 172, entry dated 3 August 1675.
23. Hooke 1935a, 195, 201 and 214, entries dated 20 November, 16 December 1675 and 25 January 1676.
24. Hooke 1935a, 225, entry dated 7 April 1676.
25. Hooke 1935a, 25, entry dated 8–14 October 1676.
26. Corporation of London Records Office City Lands Committee Papers, MS 158, dated 15 November 1676.
27. Hooke 1935a, 257, entry for 17 November 1676.
28. Corporation of London Records Office City Lands Committee Papers, MS 161, dated 13 December 1676.
29. Hooke 1935a, 262, entry dated 13 December 1676.
30. 'upon every course of stone there set' inserted above the line.
31. Corporation of London Records Office City Lands Committee Papers, MS 187, dated 9 December 1677.
32. Gunther 1930b, 527. Gunther does not give the location of the manuscript.
33. Welch 1893, 19–21.
34. Welch 1893, 21–2.
35. Corporation of London Records Office City Lands Committee Minutes (Rough), dated 6 June 1672. 'Resentment' is used here in the sense of 'grateful appreciation or acknowledgement (of a service, kindness etc.). Now obsolete, but common 1650–1750' (*Oxford English Dictionary*, 1933).

Chapter Seventeen

1. Bennett 1973.
2. Batten 1935 and 1936–7.
3. Cooper 1987, 1988a and b.
4. Bendall 1997, 384. In 1674 he was granted an extension to his title when he was appointed 'His Majesty's Cosmographer and Geographick Printer' at an annual salary of £13 6s 8d, or 20 marks (Van Eerde 1976, 133).
5. Van Eerde 1976, 123–43.
6. Leybourne 1653 and 1657.
7. Leybourne 1674, 300–1.
8. Leybourne 1674, 3.
9. Holwell 1678.
10. Gregory King (1648–1712) was the son of the land surveyor Gregory King of Lichfield. King the younger surveyed roads for John Ogilby (Bendall 1997 ii, 295).
11. Holwell 1678, 181.
12. For instance, check that the measured angles in a polygon add up to $(2n - 4)$ right angles, where n is the number of chain lines in the polygon; and plot each polygon line by line with protractor and scale, checking that the last line closes the polygon at the starting point.
13. Van Eerde 1976, 125–6.
14. Hooke 1935a, 50, entry dated 8 July 1673.
15. Hooke 1935a, 51, entry dated 19 July 1673.
16. Hooke 1935a, 55, entry dated 14 August 1673.
17. The etcher and engraver from Bohemia who produced many views of London and its buildings, including the 1669 print of John Leake's *Exact Surveigh* (Hind 1972).
18. Hooke 1935a, 55, entry dated 16 August 1673.
19. Hooke 1935a, 65, entry dated 14 October 1673.
20. Hooke 1935a, 73–4, entry dated 8 December 1673.
21. Hooke 1935a, 74, entry dated 12 December 1673.
22. Hooke 1935a, 79, 81 and 83, entries dated 9, 19 and 29 January 1674.
23. Hooke 1935a, 144, entry dated 29 January 1675.
24. Hooke 1935a, 146, entry dated 9 February 1675.
25. Hyde 1992, ix.

26. Hyde 1992, ix.
27. LTS 1992 is a recent reprint.
28. The exception is a Tudor map of Portsmouth (Harvey 1993, 69).
29. Howgego 1978, 4. In the foreword, Helen Wallis gives three terms in use in England in the seventeenth century to differentiate between ways of representing streets and buildings on maps: by orthogonal projection on to a horizontal plane ('ichnography'); by orthogonal projection on to a vertical plane ('orthography' or 'ortography'); and by an approximation of perspective projection on to a plane inclined to both the horizontal and the vertical ('scenography'). Wallis states that scenography was the most common method used for city maps in the seventeenth century. Of the three forms, ichnography and orthography are geometrically correct representations of buildings and streets (unless scenography happens to be axonometric). Nowadays any orthogonal projection on to a plane is referred to as orthographic.
30. Schofield 1987.
31. That is, an orthogonal projection of the city on to a horizontal plane by dropping a perpendicular from each significant point of detail on to the map plane, similar to William Gascoyne's 1670 plan of Whitehall Palace (Phurley 1998). Gascoyne's plan is an orthogonal projection, but it shows the internal spaces of the buildings as well as the streets around them. It is more a building survey than a land survey, and it covers only a small area of the city.
32. Hyde 1992, xi, and Johns 1989, 57–8.
33. Two recent studies of the accuracies of the surveying for the map and of the map itself (Brennan 1998 and Mayo 2001) show that when the positions of about forty features on a modern paper copy of the map are compared with the positions of the same features on present-day Ordnance Survey digital maps, the discrepancies are almost entirely attributable to the inevitable errors in measurement at the time and the dimensional stability of a succession of paper copies of the original plot. Over the full extent of the walled city average discrepancies in position are about 2–3 metres, equivalent to only a few millimetres at the scale of the map.
34. Corporation of London Records Office Comptroller's Deeds Box K, M/42A. What Hooke called 'Temple Lane' was also known as Ralph's Quay (Harben 1918, 496) and can be found as n38 in LTS 1992, 38, K16. What Hooke called 'the gully' was not Gulley Hole west of London Bridge, but 'Sabb's Quay', a narrow alley leading south out of Thames Street 'opposite to Harp Lane' as Hooke says, which can be found as n42 in LTS 1992, 38, K16.
35. LTS 1992, 38, K16.
36. Gracechurch Street.
37. Pepys 1970–83 ix, 285, entry for 22 August 1668.
38. Quoted by Reddaway 1951, 285, n. 1, and 299–300.

Bibliography

1. The pagination has a discontinuity: page 209 is followed by page 279. According to Waller the mistake arose because the book was printed at two different presses.
2. Later Margaret 'Espinasse.

SELECT BIBLIOGRAPHY

Place of publication is London unless otherwise stated.

Aarslef, Hans (1970–80). Wilkins, John. In Gillispie (1970–80), xiv, 361–81.

Abercrombie, Patrick (1923). 'Wren's plan for London after the Great Fire.' *The Town Planning Review* 10: 71–8 and 6 plates.

Ackroyd, Peter (2000). *London, the Biography*. Chatto & Windus.

Adamson, Ian (1978). 'The Royal Society and Gresham College.' *Notes and Records of The Royal Society of London* 33: 1–21.

Agassi, Joseph (1977). 'Who discovered Boyle's Law?' *Studies in the History and Philosophy of Science* 8: 189–250.

Ainsworth, G.C. (1976). *Introduction to the History of Mycology*. Cambridge University Press, Cambridge.

Ames-Lewis, Francis ed. (1999). *Sir Thomas Gresham and Gresham College*. Ashgate, Aldershot.

Andrade, E.N. da C. (1935). 'Robert Hooke and his contemporaries.' *Nature* 136 (3436): 358–61.

—— (1936). 'Hooke and his editors.' *Nature* 137 (3462): 378–81.

—— (1950). 'Robert Hooke.' *Proceedings of the Royal Society of London Series A* 201: 439–73.

—— (1951). 'Robert Hooke, inventive genius.' *The Listener* 8 February 1951, pp. 215–16.

—— (1953). 'Robert Hooke, 1635–1703.' *Nature* 171 (4348): 365–7.

Arnol'd, V.I. (1990). *Huygens and Barrow, Newton and Hooke*. Trans. E.J.F. Primrose (Nauka FLM, Moscow, 1989), Birkhäuser Verlag, Basel.

Aubrey, John (1898). *Brief Lives* ed. Andrew Clark. Clarendon Press, Oxford.

—— (1949a). *Brief Lives* ed. Anthony Powell. The Cressett Press.

—— (1949b). *Brief Lives* ed. Oliver Lawson-Dick. Secker & Warburg. Repr. 1992 Mandarin.

—— (2000). *Brief Lives* ed. John Buchanan-Brown. Penguin Books.

Bacon, Francis (2000). *The New Organon* ed. Lisa Jardine and Michael Silverthorne. Cambridge University Press, Cambridge.

Baker, T.M.M. (2000). *London. Rebuilding the City after the Great Fire*. Phillimore, Chichester.

Barbour, J.B. (1989). *Absolute or Relative Motion? Volume I The Discovery of Dynamics*. Cambridge University Press, Cambridge.

Barker, G.F. Russell. (1895). *Memoir of Richard Busby D.D. (1606–1695)*. Lawrence & Bullen.

Batten, M.I. (1935). 'A partner with Wren.' *The Times*. 14 January 1935, pp. 13–14 and 16.

—— (1936–7). 'The architecture of Dr Robert Hooke, F.R.S.' *Journal of the Walpole Society* 25: 83–113 and pls. XXXV–XL.

Beaven, A.B. (1913). *The Aldermen of the City of London.* 2 vols. The Corporation of London.

Bedford, John (1967). *London's Burning.* Abelard-Schuman.

Beier, A.L. and Finlay, R. eds (1986). *The Making of the Metropolis: London: 1500–1700.*

Bell, W.G. (1923). *The Great Fire in London in 1666.* The Bodley Head.

—— (1924). *The Great Plague in London in 1665.* The Bodley Head.

Bendall, Sarah (1997). *Dictionary of Land Surveyors and Local Map-Makers of Great Britain and Ireland 1530–1850.* 2 vols. The British Library.

Bennett, J.A. (1973). 'A study of *Parentalia,* with two unpublished letters of Sir Christopher Wren.' *Annals of Science* 30: 129–47.

—— (1975). 'Hooke and Wren and the system of the world: some points towards an historical account.' *The British Journal for the History of Science* 8 (28): 32–61.

—— (1980). 'Robert Hooke as mechanic and natural philosopher.' *Notes and Records of the Royal Society of London* 35: 33–48.

—— (1982). *The Mathematical Science of Christopher Wren.* Cambridge University Press, Cambridge.

—— (1987). *The Divided Circle, a History of Instruments for Astronomy, Navigation and Surveying.* Phaidon-Christie's, Oxford.

—— (1989). 'Hooke's instruments for astronomy and navigation.' In Hunter and Schaffer eds (1989), 21–32.

—— (1991). 'Geometry and surveying in early-seventeenth-century England.' *Annals of Science* 48: 345–54.

—— (2003). 'Hooke's instruments'. In Bennett *et al.* (2003), 62–104.

Bennett, Jim, Michael Cooper, Michael Hunter and Lisa Jardine (2003). *London's Leonardo, the Life and Work of Robert Hooke.* Oxford University Press, Oxford.

Berlinski, David (2001). *Newton's Gift.* Duckworth.

Birch, Thomas (1756–7). *The History of the Royal Society of London.* 4 vols.

Birch, W. de G. (1887). *The Historical Charters and Constitutional Documents of the City of London.* Rev. edn. Whiting.

Boyle, Robert (1999). *Works.* 14 vols, eds Michael Hunter and Edward B. Davis. Pickering & Chatto.

—— (2001). *Correspondence.* 6 vols, eds Michael Hunter, Antonio Clericuzio and L.M. Principe. Pickering & Chatto.

Brackenridge, J.B. (1995). *The Key to Newton's Dynamics.* University of California Press, Berkeley.

—— and Nauenberg, M. (2002). 'Curvature in Newton's dynamics.' In Cohen and Smith eds *The Cambridge Companion to Newton.* Cambridge University Press, Cambridge and New York, 85–137.

Brennan, James (1998). *As Burnt Surveys.* Unpublished MSc dissertation, Department of Geomatic Engineering, University College, London.

Brush, S.G. (1983). *Statistical Physics and the Atomic Theory of Matter From Boyle and Newton to Landau and Onsager.* Princeton University Press, New Jersey.

Bryden, D.J. (1992). 'Evidence from advertising for mathematical instrument making in London 1556–1714.' *Annals of Science* 49: 301–36.

Bud, R. and Warner D.J. eds (1998). *Instruments of Science.* Science Museum, London, and National Museum of American History, New York.

Burke, John G. ed. (1983). *The Uses of Science in the Age of Newton.* University of California Press, Berkeley.

Cardarelli, François (1999). *Scientific Unit Conversion.* Second edn. Springer-Verlag.

Champion, J.A.J. (1995). *London's Dreaded Visitation. The social geography of the great plague in 1665.* Historical Geography Research Series 31.

Chapman, Allan (1995). *Dividing the Circle. The Development of Critical Angular Measurement in Astronomy 1500–1850.* Second edn. John Wiley & Sons, Chichester.

Chartres, Richard and Vermont, David (1998). *A Brief History of Gresham College 1597–1997.* Gresham College.

Chilton, D. (1958). 'Land measurement in the sixteenth century.' *Transactions of the Newcomen Society* 31: 111–29 and 4 plates.

Cobb, Gerald (1942–3). *The Old Churches of London.* Second edn, Batsford.

Cohen, I.B. (1980). *The Newtonian Revolution.* Cambridge University Press, Cambridge.

—— and Smith, G. eds (2002). *The Cambridge Companion to Newton.* Cambridge University Press, Cambridge.

Colvin, Sir Howard (1995). *A Biographical Dictionary of British Architects, 1600–1840.* Third edn. Yale University Press, New Haven and London.

—— (1996). '*The Panorama as an architectural and topographical record.*' In London Topographical Society (1996), 5–13.

Conant, J.B. and Nash, L.K. eds (1964a). *Harvard Case Histories in Experimental Science Vol I.* Harvard University Press, Cambridge, Massachusetts.

—— (1964b). 'Robert Boyle's experiments in pneumatics.' In Conant and Nash eds (1964a), 1–64.

Cook, A.H. (1965). 'The absolute determination of the acceleration due to gravity.' *Metrologia* 1: 84–114.

Cook, Sir Alan (1999). *Edmond Halley, Charting the Heavens and the Seas.* Clarendon Press, Oxford.

Cooper, M.A.R. (1982). *Modern Theodolites and Levels.* Granada, Oxford.

—— (1996). 'Robert Hooke (1635–1703) proto-photogrammetrist.' *Photogrammetric Record* 15 (87): 403–17.

—— (1997, 1998a and b). 'Robert Hooke's work as Surveyor for the City of London in the aftermath of the Great Fire.' *Notes and Records of the Royal Society of London* 51: 161–74, 52: 25–38, 205–20.

—— (1999). *Robert Hooke, City Surveyor.* Unpublished PhD thesis, City University, London.

—— (2003). 'Hooke's career.' In Bennett *et al.* (2003), 1–61.

Corporation of London (1994). *The Official Guide to The Monument.* Corporation of London.

—— (2001). *The Livery Companies of the City of London.* Second edn. Corporation of London.

Cruz J.Y., Harrison J.C., Speake C.C., Niebauer T.M., McHugh M.P., Keyser P.T., Faller J.E., Jaako Mäkinen, Beruff R.B. (1991). 'A test of Newton's inverse-square law of gravitation using the 300-m tower at Erie, Colorado.' *Journal of Geophysical Research* 96 (B12): 20,073–92.

Davis, Edward B. (1994). '"Parcere nominibus": Boyle, Hooke and the rhetorical interpretation of Descartes.' In Hunter ed. (1994b), 157–75.

Deacon, Margaret (1965). 'Founders of marine science in Britain: the work of the early Fellows of the Royal Society.' *Notes and Records of the Royal Society of London* 20: 28–50.

—— (1971). *Scientists and the Sea 1650–1900.* Academic Press.

De Gandt, François (1995). *Force and Geometry in Newton's 'Principia',* trans. Curtis Wilson. Princeton University Press, Princeton, New Jersey.

Downes, Kerry (1971). *Christopher Wren.* Allen Lane, The Penguin Press.

—— (1988). *Sir Christopher Wren, the Design of St Paul's Cathedral.* Trefoil.

Drake, E.T. (1996). *Restless Genius, Robert Hooke and his Earthly Thoughts.* Oxford University Press, Oxford.

Drake, Stillman (1990). *Galileo: Pioneer Scientist.* University of Toronto Press, Toronto, Buffalo and London.

Earle, Peter (1989). *The Making of the English Middle Class.* Methuen.

Ehrlich, Mark E. (1995). 'Mechanism and activity in the scientific revolution: the case of Robert Hooke.' *Annals of Science* 52: 127–51.

Ehrlichson, Herman (1992). 'Newton and Hooke on centripetal force motion', *Centaurus* 35: 46–63.

Ellen, R.G. (1972). *A London Steeplechase.* City Press.

Elliott, James (1987). *The City in Maps, Urban Mapping to 1900.* The British Library.

'Espinasse, Margaret (1956). *Robert Hooke.* Heinemann.

Evelyn, John (1955). *Diary.* 6 vols. ed. E.S. de Beer. Clarendon Press, Oxford.

Featherstone, Ernest (1952). *Sir Thomas Gresham and His Trusts.* Mercers' Company.

Feingold, Mordechai (1984). *The Mathematicians' Apprenticeship, Science, Universities and Society in England 1560–1640.* Cambridge University Press, Cambridge.

Feisenberger, H.A. (1966). 'The libraries of Newton, Hooke and Boyle.' *Notes and Records of the Royal Society of London* 21: 42–55.

Finlay, R. and Shearer, B. (1986). 'Population growth and suburban expansion.' In Beier and Finlay (1986), 37–59.

Flamsteed, John (1975). *The Gresham Lectures,* ed. Eric G. Forbes. Mansell.

Foister, Susan (1996). 'Anthonis van den Wyngaerde's career as a topographical artist.' In London Topographical Society (1996), 1–4.

Gal, Ofer (1996). 'Producing knowledge in the workshop: Hooke's "inflection" from optics to planetary motion.' *Studies in the History and Philosophy of Science* 27: 181–205.

Geraghty, Anthony (1997). 'Jeffery book review.' *Burlington Magazine* 139 (1130): 336–7. May 1997.

—— (2001). 'Edward Woodroofe: Sir Christopher Wren's first draughtsman.' *Burlington Magazine* 143: 474–9.

Gillispie, C.C. ed. (1970–80). *Dictionary of Scientific Biography.* 16 vols. Charles Scribner's Sons, New York.

Gouk, Penelope (1980). 'The role of acoustics and music theory in the scientific work of Robert Hooke.' *Annals of Science* 37: 573–605.

—— (1982). 'Acoustics in the early Royal Society 1660–1680'. *Notes and Records of the Royal Society of London* 36: 155–75.

Gunther, R.T. ed. (1930a). *Early Science in Oxford Vol. 6. The Life and Work of Robert Hooke (Part I).* Oxford.

—— ed. (1930b). *Early Science in Oxford Vol. 7. The Life and Work of Robert Hooke (Part II).* Oxford.

—— ed. (1931). *Early Science in Oxford Vol. 8. The Cutler Lectures of Robert Hooke.* Oxford.

—— ed. (1935). *Early Science in Oxford Vol. 10. The Life and Work of Robert Hooke (Part IV).* Oxford.

Hall, A.R. (1951a). 'Robert Hooke and horology.' *Notes and Records of the Royal Society of London* 8: 167–77.

—— (1951b). 'Two unpublished letters of Robert Hooke.' *Isis* 42: 219–30.

—— (1963). 'Oldenburg and the art of scientific communication.' *The British Journal for the History of Science* 2: 277–90.

—— (1965). 'Galileo and the science of motion.' *The British Journal for the History of Science* 2: 185–99.

—— (1990). 'Beyond the fringe: diffraction as seen by Grimaldi, Fabri, Hooke and Newton.' *Notes and Records of the Royal Society of London* 44: 13–23.

—— (1992). *Isaac Newton, Adventurer in Thought.* Blackwell, Oxford.

Hambly, Edmund C. (1987). 'Robert Hooke, the City's Leonardo.' *The City University* 2 (2): 4–10.

Hanson, Julienne (1989). 'Order and structure in urban design: the plans for the rebuilding of London after the Great Fire of 1666.' *Ekistics* 334–5: 22–42.

Hanson, J.M. (1990). *Order and Structure in Urban Space: a Morphological History of the City of London.* Unpublished PhD thesis, University of London.

Harris, Frances (1997). 'Living in the neighbourhood of science: Mary Evelyn, Margaret Cavendish and the Greshamites.' In Hunter and Hutton eds (1997), 198–217.

Hartley, Sir Harold (1960). *The Royal Society, its Origins and Founders.* The Royal Society.

Harvey, P.D.A. (1993). *Maps in Tudor England.* British Library.

Henry, John (2002). *Knowledge is Power, how Magic, the Government and an Apocalyptic Vision Inspired Francis Bacon to Create Modern Science.* Icon Books, Cambridge.

Herivel, J.W. (1965). 'Newton's first solution to the problem of Kepler motion.' *The British Journal for the History of Science* 2: 350–4.

Hesse, M.B. (1966a). 'Hooke's philosophical algebra.' *Isis* 57: 67–83.

—— (1966b). 'Hooke's vibration theory and the isochrony of springs.' *Isis* 57: 433–41.

Heyman, Jacques (1998). 'Hooke's cubico-parabolical conoid.' *Notes and Records of the Royal Society of London* 52: 39–50.

—— (2003). 'Hooke and Bedlam'. In *Papers Presented at 'Hooke 2003'*, 7–8 July 2003, Gresham College and The Royal Society.

Hide, Raymond (2001). 'Zenographic longitude systems and Jupiter's differential rotation.' *Notes and Records of the Royal Society of London* 55: 69–79.

Hill, C.P. (1988). *Who's Who in Stuart Britain.* Shepheard-Walwyn.

Hind, A.M. (1972). *Wencelaus Hollar and His Views of London and Windsor in the Seventeenth Century.* Benjamin Blom, New York.

Holwell, John (1678). *A Sure Guide to the Practical Surveyor in Two Parts.*

H[ooke?], R. (1660). *New Atlantis. Begun by the Lord Verulam, Viscount St Albans: and Continued by R. H. Esquire. Wherein is set forth a Platform of Monarchical Government* . . .

—— (1661). *An Attempt for the Explication of the Phænomena, Observable in an Experiment Published by the Honourable Robert Boyle, Esq; . . . In Confirmation of a former Conjecture made by R.H.*

—— (1665). *Micrographia: Or Some Physiological Descriptions of Minute Bodies Made By Magnifying Glasses With Observations and Enquiries thereupon.* Repr. in Gunther R.T., (1938). *Early Science in Oxford, Vol. 13.* Oxford. Repr. 1961 Dover Books, New York.

—— (1674a). *An Attempt to Prove the Motion of the Earth from Observations made by Robert Hooke Fellow of the Royal Society.*

—— (1674b). *Animadversions On the first part of the Machina Cælestis Of . . . Johannes Hevelius . . .*

—— (1676). *A Description of Helioscopes, and some other Instruments made by Robert Hooke, Fellow of the Royal Society.*

—— (1677). *Lampas: or Descriptions of some Mechanical Improvements of Lamps & Waterpoises Together with some other Physical and Mechanical Discoveries Made by Robert Hooke Fellow of the Royal Society.*

—— (1678a). *Lectures De Potentia Restitutiva, or of Spring Explaining the Power of Springing Bodies. to which are added some Collections Viz . . .*

—— (1678b). *Lectures and Collections Made by Robert Hooke, Secretary of the Royal Society. Cometa containing . . . Microscopium containing . . .*

—— (1679). *Lectiones Cutlerianæ.* Repr. with a new pagination in Gunther R.T. ed. (1931).

—— (1705). *Posthumous Works*, ed. Richard Waller. London[1] (repr. Johnson Reprint Corporation, New York, 1968; Frank Cass, 1971).

—— (1726). *Philosophical Experiments and Observations of the late Eminent Dr Robert Hooke . . .* ed. William Derham. Repr. 1962. Frank Cass.

—— (1935a). *The Diary of Robert Hooke 1672–1680.* H.W. Robinson and Walter Adams eds, Taylor & Francis. Repr. 1968 Wykeham Publications.

—— (1935b). 'The Diary of Robert Hooke 1688–1690 and 1692–3.' In Gunter, R.T. ed. (1935), 69–265.

Howgego, J.L. (1978). *Printed Maps of London circa 1553–1850.* Second edn. Dawson, Folkestone.

Hull, Derek (1997). 'Robert Hooke: a fractographic study of Kettering-Stone.' *Notes and Records of the Royal Society of London* 51: 45–55.

Hunter, Lynette and Hutton, Sarah eds. (1997). *Women, Science and Medicine 1500–1700.* Sutton, Stroud.

Hunter, Michael (1989). *Establishing the New Science.* Boydell Press, Woodbridge.

—— ed. (1994a). *Robert Boyle by Himself and His Friends.* William Pickering.

—— ed. (1994b). *Robert Boyle Reconsidered.* Cambridge University Press.

—— (1994c). *The Royal Society and its Fellows 1660–1700: the morphology of an early scientific institution.* Second edn. British Society for the History of Science, Oxford.

—— (1995). *Science and the Shape of Orthodoxy.* Boydell Press, Woodbridge.

—— (2003). 'Hooke the natural philosopher.' In Bennett *et al.* (2003), 105–62.

—— and Littleton, Charles (2001). 'The work diaries of Robert Boyle: a newly discovered source and its internet publication.' *Notes and Records of the Royal Society of London* 55: 373–90.

—— and Schaffer, Simon eds (1989). *Robert Hooke New Studies.* Boydell Press, Woodbridge.

Hutton, Sarah (1997). 'Anne Conway, Margaret Cavendish and seventeenth-century scientific thought.' In Hunter and Hutton eds (1997), 218–34.

Hyde, Ralph (1992). 'Ogilby and Morgan's City of London Map.' In London Topographical Society (1992), v–xii.

Iliffe, Rob (1992). '"In the warehouse": privacy, property and priority in the early Royal Society.' *History of Science* 30: 29–68.

—— (1995). 'Material doubts: Hooke, artisan culture and the exchange of information in 1670s London.' *The British Journal for the History of Science* 28: 285–318.

Inwood, Stephen (2002). *The Man Who Knew Too Much. The Strange and Inventive Life of Robert Hooke 1635–1703.* Macmillan.

Ito, Yushi (1988). 'Hooke's cyclic theory of the earth in the context of seventeenth-century England.' *The British Journal for the History of Science* 21: 295–314.

Jardine, Lisa (2001). 'Monuments and microscopes: scientific thinking on a grand scale in the early Royal Society.' *Notes and Records of the Royal Society of London* 55: 289–308.

—— (2002). *On a Grander Scale, the Outstanding Career of Sir Christopher Wren.* HarperCollins.

—— (2003a). Hooke the man – his diary and his health. In Bennett *et al.* (2003), 163–206.

—— (2003b). *The Curious Life of Robert Hooke, the man who measured London.* HarperCollins (in press).

—— and Stewart, Alan (1998). *Hostage to Fortune, the Troubled Life of Francis Bacon.* Victor Gollancz.

Jeffery, Paul (1996). *The City Churches of Sir Christopher Wren.* Hambledon Press, London and Rio Grande.

Johns, Henry (1989). 'Introduction to the maps.' In Lobel (1989), 57–62.

Jones, P.E. ed. (1966). *The Fire Court, Calendar to the Judgments and Decrees.* 2 vols. Corporation of London.

Jones, P.E. and Reddaway, T.F. (1967). 'Introduction.' In London Topographical Society (1967), ix–xlii.

Kassler, J.C. and Oldroyd, D.R. (1983). 'Robert Hooke's Trinity College "Musick Scripts", his music theory and the role of music in his cosmology.' *Annals of Science* 40: 559–95.

Kent, P.W. (2001). *Some Scientists in the Life of Christ Church Oxford.* Oxford University Press, Oxford.

Keynes, Sir Geoffrey (1960). *A Bibliography of Dr. Robert Hooke.* Clarendon Press, Oxford.

—— (1961). *A Bibliography of the Honourable Robert Boyle.* Clarendon Press, Oxford.

King, Henry C. (1955). *The History of the Telescope.* Griffin.

Koyré, Alexandre (1952). 'An unpublished letter of Robert Hooke to Isaac Newton.' *Isis* 43: 312–37.

Lang, Jane (1956). *Rebuilding St. Paul's After the Great Fire of London.* Oxford University Press, Oxford.

Leybourne, William (1653, 1657, 1674, 1679 and 1722). *The Compleat Surveyor.* 5 edns.

Little, Bryan (1975). *Sir Christopher Wren.* Robert Hale.

Lobel, Mary D. ed. (1989). *The British Atlas of Historical Towns iii,* Oxford University Press, Oxford.

Loengard, J.S. (1989). *London Viewers and their Certificates 1508–1558.* London Record Society.

Lohne, Johs. (1960). 'Hooke versus Newton.' *Centaurus* 7 (1): 6–52.

London Topographical Society (1962a–c). *The Survey of Building Sites in the City of London after the Great Fire of 1666 Vols. 3–5.*

—— (1964). *The Survey of Building Sites in the City of London after the Great Fire of 1666 Vol. 2.*

—— (1967). *The Survey of Building Sites in the City of London after the Great Fire of 1666 Vol. 1.*

—— (1992). *The A to Z of Restoration London (The City of London, 1676).*

—— (1996). *Wyngaerde's Panorama of London circa 1544.* Eds. Sir Howard Colvin and Susan Foister.

Mach, Ernst (1960). *The Science of Mechanics.* Sixth US edn. Open Court, La Salle, Illinois.

Masters, Betty R. (1974). *The Public Markets of the City of London Surveyed by William Leybourne in 1677.* London Topographical Society.

Matthews, W.R. and Atkins, W.M. eds (1957). *A History of St Paul's Cathedral, and the Men Associated with it.* Phoenix House.

Mayo, Caroline (2001). *Is the 'A to Z of Restoration London' Accurate?* Unpublished MSc dissertation, Department of Geomatic Engineering, University College, London.

Merritt, J.F. (1998). 'Puritans, Laudians and the phenomenon of church-building in Jacobean London.' *Historical Journal* 41: 935–60.

Middleton, William S. (1927). 'The medical aspect of Robert Hooke.' *Annals of Medical History* 9: 227–43.

Milne, Gustav (1986). *The Great Fire of London.* Historical Publications Ltd, London and New Barnet, Hertfordshire.

Nakajima, Hideto (1984). 'Two kinds of modification theory of light: some observations on the Newton-Hooke controversy of 1672 concerning the nature of light.' *Annals of Science* 41: 261–78.

—— (1994). 'Robert Hooke's family and his youth: some new evidence from the will of the Rev. John Hooke.' *Notes and Records of the Royal Society of London* 48: 11–16.

Nauenberg, Michael (1994a). 'Hooke, orbital motion, and Newton's "Principia".' *American Journal of Physics* 62 (4): 331–50.

—— (1994b). 'Newton's early computational method for dynamics.' *Archives for the History of the Exact Sciences* 46: 221–51.

—— (1994c). 'Newton's "Principia" and inverse-square orbits.' *The College Mathematics Journal* 25: 212–22.

—— (1994d). 'Newton's early computational method for dynamics.' *Archives for History of the Exact Sciences* 49: 221–51.

—— (1998). 'On Hooke's 1685 manuscript on orbital mechanics.' *Historia Mathematica* 25: 89–93.

—— (1999). 'Newton's curvature method of force.' In Newton (1999), 78–82.

—— (2002). See Brackenridge 2002.

—— (2003). 'Robert Hooke's seminal contribution to orbital dynamics.' In *Papers Presented at 'Hooke 2003'*, 7–8 July 2003, Gresham College and The Royal Society.

Newton, Isaac (1959–77). *Correspondence*. 7 vols, eds H.W. Turnbull (i–iii), J.F. Scott (iv), A.R. Hall and Laura Tilling (v–vii). Cambridge University Press, Cambridge (for The Royal Society).

—— (1999). *The Principia*. Trans. I.B. Cohen and Anne Whitman, Guide by I.B. Cohen. California University Press, Berkeley, Los Angeles and London.

Niebauer T.M., Sasagawa G.S., Faller, J.E., Hilt R. and Klopping F. (1995). 'A new generation of absolute gravimeters.' *Metrologia* 32: 159–80.

O'Brien, G.W. (1970–80). 'Power, Henry.' In Gillespie (1970–80), xi, 121–2.

Ogilby, John (1675 and 1676). *Britannia*. London.

Oldroyd, David (1972). 'Robert Hooke's methodology of science as exemplified in his "Discourse of Earthquakes".' *The British Journal for the History of Science* 6: 109–30.

—— (1987). 'Some writings of Robert Hooke on procedures for the prosecution of scientific inquiry, including his "Lectures of Things Requisite to a Natural History".' *Notes and Records of the Royal Society of London* 41: 145–67.

Patterson, L.D. (1949). 'Hooke's gravitation theory and its influence on Newton [Part I].' *Isis* 40: 327–41.

—— (1950). 'Part II: the insufficiency of the traditional estimate.' *Isis* 41: 32–45.

—— (1952). 'Pendulums of Wren and Hooke.' *Osiris* 10: 277–321.

Pelseneer, Jean (1929). 'Une lettre inédite de Newton.' *Isis* 12: 237–9.

Pepys, Samuel (1970–83). *Diary*. 11 vols, eds R.C. Latham and William Matthews. Bell & Hyman.

Perks, Sydney (1922). *The History of the Mansion House*. Cambridge University Press, Cambridge.

—— (1927). *Essays on Old London*. Cambridge University Press, Cambridge.

Picard, Liza (1997). *Restoration London*. Weidenfeld & Nicholson.

Porter, Roy (2000). *Enlightenment, Britain and the Creation of the Modern World*. Allen Lane.

Porter, Stephen (1996). *The Great Fire of London*. Sutton, Stroud.

Pugliese, Patri (1982). *The Scientific Achievement of Robert Hooke*. Ph.D. thesis, Harvard University. University Microfilms International, Ann Arbor Michigan and London.

—— (1989). 'Robert Hooke and the dynamics of motion in a curved path.' In Hunter and Schaffer eds (1989), 181–205.

Pumfrey, Stephen (1991). 'Ideas above his station: a social study of Hooke's curatorship of experiments.' History of Science 29: 1–44.

—— (1995). 'Who did the work?' The British Journal for the History of Science 28: 131–56.

Pyle, Andrew, ed. (2000). Dictionary of Seventeenth-Century British Philosophers. Thoemmes Press, Bristol.

Rasmussen, S.E. (1960). London: The Unique City. Abridged edn. Penguin Books, Harmondsworth Middlesex.

Reddaway, T.F. (1951). The Rebuilding of London after the Great Fire. Edward Arnold. Repr., with some amendments and additions, of the first edn (1940) Jonathan Cape.

Robinson, H.W. (1949). 'Robert Hooke as surveyor and architect.' Notes and Records of the Royal Society of London 6: 48–55.

Rostenberg, Leona (1989). The Library of Robert Hooke. The Scientific Book Trade of Restoration England. Modoc Press, Santa Monica, California.

Rouse Ball, W.W. (1893). An Essay on Newton's 'Principia'. Macmillan, London and New York.

Russell, J.L. (1964). 'Kepler's laws of planetary motion 1609–1666.' The British Journal for the History of Science 2 (5): 1–24.

Sargeaunt, John (1898). Annals of Westminster School. Methuen.

Saunders, Ann (1997a). 'The Second Exchange 1669–1838.' In Saunders (1997b), 121–35.

—— ed. (1997). The Royal Exchange. London Topographical Society.

Schofield, John ed. (1987b). The London Surveys of Ralph Treswell. London Topographical Society.

Shapin, Steven (1988). 'The house of experiment in seventeenth-century England'. Isis 79: 373–404.

—— (1989). 'Who was Robert Hooke?' In Hunter and Schaffer eds (1989), 253–85.

—— (1994). A Social History of Truth. Civility and Science in Seventeenth-Century England. University of Chicago Press, Chicago and London.

Simpson, A.D.C. (1989). 'Robert Hooke and practical optics: technical support at a scientific frontier.' In Hunter and Schaffer eds (1989), 33–61.

Skinner, F.G. (1951). Letter reference Sc. M. 35/5980/1 to Margaret 'Espinasse from F.G. Skinner, Deputy Keeper (Weighing and Measuring) The Science Museum, London SW7'. University of Hull Margaret 'Espinasse Archives (uncatalogued). In an orange folder entitled 'Hooke: material concerning Chap 4 Surveyor & Archt'.

Speake C.C., Niebauer T.M., McHugh M.P., Keyser P.T., Faller E., Cruz Y., Harrison J.C., Jaako Mäkinen, Beruff, R.B. (1990). 'Test of the inverse-square law of gravitation using the 300-m tower at Erie, Colorado.' Physical Review Letters 65 (16): 1967–71.

Sprat, Thomas (1665). The History of the Royal Society of London, for the Improving of Natural Knowledge. Royal Society.

—— (1959). The History of the Royal Society of London, for the Improving of Natural Knowledge eds J.I. Cope and H.W. Jones. Washington University, St Louis, and Routledge & Kegan Paul.

Stephenson, Bruce (1987). Kepler's Physical Astronomy. Princeton University Press, Princeton, New Jersey.

Stevenson, Christine (1996a). 'Robert Hooke's Bethlem.' Journal of the Society of Architectural Historians 55: 254–75.

—— (1996b). Medicine and Magnificence. British Hospital and Asylum Architecture 1660–1815. Yale University Press, New Haven and London.

Stoesser-Johnston, Alison (1997). Robert Hooke and Holland: Dutch Influence on Hooke's Architecture. 3 vols. Unpublished Doctoraalscriptie Bouwkunst Rijksuniversiteit Utrecht.

—— (2000), 'Robert Hooke and Holland: Dutch influence on his architecture.' *Bulletin Konin Nederlandse Oudheidkundige Bond* 2000 (4): 121–37.

Stow, John (1994). *A Survey of London Written in the Year 1598*. Rev. 1603. Alan Sutton, Stroud.

Taylor, E.G.R. (1954). *The Mathematical Practitioners of Tudor & Stuart England 1485–1714*. Cambridge University Press, Cambridge.

—— (1993), 'Robert Hooke and the cartographical projects of the late seventeenth century (1666–1696).' *Geographical Journal* 90: 529–40.

Thurley, Simon (1998). *The Whitehall Palace Plan of 1670*. London Topographical Society.

Timbs, John (1898). *Clubs and Club Life in London*. Chatto & Windus.

Tipping, H. Avery (1924), 'Ragley Hall Warwickshire I and II.' *Country Life* 22 March, 438–45, and 29 March 476–82.

Tozer, E.T. (1990). 'Discovery of an ammonoid specimen described by Robert Hooke.' *Notes and Records of the Royal Society of London* 44: 3–12.

Turner, A.J. (1973), 'Mathematical instruments and the education of gentlemen.' *Annals of Science* 30: 51–88.

Van Eerde, K.S. (1976). *John Ogilby and the Taste of His Times*. Dawson, Folkestone.

Wallis, Helen (1994), 'Navigators and mathematical practitioners in Samuel Pepys's day.' *The Journal of Navigation* 47: 1–19.

Ward, John (1740). *The Lives of the Professors of Gresham College*.

Wattie, Margaret² (1937), 'Robert Hooke on his literary contemporaries.' *Review of English Studies* 13: 212–16.

Webster, Charles (1965). 'The discovery of Boyle's Law and the concept of the elasticity of air in the seventeenth century.' *Archives for the History of Exact Sciences* 2: 441–502.

—— (1970–80), 'Towneley, Richard.' In Gillespie (1970–80), xiii, 444–5.

Welch, Charles (1893). *History of the Monument*. Corporation of London.

Westfall, Richard S. (1967), 'Hooke and the law of universal gravitation.' *The British Journal for the History of Science* 3: 245–61.

—— (1980). *Never at Rest, a Biography of Isaac Newton*. Cambridge University Press, Cambridge.

Whiteside, Derek T. (1984), 'Newton's early thoughts on motion: a fresh look.' *The British Journal for the History of Science* 2: 118–37.

Whitrow, G. (1938). Robert Hooke. *Philosophy of Science* 5: 493–502.

Willmoth, Frances (1993). *Sir Jonas Moore. Practical Mathematics and Restoration Science*. Boydell Press, Woodbridge.

Wolpert, Lewis (1992). *The Unnatural Nature of Science*. Faber & Faber.

Woodhead, J.R. (1965). *The Rulers of London 1660–1689*. London & Middlesex Archaeological Society.

Wright, Michael (1989). 'Robert Hooke's Longitude Timekeeper.' In Hunter and Schaffer eds (1989), 63–118.

Wyngaerde, Anthonis v. d. (1996). *The Panorama of London circa 1544*, eds Howard Colvin and Susan Foister. London Topographical Society.

Young, Elizabeth and Wayland (1956). *Old London Churches*. Faber & Faber.

INDEX

Specific places and people have their own main entries. Legal and administative details of the rebuilding of London after the Great Fire are found mainly under 'London, City of'. General details of London places, especially before rebuilding began, can be found under 'London, city and Libertys of'. This distinction, which is maintained throughout the book, is explained in a note on page 223.